ENGLISH
HISTORY

The English Counties

ENGLISH HISTORY

Birdsall S. Viault, Ph.D.
Winthrop College

McGraw-Hill, Inc.

New York St. Louis San Francisco Auckland Bogotá Caracas
Lisbon London Madrid Mexico Milan Montreal New Delhi
Paris San Juan Singapore Sydney Tokyo Toronto

For Sally and Buffy

Birdsall S. Viault is a professor of history at Winthrop College, Rock Hill, South Carolina. He received his B.S. degree from Adelphi University and an M.A. degree in secondary education from the same institution. Further graduate work at Duke University led to an M.A. and Ph.D. in history. Professor Viault also holds a diploma from the Leibniz-Kolleg of the University of Tübingen, Germany.

Prior to joining the faculty at Winthrop College, Professor Viault taught at Adelphi University. He is the author of several other volumes in McGraw-Hill's College Core Books series. His articles and reviews have appeared in journals in the United States and Europe, and for a number of years he wrote on subjects related to history and current affairs in a weekly column, "Perspective," which appeared in over thirty South Carolina newspapers.

Sponsoring Editor, Jeanne Flagg
Production Supervisor, Leroy A. Young
Editing Supervisors, Meg Tobin, Patty Andrews
Front Matter Editor, Maureen Walker

English History

2 3 4 5 6 7 8 9 10 11 12 13 14 15 16 17 18 19 20 FGR FGR 9 8 7 6 5 4 3 2

ISBN 0-07-067437-X

Library of Congress Cataloging-in-Publication Data

Viault, Birdsall S.
      English history / Birdsall S. Viault.
           p.   cm.
      Includes index.
      ISBN 0-07-067437-X
      1. Great Britain — History.   I. Title.
DA30.V53   1992   91-16579
941 — dc20   CIP

Map Acknowledgments

The maps on pages 422, and 433 were reproduced from John B. Harrison, Richard E. Sullivan, and Dennis Sherman, *A Short History of Western Civilization,* 7th ed., McGraw-Hill, New York, 1990. The map on page 427 was reproduced from the 6th edition, 1985.

The maps on pages 226, and 365 were reproduced from Mortimer Chambers, et al., *The Western Experience,* 4th ed., Knopf, 1987.

Preface

This volume reviews the history of England from the earliest times to the present. It is designed to be used in two ways: as a textbook in its own right and as a supplement to any of the standard college texts.

To enhance comprehension and retention of historical material, each chapter contains a time line, an overview and summary, and a system of clearly related subheads. Dates of birth and death are given for most individuals cited. For monarchs and popes, the dates refer to their reigns and are indicated as "r."

No attempt has been made to cover the major interpretive or historical debates relating to the history of this period. Rather the reader is encouraged to consult the "Recommended Reading" sections that appear at the end of each chapter. In selecting books to be included, emphasis has been placed on recent scholarship.

Acknowledgments

It is a pleasure for me to acknowledge the assistance of those who have helped make this book possible.

Professor William Brockington of the University of South Carolina at Aiken was generous in lending me books from his personal library. Charlotte Tyson, the secretary to the Department of History at Winthrop College, assisted with the preparation of the manuscript, while the staff of the Reference Department of the Dacus Library of Winthrop College, particularly Susan Silverman, provided considerable help. I appreciate, too, the skill and judgment of Nancy Cone, who edited the manuscript, and the support and counsel of Jeanne Flagg, the sponsoring editor of this series of McGraw-Hill's College Core Books.

I must also express my appreciation to the hundreds of students I have taught over the course of some thirty years. From them I have learned much about how to make history understandable and meaningful.

I owe my greatest acknowledgment to my wife, Sally, who offered encouragement and enthusiasm throughout the project and also proofread the final page proofs with great skill.

Birdsall S. Viault
Rock Hill, South Carolina
January 1991

Contents

Maps

ENGLISH
HISTORY

CHAPTER 1

Celtic and Roman Britain

Time Line

55–54 B.C.	Julius Caesar invades Britain
A.D. 43	Emperor Claudius invades Britain
60	Queen Boudicca leads a revolt against the Romans
78–85	Julius Agricola serves as governor of Roman Britain
c. 123	The construction of Hadrian's Wall begins
c. 143	The Antonine Wall is constructed
211	Emperor Septimius Severus dies, ending his effort to conquer Scotland
314	Three bishops from Britain attend the Council of Arles

Although the British Isles have been inhabited by human beings for some 250,000 years, we may appropriately begin our history with the Celts, who crossed from the European continent and settled in the British Isles (England, Wales, Scotland, and Ireland) during the first millennium B.C. A people who occupied a large part of Iron Age Europe, the Celts consisted of numerous tribes that shared a culture dating back to the Bronze Age in Central Europe (c. 1200 B.C.). Their warrior aristocracy possessed considerable wealth and power.

In the first century B.C., the Romans began their incursions into Britain, and in the first century A.D., Britain became a province of the Roman Empire.

Celtic Britain

The earliest Celtic settlers in Britain possessed a Bronze Age culture; later Celts brought with them a knowledge of ironworking. Organized into tribes, the warlike Celts were ruled by chieftains or kings, and their simple farming society consisted of nobles, freemen, and slaves.

Celtic Religion

Celtic religion, known as druidism, involved the worship of nature deities. The druid priesthood, a powerful element in Celtic society, taught immortality and the transmigration of souls and carried out religious rituals, including some human sacrifice. The druids also sought to establish and maintain a degree of order among the warring tribes. (Although the popular imagination sometimes associates the famous monument at Stonehenge with druidism, it was probably built between 1800 and 1400 B.C., well before the time of the druids.)

Celtic Survival

In later centuries, following the conquests by the Romans and the Anglo-Saxons, some remnants of the Celts continued to survive in the more remote areas of the British Isles, including Devonshire and Cornwall in southwestern England and in Wales, Scotland, and Ireland.

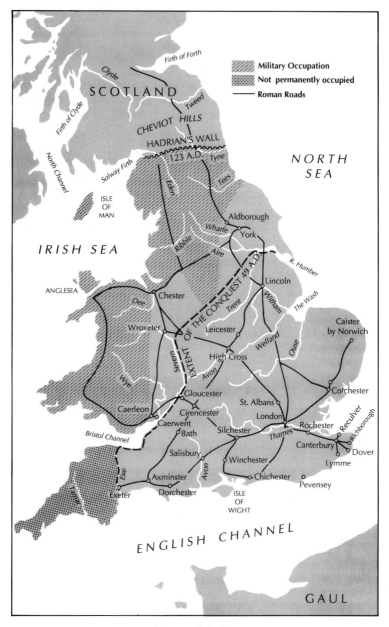

Roman Britain

Roman Britain

Julius Caesar's Invasions

Between 58 and 50 B.C., the Roman general Julius Caesar carried out his conquest of Gaul (modern France). Motivated in part by a desire to prevent the Celts of the British Isles from aiding the Gauls in their resistance to the Romans, Caesar crossed the English Channel in 55 B.C. and attacked the Celtic tribesmen in Kent, southeast of London. Caesar soon returned to Gaul, however.

In 54 B.C., Caesar again invaded Britain, advancing inland to a point near the present location of London. He collected tribute from the Celts and took hostages but did not establish a permanent occupation.

Later Caesar told of his incursions into Britain in his *Commentaries on the Gallic Wars.*

Emperor Claudius (r. A.D. 41–54)

For nearly a century after Caesar's invasions, the Romans left Britain undisturbed. Then in A.D. 43, Emperor Claudius sent an army of some forty or fifty thousand men, commanded by Aulus Plautus, to Britain. The army landed in Kent, where Claudius soon joined his forces.

Defeating the Celts, Claudius established Roman domination over southeast Britain and appointed Plautus as the first Roman governor. Plautus advanced Roman control northward.

Plautus's successors, Ostorius Scapula and Suetonius Paulinus, further extended Roman control.

Queen Boudicca's Revolt

While Suetonius Paulinus was off fighting in Wales, the Celtic Queen Boudicca led a revolt against the Romans in A.D. 60. The Romans crushed the revolt. After Boudicca was taken prisoner, she committed suicide.

Julius Agricola

From 78 to 85, Julius Agricola served as governor of Roman Britain. He completed the conquest of Wales and extended Roman domination northward to the Firth of Forth and the Firth of Clyde in southern Caledonia (modern Scotland). Following Agricola's return to Rome, however, the Caledonian tribes regained their independence.

Agricola also promoted Romanization, encouraging native Britons to adopt Roman dress and customs and use the Latin language.

Emperor Hadrian (r. 117–138)

Visiting Britain in the early second century A.D. (about 123), Emperor Hadrian ordered the construction of a wall extending some 73 miles from Solway Firth in the West to the Tyne River in the East. Hadrian's Wall was intended to protect Roman Britain from incursions by Caledonian tribesmen.

Emperor Antonius Pius (r. 138–161)

During the reign of Antonius Pius, the Romans advanced further north, building the Antonine Wall (about 143) between the Firth of Forth and the Firth of Clyde. However, the Romans had once again overextended themselves, and rebellious Caledonian tribesmen penetrated the Antonine Wall, which the Romans abandoned about 185.

Emperor Septimius Severus (r. 193–211)

In 208, Emperor Septimius Severus went to Britain, where he ordered the rebuilding of Hadrian's Wall, which had fallen into disrepair, and the repair of the Roman fortresses at Chester and York. He died at York in 211, before he completed his plans for a full-scale invasion of Scotland, which remained free of Roman control.

For the next century, peace prevailed in Roman Britain. Three Roman legions, each consisting of some thirty to forty thousand men, guarded the frontiers. The legion stationed at Carlisle protected Roman Britain against incursions from Scotland, while the legion based at Chester maintained control over Wales. The third legion, stationed at York, served as a reserve.

Emperor Caracalla (r. 211–217)

Emperor Caracalla, Septimius Severus's son and successor, granted Roman citizenship to all the free inhabitants of the Roman

Empire, including those in Britain. He acted not from altruistic motives but rather out of a desire to increase his income from taxes levied on citizens.

Roman Settlements

Towns and Other Centers

Britain remained largely a frontier outpost of the Roman Empire, although the Romans established a number of settlements. Several settlements of retired legionnaires and their families, known as *coloniae* (singular *colonia*), were established, including Lincoln, Colchester, Gloucester, and York. Existing records indicate that there was only one Roman town (*municipium*; plural *municipia*) with full legal status, namely Verulamium. Most of the towns in Roman Britain were old tribal centers, known as *civitates* (singular *civitas*). In addition, the Romans established several resorts, such as Bath, known for its healing waters.

London

Colchester served as the first capital of Roman Britain; however, London, the commercial center, soon became the center of government. Surviving records do not show that London possessed the status of either a *colonia* or *municipium*, but there is no doubt that it was the most important city in Roman Britain.

Villas

The Romans did not make any sustained effort to Romanize the Celtic villages in the countryside, although a number of large estates or villas were established with Roman or Romanized masters and native slaves or hired workers. The sites of over 600 villas have been located, primarily in the southeast.

Roman Roads

The Roman Empire was bound together by an excellent system of roads, which were better than any roads Europe would have again until the nineteenth century. In Britain, some 5000 miles of paved roads were constructed, with most of them radiating from London.

The Economy

The Roman roads encouraged economic development. Roman Britain was primarily agricultural and exported mainly grain; in addition, British mines produced metals, including tin, copper, lead, and iron, which were also exported.

Christianity

We do not know with certainty when Christianity first arrived in Roman Britain, but by the third century, Christianity was becoming widespread. In 314, three bishops from Britain attended the Council of Arles in Gaul.

St. Alban

According to tradition, the first Christian martyr in Britain was a Roman named Alban, who was killed in Verulamium in the third or fourth century. The town of St. Albans was later established on the ruins of the Roman town.

St. Patrick

By the early fifth century, St. Patrick (c. 389–461) and other British missionaries were beginning the work of carrying the Christian faith beyond Roman Britain to Ireland and southern Scotland. St. Patrick later became venerated as the patron saint of Ireland.

Although the Romans ruled Britain for four centuries, Britain never became more than a frontier outpost of the Roman Empire, and the enduring influence of Roman culture on Britain was at best slight. In time, the Roman towns, villas, and roads decayed, and the Latin language disappeared. Of all the influences that came to Britain in Roman times, Christianity proved to be the most enduring.

Recommended Reading

Arnold, C. J. *Roman Britain to Saxon England* (1984).

Birley, Anthony. *The People of Roman Britain* (1980).

Clark, Grahame. *Prehistoric Britain* (1962).

Collingwood, R. G. and I. A. Richmond. *The Archaeology of Roman Britain* (rev. ed., 1969).

Ellis, Peter Beresford. *Caesar's Invasion of Britain* (1980).

Frere, Sheppard S. *Britannia: A History of Roman Britain* (3rd ed., 1987).

Hawkes, Christopher and Jacquetta. *Prehistoric Britain* (1965).

Hawkes, Jacquetta. *Early Britain* (1949).

Hawkins, Gerald S. and John S. White. *Stonehenge Decoded* (1965).

Home, G. *Roman London* (2nd ed., 1948).

Johnson, Stephen. *Later Roman Britain* (1980).

Laing, Lloyd. *Celtic Britain* (1979).

Liversidge, Joan. *Britain in the Roman Empire* (1968).

Powell, T. G. E. *The Celts* (1958).

Salway, Peter H. *Roman Britain* (1984).

Thomas, Charles. *Christianity in Roman Britain to A.D. 500* (1981).

Todd, Malcolm. *Roman Britain, 55 B.C.–A.D. 400: The Province Beyond the Ocean* (1981).

Wacher, John. *The Towns of Roman Britain* (1974).

Webster, Graham. *Boudicca: The British Revolt Against Rome, A.D. 60* (1978).

Webster, Graham. *The Roman Invasion of Britain* (1981).

CHAPTER 2

Anglo-Saxon England

Time Line

5th century	The Anglo-Saxons conquer Roman Britain
597	Augustine begins the conversion of England to Roman Catholic Christianity
664	The Synod of Whitby leads to England's adoption of Roman Catholic Christianity
731	Venerable Bede's *History of the English Church and People* is completed
871–899	Reign of King Alfred the Great
886	The Treaty of Wedmore establishes the Danelaw
954	The English reconquer the Danelaw

961	Dunstan becomes archbishop of Canterbury
978–1016	Reign of King Ethelred the Redeless
1016–1035	Reign of King Canute
1042–1066	Reign of King Edward the Confessor
1066	The Danelaw elects Harold Godwinson as king

The barbarian invasions of the fifth century brought an end to the Roman Empire in the West, and Roman Britain came under the control of the Anglo-Saxons. Over the course of the next several centuries, Anglo-Saxon institutions developed, Roman Catholic Christianity became the religion of the land, the several Anglo-Saxon kingdoms became the united kingdom of England, and the English fought a long struggle against the Danes.

The Anglo-Saxon Conquest

The Barbarian Invasions

In the fifth century, tribes of Germanic barbarians crossed the Rhine and Danube frontiers of the Roman Empire. By the latter part of the century, the East Goths (Ostrogoths) dominated Italy, while the West Goths (Visigoths) created a kingdom in the northern and central Iberian peninsula (modern Spain and Portugal). The Vandals controlled the southern Iberian peninsula and the western part of North Africa, while the Franks established their kingdom in Gaul and western Germany. The Angles and Saxons crossed into Roman Britain.

Early Anglo-Saxon England

After invading the eastern and southeastern areas of what became England, the Anglo-Saxons gradually moved up the rivers into the interior. The Britons offered some resistance. About A.D. 500, for example, a chieftain named Arthur, who became the legendary King Arthur of the Roundtable, defeated the Anglo-Saxons at Mount Badon. But the Anglo-Saxon tide ultimately proved irresistible.

Rather than moving into the Roman towns, the Anglo-Saxons, who lived by farming and hunting, preferred to settle in the countryside. The Roman towns became depopulated and fell into ruins, the Roman villas were abandoned, and the Roman roads were neglected, although the main roads continued to be used.

Anglo-Saxon Religion

The Anglo-Saxon invaders were pagans who worshipped nature gods. Several of the days of the week acquired their names from these gods. Woden, the god of war, gave his name to Wednesday, while Thursday got its name from Thunor, the weather god. Friday was named for Frig, the goddess of fertility. The Christian Easter got its name from the Anglo-Saxon goddess Eostre, the goddess of spring.

The Heptarchy

By the beginning of the seventh century, England was dominated by a number of warring Anglo-Saxon tribes and petty kingdoms, although the Anglo-Saxons had not yet won control of the Cornish peninsula in the southwest or the area of the Cumbrian Mountains in the northwest. Further to the west were the Welsh and Irish, while the Scots and the Picts dominated the north.

Gradually the seven kingdoms of the Anglo-Saxon heptarchy developed: Northumbria, Mercia, East Anglia, Essex, Wessex, Kent, and Sussex. Of these seven, Kent, Northumbria, Mercia, and Wessex proved to be the most influential. The king who exercised at least a nominal overlordship over his fellow monarchs was known as the *Bretwalda* (Britain-ruler).

The Dominance of Mercia

Kent and Northumbria exerted successive leadership during the sixth and seventh centuries. In the early eighth century, Mercia gained control over all of England south of the Humber. King Offa II (r. 757–796) of Mercia succeeded in winning control of most of western England, and the dividing line between the Anglo-Saxons and the Welsh was drawn by an earthwork known as Offa's Dyke, which extended from North Wales to the Bristol Channel. King Offa promoted trade, signing a trade treaty with the Frankish emperor Charlemagne. Offa also improved the coinage, although the English penny got its name from another Mercian king, Penda.

Anglo-Saxon Kingdoms, Early Seventh Century

Wessex Supremacy

King Egbert (r. 802–839) of Mercia conquered Cornwall in the southwest and won nominal allegiance from the king of Northumbria. Nevertheless, Mercian power declined during the early ninth century, and dominance over England passed to Wessex.

Christianity in Anglo-Saxon England

Celtic Christianity

After the Anglo-Saxons conquered England, Christianity largely disappeared except among the surviving Celtic Christians in Wales and Ireland.

Differences from Roman Catholicism

The Celtic Christians were out of touch with the Roman Catholic Christians of the European continent, and several differences developed between Celtic Christianity and Roman Catholic Christianity. The Celtic Christians did not acknowledge the pope as the head of the church, and the Celtic church did not require its priests to be celibate. Celtic and Roman Catholic Christians also had different methods for calculating the date of Easter and differed on other matters, including ritual and liturgy, the shape of the monastic tonsure, and ecclesiastical organization.

Missionary Achievements

Celtic Christian missionaries continued their efforts to spread the faith. In 563, St. Columba, an Irish monk, established a monastery at Iona, off the coast of Scotland. The monks of Iona converted many Scots and Picts to Christianity.

St. Augustine of Canterbury

In the late sixth century, King Ethelbert (r. 560–616) of Kent expanded his domains to include most of England south of the Humber. He married Bertha, the daughter of the king of the Franks, and Frankish Roman Catholic priests came to England.

In 597, Pope Gregory I the Great (r. 590–604) sent the learned monk Augustine (d. 605) and forty monks to begin the conversion of England to Roman Catholicism. King Ethelbert gave Augustine and his monks a place to live at Canterbury, the capital of Kent. Ethelbert became one of Augustine's earliest converts, the first Anglo-Saxon king to embrace Christianity. Augustine was soon consecrated as the first archbishop of Canterbury.

Spread of Roman Catholicism

From Kent, Roman Catholic Christianity began to spread into East Anglia and Northumbria. Ethelbert's daughter married King Edwin (r. 616–632) of Northumbria, who became the dominant figure in the heptarchy soon after Ethelbert's death. As a result of his wife's influence, Edwin adopted Roman Catholicism in 627.

Celtic Resistance

However, Roman Catholicism did not spread widely in Northumbria. Instead, Celtic Christian missionaries from Scotland, led by Aidan, won many Northumbrian converts. Aidan established the great monastery of Lindisfarne ("Holy Island") off the Northumbrian coast in 635.

The Synod of Whitby (664)

At the Synod of Whitby in 664, representatives of the Celtic and Roman Catholic Christians debated their differences in the presence of King Oswy (r. 642–670) of Northumbria. Oswy decided in favor of the Roman Catholics, and England now became joined religiously with the rest of Western Europe.

Theodore of Tarsus

In 669, the pope named Theodore of Tarsus, a Greek scholar, archbishop of Canterbury. Theodore reorganized the English Church along Roman Catholic lines and increased the number of bishoprics. All English Christians now recognized the authority of the archbishop of Canterbury.

The Archbishopric of York

A second archbishopric was established in York, the capital of Northumbria, with the authority to direct the work of the church north of the Humber. Paulinus (d. 644), a Roman monk, is often regarded as the first archbishop of York.

Anglo-Saxon Society

The Class Structure

Nobility

In the early Anglo-Saxon period, there was a nobility of birth, known as eorls. Subsequently, a new nobility of wealth and service developed, known as thegns (thanes). A thegn held at least five hides of land, although some possessed considerably more. (A hide was 120 acres.) In wartime, each five-hide unit was required to provide one man for the army.

Freemen

The non-noble freemen were known as ceorls (churls). Landed ceorls generally held one hide of land. Landless ceorls worked as craftsmen in the towns or as wage-labor on the land.

Serfs

The serfs were bound to the land. They worked on the land of noble landholders and paid their overlords with a share of their produce.

Slaves

The slaves, who could be freely bought and sold, were a small class. They comprised prisoners taken in war, persons who were being punished for crimes, or persons who had lost their status as freemen because of economic hardship.

Centers of Habitation

Villages

Most Anglo-Saxons lived in small farming villages, known as tuns, which consisted of about ten to thirty families.

Towns

Larger towns, later known as boroughs, were relatively few in early Anglo-Saxon times. London, the commercial center, was the only sizable town. As trade and handicraft industry gradually developed, the towns became larger and more numerous.

Anglo-Saxon Government

The Hundreds

The hundreds were administrative and judicial units. In the midlands, a hundred usually contained about 100 hides of land (12,000 acres). Elsewhere, the size of a hundred varied from less than 20 to more than 150 hides.

The hundred court, attended by the free landholders in the hundred, met every four weeks to consider civil and criminal cases, judging them on the basis of customary law. The hundred courts also served as agencies of local government.

The Shires

The shires, later called counties, were the largest administrative units in Anglo-Saxon England.

Each shire had a shire court, which met twice a year. An official known as the ealdorman presided over the shire court and generally acted as the king's representative in the shire.

In later Anglo-Saxon times, ealdormen supervised several shires, while another official, the shire reeve (sheriff), represented the king in the shire and presided over the shire and hundred courts. The shire reeve had the particular responsibility of collecting royal revenues, including rents from royal estates and fines imposed by the shire and hundred courts. The shire reeve occasionally commanded the local militia, called the fyrd.

The King and the Witan

In Anglo-Saxon England, the king was the highest authority. But while his power was considerable, it was not absolute.

The king ruled in association with a council known as the Witan (also called the Witenagemot). The Witan did not have a clearly established membership, although it included the thegns, the ealdormen, important officials of the king's court, and the archbishops, bishops, and abbots (heads of monasteries).

The Witan met at the call of the king to advise him on important matters and acted as a court for the trial of important men and cases of major interest to the king. The Witan also had the authority to choose the king when the throne became vacant. Usually, but not always, it elected the dead king's eldest son.

A strong king could usually dominate the Witan, while a weak king frequently gave way to it. But no king could simply ignore the Witan.

Anglo-Saxon Law

The customary law of the Anglo-Saxons gradually came to be supplemented by written laws enacted by the kings and Witans. These written laws, known as dooms, dealt mostly with theft and crimes of violence. The penalties included death and mutilation, as well as fines. Imprisonment was seldom imposed as a penalty.

The Bot and the Wergeld

Anglo-Saxon law emphasized the payment of monetary compensation to an injured individual or his relatives.

A bot was paid to an injured party, while the family of a murdered man would be compensated by a wergeld. The higher the social position of the injured person, the higher was the compensation.

Determining Guilt or Innocence

The Anglo-Saxon system of justice established several methods for determining guilt or innocence.

Compurgation

In compurgation, or proof by oath, the process began with the plaintiff and defendant taking oaths. The plaintiff and defendant then would gather oath-helpers or compurgators who would swear that the charge or denial was true. These oaths had to be made with verbal accuracy and without stammering; inaccuracy or stammering were regarded as indications of guilt.

The Ordeal

If compurgation did not resolve the case, the defendant might have to undergo an ordeal.

In the ordeal of hot iron, a defendant had to carry a piece of hot iron in his hand. If the hand healed cleanly, it was a sign of innocence. If it did not, the defendant was judged guilty.

In the ordeal of hot water, a defendant picked a stone out of a pot of boiling water. Once again, if the hand healed cleanly, the defendant was deemed innocent. If it did not, he was found guilty.

In the ordeal of cold water, an accused person was tied up and thrown into a pool of water that had been blessed by a priest. If he sank, he was innocent. If he floated, he was guilty, since the blessed water had rejected him.

The Anglo-Saxon Struggle Against the Danes

The Vikings

In the ninth century, the Vikings, also known as the Norsemen, poured out of Scandinavia, assaulted the shores of Western Europe, and even pushed into the Mediterranean. To the East, they advanced deep into Russia, and some even reached Constantinople, the capital of the Byzantine Empire. Sailing westward into the Atlantic, the Vikings established settlements in Iceland and Greenland and landed in North America.

The Coming of the Danes

In English history, the Vikings are known as the Danes. The first Danish attack on England occurred about 787. Then, in the early ninth century, the Danes turned their attention to Ireland, completely overrunning it.

In 834, the Danes renewed their attacks on England. The raids gradually increased both in number and intensity, and by the late ninth century, most of northern and eastern England, including Northumbria, East Anglia, and Mercia, had come under their control. The Danes then turned against Wessex.

King Alfred the Great (r. 871–899)

King Alfred of Wessex, a talented statesman and soldier and the greatest figure in the history of Anglo-Saxon England, succeeded in pushing the Danes back. Alfred is often regarded as the first king of a united England.

The Battle of Ashdown (871)

In January 871, Alfred, who had not yet become king, defeated the Danes at the Battle of Ashdown. In the spring, following the death of his brother, King Ethelred, Alfred succeeded to the throne. During the summer, nine battles were fought, and in 872, Alfred arranged a truce.

The Treaty of Chippenham (878)

In 876, the Danes renewed their assault on Wessex. Once again defeating the Danes, Alfred and the Danish leader, Guthrum, agreed in 878 to the Treaty of Chippenham. Guthrum embraced Christianity and promised not to renew the war. Although Guthrum did not observe this commitment fully, during King Alfred's reign the Danes never again posed a serious threat to Wessex.

The Treaty of Wedmore (886)

In 884, Danes from the continent landed in Kent and won support from their fellow Danes in East Anglia. Once again, Alfred defeated the Danes. Alfred and Guthrum signed a new agreement, the Treaty of Wedmore (886), which granted to the Danes a territory known as the Danelaw, located to the north and east of London. The Danelaw included East Anglia, Essex, Mercia, and Northumbria. Alfred remained in control of all of southern England and the western midlands.

Containment of the Danes

Following Guthrum's death in 892, the Danes renewed the struggle. Alfred conducted a defensive war, and the Danes were unable to defeat him in battle.

By the time of Alfred's death in 899, both sides were exhausted. Nevertheless, Alfred had succeeded in holding the Danes back, and over a century would pass before the Danes again launched a systematic invasion of England.

Other Achievements of King Alfred

Although Alfred spent most of his time and energy combatting the threat of the Danes, he had other achievements to his credit. He actively promoted education, establishing a palace school. He also promoted a reform of the monasteries and directed a codification of the laws.

Alfred encouraged the translation of books from Latin into Anglo-Saxon. Among the works translated was the Venerable Bede's *History of the English Church and People,* which had been completed at the monastery of Lindisfarne in 731. In addition, Alfred inspired the beginning of the *Anglo-Saxon Chronicle,* which brought the narrative of English history down to Alfred's reign.

The Reconquest of the Danelaw

Alfred's son, King Edward the Elder (r. 899–924), and Edward's three sons renewed the war against the Danes in an effort to reconquer the Danelaw. By 954, the effort succeeded with the defeat of Eric Bloodaxe at the Battle of Stainmore. England was now united under the leadership of the royal house of Wessex.

The Age of Dunstan

The reign of King Edgar the Peaceful (r. 959–975) is also known as the Age of Dunstan (c. 910–988), who became archbishop of Canterbury in 961.

Educated in the palace school established by King Alfred, Dunstan entered the service of the church. He served as an adviser to King Edmund I (r. 940–946) and subsequently became abbot of the great monastery of Glastonbury. Dunstan then spent some time on the continent, where he became acquainted with the monastic reform movement that had begun at Cluny in France in 910. The Cluniac reform promoted a return to the strict observance of the rule of monastic life written by St. Benedict, an Italian monk, in the sixth century.

As archbishop of Canterbury, Dunstan promoted the monastic reform in England and encouraged the founding of new monasteries.

King Ethelred the Redeless (r. 978–1016)

In the late tenth century, the English monarchy declined as noble factions asserted themselves against the king. In 978, rebellious noblemen murdered the unpopular King Edward the Martyr (r. 975–978).

Edward's younger brother, Ethelred, became king at the age of ten. During his minority, dissension among the nobles increased. The situation did not improve after Ethelred came of age, and the king's ineffectiveness won him the nickname of "the Redeless" (lacking in counsel; sometimes he is called Ethelred the Unready).

Renewed Danish Threat

Taking advantage of the situation, the Danes renewed their pressure on England. Sporadic raiding began in 980 and grew in intensity. In 991, the Danes defeated Ethelred at the Battle of Maldon.

The Danegeld

Ethelred tried to buy off the Danes, paying a tribute known as the Danegeld. The cost of the tribute was covered by a direct tax on land, which was levied six times during Ethelred's reign.

Danish Rule

In 1013, the Danish king Sweyn forced Ethelred to flee to Normandy. Sweyn claimed the English throne, but he died a few months later.

King Canute (r. 1016–1035)

Following Sweyn's death, his son, Canute, continued the effort to conquer England. Led by Edmund Ironside, Ethelred's son, the English fought against Canute, but they were defeated at the Battle of Ashington in Essex in 1016. Edmund and Canute then signed a treaty, dividing the kingdom between them. However, Edmund suddenly died late in 1016, and Canute became the sole king of England. Canute created an empire, uniting England with Denmark and Norway. He followed the Danish pattern by dividing his kingdom into several large earldoms. In order to solidify his position among his English subjects, Canute married Ethelred's widow, Emma of Normandy, and permitted the English to retain their traditional laws and customs.

Canute's Successors

Following Canute's death, his empire collapsed. Norway had already been lost, while Denmark passed to Harthacanute, Canute's son. The English Witan voted to make Harold Harefoote, Canute's illegitimate son, regent of England with authority to govern until Harthacanute could leave Denmark. Harold then made himself king.

Following Harold's death in 1040, Harthacanute came to England to claim his throne. He died without heirs in 1042.

Wessex Restoration:
King Edward the Confessor (r. 1042–1066)

The Witan now turned back to the royal house of Wessex and elected Edward, the son of Ethelred the Redeless and Emma of Normandy, as king. Because of his religious fervor, he soon became known as Edward the Confessor.

Edward had lived in Normandy for most of his life and was not well-acquainted with England or its people. He brought to England with him many Norman nobles and priests, who were resented by the English nobility.

Earl Godwin of Wessex

Earl Godwin of Wessex was the leading figure among the king's opponents. In 1051, Godwin supported the English citizens of Dover against a French nobleman who was a friend of the king. While Edward succeeded in forcing Godwin into exile, the earl was able to return in 1052 and to renew his opposition to the king.

Responding to growing anti-Norman sentiment, the Witan removed Robert of Jumièges as archbishop of Canterbury, replacing him with Stigand, an English supporter of Godwin. The pope refused to acknowledge Stigand, however, regarding him as a usurper.

Following Godwin's death in 1053, the earldom of Wessex passed to his son, Harold Godwinson.

King Harold (r. 1066) and His Opponents

In January 1066, the childless King Edward the Confessor died, after allegedly having named Harold Godwinson as his successor. The Witan soon confirmed the dead king's action.

Harold of Norway

King Harold faced two opponents. The first was Harold Hardrada, the king of Norway, whose claim was based on the fact that England had been part of the domains ruled by his predecessor, Canute. Harold Hardrada had the support of Tostig, the earl of Northumbria, who was the brother of King Harold (Godwinson). When the thegns of Yorkshire had declared Tostig an outlaw in 1065, he had taken refuge in Flanders. Harold Hardrada and Tostig threatened to invade England to challenge Harold.

William of Normandy

Harold's second opponent was his cousin, William, the duke of Normandy, who also claimed the English throne and was preparing an invasion force.

Anglo-Saxon Literature

In addition to the Venerable Bede's *History of the English Church and People* and the *Anglo-Saxon Chronicle* [see p. 19], the literary heritage of Anglo-Saxon England includes the work of the poet Caedmon and the epic poem *Beowulf.*

Caedmon

Caedmon, a seventh-century poet and the first English poet known by name, was a Northumbrian herdsman who became a lay brother in the abbey of Whitby. *Caedmon's Hymn,* written about 665, may well be the first literary work composed in England.

Beowulf

Beowulf, the oldest English epic, tells the story of a Scandinavian hero. Probably written in Northumbria in the early eighth century, it provides a striking picture of early Germanic life. The earliest surviving manuscript of *Beowulf* was written in Saxon in the late tenth century.

The history of England from the ninth century to the early eleventh century was dominated by the long struggle of the English against the Danes. Although the royal house of Wessex regained the throne in the person of Edward the Confessor, soon after his death England was conquered by the Normans, and a new era in English history began.

Recommended Reading

Ashe, Geoffrey. *The Quest for Arthur's Britain* (1968).

Barlow, Frank. *Edward the Confessor* (1970).

Barlow, Frank. *The English Church, 1000–1066* (2nd ed., 1979).

Blair, Peter Hunter. *An Introduction to Anglo-Saxon England* (2nd ed., 1977).

Brown, P. David. *Anglo-Saxon England* (1978).

Bryant, Arthur. *The Story of England: Makers of the Realm* (1953).

Campbell, James, ed. *The Anglo-Saxons* (1982).

Crossley-Holland, Kevin, ed. *The Anglo-Saxon World* (1983).

Duckett, Eleanor S. *Alfred the Great: The King and His England* (1957).

Duckett, Eleanor S. *Anglo-Saxon Saints and Scholars* (1947).

Duckett, Eleanor S. *St. Dunstan of Canterbury: A Study of Monastic Reform in the Tenth Century* (1955).

Farmer, D. H., ed. *The Age of Bede* (rev. ed., 1983).

Fell, Christine, et al. *Women in Anglo-Saxon England and the Impact of 1066* (1986).

Finberg, H. P. R. *The Formation of England, 550–1042* (1974).

Laing, Lloyd and Jennifer Laing. *Anglo-Saxon England* (1979).

Loyn, Henry R. *The Governance of Anglo-Saxon England, 500–1087* (1984).

Loyn, Henry R. *The Vikings in Britain* (1977).

Mayr-Harting, Henry. *The Coming of Christianity to Anglo-Saxon England* (1972).

Stenton, Frank M. *Anglo-Saxon England* (3rd ed., 1971).

Whitelock, Dorothy. *From Bede to Alfred: Studies in Early Anglo-Saxon Literature and History* (1980).

Wilson, David. *The Anglo-Saxons* (3rd ed., 1981).

CHAPTER 3

The Normans

Time Line

1107	King Henry I and Anselm agree to the Compromise of Bec
1128	Matilda marries Geoffrey of Anjou
1135–1154	Reign of King Stephen
1153	The Treaty of Wallingford recognizes Henry of Anjou as King Stephen's heir

In 1066, William, the duke of Normandy, crossed the English Channel and began his conquest of England. The Norman Conquest was an important turning point in English history.

William the Conqueror established a powerful monarchy and created the best-organized state to exist in Western Europe since the fall of the Roman Empire in the West some 600 years earlier.

As a consequence of the Norman Conquest, the Norman nobility replaced the old Anglo-Saxon nobility, and the institutions of Norman feudalism fused with Anglo-Saxon traditions. England was brought into closer contact with the European continent. While the English in many cases gained from this contact, England often became embroiled in French affairs.

The Norman Conquest

Normandy

In the early tenth century, a Viking known as Rollo or Rolfe created a duchy in northwestern France known as Normandy, the land of the Northmen. The Normans adopted the Roman Catholic faith, and the dukes of Normandy expanded their territorial holdings, developing a powerful state with its capital at Rouen.

In theory, the dukes of Normandy were feudal vassals of the king of France. In fact, however, the French kings of the tenth and eleventh centuries were relatively weak, and the dukes of Normandy could act independently.

Born in 1027, William the Bastard, the illegitimate son of Duke Robert the Devil, became duke in 1035 at the age of eight. When William came of age, he increased his power at the expense of the

Norman nobility and defended Normandy's independence against the king of France.

The Invasion of Tostig and Harold Hardrada

In 1066, Tostig, the exiled earl of Northumbria and brother of England's King Harold (r. 1066), and Harold Hardrada, the king of Norway, landed an invasion force in Yorkshire. King Harold rushed northward to meet the invaders, defeating them at the Battle of Stamford Bridge on September 25. Both Tostig and Harold Hardrada were killed in the battle. Meanwhile, William of Normandy was preparing his own assault on England.

The Norman Invasion

Three days after the Battle of Stamford Bridge, on September 28, 1066, Duke William landed at Pevensey in southern England.

Duke William's Claim

William based his claim to the English crown on commitments purportedly made by King Edward the Confessor and King Harold (see Chapter 2). First, William claimed that the childless Edward the Confessor had promised him the succession while visiting Normandy in 1051. Then, in 1064, Harold had visited William in Normandy. On that occasion, William insisted, Harold had made a similar promise.

The Battle of Hastings

William's army employed primarily horsemen with coats of mail; the infantry was subordinate. In contrast, Harold's army consisted mostly of infantry.

The two armies met near Hastings in Sussex on October 14, 1066. William won a decisive victory, and Harold died in the battle.

King William the Conqueror
(r. 1066–1087)

William's Coronation

Following his victory at Hastings, William advanced northward and encircled London. The English leaders gave way, and the Witan acknowledged him as king. William was crowned in London's Westminster Abbey on Christmas Day 1066.

Suppression of Opposition

In 1067, while William I, known after Hastings as William the Conqueror, was away in Normandy, revolts broke out in England. By 1069, a general war was underway.

By 1071, however, William succeeded in crushing the revolts. The Normans now carried out a campaign of devastation, especially in northern England, to make sure that the rebellion would not be renewed.

Securing His Position

In order to strengthen his position further, William built a series of castles at key points in England and along the Welsh border. Both the Tower of London and Windsor Castle, located a few miles outside the capital, began as Norman castles.

In 1072, William advanced into Scotland, and he also pushed into Wales, building a castle at Cardiff. On the continent, he conquered Maine, southwest of Normandy, in 1073.

Norman Feudalism

William the Conqueror confiscated the lands of the English nobility who had opposed him. He kept a large portion of these lands for himself and distributed the remainder to his Norman nobles.

According to the feudal principle, all land belonged to the king, who was the suzerain (feudal overlord) of those who received land from him. Those to whom the king made grants of land, known as fiefs, were his vassals. These vassals of the king, known as tenants-in-chief, took oaths of fealty to their suzerain, pledging their loyalty and military and other service.

Subinfeudation

In turn, the king's vassals distributed part of their fiefs to lower-ranking members of the nobility, who were obliged to help their overlords fulfill their service obligations to the king. This process, known as subinfeudation, continued down through the various ranks of the nobility. On one level, a great baron might hold a large number of manors (estates). On the lowest level, a knight might hold only one. In each instance, the individual who granted the fief became the suzerain of the person who received it. In turn, the recipient became the vassal of his suzerain.

Feudal Obligations

Each suzerain was obligated to provide protection for his vassals, while the vassals owed loyalty and service to their suzerain. Vassals were generally obliged to provide a specific number of knights to their suzerain, customarily for forty days of service a year. The vassals could also be called upon to attend their suzerain's court to assist in the administration of justice. In addition, vassals were obliged to contribute to the ransom of their suzerain if he was captured by an enemy and to entertain their suzerain on visits. If a vassal failed to meet his obligations or if he was convicted of a serious crime, the fief could revert to the suzerain.

Royal Supremacy

In the feudal system of Norman England, William the Conqueror made certain that his position as the supreme feudal overlord would remain unchallenged. He did not want his nobility to gain the sort of independence of royal authority enjoyed by the French nobility of this era.

William distributed fiefs to his nobility in scattered holdings so the nobles would be unable to establish strong power bases. The only exception to this occurred along the frontiers or marches, as they were known, where noblemen received large fiefs in exchange for providing protection against the troublesome Welsh and Scots.

In every county, the king remained the largest landholder. Furthermore, lesser vassals swore feudal oaths of allegiance to the king that took precedence over their oaths to their immediate suzerains. William also retained the old Anglo-Saxon militia, the *fyrd,* and used it against a group of rebellious nobles in 1075. In addition, William retained the old Anglo-Saxon shire and hundred courts, which operated under royal authority. This prevented the feudal nobility from gaining too much control over the local administration of justice.

The local sheriffs remained under royal control and became the king's chief agents in local government.

The Manors

The manors were largely self-sufficient estates, consisting of the manor house, the village, and fields, pastures, orchards, and woods.

Serfs.   The workers on the manors were usually serfs, who were bound to the land and could not leave without the permission of the lord of the manor. The serfs farmed both the land allotted to them and the lord's land (the desmesne). The serfs were also required to pay rent, usually in kind, to the lord.

Freemen.   Most of the coerls (see Chapter 2) who still possessed their freedom at the time of the Norman Conquest became serfs, but a few maintained their status as freemen. These freemen paid rents, usually in produce but occasionally in money, to the lords for their use of the land.

The Domesday Book

In 1085, William I appointed a commission to undertake what became known as the Domesday inquest, a thorough survey of the economic resources of the kingdom for purposes of taxation. Royal clerks subsequently rearranged the survey data in two volumes, known as the Domesday Book, which provides extensive information regarding England's landholding and feudal conditions in the generation after the conquest.

William I's Government

The Great Council

At first, the king's great council *(magnum concilium)* resembled the Anglo-Saxon Witan, including among its members the most important noblemen and the bishops and abbots. As the feudal system developed, the great council's membership came to be based on landholding. The great council included only the king's tenants-in-chief (the barons) and the bishops and abbots who had the status of barons in the feudal system.

The great council customarily met three times a year. Its membership totaled about 500, although a smaller number attended its meetings. The king could seek the advice of the great council, and he could ask it to endorse his decrees, although he was not obliged to do so. The great council also had extensive judicial functions.

The Curia Regis

In addition, a smaller permanent council, the *curia regis,* consisted of noblemen serving the king and officials of the royal household. Among the king's officials were the chancellor, a royal secretary who prepared documents, and the justiciar, the head of the royal judicial system who also acted as the king's chief assistant in administrative matters. In the king's absence, the justiciar customarily served as regent. In time, the *curia regis* evolved into a body of specialized officials who supervised the work of the government.

William I and the Church

The pope supported William's invasion of England in 1066 after William promised to remove Stigand as archbishop of Canterbury (see Chapter 2). Nevertheless, William was determined to control the church.

Lanfranc's Reforms

Lanfranc, an Italian theologian whose selection was endorsed by the pope, served as archbishop of Canterbury from 1070 to 1089. He had previously headed the monastery of Bec in Normandy. Norman churchmen replaced most of the Anglo-Saxon bishops.

William supported Lanfranc's efforts to reform the English church. These reforms included enforcing clerical celibacy and monastic discipline, improving the education of the clergy, and eliminating simony (the sale of church offices).

William's Ecclesiastical Claims

While William I cooperated with Pope Gregory VII (r. 1073–1085) in his campaign to reform the church, he refused to accept the pope's assertion that temporal rulers should acknowledge the supremacy of papal authority. The king would not permit the pope to control the selection of bishops and abbots. Instead, he insisted that they be elected in his presence or in the presence of his representative. In addition, the king refused to allow appeals to papal courts without his permission, and no papal letters or legates could be received in England without his consent. Furthermore, no vassal (tenant-in-chief) of the king could be excommunicated without the king's approval.

System of Church Courts

William separated the systems of secular and ecclesiastical justice. Bishops would no longer preside over hundred courts, as they had occasionally done, nor could clergy be tried in these courts. New church courts would try all cases involving members of the clergy and cases covered by canon law (the law of the church). The creation of this system of church courts paved the way for the conflict between the English state and the church later in the Middle Ages.

William the Conqueror's Last Years

During the final years of his reign, William became embroiled in a conflict with King Philip I of France (r. 1060–1108), who supported William's eldest son, Robert, in a revolt against his father. Open warfare broke out in 1087. During the conflict, William suffered a fatal injury when he was thrown from his horse. He died at Rouen, Normandy's capital, on September 9, 1087.

Norman Culture

The Norman conquest led to increased ties between England and the European continent. Normans held the key positions in the government and the church, and they maintained their contacts with the continent. In addition, English trade with the continent increased.

Language

Under the Normans, French became the language of government and law, and educated people were fluent in both French and Latin. English was largely reduced to the status of a spoken language, where it remained until the fourteenth century. English grammar gradually became simplified, and the vocabulary was enriched with French words.

Literature

Most writers of the Norman period wrote in Latin. Chroniclers kept records of events. The best known of these chroniclers, William of Malmesbury (d. c. 1143), wrote a notable account of the reigns of Henry I and Stephen.

Eadmer (d. 1124), a monk at Canterbury, wrote a six-volume history of England during the period from 1066 to 1122, as well as a biography of Archbishop Anselm.

Geoffrey of Monmouth (c. 1100–1154) wrote a history of the kings of Britain that is one of the sources of the legend of King Arthur and Merlin the magician.

Architecture

In addition to building castles, the Normans built some 300 churches and several monasteries. New cathedrals were erected in some of the major cities, including Chester, Durham, Lincoln, and Norwich.

Norman architecture was a type of the Romanesque style that was typical of Western European architecture during the eleventh and twelfth centuries. It was characterized by the use of round arches, massive, heavy walls, and small windows.

King William Rufus (r. 1087–1100)

The Succession to William the Conqueror

When William the Conqueror died in 1087, he left the duchy of Normandy to Robert, his eldest son. The English crown passed to William's second son, William II, known as William Rufus (William the Red-Faced). The succession was determined by William the Conqueror, without a vote of the Great Council.

Many of the Norman barons in England preferred Robert, and a rebellion against William Rufus, led by Bishop Odo of Bayeux, William I's brother, broke out in 1088. Although William I had exiled Odo from England, he had returned. Robert failed to support the revolt fully, and William Rufus suppressed it.

William Rufus and the Church

Following the death of Lanfranc in 1089, William Rufus left the position of archbishop of Canterbury vacant for four years, collecting its revenues for himself. He did the same with several other vacant bishoprics.

When the king fell ill in 1093, he became repentant. At the king's urging, Anselm, the Italian-born abbot of the monastery of Bec in Normandy, agreed to become archbishop of Canterbury.

Following William Rufus's recovery, he became involved in a quarrel with Anselm, who was a strong defender of the rights and privileges of the church. Anselm opposed the king's confiscation of church lands, as well as the king's efforts to gain more complete control over the selection of bishops. In 1097, following several years of conflict, William allowed Anselm to go into exile.

Territorial Expansion

When Robert went on the First Crusade (see Chapter 4) in 1096, William Rufus gained control of Normandy. He also invaded Wales and Scotland, compelling the Scottish king Malcolm III to do him homage and annexing Cumberland.

These expansionist activities proved expensive, and William raised money by pressuring the nobility almost to the point of extortion and by selling church offices.

The Death of William Rufus

On August 2, 1100, while hunting in the New Forest in Hampshire, William Rufus was shot through the heart. It might have been an accident, but perhaps it was murder, arranged by the king's younger brother, Henry.

King Henry I (r. 1100–1135)

Following his brother's death, Henry quickly made good his claim to the throne. Robert, Henry's oldest brother, was unable to assert his claim, since he had not yet returned from the First Crusade. To strengthen his position, Henry I, known as Henry Beauclerc, married Edith, the daughter of the king of Scotland and great-granddaughter of Edmund Ironside (see Chapter 2). He imprisoned Ranulf Flambard, the bishop of Durham who had been William Rufus's unpopular justiciar.

Henry I's Coronation Charter

In his coronation charter, Henry I promised to redress grievances, to abide by the laws of Edward the Confessor, and to keep a "firm peace" in England. Although these pledges were too vague to restrict Henry's freedom of action, the coronation charter recognized, at least by implication, that the king was subject to the law. This provided a precedent for the Magna Carta, which the barons forced King John to sign in 1215 (see Chapter 4).

Conflict with Robert

In 1101, Robert returned from the Holy Land and invaded England, landing at Portsmouth. Robert won the support of several English barons, including Ranulf Flambard who had escaped from his imprisonment in the Tower of London.

The conflict was resolved by diplomacy when Henry agreed to pay Robert a large annual pension. Henry was confirmed as king of England and Robert as duke of Normandy.

Acquisition of Normandy

Robert proved to be an ineffective ruler of Normandy, and the duchy sank into chaos. Encouraged by several Norman barons, Henry invaded Normandy in 1106. Defeating Robert in the Battle of Tinchebrai, Henry imprisoned him in Cardiff Castle, where he died at the age of 80 in 1134. Thus, forty years after the Norman conquest of England in the Battle of Hastings, Henry I of England conquered Normandy.

Henry I and the Church

Conflict with Anselm

Early in his reign, to get into the good graces of the church, Henry I recalled Anselm to Canterbury. A conflict soon developed between royal and ecclesiastical authority, however. Henry insisted that Anselm pay him homage as his feudal tenant-in-chief, but the archbishop refused to do so. A second conflict involved investiture. Pope Gregory VII had declared that the investiture of a bishop with his staff and ring, the symbols of his office, could be performed only by a churchman. This appeared to threaten the king's power to control appointments to high church office, and Anselm supported the papal position. Henry responded by seizing church lands and exiling the archbishop.

Compromise of Bec

Under the terms of the Compromise of Bec of 1107, Henry and Anselm agreed that churchmen would render homage for their fiefs, thereby acknowledging that they were feudal vassals of the king. The compromise also provided that, while bishops would be elected in the presence of the king or a royal official, the church would invest them with their symbols of office.

This compromise represented a royal victory, since the king could readily influence the election of bishops by the cathedral chapters (the clergy of a cathedral). The question of who actually invested them with their symbols of office was of little practical significance.

When Anselm died in 1109, Henry left the archbishopric of Canterbury vacant for several years, and the income went to the royal treasury.

Henry I's Government

Henry I reformed the great council by requiring the attendance of a select group of barons, while the king's chief officials constituted the small council, the *curia regis*.

The Exchequer

When the *curia regis* met with a staff of clerks to deal with financial matters, it was called the Exchequer. This name probably came from the checkered cloth that covered the table of accounts. The Exchequer audited the reports of the sheriffs, who collected most of the royal revenues, twice a year and generally kept tabs on the sheriffs and other local officials, making certain that the king received the revenues due him.

Itinerant Justices

Henry I, who gained the title "lion of justice," also began the practice of sending out itinerant justices, who went from the *curia regis* to the shire courts to administer justice in the name of the king. During the reign of Henry I, this practice was just getting under way. It would be considerably expanded later in the century during the reign of King Henry II (see Chapter 4).

The Decline of Feudalism

Less than a century after its establishment by William the Conqueror, the feudal system began to decline in England. Henry I began to take money payments, known as scutage (shield money), from bishops in lieu of service. The barons also began to accept money payments from their knights instead of military service. Subsequently, Henry I's successor, King Stephen, preferred to fight his battles with hired mercenaries rather than a feudal army.

The Growth of Towns

The decline of feudalism was accompanied by a growth of towns, which was fostered by the revival of trade. Wealthy towns were able to buy charters from the king, giving them rights of self-government.

Matilda and Stephen

Matilda's Claim to the Throne

Henry I's only son, William, drowned in 1120, while returning to England from Normandy in a ship manned by a drunken crew. Henry called on the English barons to recognize his daughter Matilda as his heir. The barons agreed to do so, hoping to benefit from the reign of a woman.

In 1128, Matilda, at that time the widow of the Holy Roman Emperor Henry V, married Geoffrey, the son of the Count of Anjou. Geoffrey was known as the Plantagenet because of the sprig of broom (*genista*) he wore in his helmet.

The Accession of King Stephen

On December 1, 1135, Henry I suddenly died. Despite their earlier oaths, the barons gave the crown to Stephen of Blois, the grandson of William the Conqueror and nephew of Henry I. Stephen (r. 1135–1154) had the powerful support of his brother Henry, the bishop of Winchester and abbot of Glastonbury who was also the papal legate. Matilda fled to Normandy.

Stephen quickly proved to be an ineffective ruler, unable to control the barons who acted with increasing independence of royal authority.

Civil War

In 1139, Matilda returned to England to challenge Stephen. Several years of indecisive civil war ensued, although Geoffrey of Anjou did succeed in conquering Normandy.

Treaty of Wallingford

When Geoffrey died in 1151, Matilda gave her claim to the English throne to their eldest son, Henry of Anjou. The ruler of Normandy, Anjou, and Maine, Henry invaded England in 1152. Under the terms of the Treaty of Wallingford, signed in November 1153, Stephen would remain king for the rest of his life. Henry of Anjou was recognized as his heir. The settlement also provided for the razing of over 1000 illegal castles built by the barons after 1135.

The Accession of Henry II, First of the Angevins

In October 1154, Stephen died, and Henry of Anjou succeeded to the throne as Henry II. The direct line of Norman kings ended, and England now had a new royal family, the Angevins, also known as the Plantagenets.

During King Stephen's reign, the prestige and power of the monarchy established by William the Conqueror had declined as the nobility asserted its claims against the crown. The anarchy of these years showed the need for an effective monarch who could provide the country with a stable government. This was the task that confronted Henry of Anjou, who became King Henry II at Stephen's death.

Recommended Reading

Appleby, John T. *The Troubled Reign of King Stephen* (1970).

Barlow, Frank. *The English Church, 1066–1154* (1979).

Barlow, Frank. *The Feudal Kingdom of England, 1042–1216* (3rd ed., 1972).

Barlow, Frank. *The Norman Conquest and Beyond* (1983).

Barlow, Frank. *William Rufus* (1983).

Boase, T. S. R. *English Art, 1100–1216* (1953).

Brown, R. Allen. *The Normans* (1984).

Brown, R. Allen. *The Normans and the Norman Conquest* (2nd ed., 1986).

Clapham, A. W. *English Romanesque Architecture,* 2 vols. (1930–1934).

Davis, R. H. C. *King Stephen, 1135–1154* (1967).

Douglas, David C. *The Norman Achievement, 1050–1100* (1969).

Douglas, David C. *The Norman Fate, 1100–1154* (1976).

Douglas, David C. *William the Conqueror: The Norman Impact Upon England* (1964).

Evans, Gillian R. *Anselm and a New Generation* (1980).

Gibson, Margaret. *Lanfranc of Bec* (1978).

Green, Judith A. *The Government of England Under Henry I* (1986).

Hallam, Elizabeth M. *Domesday Book Through Nine Centuries* (1986).

Hinde, Thomas. *The Domesday Book: England's Heritage, Then and Now* (1985).

Hollister, C. Warren. *The Impact of the Norman Conquest* (1969).

Hollister, C. Warren. *The Military Organization of Norman England* (1965).

Howarth, David. *1066: The Year of the Conquest* (1977).

Le Patourel, John. *The Norman Empire* (1976).

Lloyd, Alan. *The Making of the King, 1066* (1966).

Rowley, Trevor. *The Norman Heritage, 1066–1200* (1983).

Sawyer, Peter, ed. *Domesday Book: A Reassessment* (1985).

Vaughn, Sally N. *The Abbey of Bec and the Anglo-Norman State, 1034–1136* (1981).

CHAPTER 4

Henry II and His Sons

Time Line

1154–1189	Reign of King Henry II
1162–1170	Thomas à Becket serves as archbishop of Canterbury
1164	King Henry II issues the Constitutions of Clarendon
1166	King Henry II issues the Assize of Clarendon
1170	The Inquest of Sheriffs is conducted
1176	King Henry II issues the Assize of Northampton
1189–1199	Reign of King Richard I
1190	King Richard I embarks on the Third Crusade
1194	King Richard I returns to England

1199–1216	Reign of King John
1204	King John loses Normandy to King Philip Augustus of France
1208	Pope Innocent III imposes an interdict on England
1213	King John acknowledges Stephen Langton as archbishop of Canterbury
1214	King Philip Augustus's victory at the Battle of Bouvines ends King John's hope of regaining his French domains
1215	King John signs the Magna Carta

King Henry II, the first of the Angevin, or Plantagenet, kings of England, was a capable, intelligent, and energetic monarch, who combatted the anarchy that had developed during the reign of King Stephen. One of the greatest of England's kings, he is known for his enduring contributions to the English system of justice and also for his bitter conflict with Thomas à Becket, the archbishop of Canterbury.

Henry II's two sons, who succeeded him, proved to be less capable rulers. For most of his reign, King Richard I was absent from England, fighting either on the Third Crusade or in France. King John confronted three opponents—King Philip Augustus of France, Pope Innocent III, and the English barons—and was defeated by all three.

King Henry II (r. 1154–1189)

The Angevin Empire

When Henry II became king at the age of twenty-one, he possessed an impressive empire, which extended from Scotland to the Pyrenees.

French Territory

In addition to England, Henry held extensive territory in France, including Normandy, Anjou, Maine, and Touraine. In 1152, he married Eleanor of Aquitaine (c. 1122–1204), whose marriage to King Louis VII of France (r. 1137–1180) had been dissolved by an annulment earlier

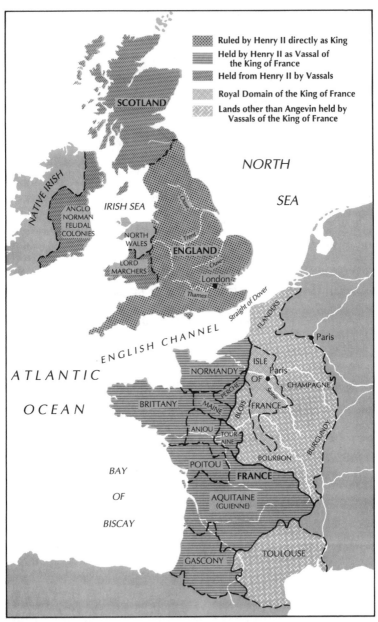

Dominions of Henry II

that year. By his marriage, Henry gained Aquitaine, Auvergne, Guienne, and Poitou. Subsequently he acquired control of Brittany and Toulouse. Henry II was very interested in his French domains and spent two years in France for every year he spent in England.

British Territory

During King Stephen's reign, Scotland had acquired the counties of Cumberland, Northumberland, and Westmoreland in northern England. Henry II regained control of these counties and compelled King Malcolm of Scotland to do homage to him as overlord. He was also recognized as overlord of Wales, although his control there was far from complete. In Ireland, effective English control was limited to the area known as the Pale, the region around Dublin.

Royal Administration

King Henry II's first task was to restore order in England in the wake of the anarchy that had developed during King Stephen's reign. He drove the mercenary soldiers employed by Stephen and Matilda out of the country and restored royal control over the rebellious barons, ordering the destruction of castles that had been built without the king's permission. He required not only his tenants-in-chief but the subvassals as well to do homage to him as their feudal overlord.

The Inquest of Sheriffs

In 1170, Henry II carried out a broad survey of local government, known as the Inquest of Sheriffs, and then acted to eliminate the corrupt practices the survey revealed. Most of the barons who served as sheriffs were replaced with men who would loyally serve the interests of the king.

The Exchequer

Henry II strengthened the Exchequer, which had originally been established by King Henry I (see Chapter 3). The Exchequer served not only as a financial agency but also as a court of law and became, in effect, a separate department of the royal administration, distinct from the *curia regis.*

Revenue

Although Henry II ended the collection of the Danegeld, he considerably increased royal revenues. In the past, churchmen had paid scutage in lieu of performing military service. Henry II collected scutage from the nobility, as well, using the income to employ mercenary soldiers instead of demanding military service from his reluctant vassals.

In 1188, Henry II levied an income and personal property tax known as the Saladin Tithe.

Judicial Reforms

The judicial reforms enacted by King Henry II created a new system of royal law common to the entire kingdom in place of the local law of the feudal barons. These legal principles and practices established the foundations of English common law.

Itinerant Justices

Henry II expanded the system of itinerant justices inaugurated by King Henry I, developing it as a regular and normal procedure. The kingdom was divided into circuits, and royal judges traveled these circuits, bringing royal justice to the counties. The presence of a royal justice in a county court converted it into a royal court.

In addition to their judicial work, the itinerant justices also performed administrative functions on behalf of the king.

The Assize of Clarendon (1166)

In the Assize of Clarendon, Henry II required small groups of men in each hundred to report violations of the law to the sheriffs and royal justices. These juries, known as presentment juries, are the ancestors of modern grand juries.

Henry II also introduced the use of petit juries (trial juries) to determine the guilt or innocence of accused individuals. These trial juries replaced the old methods of compurgation and trial by ordeal (see Chapter 2).

The Assize of Northampton (1176)

The Assize of Northampton established the principle that a serious crime (felony) was not simply a local matter but an offense against the king. Therefore, those accused of felonies should be tried by itinerant justices in the royal courts.

Writs

Another principle established during the reign of Henry II was that the king was responsible for the protection of property rights.

Two writs simplified the resolution of disputes over inherited land and substantially reduced the power of the barons' feudal courts.

The Writ of Right

The Writ of Right recognized the right of a feudal baron to try in his own feudal court cases related to the ownership of land. However, it was illegal for a feudal baron to deprive any person of his property without a trial or to prevent an heir from taking possession of land to which he was entitled. Wronged persons could appeal to royal justice for redress.

The Writ Praecipe

The Writ *Praecipe* went beyond the Writ of Right, instructing sheriffs to order that land which had been taken improperly be restored to the plaintiff or to require the defendant to appear in a royal court to explain his noncompliance.

The Court of Common Pleas

In 1178 the king assigned a group of five barons from the *curia regis* to sit permanently as a judicial body, dealing with many cases that did not fall under the jurisdiction of the Exchequer Court. This new court subsequently became known as the Court of Common Pleas.

King Henry II and the Church

During the reign of King Stephen, the church had acquired new privileges and a greater independence of royal authority. Church courts, governed by canon law, claimed the right to try all cases involving clergymen, whatever their offense. Many persons could claim the status of clergymen (benefit of clergy), even though their actual connection with the church was slight. Church courts did not impose the death penalty, and even for serious crimes, church courts often imposed only a fine.

Election of Thomas à Becket
as Archbishop of Canterbury

In 1161, Theobald, the archbishop of Canterbury, died. The following year, Henry II secured the election of Thomas à Becket (1118–1170) to the office. Becket was a close friend of the king and had served as royal chancellor from 1154, acting as a loyal supporter of royal authority. Henry expected that he would continue to do so. After becoming archbishop, however, Becket was determined to uphold the rights and privileges of the church.

The Constitutions of Clarendon (1164)

Under the terms of the Constitutions of Clarendon, issued by Henry II in 1164, clergymen accused of crimes would be charged in a royal court and tried in a church court. If convicted, they would be deprived of their clerical status and be returned to a royal court for sentencing.

The Constitutions of Clarendon also restated the restrictions which William the Conqueror had imposed on the church. Appeals from English church courts to papal courts without royal consent were prohibited, and no clergyman could leave England without the king's consent. Furthermore, no tenant-in-chief could be excommunicated without the king's approval, and the king's influence over the election of bishops and abbots was increased.

Becket reluctantly agreed to accept the Constitutions of Clarendon but then went to the continent, where he secured papal release from his promise.

Becket's Murder

In 1170, Henry II and Becket patched up their quarrel, and the archbishop returned to England. A new conflict quickly developed, however. When Henry expressed his anger at the archbishop, four of his knights went to Canterbury in December 1170 and murdered Becket in his cathedral. The archbishop was soon canonized as St. Thomas of Canterbury, and his shrine became a popular pilgrimage destination.

Henry's Concessions to the Church

The shocking murder caused Henry to lose most of the gains he had made at the expense of the church. In 1172, the king reached an accord with the church, agreeing to permit church courts to have full jurisdiction over clergy accused of crimes and to allow appeals to Rome without royal interference.

Religion and Learning

During the twelfth century, the Christian church in Western Europe displayed great energy. In England, as on the continent, the Cistercian reform movement that had begun at Cîteaux in France inspired the founding of many new monasteries and the reformation of older ones.

Two churchmen, John of Salisbury and William of Newburgh, were the leading intellectual figures in late twelfth-century England.

John of Salisbury

John of Salisbury (c. 1110–1180), who at the end of his career became bishop of Chartres in France, wrote the *Polycraticus,* an important treatise on politics, and the *Metalogicus,* a consideration of the intellectual life and philosophical controversies of the age.

William of Newburgh

A monastic chronicler, William of Newburgh (c. 1136–c. 1198) wrote, in Latin, a history of England from 1066 to 1198, presenting a commentary on contemporary events, especially an analysis of the causes and results of the anarchy during the reign of King Stephen.

Henry II's Sons

Henry II fathered four legitimate sons. In 1170, he had Henry, the eldest, crowned as his successor to the English throne. Henry would also inherit Normandy, Anjou, and Maine. Geoffrey had married the heiress of Brittany and was thus assigned this territory, while Richard was to become the duke of Aquitaine. John, who was only five years old in 1170, was not included in this distribution of his father's possessions and became known as John Lackland. When he was eight, John was promised the overlordship of Ireland.

Revolts Against Henry II

The royal brothers were not satisfied with their father's action. Inspired by their mother, Eleanor of Aquitaine, who no longer lived with Henry II, and later by King Philip Augustus (r. 1180–1223) of France, they rebelled against their father.

Henry II succeeded in crushing the great revolt of 1173–1174, led by Henry, Geoffrey, and Richard. Although Henry and Geoffrey both predeceased their father, the plotting continued. In 1189, Richard and John joined King Philip Augustus in a war against the king. In July of that year, Henry II died at Chinon in France.

King Richard I (r. 1189–1199)

King Richard I, known as Richard the Lionhearted, was a knight who loved adventure and had a distinct talent for warfare. During his ten-year reign, he spent only six months in England. The rest of the time he was either fighting on the Third Crusade or on the continent.

Royal Administration

The effectiveness of the royal administration established by King Henry II was demonstrated by its successful operation during Richard's long absences.

Prior to embarking on the Third Crusade, Richard divided authority between two justiciars. Hugh de Puiset, the bishop of Durham, exercised authority in the north, while William Longchamp, the bishop of Ely, held power in the south. Longchamp succeeded in driving de Puiset from power, but then, in 1191, was replaced by a new justiciar, Walter de Coutances, the archbishop of Rouen in Normandy.

Suppression of Conspiracy

John, Richard's younger brother, conspired against the king during his absence, and then, when Richard was captured during his return from the Holy Land, John claimed the throne. Although he was rejected in England, John received recognition as king from King Philip Augustus of France. In 1193, Richard named a new justiciar, the archbishop of Canterbury, Hubert Walter (d. 1205), who successfully defended the king's interests. When Richard won release from his captivity in 1194, he returned to England and reestablished his authority.

The Crusades

The First and Second Crusades

The Crusades represented the efforts of Western European Christians during the Middle Ages to regain control of the holy places in Palestine that had come under Muslim control several centuries earlier. The First Crusade, launched by Pope Urban II in 1095, resulted in the capture of Jerusalem in 1099 and the establishment of a Christian kingdom of Jerusalem.

The Muslims then succeeded in recapturing Edessa, endangering the survival of the Christian kingdom. The Second Crusade, from 1147 to 1149, failed to retake Edessa.

During the late twelfth century, Saladin, the ruler of Egypt and Syria, united the Muslims under his leadership, and in 1187 he captured Acre and Jerusalem.

King Richard and the Third Crusade

Late in his reign, King Henry II had begun plans for participating in a crusade to retake Jerusalem and the Holy Land. After inheriting the crown, Richard the Lionhearted enthusiastically continued the preparations, raising an army in England and his French domains.

In 1190, Richard set forth on the Third Crusade, joined by the Holy Roman Emperor Frederick Barbarossa (r. 1155–1190) and King Philip Augustus of France. Although Barbarossa drowned en route, Richard and Philip Augustus continued on their mission.

Conquests in the East

Richard captured the island of Cyprus, married Berengaria of Navarre, and took Acre in July 1191. After quarreling with Richard, Philip Augustus returned to France. Richard remained in the Holy Land for another year, and on two occasions, he and his troops came within sight of Jerusalem, although they never succeeded in entering the city. In October 1192, Richard left for home.

Capture and Imprisonment

During his return journey, Richard was captured by Leopold, the duke of Austria, who turned him over to the Holy Roman Emperor Henry VI (r. 1191–1197). Richard's subjects had to pay the emperor a large ransom to win their king's release.

The Last Years of Richard the Lionhearted

Returning to England in 1194, Richard restored his authority and then went to France, where he spent the final five years of his reign in a sporadic struggle with King Philip Augustus for control of his French domains. Richard died in April 1199 of a crossbow wound suffered in a skirmish with one of his own vassals.

King John (r. 1199–1216)

As king of England, John became involved in conflicts with King Philip Augustus of France, Pope Innocent III (r. 1198–1216), and the English barons, suffering defeat at the hands of all three.

Conflict with King Philip Augustus

King Philip Augustus wanted to extend his control over the English possessions in France, which included about half the country.

King John's Disputed Marriage

In 1199, John secured an annulment of his marriage to his childless first wife, Isabel of Gloucester, and the following year he married Isabel of Angoulême, who had previously been betrothed to Hugh the Brown, one of the vassals of Philip Augustus. Hugh appealed to his feudal suzerain for justice. Technically, King John's holdings in France made him a vassal of the French king, and Philip Augustus summoned him to his feudal court in Paris, using the royal marriage as a pretext to challenge the English ruler.

King John's Losses

When King John refused to comply with the summons, Philip Augustus induced most of the nobility in the English-held territory in France to acknowledge him as their feudal overlord. The French king then moved against John's territory, seizing Normandy in 1204. By 1206, Philip Augustus had occupied Anjou, Maine, Touraine, Brittany, and most of Poitou. Only Aquitaine remained under King John's control.

The Battle of Bouvines (1214)

In an attempt to regain his domains in France, John hired mercenaries and made an alliance with the Holy Roman Emperor Otto IV (r. 1209–1215). In the Battle of Bouvines of July 1214, Philip Augustus defeated John's allies, Otto IV and the count of Flanders. Confronted by superior French forces, King John signed a truce with the French king and returned to England. The Battle of Bouvines proved to be decisive, leaving Philip Augustus supreme in France.

Conflict with Pope Innocent III

Following the death in 1205 of Hubert Walter, the archbishop of Canterbury, a dispute developed between King John and the clergy of Canterbury over Walter's successor. Pope Innocent III refused to accept the candidate supported by either party and arranged in 1207 for the selection of Stephen Langton (c. 1155–1228), a well-known English theologian. John refused to accept Langton.

Interdict and Excommunication

In March 1208, Pope Innocent III imposed an interdict on England, which remained in effect for six years. The interdict halted all church services. The only sacraments which could be administered were baptism and extreme unction. In retaliation, John seized church lands and revenues. The pope responded by excommunicating King John in November 1209, and many bishops and abbots left England and sought refuge on the continent.

In 1212, Innocent III declared John deposed and freed his subjects of their obligations to him. This encouraged the English barons in their opposition to the king, while King Philip Augustus, for his part, began to organize his forces for an invasion of England.

King John's Surrender

Faced by the revolt of the barons and the threat of a French invasion, John submitted to the pope in April 1213. He agreed to recognize Stephen Langton as archbishop of Canterbury and to return the church lands he had seized. In addition, he promised to compensate the church for its losses and to allow exiled clergymen to return to England. John also agreed that he would hold England as a fief from the pope.

While King John paid a substantial price in order to make peace with Pope Innocent III, the pope now became his protector. King Philip Augustus had to cancel his plans for an invasion of England in order to avoid a conflict with the pope.

Conflict with the Barons

King John's defeat by the French and the pope weakened his position. In addition, his wars in France had been expensive, and his demands for money to support his wars, diplomacy, and extravagant lifestyle had angered the English barons.

Magna Carta

The rebellious barons forced King John to sign the Magna Carta at Runnymede on the Thames River outside London on June 15, 1215.

Provisions.   The Magna Carta was, above all, a feudal document, in which the king promised not to interfere with the traditional rights and privileges of the barons. In addition, in the sixty-three clauses of the Magna Carta, King John promised to maintain the rights of the church and the liberties of the towns. In one of its most famous provisions, the Magna Carta declared that no freeman would be detained or punished except "by the lawful judgment of his peers and by the law of the land."

Mechanism for Enforcement.   The Magna Carta established a committee of twenty-five barons to enforce the agreement. If the king failed to keep his commitment, the barons were entitled to act to compel his obedience.

The main significance of the Magna Carta was that it established the principle that the king himself was subject to the law. In that sense, the Magna Carta may be viewed as the first step in the creation of constitutional government in England.

Renewed Strife

Although King John signed the Magna Carta, he sought to avoid abiding by its provisions. At the king's urging, Pope Innocent III freed him from his commitment in August 1215. After John employed continental mercenaries in an effort to restore his full authority, the barons rose in revolt, inviting Louis, the son of King Philip Augustus, to come to England and become their king.

In the midst of this new crisis, King John suddenly died in October 1216. The king's death spared England a new civil war.

During his long reign, King Henry II established effective instruments of royal government that continued to function under the absent King Richard and the incompetent, or at least unsuccessful, King John. As a consequence, despite momentary setbacks, the powerful English monarchy became even more powerful.

The prospect of the king becoming a despot evoked the opposition of the barons, who forced King John to sign the Magna Carta in 1215. By the time of John's death, the issue of placing limitations on royal absolutism was not yet resolved. Later generations, however, could cite the important principles established by the Magna Carta: that the king himself was subject to the law and that if the king did not observe the law, his subjects could legitimately seek to force him to do so.

Recommended Reading

Appleby, John T. *England Without Richard, 1189–1199* (1965).

Appleby, John T. *John, King of England* (1960).

Barlow, Frank. *The Feudal Kingdom of England, 1042–1216* (1965).

Barlow, Frank. *Thomas Becket* (1986).

Cheney, C. R. *From Becket to Langton: English Church Government, 1170–1213* (1956).

Cheney, C. R. *Hubert Walter* (1967).

Gillingham, John. *The Angevin Empire* (1984).

Gillingham, John. *Richard the Lionheart* (1978).

Holt, J. C. *Magna Carta and Medieval Government* (1985).

Jolliffe, J. E. A. *Angevin Kingship* (2nd ed., 1963).

Jones, Thomas B. *The Becket Controversy* (1970).

Keefe, Thomas K. *Feudal Assessments and the Political Community Under Henry II and His Sons* (1983).

Kelly, Amy. *Eleanor of Aquitaine and the Four Kings* (1950).

Kibler, William W., ed. *Eleanor of Aquitaine: Patron and Politician* (1976).

Pernoud, Régine. *Eleanor of Aquitaine* (1968).

Powicke, F. M. *The Loss of Normandy, 1189–1204* (2nd ed., 1961).

Powicke, F. M. *Stephen Langton* (1928).

Saltman, Avrom. *Theobald, Archbishop of Canterbury* (1956).

Warren, W. L. *Henry II* (1973).

Warren, W. L. *King John* (1961).

Wilkes, Michael, ed. *The World of John of Salisbury* (1984).

CHAPTER 5

The Thirteenth Century

Time Line

1216–1272	Reign of King Henry III
1221	The first Dominican friars arrive in England
1223	The first Franciscan friars arrive in England
1258	The barons draw up the Provisions of Oxford
1259	The Treaty of Paris leaves King Henry III with Gascony as his only possession in France
1265	Simon de Montfort's Parliament meets
c. 1267	Roger Bacon publishes *Opus Majus*
1272–1307	Reign of King Edward I

1278	The Statute of Gloucester reduces the authority of the baronial courts
1279	The Statute of Mortmain restricts the further acquisition of land by the church
1283	The Statute of Acton Burnell provides for imprisonment for debt
1284	Wales is annexed by the English crown
1285	The Second Statute of Westminster (*De Donis Conditionalibus*) provides for keeping landholdings intact
1290	King Edward I expels the Jews from England
	The Third Statute of Westminster (*Quia Emptores*) prohibits subinfeudation
1292	Scotland's king, John Balliol, does homage to King Edward I
1295	The Model Parliament meets
1303	King Edward I makes peace with King Philip IV of France
1314	The Scots defeat the English at the Battle of Bannockburn

---

During the long reign of King Henry III, the conflict between the king and barons that had begun in the previous reign of King John continued. This conflict contributed to the emergence of Parliament as a significant factor in English government.

In religion and learning, the thirteenth century was particularly fruitful. The Franciscans, Dominicans, and other orders of friars reinvigorated the spiritual life of England. The universities of Oxford and Cambridge came to rival their counterparts on the continent, while English scholars contributed to the intellectual resurgence of Western Europe. In architecture, English Gothic claimed its place among the architectural achievements of the Middle Ages.

King Edward I, whose reign began in 1272, appeared to have learned from his father's misfortune that the king was indeed subject to the law, although the monarch remained capable of exercising extensive authority. While Edward I was a talented military leader, his reign is particularly important for its legal developments and the further evolution of Parliament.

King Henry III (r. 1216–1272)

King Henry III began his long reign at the age of nine. William Marshal (d. 1219), the regent, succeeded in ending the civil war that had begun in the final months of King John's reign (see Chapter 4).

Following William Marshal's death in 1219, Hubert de Burgh (d. 1243), the justiciar, became regent. In 1232, Henry III began to rule in his own right and dismissed de Burgh.

Disaffection of Barons

Peter des Roches (d. 1238) from Poitou in France, the bishop of Winchester, now became the most influential figure in the royal household. Mercenaries from Poitou came to England to protect the king and his court, while other foreigners received important positions in the government and church. This influx of foreigners increased after the king's 1236 marriage to Eleanor of Provence, adding to the growing resentment of the English barons. Also contributing to baronial resentment were the king's violations of the rights of the barons established by the Magna Carta, his avoiding consultation with the Great Council, and his extravagance.

Foreign Adventures

France

King Henry III sought to regain the Angevin Empire in France. This costly struggle ended with the signing of the Treaty of Paris in 1259, which left the king in control only of Gascony (southern Aquitaine).

Sicily

In 1254, King Henry III became involved in a papal scheme to win the crown of Sicily for his second son, Edmund of Lancaster. The English would have had to raise and equip an army to conquer Sicily and, in addition, Henry agreed to compensate the pope for the costs of earlier fighting in Sicily by the papal army. In 1255, both the Great Council and the clergy refused to grant the king any money to fight a Sicilian war. The ill-fated venture ended with an intensification of the barons' already considerable resentment of the king's policies.

The Emergence of Parliament

Origin

The emergence of Parliament was the most important development in English government and politics during the thirteenth century. The word "parliament" is derived from the French word *parler* "to speak". Originally the term was loosely applied to a meeting where the king discussed important issues with royal officials and influential subjects, who advised him on matters of policy and taxation. After the mid-thirteenth century, however, the term was usually reserved for meetings of the Great Council.

Development of Powers

During the thirteenth century, the composition of Parliament varied and it met only occasionally, whenever the king summoned it. At meetings of Parliament, the king could discuss issues facing the country, explain royal policy, solicit advice, and become informed about his subjects' opinions. Parliament could petition the king, and it also acted as the highest court in England. The key to Parliament's growing influence, however, was its power of the purse. By the end of the thirteenth century, Parliament had acquired the power to approve all extraordinary taxes.

The Provisions of Oxford (1258)

The growing resentment against King Henry III burst forth in a revolt of the barons in 1258. Simon de Montfort (c. 1208–1265), the French-born earl of Leicester and the king's brother-in-law, led the revolt.

When the Great Council met in 1258, the rebellious barons compelled the king to accept the Provisions of Oxford, which stipulated that the Great Council would be called into session three times each year. In addition, a Council of Fifteen, dominated by the barons, would supervise the government. In particular, the council had the power to appoint three of the king's chief officials: the chancellor, the treasurer, and the justiciar. In essence, the Provisions of Oxford created a dictatorship of the barons in place of royal despotism.

Reassertion of Royal Authority

Divisions soon developed among the barons, enabling King Henry III to reassert his authority. With the aid of foreign mercenaries, the king dismissed the Council of Fifteen and recovered control of the government.

The Barons' War

In an effort to avert civil war, King Henry III and the barons agreed to invite the saintly King Louis IX (r. 1226–1270) of France to arbitrate their quarrel. In the Mise of Amiens (1264), Louis IX decided in favor of his fellow monarch.

The barons refused to accept this decision and went to war against the king. Led by Simon de Montfort, the barons defeated the king and his supporters in the Battle of Lewes (May 1264), taking the king and his son, Edward, prisoner.

Simon de Montfort's Parliament (1265)

While King Henry III retained the throne, for the next fifteen months Simon de Montfort was, in effect, England's ruler, heading a council of nine barons.

Simon summoned a meeting of the Great Council (Parliament), which included not only the customary barons and clergy but also two representative knights from each shire (county) and two representative burgesses from each borough (town). While shire representatives had attended earlier meetings of the Great Council, it is likely that this was the first time that representatives of the towns were invited to attend. Simon's Parliament of 1265 was the most representative body ever assembled up to this point in English history and thus marked an important step in the development of Parliament.

King Henry III's Last Years

In May 1265, Henry III's son, Prince Edward, escaped from imprisonment and assembled an army. In August, he defeated the barons in the Battle of Evesham. Simon de Montfort was killed in the battle, and Henry III regained power. Henry III then began gradually to turn control of the government over to his son.

Despite the barons' defeat, some of the reforms they sought survived. For example, the Statute of Marlborough (1267) established new legal procedures to protect feudal rights. Nevertheless, the restrictions on the king's power established by the Provisions of Oxford were not restored.

Religion

In medieval England, as elsewhere in Europe, monasteries played an important role in religious life. In 1100, 88 English monasteries existed; by 1200, there were nearly 400. Many of the monasteries had become wealthy landholders and were more concerned with secular affairs than with spirituality.

The Friars

In the early thirteenth century, new religious orders appeared, whose members, rather than retiring from the world beyond monastery walls, conducted an active ministry among the people.

Franciscans

The Franciscans, inspired by the ideals of their Italian founder, St. Francis of Assisi (c. 1182–1226), embraced poverty and served the needs of the poor and the sick.

Dominicans

The Dominicans, founded by the Spaniard St. Dominic (c. 1170–1221), were above all preachers and teachers and were active in the struggle against heresy. The first Dominicans reached England in 1221, while the first Franciscans arrived in 1223.

Other Orders

Two other orders of friars, the Carmelites and the Augustinians (known in England as the Austin friars), followed during the 1240s. By 1300, the friars had established about 150 houses in England.

Learning

The Universities

The universities, chartered bodies of teachers and students, were the great educational innovation in Western Europe during the High

Middle Ages. The universities generally offered education in four areas: the liberal arts, law, medicine, and theology.

Oxford

At first, English students attended the universities in Paris and other continental cities. During the twelfth century, an English university developed from a local school in Oxford. It received a royal charter from King Henry III in 1248.

Cambridge

In the early thirteenth century, a conflict between the university community and townspeople in Oxford caused some academics to go to Cambridge, where they founded a second university.

Scholars

Robert Grosseteste

Robert Grosseteste (c. 1175–1253), the first chancellor of Oxford University who later became the bishop of Lincoln, was a student and teacher of mathematics, science, medicine, and law and wrote extensively on scientific methodology.

Roger Bacon

Roger Bacon (c. 1214–c. 1294), a Franciscan and student of Grosseteste's at Oxford, also studied in Paris. He was critical of his contemporary's unquestioning acceptance of the ancient Greek philosopher Aristotle and of many ideas of the scholastic philosophers, especially St. Thomas Aquinas. Bacon taught the inductive method of reasoning in the study of science. In his *Opus Majus* (c. 1267), Bacon presented an encyclopedic compendium of information on grammar, philosophy, mathematics, and physics.

Duns Scotus

Duns Scotus (c. 1266–1308), a Franciscan theologian who taught at Oxford, was a critic of St. Thomas Aquinas. Duns Scotus emphasized the limits of human reason in acquiring a knowledge and understanding of God and religious truth. Rejecting Aquinas's view that the truth of many Christian teachings could be rationally demonstrated, he insisted that they could only be accepted by faith. Aquinas's supporters, the Thomists, called Duns Scotus's partisans "Dunces," a word that has remained a part of the English vocabulary.

Henry de Bracton

Henry de Bracton (d. 1268), a legal scholar and royal justice, wrote *On the Laws and Customs of England,* a comprehensive treatise on English law.

Roger of Wendover and Matthew Paris

Roger of Wendover (d. c. 1236) and Matthew Paris (d. 1259), both of the Abbey of St. Albans, were prominent chroniclers. Roger of Wendover wrote the *Flowers of History,* a general chronicle beginning with the Creation. He presented a particularly distorted and hostile account of the reign of King John. Following Roger's death, Matthew Paris continued the chronicle.

Architecture

During the late twelfth century, the graceful Gothic style, developed on the continent, began to supplant the heavy Norman Romanesque.

Early Gothic

Early English Gothic (late twelfth to late thirteenth centuries) was fresh and almost severe in its simplicity, employing steeply pitched roofs and lancet windows (windows with sharply pointed arches). Salisbury Cathedral provides one of the purest examples of Early English Gothic, while Lincoln Cathedral, often described as the finest of all English cathedrals, is the richest example of the style.

Decorated Gothic

In the Decorated Gothic style (late thirteenth to late fourteenth centuries), decorations developed from straight geometric designs into more curvilinear patterns based on shapes found in nature. The windows were broader, while the spires were more heavily decorated than in the Early English style. The cathedrals of Bristol, Ely, and Exeter provide outstanding examples of the Decorated Gothic style.

Perpendicular Gothic

The name Perpendicular Gothic (late fourteenth to mid-sixteenth centuries) is applied to the style developed during the final period of

Gothic architecture in England and is derived from the predominantly vertical lines of its tracery and paneling. The arches were characterized by flatter points, and the towers were square. The Perpendicular style was employed in the reconstruction of the nave of Canterbury Cathedral, and a number of elaborate college chapels at Oxford and Cambridge were built in this style.

Towns and Economic Activity

Towns

The Middle Ages brought a substantial increase in England's population from about 2 million at the time of the Norman Conquest to over 4 million by the mid-fourteenth century. Although most of the people lived in rural areas, towns gradually increased in size and number. By 1300, there were about 200 towns in England, but few had more than 5000 inhabitants. London, with some 40,000 people, was the only substantial city. The seaport of Bristol, with a population of 12,000, was the country's second-largest city, while York was the leading city in the north.

Self-Government

Since the time of William the Conqueror, towns had been subject to the authority of the king or local lords and to the sheriffs and baronial courts. But, while feudal law effectively regulated the affairs of the nobility and peasants, towns did not fit into the framework of the feudal system. Towns thus sought charters, often buying them from the king or local barons. These chartered towns were independent corporations, like the monasteries and universities, with rights of self-government, including the rights to elect their own mayors and officials, to collect taxes, to maintain their own courts, and to deal directly with the king. According to tradition, serfs who fled to towns would gain their freedom if they remained unapprehended for a year and a day.

Representation in Parliament

Towns gradually acquired a role in the government of the kingdom, especially after the burgesses (townsmen) gained representation in Parliament. The townspeople were inclined to support the king, who represented the cause of order and stability, against the contentious feudal nobility.

Trade

Markets and Fairs

Each town had a market, usually held weekly, where mainly local trade was conducted. A number of large towns held fairs once or twice a year, attracting merchants from all over England as well as a growing number of continental merchants.

Exports and Imports

During the Middle Ages, England's main exports included grain, salt, hides, tin, lead, and iron. In addition, England exported a large quantity of raw wool to Flanders, the center of the Western European woolen textile industry. Among England's major imports were furs, silver, linen, wax, and tar, as well as wine, silk, jewels, dyes, and spices.

Guilds

The guilds regulated economic activities in the towns.

Merchant Guilds

The first guilds to be organized were the merchant guilds, which consisted of townsmen who were engaged in trade. Members of a merchant guild held a monopoly on the right to trade in the town, and the guild's members were bound by its regulations controlling prices and competition.

Craft Guilds

Gradually craft guilds developed. These were composed of people in a town who engaged in a particular craft: carpenters, weavers, masons, shoemakers, tanners, goldsmiths, etc. The craft guilds regulated the production and sale of goods.

Craftsmen passed through three stages: apprentices, journeymen, and masters, although many journeymen never reached the rank of master. Following an apprenticeship, which customarily lasted seven years, an individual became a journeyman. If a journeyman could garner sufficient resources to establish his own shop, he could become a master craftsman.

Care of Members

Both merchant guilds and craft guilds also served social and philanthropic functions, including taking care of members who were ill or aged.

Banking and Finance

The medieval church condemned the charging of interest as usury; therefore, Christians were prohibited from lending money. Some, even churchmen, did so, finding some subterfuge to escape the strictures of the church. But most moneylenders in medieval England were Jews. Since money was in scarce supply, moneylenders charged high rates of interest.

Anti-Semitism

The Crusades promoted a growth of religious fervor, which was often directed against the Jews. In England, as elsewhere in Western Europe, anti-Jewish riots claimed many victims, and Jews were subject to other forms of persecution and discrimination.

On a number of occasions, the English kings levied taxes on the accumulated wealth of the Jews. Then, in 1290, King Edward I expelled the Jews from England. Some 16,000 left the country.

Italian Bankers

Italian bankers now moved in. Many of these bankers came from the northern Italian province of Lombardy, and the center of their operations in London came to be known as Lombard Street.

King Edward I (r. 1272–1307)

King Edward I was an energetic and efficient ruler and a vigorous warrior. He left an enduring mark on England's law and institutions.

Annexation of Wales

Soon after King Edward I's accession, a revolt broke out in Wales, which the king suppressed in 1277. The Statute of Wales, adopted in 1284, provided for the annexation of Wales by the English crown. Wales was divided into shires, and English law was introduced. Nevertheless, Welsh unrest continued.

In 1301, King Edward I gave his son, Edward, the title of Prince of Wales. Since that time, the title has traditionally been bestowed on heirs to the throne.

Conflict with Scotland

While King Edward I was able to add Wales permanently to the domains of the English monarchy, he was less successful in his efforts to subdue Scotland.

During the early years of his reign, Edward refrained from pressing his claims in Scotland. The death of the Scottish king, Alexander III, in 1286, however, initiated a series of events which offered Edward an opportunity to intervene.

Claimants to the Throne

Following Alexander III's death, his young granddaughter Margaret, the "Maid of Norway" (1283–1290), was proclaimed queen, and the Scots accepted Edward's proposal that she be betrothed to his son. This would, in time, have led to the union of Scotland with England. In 1290, Margaret suddenly died, however, and now some thirteen rival claimants to the Scottish throne appeared. Of the thirteen, John Balliol and Robert Bruce had the strongest claims.

John Balliol

With the support of King Edward I, John Balliol (r. 1292–1296) became king and did homage to Edward for the fief of Scotland. To the irritation of the Scots, Edward took seriously his position as feudal overlord and in 1294 demanded that Balliol provide manpower for England's war against France. The Scots responded by making an alliance with France in 1295, beginning a relationship that lasted for almost 300 years.

William Wallace

In 1296, Edward I pushed into Scotland, deposed Balliol, and asserted his control over the country. The following year, however, the Scots, led by William Wallace (r. 1297–1305), defeated the English at the Battle of Stirling Bridge and then invaded northern England. The seesaw struggle continued, as Edward defeated the Scots in the Battle of Falkirk in 1298. In 1305, Wallace was handed over to the English, who executed him.

Robert Bruce

The rebellious Scots found a new leader in Robert Bruce (r. 1306–1329), who was soon defeated by the English in the Battle of Methven in 1306. Unrest continued in Scotland, however. In 1307, Edward began a new push against the Scots, but he died just south of the Scottish border. The new king, Edward II, halted the invasion and returned to London.

Scottish Independence

Conflict between the Scots and the English continued. Finally, at the Battle of Bannockburn in 1314, the Scots defeated the English, regaining the independence that they still possessed when King James VI of Scotland inherited the English crown in 1603, becoming King James I of England (see Chapter 8).

Relations with France

King Philip IV of France (r. 1285–1314), known as Philip the Fair, hoped to take Gascony away from the English, while King Edward I hoped to recover the lost English possessions in France. When Edward refused to respond to a summons by Philip, his feudal overlord in Gascony, the French king declared Gascony forfeit. In 1294, Edward went to war, but his effort was weakened by his campaigns in Wales and Scotland. Philip the Fair, for his part, was distracted by a conflict with the count of Flanders. In addition, both Edward I and Philip the Fair were embroiled in disputes with Pope Boniface VIII. In 1303, the two kings made peace, and Edward retained Gascony.

King Edward I and the Church

While King Edward I was personally devout, he was determined to place limits on the power of the church, which was the greatest landowner in England.

Statute of Mortmain

In the Statute of Mortmain (1279), the king sought to restrict the further acquisition of land by the church. The statute provided that land could not be sold or donated to the church without the king's consent.

Conflict with Pope Boniface VIII

King Edward I also sought to impose taxes on the clergy. In 1296, however, Pope Boniface VIII (r. 1294–1303) issued the bull *Clericos laicos,* which maintained that no tax could be levied on the clergy without papal consent. The king responded by confiscating church property. Ultimately the king and pope agreed to a compromise whereby the clergy agreed to make "voluntary" gifts to the king.

Royal Administration

The reign of King Edward I produced a series of important statutes that made English common law clearer and more consistent and served to strengthen the king's government and to reduce the power and privileges of the barons.

The Statute of Gloucester (1278)

The Statute of Gloucester required the barons to demonstrate by what authority (*quo warranto*) they conducted their private courts and enjoyed other privileges. Protests by the barons led Edward I to agree that possession of privileges from the first year of the reign of Richard I (i.e., 1189–1190) entitled the barons to continue to exercise them. Despite this setback, Edward I continued his efforts to restrict the baronial courts and to establish the primacy of royal justice.

The Second Statute of Westminster (1285)

The Second Statute of Westminster, known also as *De Donis Conditionalibus,* provided that land should be passed to heirs in accord with the order established in the original charter. This practice, known as entail, was designed to keep landholdings intact.

The Third Statute of Westminster (1290)

The Third Statute of Westminster, also known as *Quia Emptores,* prohibited further subinfeudation by requiring that buyers of land would become the direct vassals or tenants of the seller's overlord, who was frequently the king.

Effects of the Westminster Statutes

The Second and Third Statutes of Westminster both reflected and encouraged the decline of feudalism and the change in relationship from one of lord and vassal to that of seller and buyer or landlord and tenant.

The Statute of Acton Burnell (1283)

The Statute of Acton Burnell, also known as the Statute of Merchants, aided merchants by providing that a person could legally be imprisoned for the nonpayment of debt.

Royal Courts

As the baronial courts declined in significance, the royal courts expanded their jurisdiction and became more specialized. By the reign of King Edward I, two separate central courts of the common law had evolved out of the *curia regis*. The Exchequer Court dealt with tax cases, while the Court of Common Pleas dealt with civil cases. A third court, the Court of King's Bench, was developing, with jurisdiction over criminal cases or pleas of the crown.

The Model Parliament (1295)

During the thirteenth century, the kings increasingly came to realize the value of including representative knights from the shires and burgesses from the towns in meetings of Parliament. Between 1290 and 1310, King Edward I summoned representative knights and burgesses to thirteen of his thirty-four Parliaments.

Representation

The Model Parliament of 1295 included representatives of all forty shires and some 114 chartered boroughs. The term "Model Parliament" is misleading, however, since subsequent Parliaments did not necessarily follow its pattern of representation. In fact, twelve of the twenty Parliaments summoned by King Edward I after 1295 contained no representatives of the shires and boroughs at all, while only three fully imitated the pattern of the Model Parliament. Furthermore, the members of the Model Parliament were grouped in three orders — clergy, barons and knights, and burgesses — similar to the French Estates General. It was only later, in the fourteenth century, that Parliament took on its enduring form, with the burgesses and knights meeting separately, marking the origin of the House of Commons, while the meetings of the barons and bishops developed into the House of Lords. In addition, after 1295, the lower clergy ceased to attend meetings of Parliament, choosing instead to meet in its own convocations of Canterbury and York.

Powers

Although the influence of the representative knights and burgesses in Parliament would remain limited for some generations to come, they did have the ability to present petitions. This marked the origins of Parliament's development as a legislative body. The knights and burgesses could petition the king, with or without the support of the barons, for the redress of specific or general grievances. If the king granted a petition, his council might then prepare an appropriate statute. In time, Parliament's judicial functions decreased in importance, while its legislative functions increased. During the reign of King Edward I, however, this development was only in its earliest stages.

The Confirmation of Charters

In 1297, when King Edward I was fighting in France and running short of money, he was forced to agree to the Confirmation of Charters. In this document, the king reaffirmed the Magna Carta and promised that direct non-feudal taxes would no longer be levied without the consent of Parliament. This represented an important step in Parliament's acquisition of the power of the purse, which gave it greater leverage in its dealings with the king.

The thirteenth century brought important developments to England in many areas, but especially in government. King Henry III's misrule provoked a baronial revolt that threatened the fundamental authority of the monarchy. However, Henry III's son and successor, King Edward I, proved to be a strong and effective king who succeeded in restoring the monarchy to its position of leadership. Edward I's important contributions to law and justice won him the nickname of the "English Justinian." During his thirty-five-year reign, feudalism declined in significance, and Parliament became more firmly established in the English pattern of government. As a warrior, Edward I brought Wales fully under English control, although he was less successful in his efforts to subdue Scotland.

Recommended Reading

Barrow, G. W. S. *Kingship and Unity: Scotland, 1000–1306* (1981).

Bolton, J. L. *The Medieval English Economy, 1150–1500* (1980).

Bony, Jean. *The English Decorated Style: Gothic Architecture Transformed, 1250–1350* (1979).

Braun, Hugh. *An Introduction to English Mediaeval Architecture* (1951).

Brieger, Peter H. *English Art, 1216–1307* (1957).

Chancellor, John. *The Life and Times of Edward I* (1981).

Davies, R. R. *Conquest, Coexistence and Change: Wales, 1063–1415* (1987).

Galbraith, V. H. *Roger Wendover and Matthew Paris* (1944).

Knowles, David. *The Religious Orders in England*, vol. I (1962).

Labarge, Margaret W. *Simon de Montfort* (1962).

Leff, Gordon. *Paris and Oxford Universities in the Thirteenth and Fourteenth Centuries: An Institutional and Intellectual History* (1968).

McEvoy, James. *The Philosophy of Robert Grosseteste* (1982).

Miller, Edward and John Hatcher. *Medieval England: Rural Society and Economic Change, 1086–1348* (1978).

Moorman, John R. H. *Church Life in England in the Thirteenth Century* (1955).

Ormond, Mark, ed. *England in the Thirteenth Century* (1986).

Painter, Sidney. *William Marshal* (1933).

Power, Eileen. *The Wool Trade in English Medieval History* (1941).

Powicke, F. M. *The Thirteenth Century, 1216–1307* (2nd ed., 1962).

Prestwich, Michael. *Edward I* (1988).

Reynolds, Susan. *An Introduction to the History of English Medieval Towns* (rev. ed., 1982).

Treharne, R. F. *The Baronial Plan of Reform, 1258–1263* (rev. ed., 1971).

Treharne, R. F. *Essays on Thirteenth-Century England* (1971).

Vaughan, Richard. *Matthew Paris* (1958).

Williams, Gwyn A. *Medieval London: From Commune to Capital* (1963).

CHAPTER 6

The Fourteenth and Fifteenth Centuries

Time Line

1307–1327	Reign of King Edward II
1311	The Ordinances of 1311 establish baronial domination over the king
1327	Parliament deposes King Edward II
1327–1377	Reign of King Edward III
1337	The Hundred Years' War begins
1340	The English navy defeats the French at the Battle of Sluys
1346	The English capture King David II of Scotland at the Battle of Neville's Cross

	The English defeat the French at the Battle of Crécy
1348–1349	The Black Death strikes England
1356	The English defeat the French at the Battle of Poitiers
1357	In the Treaty of Berwick, the Scots agree to pay a large ransom for King David II
1360	The Treaty of Brétigny awards England Aquitaine, Ponthieu, and Calais
1377–1399	Reign of King Richard II
1381	Wat Tyler and Jack Straw lead the Peasants' Revolt
1399–1413	Reign of King Henry IV
1413–1422	Reign of King Henry V
1415	The English defeat the French at the Battle of Agincourt
1420	The Treaty of Troyes recognizes King Henry V as heir to the French throne
1422–1461	Reign of King Henry VI
1429	Joan of Arc lifts the English siege of Orleans
1431	Joan of Arc is burned at the stake
1450	Jack Cade leads a revolt in southern England
1453	The Hundred Years' War ends
1454	The Wars of the Roses begin
1461	The Yorkists win the Battle of Towton, ending Lancastrian rule
1461–1483	Reign of King Edward IV
1483–1485	Reign of King Richard III
1485	Henry Tudor wins the Battle of Bosworth Field

For England, the fourteenth and fifteenth centuries were a time of turmoil and intensifying violence: the period of the Hundred Years' War, the Black Death, the Peasants' Revolt, and the Wars of the Roses. The authority of the monarchy declined, but so, too, did that of the nobility, which exhausted itself in the wars in France and at home. The decline of the nobility hastened the end of feudalism and contributed to the expansion of Parliament's authority. In religion, the movement led by John Wycliffe presented a challenge to the Roman Catholic Church.

While demoralization and decline mark much of the history of these centuries, there was also growth. Industry and commerce expanded, advances in education occurred, and the English language and English literature emerged. In addition, the Hundred Years' War did much to stimulate the development of English national consciousness.

King Edward II (r. 1307–1327)

King Edward II proved to be a weak monarch, dependent on favorites. Piers Gaveston (d. 1312), a Gascon knight, was the king's favorite counselor during the first years of his reign. Edward II married Isabella (1296–1358), the daughter of King Philip IV of France (r. 1285–1314).

The Ordinances of 1311

In the Parliaments of 1309 to 1312, Thomas, the earl of Lancaster (c. 1277–1322) and the king's first cousin, led the barons' effort to reassert their influence. Gaveston was banished to Ireland, and the barons compelled the king to accept the Ordinances of 1311. They provided that Parliament should be called into session at least twice a year and established a council of twenty-one Lords Ordainers with authority to control the appointment of the chief administrative and household officials. Furthermore, the Ordinances barred the king from declaring war without Parliament's approval.

The King's Defiance

As in the past when the barons had sought to place restrictions on the king's authority, the king's acceptance of the Ordinances was only temporary. In 1312, Edward II defied the Lords Ordainers and recalled Gaveston. The barons then retaliated by having Gaveston executed.

Civil War

Following the Scots' defeat of the English at the Battle of Bannockburn in 1314 (see Chapter 5), the barons forced the king to agree to the reinstitution of the Ordinances of 1311. Disunity among the barons, high taxes, and Scottish raids on northern England combined to foment a civil war. At the Battle of Boroughbridge, fought in March 1322, the king's army defeated the earl of Lancaster, who was tried for treason and executed. But the triumph of Edward II and Hugh Despenser (1262–1326), the king's new favorite, proved brief.

The Revolt of Queen Isabella and Roger Mortimer

In 1325, Queen Isabella went to Paris to negotiate the continuing Anglo-French dispute over Gascony with her brother, King Charles IV. Refusing to return to England, she became the mistress of Roger Mortimer (c. 1287–1330), who had been the most powerful of the Welsh marcher lords. Mortimer had been imprisoned following the Battle of Boroughbridge but had escaped to France in 1323.

Victory of the Rebels

Isabella and Mortimer launched a conspiracy against King Edward II. Landing in England in 1326, they quickly took London. The rebels executed Despenser and imprisoned Edward II.

Deposition of Edward II

In January 1327, a Parliament controlled by the rebels deposed Edward II in favor of his son, Edward, the duke of Aquitaine, a boy of fifteen, who had returned to England with his mother and her lover. In September, Edward II was murdered.

King Edward III (r. 1327–1377)

During the first years of King Edward III's reign, power was exercised by a regency headed by his mother, Queen Isabella, and Roger Mortimer. In 1330, at the age of eighteen, the king rebelled against his guardians, having his mother imprisoned and Mortimer condemned as a traitor and hanged. Edward III did not threaten the rights and privileges of the barons, who supported the king in his wars.

Relations with Scotland

In Scotland, King Edward III supported Edward Balliol (d. 1363) in his struggle against David Bruce (King David II; r. 1329–1371), the son of Robert Bruce (see Chapter 5).

Treaty of Newcastle (1334)

In 1333, at the Battle of Halidon Hill, Edward III and Balliol won a decisive victory. David II fled to France. Under the terms of the Treaty of Newcastle of 1334, Edward Balliol ceded most of Lothian in southern Scotland to England and did homage to Edward III for the rest of Scotland. Repudiating Balliol, the Scots carried out sporadic resistance to the English.

Renewed Conflict

In 1341, with French support, David II drove the English out of Scotland, and in 1346, he invaded England. At the Battle of Neville's Cross, fought in October 1346 near Durham in northern England, the English took David captive.

Treaty of Berwick (1357)

By this point, King Edward III was deeply involved in his war with France and sought a settlement with the Scots. Under the terms of the Treaty of Berwick of 1357, the Scots paid a large ransom for their king. David II regained his throne and ruled Scotland until his death in 1371.

King Edward III and the Barons

For nearly twenty-five years, King Edward III fought an intermittent war against France. Baronial discontent festered, and the barons took advantage of a quarrel betweens the king's sons, Edward the Black Prince (1330–1376) and John of Gaunt (1340–1399).

In April 1376, the "Good Parliament" censured John of Gaunt's conduct of the war and impeached several of his associates.

Death of the Black Prince

In June 1376, the Black Prince died, and his ten-year-old son, Richard of Bordeaux, became heir to the throne. He succeeded his grandfather in 1377, becoming King Richard II.

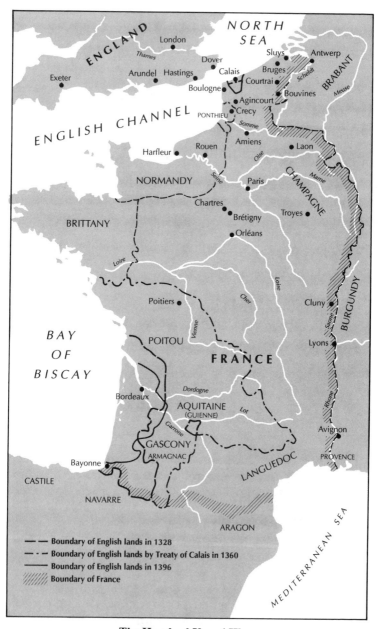

The Hundred Years' War

The Hundred Years' War

For more than a century, from 1337 to 1453, England fought an intermittent war against France. This Hundred Years' War was a continuation of the long struggle between the kings of England and France over English royal possessions in France. Ever since the time of William the Conqueror, who had joined his French holdings with England, these possessions had been an obstacle in the path of the French kings' efforts to extend their authority over the entire country.

Immediate Causes

Gascony

In 1294, King Philip IV had attempted to take Gascony in southwestern France from the English, and the French continued to interfere with English rule over the province. King Edward III became convinced that only a full-scale war could prevent a French takeover of Gascony.

Economic Rivalry

Several other factors also contributed to the outbreak of war. Edward III wanted to defend England's economic interests in Flanders. The count of Flanders was becoming increasingly subject to the domination of the French king, and this threatened England's profitable wool trade.

In 1337, Edward III and the Flemish merchants joined in an alliance against King Philip VI of France and the pro-French count. The same year, Philip VI declared Gascony forfeit because the English had refused to accept the judicial decisions of its French overlord.

Scotland

Also contributing to the outbreak of war was Edward III's resentment of the French alliance with Scotland.

King Edward III's Claim to the French Throne

Edward III's conflict with the French encouraged him to assert his claim to the French throne. The old Capetian dynasty, which had provided France's kings since the late tenth century, had died out following the deaths without heirs of the three sons of King Philip IV.

Philip IV's daughter, Isabella, was the mother of Edward III. As the grandson of Philip IV, Edward was, in fact, the closest living male heir to the French throne. The French courts, however, had invalidated Edward III's claim by citing the old Salic Law, which barred inheritance through the female line, and had awarded the French crown to Philip IV's nephew, Philip of Valois. He succeeded to the French throne as King Philip VI (r. 1328–1350), the first king of the Valois dynasty.

The First Phase, 1337–1360

Following several minor naval engagements, King Edward III invaded northern France through the Low Countries in 1338, but this invasion accomplished little.

The Battle of Sluys (1340)

In 1340, the English fleet defeated the French navy in the Battle of Sluys, off the coast of Flanders. This victory gave the English control of the English Channel for the next generation.

The Battle of Crécy (1346)

At the Battle of Crécy, fought in August 1346, the army commanded by King Edward III and the Black Prince inflicted a devastating defeat on a larger French force. The English owed their victory to their superior tactics and to the invention of the longbow, which enabled the English infantrymen to defeat the mounted French knights, who wore heavy coats of mail.

Following their victory at Crécy, in 1347 the English took the French channel port of Calais, which they held for the next two centuries. For the next several years, the Black Death forced an intermission in the war.

The Battle of Poitiers (1356)

In September 1356, an English army led by the Black Prince defeated the French near Poitiers. The French king, John II (r. 1350–1364), and more than 1000 French knights were taken prisoner.

The Treaty of Brétigny (1360)

Under the terms of the Treaty of Brétigny, King Edward III agreed to renounce his claim to the French throne and acquired control of Aquitaine and some adjoining territory, as well as Ponthieu and Calais. The French agreed to pay the immense ransom of £500,000 for the release of King John II. When the French failed to raise the ransom money and failed to carry out other provisions of the treaty, King John voluntarily returned to imprisonment in London, where he died in 1364.

The Second Phase, 1369–1396

During the late fourteenth century, the English suffered several setbacks in the war, resulting from several factors, including the Black Death, the Black Prince's misrule in Aquitaine, the senility of King Edward III, and the rivalry between the king's sons, the Black Prince and John of Gaunt. In addition, the French possessed a capable new king in the person of Charles V (r. 1364–1380).

French Victories

The war was renewed in 1369, with the Black Prince pushing against the French from Aquitaine, while John of Gaunt advanced from Calais into Normandy. The tide of war soon turned, however, and the French won a series of victories on land and at sea. By the time of King Charles V's death in 1380, England held only Calais and a strip of territory along the French coast from Bayeux to Bordeaux.

Truce

Under the terms of an uneasy truce arranged in 1396, England's King Richard II agreed to marry the eight-year-old daughter of King Charles VI of France.

The Third Phase, 1414–1453

In the early fifteenth century, King Charles VI (r. 1380–1422) lapsed into insanity, and France came to be divided between the king's uncle, the duke of Burgundy, and the king's brother, the duke of Orleans. Taking advantage of the disorder in France, England's King Henry V (r. 1413–1422) formed an alliance with the Burgundians and renewed the war.

The Battle of Agincourt (1415)

Henry V inflicted a crushing defeat on the French in the Battle of Agincourt in October 1415. As a consequence of the battle itself and the English massacre of their prisoners, French losses are estimated at 7000, while English dead numbered about 500.

The Treaty of Troyes (1420)

Burgundians.   In August 1417, Henry V returned to France and, by the spring of 1418, had conquered Normandy. In May 1418, the Burgundians seized Paris, and Duke John the Fearless of Burgundy (r. 1404–1419) united the French nobility under his leadership. The issue now was whether the Burgundians would maintain their alliance with the English or would turn against them in defense of the French monarchy.

In September 1419, Duke John the Fearless was murdered. His son, Duke Philip the Good (r. 1419–1467), succeeded him.

Negotiation of Treaty.   In 1420, Duke Philip the Good, acting in the name of the insane King Charles VI, negotiated the Treaty of Troyes with King Henry V. The English king became engaged to Catherine (1401–1437), Charles VI's daughter, and was recognized as heir to the French throne. Until the death of Charles VI, Henry V would rule France as regent, in association with Philip the Good. The Dauphin, the eldest son of Charles VI, was thus disinherited.

Deaths of English and French Kings.   In August 1422, however, King Henry V died, leaving his nine-month-old son, Henry VI (r. 1422–1461), with his claims in France. King Charles VI died a few months later. Both England and France were now ruled by regencies.

Joan of Arc

The war was soon renewed, and the English did well against the French Dauphin, who became King Charles VII (r. 1422–1461). Since the English controlled both Paris and Rheims, the Dauphin could not be formally crowned.

French territories south of the Loire River, with the exception of Gascony, remained loyal to the Dauphin. In October 1428, the English laid siege to Orleans, the Dauphin's last stronghold.

Crowning of the Dauphin.   At this critical point in the war, Joan of Arc (c. 1412–1431) appeared. A young peasant girl, she was convinced that God had given her the mission of saving France. She persuaded the Dauphin to provide her with an army, and she succeeded in lifting the siege of Orleans in May 1429. In July, Joan accompanied the Dauphin through enemy-controlled territory to Rheims, where he was crowned king of France.

Execution of Joan.   Joan of Arc failed, however, in her effort to free Paris, and in May 1430, she was captured by the Burgundians, who sold her to the English. The English turned her over to French churchmen who supported the English cause, and she was tried by a church court. Condemned as a witch and a heretic, Joan of Arc was burned at the stake in Rouen on May 10, 1431. Despite her death, Joan of Arc inspired the French with a spirit of national revival.

The End of the War

In 1435, the Burgundians abandoned their alliance with England in return for concessions of French territory. The following year, the French seized Paris and then moved systematically to drive the English from most of northern France. In 1448, the French took Maine and from 1449 to 1451 regained Normandy. After the French took Bordeaux in 1453, the war ended with only the channel port of Calais remaining in English hands.

The Significance of the War

The Hundred Years' War began as a feudal and dynastic conflict but increasingly became a war between two countries, which encouraged the development of nationalism in both England and France.

Impact on English Foreign Relations

Although England was defeated, the loss of its holdings in France freed the English from continental entanglements. This ultimately enabled the English to turn their attention to the world beyond Europe, where they gradually created a great empire.

Impact on English Government

The war also had a significant impact on England's government. Parliament had earlier won the right to approve new taxes. During the war, the king's need for money to fight the French compelled him to summon Parliament into session more frequently, which made it possible for Parliament to pressure the king for more concessions. It was during the Hundred Years' War that the knights and burgesses began to meet separately from the barons and bishops in order to discuss money matters. This separate meeting of the knights and burgesses marked the beginning of the division of Parliament into two houses, the House of Commons and the House of Lords.

Changes in Warfare

Finally, the Hundred Years' War brought changes to the nature of warfare, as infantrymen armed with longbows ended the invincibility of knights on horseback. This development helped promote the emergence of professional armies supported by direct taxation in place of forces raised by feudal levies.

The Black Death

In the mid-fourteenth century, an epidemic of bubonic plague swept out of Asia and spread along the trade routes into Europe, striking England in 1348–1349. Close to one-third of England's population succumbed to the ravages of the Black Death.

Economic Effect

The decline in the labor supply led to a substantial increase in wages. While prices generally increased, rents declined, and the rental of farm land increasingly replaced the manorial system based on serfdom. This promoted the creation of a large class of small peasant farmers. The growing of grain declined, while sheep raising increased, since it required less labor.

The Statute of Laborers (1351)

Facing an economic squeeze, the landholders secured the passage in 1351 of the Statute of Laborers, which froze both wages and prices. However, the law had little practical effect other than to enrage the peasants.

Religion

During the fourteenth century, the English church experienced a decline. The monarchy emphasized political factors, rather than spiritual ones, in the appointment of bishops, while many clergy neglected their religious duties, preferring more worldly pursuits. During the

Babylonian Captivity of the papacy from 1305 to 1378, a series of French popes resided at Avignon in southern France, rather than in Rome, and were subservient to the French monarchy. This increased English resentment of the papacy and its demands, since England was at war with France, and England responded by penalizing the papacy.

Legislative Restrictions on the Papacy

The Statute of Provisors (1351) prohibited papal appointments to church office in England without royal consent, while the Statute of Praemunire (1353) barred appeals to papal courts by prohibiting the trial of any cases involving the church outside of England. In 1366, Parliament ended the payment of an annual tribute to the pope that had begun in the reign of King John during the early thirteenth century.

John Wycliffe and the Lollards

John Wycliffe (c. 1324–1384), a scholar who taught at Oxford University, launched an attack on the wealth and power of the Catholic church, opposing both the collection of papal taxes in England and the ownership of property by the church.

Teachings

Wycliffe insisted that the Bible was the only source of Christian doctrine, and to make the Bible more accessible to literate Englishmen he translated it into English. He rejected the authority of the papacy and the hierarchy of the church, regarding them as both unscriptural and unnecessary. He also rejected the Roman Catholic doctrine regarding the Eucharist, which taught that the consecrated bread and wine were miraculously transformed into the body and blood of Christ. The ideas of Wycliffe foreshadowed the Protestant Reformation of the sixteenth century.

Lollards

Wycliffe won a number of followers, known as Lollards, who continued to promote his teachings after his death. During the late fourteenth century, the church condemned the Lollards as heretics and, with the support of the government, the movement was suppressed. But Wycliffe's ideas had already spread to Bohemia, where they influenced John Hus (c. 1369–1415), a teacher at the university in Prague.

King Richard II (r. 1377–1399)

King Richard II, the son of the Black Prince, succeeded his grandfather, King Edward III, at the age of ten.

The Lords Appellant

During Richard II's minority, the great barons contended with one another in a struggle for power. The duke of Gloucester led the faction known as the "Lords Appellant," so called because they "appealed" for the king's advisers to be punished for treason. The Lords Appellant dominated the "Merciless Parliament" of February 1388, which condemned to death or banished the king's advisers. Five Lords Appellant then took control of the government.

In May 1389, at the age of twenty-two, Richard II took power into his own hands, but he quickly proved to be an ineffective and unpopular ruler.

The Peasants' Revolt (1381)

The Peasants' Revolt of 1381 resulted from several factors, including the dislocations brought by the Black Death, hostility to the Statute of Laborers, and the poll taxes of 1377, 1379, and 1380.

March on London

Directed against both the landowners and the king's government, the revolt began in Essex, in southeastern England, in May 1381 and quickly spread to Kent. Led by Wat Tyler (d. 1381) and Jack Straw, the rebels marched on London, burning landlords' houses and manor rolls as they went.

Reaching London, the rebels carried out a two-day rampage of killing and plundering. They murdered hated royal officials, burned officials' houses, and freed prisoners.

King Richard II's Intervention

The government was paralyzed, and the fourteen-year-old King Richard II and his ministers took refuge in the Tower of London.

On June 14, the king bravely met with the rebels' leader, Wat Tyler, promising reforms, including abolition of the poll tax and peasants' obligation to work on the lord's desmesne.

When Tyler increased his demands, he was killed on June 15. Richard II then calmed the angry rebels by promising that he would be their leader and urging them to disperse. The rebels left London, and the revolt subsided. The king's promises of reform were not kept. Subsequent acts of rebellion were suppressed, and the peasants continued to suffer from exploitation.

The Overthrow of King Richard II

In 1397, King Richard II began to act in an increasingly despotic fashion. Taking revenge on the Lords Apellant, he had the duke of Gloucester and the earl of Arundel executed and the earl of Warwick exiled from the kingdom.

Victory of Henry of Bolingbroke

In February 1399, John of Gaunt, the duke of Lancaster and the king's uncle, died. Richard II barred the rightful heir, Henry of Bolingbroke, John of Gaunt's son, from inheriting the duchy of Lancaster and seized the property of the house of Lancaster. This act frightened England's property holders.

Returning from exile in July 1399, Henry of Bolingbroke landed in Yorkshire and quickly gathered support. Richard II was taken prisoner.

Crowning of Henry

Parliament forced the king to abdicate and awarded the crown to Henry of Bolingbroke, whose claim was based on heredity (his father, John of Gaunt, was a younger son of King Henry III) and on conquest. He became the first king of the House of Lancaster, King Henry IV. In establishing Henry IV on the throne, Parliament demonstrated its growing authority, since it had not only deposed a king but had selected as his successor an individual who was not a direct heir to the throne. The former king, Richard II, died in February 1400. Whether he was murdered, starved to death, or committed suicide has never been determined.

The Lancastrian Kings

King Henry IV (r. 1399–1413)

The reign of King Henry IV began a century of conflict over the succession to the throne, with rival factions using Parliament as an instrument in their struggle.

In an effort to defend his possession of the throne, Henry IV dealt cautiously with the nobility, Parliament, and the church. When Parliament denied him money, the king borrowed from London merchants. During these years, the power of Parliament continued to increase. Above all, Parliament insisted that the king's redress of grievances should precede the granting of money. Parliament also insisted on its rights to freedom of debate and to audit the king's accounts, and the House of Commons gained the authority to originate money bills.

Revolt Against King Henry IV

Encouraged by the French and their Scottish allies, Owen Glendower (c. 1359–1415) and Sir Edmund Mortimer (1376–1409) of Wales joined with the powerful Percy family of Northumberland in a revolt against King Henry IV. In several engagements fought between 1403 and 1408, the king succeeded in suppressing the revolt, although unrest continued in Wales.

Capture of the Scottish Prince

King Henry IV captured James, the young heir to the Scottish throne, in 1406. The English held him hostage for nineteen years, thus effectively neutralizing the Scots, preventing them from aiding their French ally in war against England.

King Henry V (r. 1413–1422)

King Henry V was not as threatened by revolt as his father had been. His chief opponent, Sir John Oldcastle (c. 1378–1417), was an influential follower of John Wycliffe. The king had Oldcastle imprisoned in the Tower of London. After he escaped, Oldcastle was charged with plotting against the king. In 1417, he was captured in Wales and executed. King Henry V focused his attention on the war against France, and his victories marked the height of England's successes in the Hundred Years' War.

King Henry VI (r. 1422–1461)

King Henry VI inherited the throne at the age of one. During his minority, his uncles, the dukes of Bedford and Gloucester, controlled the government and ran the war in France.

In 1445, Henry VI married Margaret of Anjou (c. 1430–1482), an ambitious woman who became extremely unpopular in England. She exercised considerable authority, particularly during her husband's periods of insanity.

Opposition to the King

The unpopularity of the queen and setbacks in France increased discontent with Henry VI and his unsuccessful ministers, William de la Pole, the duke of Suffolk (1396–1450), and Edmund Beaufort, the duke of Somerset (d. 1455). In 1450, Royal Navy captains murdered de la Pole, a favorite of the queen.

Also in 1450, Jack Cade of Kent led a revolt in southern England. When the rebels reached London, the frightened government promised them amnesty. Although Cade was captured and executed, the unrest continued for some time.

To compound the government's problems, King Henry VI was not only incompetent but also suffered from increasing episodes of insanity. By the end of the Hundred Years' War in 1453, the country stood on the brink of civil war.

The Wars of the Roses

The civil war that broke out in England shortly after the end of the Hundred Years' War is known as the Wars of the Roses. Its name originated from the emblems of the contending royal houses, the white rose of the House of York and the red rose of the House of Lancaster. (In fact, the Lancastrians did not adopt their emblem until the war had ended.) The Wars of the Roses were, above all, a struggle among members of the nobility and landed gentry, who sided with the contending houses primarily for reasons of their own self-interests.

Causes

The war resulted, above all, from the incompetence and periodic insanity of the Lancastrian King Henry VI. The decline of royal authority encouraged factionalism among the nobility and offered an open invitation to revolt.

Revolt was also encouraged by the defeat in France and the hostility to Queen Margaret and the king's advisers, especially Edmund Beaufort, the duke of Somerset.

The Question of Succession

Until 1453, King Henry VI remained childless. Richard, the duke of York, the grandson of King Edward III's third son, had the best claim to the throne, although he was challenged by the duke of Somerset. While Somerset's family, the Beauforts, were descendants of John of Gaunt (the second son of King Edward III), they had specifically been barred from the succession by an act passed in 1407 with the approval of King Henry IV, the founder of the Lancastrian house.

In 1453, the issue of the succession was complicated when Queen Margaret gave birth to a son. To compound matters, that same year the king experienced the first of his episodes of insanity.

Rebellion of the Duke of York

With the king unable to govern, the House of Lords named Richard, duke of York, lord protector. Then, when the king recovered in 1454, the duke of York was removed from office and his rival, the duke of Somerset, was released from prison. The duke of York responded by going to war. This act began the Wars of the Roses, which lasted until 1485. During most of the civil war, the Yorkists controlled the government.

Battles and Their Aftermath

Battle of St. Albans (1455)

The Yorkists won the Battle of St. Albans in May 1455, and the duke of Somerset was killed. Queen Margaret was now the leader of the Lancastrians.

The duke of York became lord protector later in the year, when King Henry VI once again lapsed into insanity. The king regained his authority when he recovered in 1456. In 1459, the leading Yorkists fled into exile.

Battle of Northampton (1460)

In 1460, the Yorkists returned and renewed the war, defeating the Lancastrians in July at the Battle of Northampton. Capturing the king, the duke of York hurried to London to assert his claim to the throne. A compromise was arranged whereby Henry VI would remain king, but the duke of York and his heirs were recognized as the king's successors.

Battle of Wakefield (1460)

Queen Margaret, whose son had been disinherited, raised an army and defeated the Yorkists at the Battle of Wakefield in December 1460. The duke of York died in this battle, and his claim to the throne passed to his son, Edward. Richard Neville, the earl of Warwick (1428–1471), became the effective leader of the Yorkists.

Battle of Mortimer's Cross (1461)

Although Queen Margaret's army succeeded in rescuing King Henry VI from captivity, the Yorkists defeated the Lancastrians at the Battle of Mortimer's Cross on February 2, 1461. Entering London in March, Edward, the nineteen-year-old Yorkist claimant, proclaimed himself king as King Edward IV.

Battle of Towton (1461)

Leading his army to northern England, Edward IV defeated the Lancastrians at the Battle of Towton later in March. King Henry VI fled to Scotland with his wife and child. Four years later, he was captured and imprisoned in the Tower of London. Although he regained his crown briefly in 1470–1471, the Battle of Towton brought the effective end of the sixty-two years of Lancastrian rule.

King Edward IV (r. 1461–1483)

King Edward IV, the first Yorkist king, devoted most of his efforts, especially during the first years of his reign, to the continuing struggle against the Lancastrians and to his conflict with his one-time ally, Richard Neville, the earl of Warwick.

Conflict with the Earl of Warwick and the Lancastrians

The cousin of Edward IV, the earl of Warwick (known as Warwick the Kingmaker), had helped the king win his throne. During the first years of his reign, Edward IV permitted Warwick to dominate the government. In 1464, however, the king turned against Warwick.

In 1469, Warwick formed an alliance with Queen Margaret and the Lancastrians. Taking London the next year, the rebels restored King Henry VI to the throne.

The Lancastrian recovery of power proved brief. In April 1471, Edward IV defeated the Lancastrians at the Battle of Barnet, where

Warwick was killed. Then, at the Battle of Tewkesbury in early May, Edward IV defeated Queen Margaret's army. King Henry VI and the queen were captured, and the Prince of Wales, their only son, was killed. Later that month, Henry VI was murdered in the Tower of London, bringing an end to the direct Lancastrian line. For the next twelve years, Edward IV was relatively secure in his possession of the throne.

War with France

In 1475, allied with his brother-in-law, Charles the Bold, the duke of Burgundy (r. 1467–1477), King Edward IV invaded France. Despite the protests of Charles the Bold, the English made a deal with King Louis XI, who agreed to make annual payments to the English of £10,000. This subsidy reduced the king's dependence on Parliament for money.

King Richard III (r. 1483–1485)

In 1483, King Edward IV died unexpectedly, leaving two young princes to be protected by either the unpopular queen mother, Elizabeth Woodville (1437–1492), or their uncle, Richard, the duke of Gloucester.

Seizure of the Throne

While Richard had been a loyal supporter of his brother, Edward IV, he was now determined to take the crown for himself. He ordered the arrest of the queen mother's supporters and pressured the Great Council into making him lord protector. He imprisoned the young brothers—the thirteen-year-old lawful, although uncrowned, King Edward V and the twelve-year-old Richard, duke of York—in the Tower of London. He claimed falsely that the boys were illegitimate and that he was the legitimate heir to the throne. In July 1483, Richard, the duke of Gloucester, was crowned King Richard III. The two princes were murdered in the tower. The precise nature of the role of Richard III in the murders has remained a subject of historical controversy.

. Emergence of Henry Tudor

Richard III was an arbitrary ruler, and opposition to him mounted. The duke of Buckingham, who had supported the king in his seizure of the throne, now turned against him, giving his support to Henry Tudor, the earl of Richmond.

Henry Tudor possessed a weak claim to the throne. He derived his claim from his mother, who was a descendant in the Beaufort line of John of Gaunt (the duke of Lancaster and son of Edward III), by his mistress, Catherine Swinford. While Parliament had legitimized the children of this union, they were specifically barred from the succession. But the deaths of King Henry VI and the Prince of Wales in 1471 had made Henry Tudor the head of the Lancastrians.

The duke of Buckingham's plot was discovered, and the duke was executed. While Richard III thus held on to his throne, his unpopularity continued to mount.

The Battle of Bosworth Field (1485)

Henry Tudor sought refuge in France, where he gained the support of King Louis XI and raised an army. Landing in Wales in August 1485, Henry advanced into England, where the opponents of Richard III rallied to his cause.

The armies of Henry Tudor and the king met in the Battle of Bosworth Field. King Richard III, the last of England's Yorkist kings, was killed, and his army was dispersed.

End of the Wars of the Roses

Following his victory, Henry Tudor went on to London, where he was crowned King Henry VII, the first of the Tudor dynasty to rule England. Parliament confirmed his accession to the throne, and he married Princess Elizabeth, the daughter of the Yorkist King Edward IV. This act helped unite the opposing houses of Lancaster and York.

Effects of the Wars of the Roses

The Battle of Bosworth Field was the last battle of the Wars of the Roses. This civil war had decimated the nobility and had also brought the decline of Parliament's authority. In a more positive vein, the Wars of the Roses had helped promote a growing spirit of cooperation between the prosperous middle classes and the king against their common enemy, the nobility, who were held responsible for the anarchy into which England had sunk.

Economic Developments

During much of the Middle Ages, England had been a producer and exporter of raw wool. In the late fourteenth century, however, England began to develop its own woolen textile industry. As the manufacture and export of woolen textiles increased, it contributed to the expansion of England's merchant fleet and the development of merchant organizations. The Navigation Act of 1381 required English merchants to use English ships for the export or import of goods.

Culture

Language

During the fourteenth century, anti-French sentiment engendered by the Hundred Years' War encouraged the increased use of English, rather than French, in the life of official England. In 1362, English replaced French as the language of the courts of law, while in 1363, the chancellor opened Parliament with an address in English. John Wycliffe wrote and preached in English and prepared an English translation of the Bible, while John Gower (1330–c. 1408) wrote his later poems in English.

Literature

William Langland

William Langland (c. 1332–c. 1400) and Geoffrey Chaucer (c. 1340–1400) were the most important English writers of the fourteenth century. The poem *Piers Plowman* (1362), traditionally ascribed to Langland, is an allegory attacking the corrupt society of the time.

Geoffrey Chaucer

Chaucer's most famous work, the *Canterbury Tales,* is a collection of stories presented in poetic form, supposedly told by a diverse group of pilgrims journeying to the shrine of St. Thomas à Becket in Canterbury. The stories reveal Chaucer's profound insight into human nature and are strongly secular in spirit. Chaucer took particular delight in revealing the foibles and corruption of members of the clergy.

Thomas Malory

No fifteenth-century English poet achieved the stature of Chaucer. In prose, the most important writer of the fifteenth century was Sir Thomas Malory (d. 1471), who wrote *Morte D'Arthur* (1469), a retelling of the legend of King Arthur and his knights of the round table.

Philosophy

The noted scholastic philosopher William of Ockham (d. c. 1349) was a Franciscan who studied and taught at Oxford. Like Duns Scotus before him (see Chapter 5), William of Ockham rejected the idea that reason could serve as a valid guide in matters of faith. He also staunchly defended the Franciscan ideal of poverty against the efforts of the pope to modify it. In this dispute, he became a strong opponent of the claims of papal sovereignty.

Law

Sir John Fortescue (c. 1394–c. 1476) wrote *De Laudibus Legum Angliae,* a treatise on English common law.

Sir Thomas Littleton (c. 1407–1481) wrote treatises on estates and the law of real property.

Printing

The invention of printing with movable metal type is generally credited to Johannes Gutenberg (c. 1400–1468), who established a press at Mainz in the German Rhineland. About 1456, Gutenberg produced his superbly printed edition of the Bible.

In 1477, William Caxton (c. 1421–1491) set up the first printing press in England, printing about 100 books.

The printing press had an immense impact, enabling the rapid spread of new knowledge and ideas among the educated classes.

Henry Tudor's victory at Bosworth Field in 1485 brought an end to the turmoil that had afflicted England during the fourteenth and fifteenth centuries. England stood in need of a strong government that could restore peace, order, and prosperity to the country. The new Tudor dynasty provided that government.

Recommended Reading

Alexander, Grant. *Independence and Nationhood: Scotland, 1306–1469* (1984).

Barber, Richard. *Edward, Prince of Wales and Aquitaine: A Biography of the Black Prince* (1978).

Bean, J. M. W. *The Decline of English Feudalism, 1215–1540* (1968).

Bridbury, A. R. *Economic Growth: England in the Later Middle Ages* (1975).

Chambers, E. K. *English Literature at the Close of the Middle Ages* (1945).

Chrimes, S. B. *Lancastrians, Yorkists, and Henry VII* (1964).

Cottle, Basil. *The Triumph of England, 1300–1500* (1969).

Davies, R. G. and J. H. Denton, eds. *The English Parliament in the Middle Ages* (1981).

DuBoulay, F. R. H. *An Age of Ambition: England in the Late Middle Ages* (1970).

Edwards, Sir Goronwy. *The Second Century of the English Parliament* (1979).

Evans, Joan. *English Art, 1307–1461* (1949).

Fryde, E. B. *The Great Revolt of 1381* (1969).

Fryde, Natalie. *The Tyranny and Fall of Edward II, 1321–1326* (1979).

Goodman, Anthony. *The Wars of the Roses: Military Activity and English Society, 1452–97* (1981).

Hilton, R. H. *The Decline of Serfdom in Medieval England* (1969).

Hilton, R. H. *The English Peasantry in the Later Middle Ages* (1975).

Hutchison, Harold F. *Henry V: A Biography* (1967).

Hutchison, Harold F. *The Hollow Crown: A Life of Richard II* (1961).

Jacob, Ernest Fraser F. *The Fifteenth Century, 1399–1485* (1961).

Kendall, Paul Murray. *Warwick the Kingmaker* (1957).

Kendall, P. M. *The Yorkist Age* (1962).

Kenny, Anthony. *Wycliffe* (1985).

Kirby, J. L. *Henry IV of England* (1970).

McKisack, May. *The Fourteenth Century, 1307–1399* (1959).

Maddicott, J. R. *Thomas of Lancaster, 1307–1322: A Study in the Reign of Edward II* (1970).

Myers, A. R. *England in the Late Middle Ages* (1952).

Norton-Smith, John. *Geoffrey Chaucer* (1974).

Packe, Michael. *King Edward III* (1982).

Ross, Charles. *Edward IV* (1974).

Ross, Charles. *Richard III* (1981).

Seward, Desmond. *The Hundred Years War: The English in France, 1337–1453* (1978).

St. Aubyn, Giles. *The Year of Three Kings: 1483* (1983).

Thompson, John A. F. *The Transformation of Medieval England, 1370–1529* (1983).

Tuck, Anthony. *Richard II and the English Nobility* (1974).

Wilkinson, Bertie. *The Later Middle Ages in England, 1216–1485* (1969).

Wolffe, B. P. *Henry VI* (1981).

CHAPTER 7

The Tudor Century:
Henry VII and Henry VIII

Time Line

1485–1509	Reign of King Henry VII
1492	The Treaty of Etaples ends the war between England and France
1494	Poynings's Acts extend English control over Ireland
1497–1498	John Cabot explores the northeast coast of North America
1509	Catherine of Aragon marries Henry, the son of King Henry VII
	John Colet establishes St. Paul's School in London

1509–1547	Reign of King Henry VIII
1512–1514	England joins with King Ferdinand of Spain and the Holy Roman Emperor Maximilian in a war against France
1513	King James IV of Scotland is killed at the Battle of Flodden Field
1516	Thomas More publishes *Utopia*
1522–1526	England joins with the Holy Roman Emperor Charles V in a war against France
1527	King Henry VIII requests a papal annulment of his marriage to Catherine of Aragon
1532	King Henry VIII names Thomas Cranmer archbishop of Canterbury
1533	King Henry VIII marries Anne Boleyn
1534	Parliament passes the Act of Supremacy
1536	The Act of Union joins Wales with England
1536–1539	The English monasteries are dissolved
1539	Parliament enacts the Six Articles
1542	The English defeat the Scots at the Battle of Solway Moss
1544–1546	England joins with Emperor Charles V in a war against France

The first of England's Tudor monarchs, Kings Henry VII and Henry VIII, proved to be skillful politicians who succeeded in establishing an identity between their interests and objectives and those of the nation. They provided orderly and effective government, winning the support of the prosperous middle classes, who appreciated the peace and stability the kings brought to the land. As a consequence, the power of the monarchs increased, while the authority of Parliament declined.

In religion, King Henry VIII began the English Reformation, breaking the ties between England and the Roman papacy and creating what amounted to a national Catholic church.

King Henry VII (r. 1485–1509)

King Henry VII, who won his throne at the Battle of Bosworth Field, was a ruthless and efficient ruler who restored peace and order to his kingdom and reestablished the authority of the monarchy.

Defeat of Yorkist Conspiracies

Early in his reign, King Henry VII used force to suppress several rebellions and to defeat rival claimants to the throne. The central figures in these plots were Margaret of Burgundy, the sister of the Yorkist King Edward IV and the widow of Duke Charles the Bold of Burgundy, and Gerald Fitzgerald, the eighth earl of Kildare and lord deputy of Ireland.

In 1487, the king crushed a revolt led by Lambert Simnel. Although the revolt had been serious, the king regarded Simnel as beneath the dignity of execution and made him a scullion in the royal kitchen.

A decade later, in 1497, the king defeated a revolt led by Perkin Warbeck (1474–1499), who was executed two years later.

Decline of the Nobility

The factionalism and ambitions of the nobility had long been a cause of disorder in England, but their decline had been hastened by the Hundred Years' War and the Wars of the Roses. In order to further this decline, King Henry VII chose his ministers mainly from the prosperous middle classes, who supported the king in his effort to prevent the nobility from regaining its influence and power. In his campaign against the nobility, Henry VII vigorously enforced an act adopted earlier against livery and maintenance, which had deprived the nobles of the right to maintain private armies.

The Court of the Star Chamber

King Henry VII also used the Court of the Star Chamber as a powerful instrument of royal authority in his campaign against the nobility. (The court gained its name from the starred ceiling of the room in which it met.)

Powers

The Court of the Star Chamber had jurisdiction over cases involving livery and maintenance, riots and other civil disorders, the misconduct of sheriffs, the bribery of juries, and similar matters. Its procedures were more flexible than those of the courts of the common law, and it could use methods of obtaining evidence that the courts of the common law could not. The Court of the Star Chamber tried cases without juries and was therefore beyond bribery and intimidation.

Uses

In the time of Henry VII, the Court of the Star Chamber was popular, since it helped the king restore order to the country. In the seventeenth century, however, the court became unpopular when the Stuart kings used it as a weapon in their conflict with Parliament (see Chapter 9).

King Henry VII and Parliament

Jealous of his authority as king, Henry VII sought to rule without Parliament insofar as that was possible. During his reign, Parliament met only five times and only once during his final twelve years.

Henry VII's frugality freed him from dependence on Parliament for grants of money. The king strove to reduce the expenses of government and secured money by collecting the high fines imposed by his courts and by seizing the lands of his opponents. He also benefited from the expansion of trade, which increased his income from customs duties.

When Parliament did meet, Henry VII succeeded in managing it, both because of his skill and because his objectives coincided with the interests of the prosperous classes that dominated Parliament.

Foreign Affairs

King Henry VII pursued a prudent foreign policy, generally avoiding war and other costly continental entanglements and seeking to achieve his foreign policy objectives through diplomacy and marriage alliances.

Scotland

Under the terms of an agreement reached in 1499, Henry VII's daughter, Margaret Tudor (1489–1541), married King James IV (r. 1488–1513) of Scotland in 1503. While this agreement led only to a temporary improvement in Anglo-Scottish relations, the marriage laid the basis for the eventual union of the English and Scottish crowns.

Spain

In the Treaty of Medina del Campo, signed in 1489, Henry VII arranged for his son, Arthur, to marry Catherine of Aragon (1485–1536), the daughter of King Ferdinand (r. 1479–1516) and Queen Isabella (r. 1474–1504) of Spain. The marriage took place in 1501, but Arthur died five months later. Henry VII negotiated a new treaty with Spain in 1503, which provided for the marriage of Catherine to his second son, Henry. This marriage took place in 1509.

France

Under the terms of the Treaty of Medina del Campo, England agreed to support Spain in a war against France. Although the Spanish made a separate peace with the French in 1491, thereby deserting Henry VII, the English continued the war. The French king, Charles VIII (r. 1483–1498), was more interested in fighting in Italy than he was in fighting the English and quickly agreed to the Treaty of Etaples of 1492. The treaty provided for the French payment of substantial annual subsidies to Henry VII.

The venture thus ended in a triumph for Henry VII, who had secured the marriage alliance with Spain and had done little fighting, while the French subsidies paid for the cost of the war.

Ireland

Since the early fourteenth century, the English-controlled area around Dublin, known as the Pale, had been shrinking. Furthermore, the English in Ireland were inclined both to oppose English rule, preferring to regulate their own affairs, and to support the Yorkist cause.

In theory, English rule in Ireland was exercised by an English viceroy although, in fact, this official rarely went near Ireland. Whatever English authority existed in Ireland was exercised by an Anglo-Irish lord deputy. For a number of years, the earls of Kildare had held this office. King Henry VII deprived the pro-Yorkist earl of his position and, in 1494, sent Sir Edward Poynings (1459–1521) to Ireland as his replacement. Poynings secured adoption by the Irish Parliament of several laws, known collectively as Poynings's Acts, that extended the control of the English king in Ireland. No acts of the Irish Parliament would take effect without the approval of the English crown, but acts of the English Parliament would be applicable to Ireland.

In 1497, when the danger of Yorkist plots ended, the earl of Kildare was restored to office as lord deputy. It had become apparent that the support of the Kildare family was necessary to maintain order in Ireland.

Exploration

The late fifteenth century was a great age of European exploration. The efforts of the Portuguese to find a route east by sea to the Indies resulted in the arrival of Vasco da Gama (c. 1469–1524) in India in 1498, while the Spanish quest for a route west by sea to the Indies led to the voyage of Christoper Columbus (1451–1506) in 1492.

John Cabot

The first English voyages were financed by the wealthy merchants of Bristol. In 1497 and 1498, John Cabot (c. 1450–c. 1498), a Genovese sailor who lived in Bristol, made two voyages along the northeast coast of North America, searching for a northwest passage leading to Asia.

Although Cabot's voyages were a private undertaking, King Henry VII granted him a monopoly of trade in any lands he might discover, and English claims to North America were based on Cabot's voyages. They did not, however, produce any profitable trade, and the Bristol merchants and the king soon lost interest in the venture.

Economic Developments

Encouragement of Commerce

King Henry VII's economic policies won him increasing support from England's prosperous classes, especially the merchants. The king encouraged foreign commerce and, in particular, demanded from foreign merchants who enjoyed privileges in England reciprocal privileges for English merchants. The Intercursus Magnus Treaty, signed with the Netherlands in 1497, provided for trade reciprocity, while the Intercursus Malus Treaty, signed with the Flemish towns in 1506, gave a monopoly of the lucrative English wool trade to the Merchants Adventurers, an English trading company that specialized in the trade in woolen textiles. In addition, a high duty was placed on the export of raw wool in order to promote the English manufacture and export of woolen textiles, while the Navigation Act of 1485 gave further encouragement to the development of the English merchant fleet. This act provided that Bordeaux wines imported into England had to be carried in English ships manned by English, Welsh, or Irish seamen.

Decline of the Craft Guilds

By the late fifteenth century, England's craft guilds were declining in importance and were being replaced by the domestic system. In this system, merchants supplied workers in their cottages with materials and then bought the finished goods. The domestic system developed first in the important woolen textile industry.

Agriculture

During the fifteenth century, the enclosure movement had gained momentum in England, as great landowners enclosed open fields and common lands in order to create larger farms or to provide pastures for sheep raising, which was increasingly profitable. This practice deprived tenant farmers of their livelihood. At the behest of King Henry VII, Parliament passed acts designed to regulate enclosures. This legislation had little impact, however, since enclosures resulted from a natural economic development that legislation could not readily control.

King Henry VIII (r. 1509–1547)

King Henry VIII inherited a secure throne and a full treasury, which his extravagance soon dissipated.

Relations with France

War, 1512–1514

Since 1494, Italy had been Europe's battleground, becoming the objective of French and Spanish ambitions. In 1511, King Ferdinand of Spain, Henry VIII's father-in-law, induced the English to join the

Holy League, which Pope Julius II (r. 1503–1513) had organized in an effort to drive the French out of Italy. The following year, England joined Spain and the Holy Roman Emperor Maximilian (r. 1493–1519) in a war against France.

Leading an English army to northern France, Henry VIII won the Battle of the Spurs and seized Tournai. Henry VIII's allies then abandoned him, making peace with King Louis XII (r. 1498–1515).

Peace Terms

In 1514, Henry VIII made peace with the French on favorable terms, arranging for the marriage of the decrepit King Louis XII to his seventeen-year-old sister, Mary. The French also agreed to pay Henry VIII an annual subsidy, and the English kept Tournai as security for payment. The death of King Louis XII in 1515 ended the marriage and the French alliance with England.

Renewed War, 1522–1526

France's new king, Francis I (r. 1515–1547) of the House of Valois, renewed French aggression in Italy, taking Milan.

Meanwhile, King Ferdinand of Spain died in 1516, and the crown passed to his grandson, Charles of Hapsburg, who became King Charles I (r. 1516–1556) of Spain. In 1519, Charles's paternal grandfather, Holy Roman Emperor Maximilian, died, and Charles now inherited the imperial crown, becoming Holy Roman Emperor Charles V (r. 1519–1558). In order to consolidate his position in Spain, Charles made a temporary peace with France, but a renewal of the Hapsburg-Valois conflict was virtually inevitable.

Alliance with Spain.   In an effort to maintain the balance of power on the European continent, England supported Spain in this conflict. Cardinal Thomas Wolsey (c. 1473–1530) was one of the first advocates and practitioners of the developing doctrine of the balance of power. According to this doctrine, no one state should become powerful enough to threaten the interests or the independence of the others. Therefore, the weaker states should join together to contain any state that threatened to become too powerful.

Costly Expeditions.   Forming an alliance with Charles V, England went to war against France in 1522. English expeditions to France in 1522 and 1523 accomplished little, however, and proved costly. In 1523, King Henry VIII summoned Parliament, which had not met in eight years, to ask for money to support the war. Although the king secured funds, the wrangle with Parliament made him realize that the pursuit of the war would endanger his popularity, and he decided to mark time.

In 1525, Emperor Charles V decisively defeated the French at Pavia in Italy, taking King Francis I prisoner. Two years later, Charles V sacked Rome and imprisoned the pope.

Henry VIII was now concerned about the growth of Hapsburg power and was also annoyed by Charles V's refusal to help England gain territory in France.

Attempts at French Alliance

In an effort to restore the balance of power, Henry VIII made peace with France in 1526 and then sought to form an alliance with the French, directed against Charles V. However, this pro-French policy proved unpopular among Henry's subjects, and the king was unable to secure the finances necessary to wage war against Charles V. Futhermore, the king was about to become involved in his reform of the English church, which required him to devote his full attention to domestic affairs.

King Henry VIII and the Reformation

The Continental Reformation

In the early sixteenth century, the Protestant Reformation began on the European continent. In 1517, Martin Luther (1483–1546) initiated the Reformation in the German state of Saxony, and Lutheranism soon spread throughout much of Germany and into Scandinavia. In Switzerland, the French-born John Calvin (1509–1564) became the leader of the Reformation in Geneva in 1536. Calvinism soon became the predominant religion in most of Switzerland and the northern Netherlands, as well as in Scotland.

Although Luther, Calvin, and other Protestant reformers disagreed on many doctrinal matters, they were united in their rejection of the papacy and on their insistence that the Bible was the only valid source of Christian doctrine.

King Henry VIII's Conflict with the Papacy

King Henry VIII always regarded himself as a Catholic. In 1521, he wrote *Defense of the Seven Sacraments,* an anti-Lutheran tract.

Pope Leo X (r. 1513–1521) bestowed on him the title "Defender of the Faith," which is still used by England's monarchs. Thus, Henry VIII's conflict with the papacy did not involve theological matters but rather a more personal situation.

Attempt to Annul Marriage.   The sequence of events that resulted in the English Reformation began with the king's desire to secure an annulment of his marriage to Catherine of Aragon. She had given birth to six children, but only one had survived, the future Queen Mary. There was, however, no precedent in English history for a reigning queen, and Henry became increasingly concerned with securing a male heir to the throne in order to continue the Tudor line and to avoid a renewed conflict over the succession. He had also become infatuated with Anne Boleyn (1507–1536), a lady-in-waiting at the court.

In 1527, the king requested Pope Clement VII (r. 1523–1534) to grant him an annulment, contending that his marriage to Catherine was invalid. She was the widow of Henry's older brother, Arthur. According to canon law, a man was not permitted to marry his brother's widow. Pope Julius II (r. 1503–1513) had granted a dispensation to permit the marriage, but Henry now argued that the dispensation should not have been granted.

Not only did Pope Clement VII hesitate to reverse the decision of a predecessor, but his freedom of action was restricted by the fact that the Holy Roman Emperor Charles V, Catherine of Aragon's nephew, dominated Italy at the time.

Dismissal of Wolsey.   Henry VIII became increasingly impatient. In 1529, he dismissed Cardinal Wolsey, his lord chancellor, replacing him with Thomas More (1478–1535). However, Thomas Cromwell (c. 1485–1540) now became the king's chief adviser.

The Reformation Parliament

In 1529, Henry VIII summoned Parliament, which remained in session for seven years, becoming known as the Reformation Parliament.

In 1531, Henry VIII compelled the English clergy to acknowledge him as their "only and supreme lord, and as far as the law of Christ allows, even supreme head." The king acquired the authority to control appointments to church offices. The following year, Parliament prohibited the payment to the pope of annates, the first year's income of newly appointed archbishops and bishops. In addition, Parliament forbade appeals to papal courts and barred all payments by the English church to the pope. These efforts to coerce the pope failed.

Marriage to Anne Boleyn

In 1532, Henry VIII made the subservient Thomas Cranmer (1489–1556) archbishop of Canterbury. In January 1533, the king secretly married Anne Boleyn, who gave birth in September to a daughter, Elizabeth, rather than the male heir Henry had hoped for. In May 1533, Cranmer granted the king the annulment of his marriage to Catherine of Aragon.

The Act of Supremacy and the Six Articles

In 1534, Parliament passed the Act of Supremacy, which declared the king to be the "only supreme head on earth" of the English church. While England rejected papal supremacy, the English church under Henry VIII remained Catholic in its doctrine and practice. In 1539, Parliament enacted the Six Articles, defining the doctrine of the English church. On all points, except papal supremacy, the Six Articles reaffirmed Catholic teaching and rejected Protestant beliefs.

English Translation of the Bible and the Worship Service

In 1537, Henry VIII authorized the publication of an English translation of the Bible, based on the earlier translations of William Tyndale (c. 1494–1536) and Miles Coverdale (1488–1569). In 1539, the king ordered that the English translation of the Bible be placed in all churches. Several years later, he ordered that parts of the worship service of the English church be translated from Latin into English. These actions served to encourage the spread of Protestant ideas in England, although that was not the king's intention.

Dissolution of the Monasteries

King Henry VIII took action against the English monasteries, which were regarded as strongholds of support for the papacy. The king instructed Thomas Cromwell to investigate corruption and immorality in the monasteries and to develop a case for their dissolution. An act of Parliament passed in 1536 dissolved the smaller monasteries, while the larger ones were dissolved in 1539. The king seized the monastic lands, which amounted to about ten percent of the land in England, and sold most of these lands to well-to-do landed gentry. This brought great wealth to the king, further reducing his need to ask Parliament for direct taxes, while those who acquired the land gained a financial stake in supporting the king's break with Rome.

The Act of Succession of 1534

The Act of Succession passed by Parliament in March 1534 declared Mary, Henry VIII's daughter by Catherine of Aragon, illegitimate and named Elizabeth, his daughter by Anne Boleyn, successor to the throne. In addition to declaring Anne Boleyn the king's lawful wife, the act required the king's subjects to take an oath to defend the act and all other acts of the Reformation Parliament.

Opposition to the Reformation

King Henry VIII encountered some opposition to his break with Rome.

Executions of More and Fisher.   Thomas More, the former lord chancellor, and John Fisher (1459–1535), the bishop of Rochester, refused to swear the oath required by the Act of Succession of 1534 and were executed in 1535.

Suppression of Pilgrimage of Grace.   In 1536, a revolt, known as the Pilgrimage of Grace, broke out in conservative northern England, but Henry easily suppressed it.

Support of Subjects

Most Englishmen supported their king. Many resented the great wealth of the Catholic church, as well as the taxes and fees it levied. Furthermore, English hostility to the papacy had grown during the period of the Babylonian Captivity in the fourteenth century (see Chapter 6), when the papacy was dominated by France, England's traditional enemy. In addition, those who had bought monastic property strongly supported the king.

King Henry VIII's Last Years

The King's Marriages

Henry VIII's marriage to Anne Boleyn was followed by four others. Although Anne gave birth to a daughter, the future Queen Elizabeth I, she did not produce the son Henry desired. She was convicted of adultery and beheaded in May 1536.

Ten days later, the king married Jane Seymour (c. 1509–1537), who died a few days after giving birth to a son, the later King Edward VI.

In early 1540, Thomas Cromwell arranged for Henry VIII to marry Anne of Cleves (1515–1557). Cromwell wanted to ally England with the Protestants of Germany, but Henry found Anne unattractive and the marriage lasted only a few months. After divorcing Anne, who received a substantial financial settlement, the king had Cromwell executed on a charge of treason.

In the summer of 1540, Henry married Catherine Howard (c. 1521–1542). Accusing her of adultery, the king had her beheaded in 1542.

Henry married his sixth wife, Catherine Parr (1512–1548) in 1543. She succeeded in outliving the king.

The Act of Succession of 1543

The Act of Succession of 1543 replaced the act adopted in 1534, providing for the succession to the throne of Henry VIII's three children, Edward, Mary, and Elizabeth, in that order.

Conflict with Scotland

Battle of Flodden Field (1513).   Early in King Henry VIII's reign, the English inflicted a crushing defeat on the Scots. In 1513, King James IV of Scotland invaded England. In the Battle of Flodden Field, fought in September, James IV was killed, along with much of his country's elite.

James V of Scotland.   Scotland's new king, James V (r. 1513–1542), was an infant, but when he came of age, Scotland's traditional alliance with France was renewed. Cardinal David Beaton (1494–1546), the king's chief adviser, was strongly pro-French. In 1536, James V married Madeleine, the daughter of King Francis I, and when she died, he married Mary, daughter of the French duke of Guise (1515–1560).

Battle of Solway Moss (1542).   War between England and Scotland broke out in 1542. In November, the English defeated the Scots at the Battle of Solway Moss. A month later, King James V died, leaving his crown to his week-old daughter, Mary Stuart, who later became known as Mary Queen of Scots (1542–1587).

Continued Warfare.   Concerned about the Scottish alliance with France, Henry VIII decided to take the initiative against the French.

Signing a treaty with the Holy Roman Emperor Charles V in late 1543, the king sent English troops to France, where they occupied the Channel port of Boulogne. In 1544, Charles V signed a separate peace with France, leaving England in the lurch. The costly war continued until June 1546, when Henry VIII and Francis I reached a settlement that allowed England to retain Boulogne for eight years.

Meanwhile, England's war against Scotland continued. In 1544, the English burned Edinburgh, and in May 1546, Cardinal Beaton was assassinated. Nevertheless, the pro-French elements among Scotland's leaders retained their dominance, and Scotland remained an implacable enemy of England.

Incorporation of Wales

The Act of Union of 1536 incorporated Wales completely into England, and the twelve Welsh counties received twenty-four representatives in Parliament. An act passed in 1543 united Welsh legal and administrative procedures with those of England.

Attempt to Subdue Ireland

In Ireland, English control remained limited to the region around Dublin known as the Pale. Elsewhere, Irish chieftains ruled. Most of the Irish were Roman Catholics and were hostile to King Henry VIII's religious policy.

King Henry VIII sought to strengthen the English hold on Ireland. As lord deputy, he replaced the Anglo-Irish earl of Kildare with an Englishman, which led to an unsuccessful revolt by Kildare's supporters.

In 1541, Henry assumed the titles of king of Ireland and head of the Irish church, and he distributed confiscated monastery lands to his supporters in Ireland. He failed, however, to win the support of most of the Irish people.

The Beginning of the English Renaissance

The Renaissance began in Italy in the fourteenth century and gradually spread northward across the Alps to the rest of Europe. The Renaissance brought an intensification of interest in the classical civilizations of ancient Greece and Rome, as well as an intensification of the secular spirit in Western European civilization, resulting in an increasing concern with the things of this world rather than eternity and a new emphasis on the individual and individual accomplishment.

The Oxford Humanists

During the Renaissance, humanist scholars studied and found inspiration in classical literature. In England, many of the first humanists had ties to Oxford University.

William Selling

William Selling was one of the first English scholars to study in Italy, going to the homeland of the Renaissance in 1464. Returning to England, he became the prior of Canterbury and made the monastic school there a center of the new learning.

Thomas Linacre

Thomas Linacre (c. 1460–1524), a pupil of Selling's, spent several years in Italy studying the classics and medicine and earning a medical degree.

William Grocyn

William Grocyn (c. 1446–1519), a friend of Linacre's, studied Greek in Italy. In the early 1490s, both Linacre and Grocyn returned to Oxford as teachers, doing much to establish humanism there.

John Colet

John Colet (c. 1467–1519), a student of Linacre's and Grocyn's, studied in Italy and returned to England in 1497 to teach at Oxford. From 1497 to 1504, he delivered a series of lectures at Oxford on the Epistles of St. Paul. While Colet knew little or no Greek, he brought a humanistic point of view to bear in these lectures. In 1505, Colet became dean of St. Paul's cathedral in London. He organized a new school at St. Paul's in 1509, which emphasized the study of Greek and Latin languages and literature. By the late sixteenth century, Greek was taught in many other English schools that prepared students for the universities.

Thomas More

Thomas More (1478–1535), who studied under Linacre, Grocyn, and Colet, was England's greatest humanist. After studying the classics at Oxford, he studied law at the Inns of Court in London. Entering the service of the monarchy, he became lord chancellor (see p. 105).

More's most famous work is *Utopia* (1516), which he wrote in Latin. *Utopia* (meaning "nowhere" in Greek) described an imaginary island where an ideal cooperative society flourished. In this society based on reason and tolerance, the citizens practiced a Christianity that was free of ignorance and superstition. There was no private property and no desire for profit, and there was no war, except in self-defense. More contrasted this society with the evils existing in his own society.

Erasmus

The Dutch-born Desiderius Erasmus (1466–1536), the most famous of the humanists of the Northern Renaissance, spent several years in England, including a stint as a professor at Cambridge.

In his most famous work, the satirical *Praise of Folly* (1512), Erasmus ridiculed many attitudes of his own time, among them ignorance, superstition, and greed. His satire was especially sharp when it was directed against churchmen who manifested these qualities.

Erasmus also used his knowledge of the classical languages in an effort to achieve a deeper understanding of the Bible. In 1516, he published an annotated edition of the New Testament in Greek, which revealed several significant errors in the Latin Vulgate, the biblical text authorized by the Roman Catholic Church.

Kings Henry VII and Henry VIII were strong and successful monarchs who were able to use Parliament for their own purposes. Henry VII's greatest achievement was his restoration of order and stability to the kingdom following the turmoil of the Wars of the Roses. While Henry VIII succeeded in breaking England's ties with the papacy, the religious reformation he initiated marked the beginning of a new era of turmoil in the life of the English nation.

Recommended Reading

Alexander, Michael Van Cleave. *The First of the Tudors: A Study of Henry VII and His Reign* (1980).

Beckingsale, B. W. *Thomas Cromwell, Tudor Minister* (1978).

Bindoff, S. T. *Tudor England* (1950).

Chambers, R. W. *Thomas More* (1958).

Chrimes, S. B. *Henry VII* (1972).

Dickens, A. G. *Thomas Cromwell and the English Reformation* (1959).

Elton, G. R. *England Under the Tudors* (2nd ed., 1974).

Elton, G. R. *Reform and Reformation: England, 1509–1558* (1977).

Ferguson, Arthur B. *The Articulate Citizen and the English Renaissance* (1965).

Ferguson, Charles W. *Naked to Mine Enemies: The Life of Cardinal Wolsey* (1958).

Fox, Alistair. *Thomas More, History and Providence* (1982).

Guy, John. *Tudor England* (1988).

Haigh, Christopher, ed. *The English Reformation Revised* (1987).

Heal, Felicity and Rosemary O'Day, eds. *Church and Society in England: Henry VIII to James I* (1977).

Hughes, Philip. *The Reformation in England* (5th ed., 1963).

Ives, E. W. *Anne Boleyn* (1986).

Mackie, J. D. *The Earlier Tudors, 1485–1558* (1983).

Marius, Richard. *Thomas More: A Biography* (1985).

Mattingly, Garrett. *Catherine of Aragon* (1941).

Morris, Christopher. *The Tudors* (rev. ed., 1976).

Paul, John E. *Catherine of Aragon and Her Friends* (1966).

Powicke, F. M. *The Reformation in England* (1941).

Ridley, Jasper. *Thomas Cranmer* (1962).

Scarisbrick, J. J. *Henry VIII* (1968).

Scarisbrick, J. J. *The Reformation and the English People* (1984).

Simons, Eric N. *Henry VII: The First Tudor King* (1968).

Smith, Lacey Baldwin. *Henry VIII: The Mask of Royalty* (1971).

Smith, Lacey Baldwin. *A Tudor Tragedy: The Life and Times of Catherine Howard* (1961).

Williams, Penry. *The Tudor Regime* (1979).

Youings, Joyce A. *The Dissolution of the Monasteries* (1971).

Youings, Joyce A. *Sixteenth-Century England* (1984).

CHAPTER 8

The Tudor Century:
Edward VI, Mary I, and Elizabeth I

Time Line

1547–1553	Reign of King Edward VI
1549	The Act of Uniformity requires the use of the *Book of Common Prayer* in England's churches
	Kett's Rebellion breaks out near Norwich
1551	The Forty-two Articles reflect the growth of Calvinist doctrine in the Anglican Church
1553–1558	Reign of Queen Mary
1554	Cardinal Reginald Pole receives England back into the Roman Catholic Church

1555–1556	Queen Mary's persecution of Protestants earns her the nickname of "Bloody Mary"
1558	England loses Calais to the French
1558–1603	Reign of Queen Elizabeth I
1559	The Act of Supremacy establishes the monarch as "supreme governor" of the Church of England
1563	The Thirty-nine Articles define the teachings of the Anglican Church
1568	Mary Queen of Scots flees to England
1570	Pope Pius V excommunicates Elizabeth I
1572	The Puritans set forth their demands in the "Admonitions to Parliament"
1577–1580	Sir Francis Drake circumnavigates the globe
1585	An English colony is established on Roanoke Island
1587	Mary Queen of Scots is executed
1588	The English defeat the Spanish Armada

During the second half of the sixteenth century, from the death of King Henry VIII in 1547 to the death of Queen Elizabeth I, the last Tudor monarch, in 1603, religion remained the central issue confronting the monarchy. Under King Edward VI, the Church of England (Anglican Church) became more Protestant in doctrine and practice, but Queen Mary, Edward's older sister, attempted to restore Roman Catholicism. This, as well as her marriage to King Philip II of Spain, an ardent Roman Catholic, proved extremely unpopular with her subjects.

Queen Elizabeth I led England during one of the most glorious periods in its history. In religion, she sought to find a broad, moderate settlement that would satisfy the great majority of her subjects. In foreign affairs, England solidified its rule in Ireland, while the defeat of the Spanish Armada marked the definitive emergence of England as a major European and world power. In literature, the Elizabethan Age proved to be a time of particular genius.

King Edward VI (r. 1547–1553)

King Edward VI ascended to the throne at the age of nine. Edward Seymour (c. 1506–1552), the duke of Somerset and Edward's uncle, headed the regency council of sixteen, which governed England.

In 1549, John Dudley (c. 1502–1553), the earl of Warwick who subsequently became the duke of Northumberland, replaced Somerset as the most powerful figure in the government. In 1552, the efforts of Dudley and his allies led to Somerset's execution on charges of high treason.

Religion

During Edward VI's reign, the dukes of Somerset and Northumberland both encouraged the trend toward Protestantism. In 1547, Parliament repealed the Six Articles (see Chapter 7), as well as the laws against heresy, and an act of Parliament permitted priests to marry.

The Act of Uniformity of 1549

Protestant ideas were expressed in the worship of the Church of England, set forth in the majestic English of Archbishop Thomas Cranmer's *Book of Common Prayer.* The Act of Uniformity of 1549 required the use of the English prayer book in the country's churches.

The Forty-two Articles

In 1551, Parliament adopted the Forty-two Articles, setting forth the doctrine of the Anglican Church. The Forty-two Articles reflected the growing influence of Calvinist teaching.

The Act of Uniformity of 1552

A new Act of Uniformity, adopted in 1552, required the use of a revised *Book of Common Prayer* that reflected the growth of Protestant influence. In particular, the service of Holy Communion became more Protestant in tone. In addition, the act required all the people to attend Anglican worship services.

Foreign Affairs

From his father, King Henry VIII, Edward VI inherited problems with both Scotland and France.

Scotland

The duke of Somerset initiated an English invasion of Scotland in an effort to force the Scots to conclude the negotiations, begun by Henry VIII, for the marriage of Edward VI to the four-year-old Mary Stuart. Although the Scots were defeated in 1547 at the Battle of Pinkie, near Edinburgh, they nevertheless sent their young queen to France, where she was later betrothed to Francis, the heir to the French throne.

France

In 1549, war broke out between England and France after the French attacked the English-held town of Boulogne, which the English surrendered.

Kett's Rebellion

The extravagance of King Henry VIII had depleted the royal treasury, causing the king to debase the coinage, a policy continued by the duke of Somerset. Gold coins almost completely disappeared from circulation, and silver coins were not accepted at face value. This debasement of the coinage encouraged inflation and added to the miseries of the poor. Agrarian resentment was increased further by the continuing enclosure of land (see Chapter 7), the destruction of forests to make more pastureland, and rent increases.

In 1549, the mounting discontent burst forth in Kett's Rebellion, which broke out near Norwich under the leadership of Robert Kett. The revolt was suppressed, and Kett and 1000 of his followers were executed.

Lady Jane Grey

Recognizing the likelihood that tuberculosis would soon claim the life of King Edward VI, Northumberland developed a plan to maintain his power by depriving the king's Catholic sister, Mary, of the succession. According to this plan, Northumberland's son, Lord Guildford Dudley, would marry Lady Jane Grey (1537–1554), the granddaughter of King Henry VIII's sister, Mary, and Edward VI would then designate Lady Jane as his heir. The dying king agreed to do so.

Following Edward VI's death in July 1553, the sixteen-year-old Lady Jane was proclaimed queen. Much of the country supported

Mary, however, and rallied to her cause. While many in England were not happy with the prospect of a Catholic queen, the plotting of Northumberland against the rightful heir to the throne was even more distasteful. As Northumberland's army moved against Mary's forces, many of his soldiers deserted.

The "reign" of Lady Jane Grey ended after only nine days. Although Northumberland repudiated Protestantism and begged for his life, he was executed.

Queen Mary I (r. 1553–1558)

Mary Tudor, England's first reigning queen, had been raised as a Roman Catholic and believed her mission was to restore Roman Catholicism in England and to forge an alliance with Catholic Spain, the homeland of her mother, Catherine of Aragon.

The Restoration of Roman Catholicism

Soon after Queen Mary's accession to the throne, Parliament repealed the religious legislation of Edward VI's reign and reenacted the old laws against heresy. Parliament refused, however, to repeal the Act of Supremacy of 1534 or to restore the confiscated monastic lands (see Chapter 7). The action of Parliament restored the religious situation as it had been at the time of King Henry VIII's death in 1547.

Acting on her own authority, the queen forced continental Protestants to leave England and installed Catholic bishops in office. Stephen Gardiner (c. 1493–1555), the bishop of Winchester, became lord chancellor. Queen Mary remained determined to bring the English Church back into union with the Roman papacy.

Mary's Marriage

In July 1554, Queen Mary married Philip of Hapsburg, the son of the Holy Roman Emperor Charles V. Two years later, Philip, an ardent supporter of the Roman Catholic cause throughout Europe, became King Philip II (r. 1556–1598) of Spain.

Wyatt's Revolt

The queen's marriage provoked three revolts in England during 1554. The most serious broke out in Kent, where Sir Thomas Wyatt won the support of troops that had turned against the queen. Loyal troops suppressed the revolt, and Wyatt was executed. Lady Jane Grey and her husband were also executed, although they had not been involved in the revolt.

Reunion with the Roman Papacy

Although her marriage was unpopular in England, Mary believed it would help her in her effort to restore Roman Catholicism. Mary's third Parliament, elected in 1554, proved sympathetic to the Catholic cause. In November 1554, soon after the queen's marriage, Cardinal Reginald Pole (1500-1558), the papal legate, went before a session of Parliament and received England back into the Roman Catholic Church. In the Act of Repeal of 1554, Parliament repealed the Act of Supremacy of 1534 and other anti-papal laws dating from the reign of Henry VIII. However, there was no attempt to restore the confiscated monastic lands.

Persecution of Protestants

During 1555 and 1556, Mary stepped up the persecution of Protestants. Some 300 who refused to recant were burned at the stake, including the Protestant bishops Hugh Latimer (c. 1485-1555) and Nicholas Ridley (c. 1500-1555), as well as the former archbishop of Canterbury, Thomas Cranmer. The persecutions led to the queen's acquisition of the nickname "Bloody Mary."

Foreign Affairs

In March 1557, Philip II returned to England after an absence of nineteen months and secured Mary's support in a war against France. The war did not go well for England, which lost Calais, its last possession in France, in January 1558.

Queen Elizabeth I (r. 1558-1603)

When Queen Elizabeth I, the last of the Tudors to rule England, ascended to the throne after Mary died in November 1558, the country was torn by religious discord. France, Scotland, and Spain were either actual or potential enemies. The new queen's objectives were to find a religious settlement acceptable to the overwhelming majority of her subjects and to keep England out of war.

Queen Elizabeth I proved to be a strong monarch who never let her advisers dominate her. Sir William Cecil, who later became Lord Burghley (1520–1598), was the queen's chief counselor for forty years.

Early in her reign, it was widely believed that the queen would marry Robert Dudley, the earl of Leicester and the son of the duke of Northumberland who had ruled England during the reign of King Edward VI. She did not, and although other prospective consorts appeared, she remained unmarried.

Religious Policy

Concerned about the impact of religious discord on national unity, Queen Elizabeth I sought a religious settlement that would satisfy the great majority of her subjects.

The Act of Supremacy of 1559

In 1559, Elizabeth's first Parliament, a thoroughly Protestant body, repealed the heresy laws of Queen Mary's reign and enacted a new Act of Supremacy, which established the monarch as the "supreme governor" of the Church of England. Officials of state and church were required to take an oath of allegiance to the queen as head of the church.

The Act of Uniformity of 1559

The Act of Uniformity, also adopted in 1559, endorsed a modified version of the 1553 *Book of Common Prayer* and decreed its use in the country's churches. Matthew Parker (1504–1575), a Protestant scholar, became archbishop of Canterbury, and Catholic bishops were removed from office.

The Thirty-nine Articles

In 1563, a church convocation defined the teachings of the Anglican Church in the Thirty-nine Articles. While the church was generally Protestant, it continued to be governed by bishops. Above all, however, the Elizabethan religious settlement emphasized both compromise and ambiguity in wording in an attempt to unite as many as possible of the queen's subjects in the national church.

Opposition to the Elizabethan Religious Settlement

The Protestants

Although the Elizabethan compromise won broad acceptance, many ardent Protestants opposed the settlement because it did not go far enough in making the Anglican Church truly Protestant. The term "Nonconformists" is generally applied to those Protestants who refused to conform to the Church of England and held worship services where the *Book of Common Prayer* was not used.

Puritans.   Some of these Nonconformists, known as Puritans, wanted to purify the church of all remaining Catholic elements. In particular, many Puritans wanted to replace the bishops with the presbyterian system of representative church government practiced in Scotland. They set forth their demands in the "Admonitions to Parliament" of 1572.

Separatists.   The Separatists, who were more radical Protestants, wanted a complete break with the established Church of England. Led by Robert Browne (c. 1550–1633) and others, they favored a congregational form of church government and the separation of church and state. The Pilgrims who settled at Plymouth in 1620 were Separatists.

Both the Puritans and the Separatists were influenced by the teachings of the continental reformer John Calvin.

Government Repression.   The government acted against the Nonconformists. In 1583, the powers of the Court of the High Commission, which had been created in 1559, were expanded, enabling it to try cases involving Nonconformists. In the same year, John Whitgift (c. 1530–1604), a vigorous opponent of the Nonconformists, became archbishop of Canterbury, while a law enacted in 1593 provided for the exile of those who rejected royal supremacy in religious affairs or attended Nonconformist services.

The Roman Catholics

In 1570, Pope Pius V (r. 1566–1572) excommunicated Queen Elizabeth I and absolved her subjects of their obligations to her.

In 1568, an English Roman Catholic seminary had been established at Douai in Flanders, and by 1580, over 100 Roman Catholic priests, led by Jesuits, were active in England, ministering to English Catholics and encouraging Catholic opposition to the queen.

Countering this Catholic opposition, the government increased fines for nonattendance at Anglican religious services, while celebrating or attending Roman Catholic masses was punished with imprisonment. Roman Catholic priests were charged with treason. Some 200 to 300 Roman Catholics lost their lives during Elizabeth's reign, both as the result of persecution and because of their involvement in plots against the queen. The number executed during Elizabeth's reign approximately equaled the victims of religious persecution during the earlier reign of Queen Mary.

Mary Queen of Scots

Many Roman Catholic opponents of the Elizabethan religious settlement supported the claim of Mary Queen of Scots (1542–1587), who was a great-granddaughter of King Henry VII, to the English throne. The Catholics regarded Elizabeth, the daughter of Anne Boleyn, as illegitimate, since in their view Henry VIII's marriage to his first wife, Catherine of Aragon, had never been properly annulled; thus, Mary Queen of Scots was the rightful heir to the throne.

The Scottish Reformation

Introduction of Calvinism.   During the sixteenth century, Scotland converted to Calvinism as a result of the work of the reformer John Knox (1505–1572) and others. After becoming a disciple of John Calvin in Geneva, Knox returned to Scotland in 1558. The same year, the Scottish queen, Mary Stuart (Mary Queen of Scots), the daughter of King James V (r. 1513–1542), married the French Dauphin, who became King Francis II in July 1559.

Break with Roman Catholicism.   The queen's marriage increased Scottish fears of being incorporated into a French Catholic empire. A group of four Protestant noblemen organized the Lords of the Congregation and called on the regent, Mary of Guise (1515–1560), Mary Stuart's French-born mother, to introduce reforms in the Scottish church. The demands were rejected, and in 1559, civil war broke out in Scotland. England aided the rebels. Under the terms of the Treaty of Edinburgh of 1560, French and English troops withdrew from Scotland, and the alliance between Scotland and France came to an end.

Also in 1560, the Scottish Parliament broke with Roman Catholicism and reorganized the Scottish church along Calvinist lines, introducing a presbyterian form of church government. Following the death of Mary of Guise in 1560, a council of twelve nobles was established to govern Scotland until Mary Stuart returned from France.

Mary Stuart's Reign

Following her husband's death in December 1560, Mary Stuart returned to Scotland in August 1561. Hostile to her country's conversion to Calvinism, Mary also held the ambition of acquiring the English crown. But her personal life complicated her political ambitions.

Scandals.   In July 1565, Mary married her cousin, Lord Darnley (1545–1567), a grandson of England's King Henry VII. Mary's marriage to the Catholic Darnley proved unpopular with the Protestant lords, but Mary easily suppressed their revolt.

When Darnley's dissipated character proved him unfit to be king, Mary turned to David Rizzio (c. 1533–1566), her private secretary, as confidant. The jealous Darnley then murdered Rizzio in March 1566. In June 1566, Mary gave birth to a son, the future King James VI of Scotland and King James I of England, but she had come to hate Darnley. She fell in love with the earl of Bothwell (c. 1536–1578), a Protestant, who engineered Darnley's murder in February 1567. Divorcing his wife, Bothwell married Mary in a Protestant ceremony in May of that year.

Abdication and Flight.   These events infuriated both the Protestants and Catholics, and a revolt broke out. Bothwell fled Scotland, and Mary was imprisoned and forced to abdicate. Escaping in May 1568, Mary fled to England, where she came to pose a serious threat to Queen Elizabeth I.

Plots Against Queen Elizabeth I

Old Nobility.   The old nobility of northern England hatched a plot centering on Mary Queen of Scots and the duke of Norfolk (1536–1572). According to the scheme, the duke would marry Mary and reign with her following Elizabeth's overthrow or death, restoring power to the old nobility. The revolt began in 1569 but was quickly suppressed. The duke of Norfolk was briefly imprisoned in the Tower of London, and about 800 rebels were executed.

Continental Conspiracy.   In 1571, Roberto di Ridolfi, an Italian banker and papal agent, launched another plot, in association with the duke of Norfolk and with the support of King Philip II of Spain. The marriage of Mary to the duke of Norfolk would be the signal for an English Catholic uprising and a Spanish invasion. The plot was uncovered before it could be carried out. Convicted of treason, the duke of Norfolk was executed in 1572.

Throckmorton.   In 1583, Francis Throckmorton (1554–1584) acted as an intermediary between the Spanish, the French, and Mary. Following his arrest, Throckmorton confessed and was executed.

Execution of Mary.   In 1586, Anthony Babington (1561–1586) hatched a plot to kill Elizabeth and place Mary on the throne. Elizabeth now agreed to Mary's execution, signing the death warrant in February 1587.

Conflict with France

In 1559, the Treaty of Cateau-Cambrésis ended the war between France and her enemies, England and Spain. King Francis II nevertheless continued to support the claim of his wife, Mary Queen of Scots, to the English throne, but his death in 1560 ended this support.

In 1562, a religious civil war broke out in France between the Calvinist Huguenots and the Roman Catholics. England intervened in support of the Huguenots, sending troops to the seaport city of Le Havre. This intervention quickly proved unwise, however, and the English garrison at Le Havre surrendered in 1563. The English subsequently provided secret aid to the Huguenots, while at the same time seeking to restrain the French by considering offers for the marriage of Queen Elizabeth to King Charles IX (r. 1560–1574) of France or one of his two brothers, the dukes of Anjou and Alençon.

Conflict with Spain

Queen Elizabeth, who never married, also used the possibility of marriage as an instrument of diplomacy in her relations with Spain. Early in her reign, Spain's King Philip II, who had previously been married to England's Queen Mary, proposed marriage to Elizabeth. When the queen procrastinated, Philip lost patience and took a French wife.

Despite the talk of a possible marriage alliance, England and Spain remained both antagonists in religion and commercial rivals. Having been rebuffed by Queen Elizabeth as a marriage partner, King Philip II supported the claims of Mary Queen of Scots; following her death, he claimed the English crown for himself. For its part, England provided assistance to the Netherlands, which had rebelled against Spanish rule.

English Interference with Spanish Trade

The English also sought to gain a share of the slave trade between West Africa and the Spanish colonies in the West Indies. In 1562, Sir John Hawkins (1532–1595) sold a cargo of 400 slaves on the island of Santo Domingo and took home a cargo of sugar, hides, pearls, and a little gold. Making another voyage in 1564, Hawkins sold slaves on the northern coast of South America, returning to England with a valuable cargo. On his third voyage in 1567, Hawkins met resistance from the Spanish near Vera Cruz, Mexico, and only two of his ships made their way back to England.

English Raiders

The English now turned to raids against Spanish shipping and colonies, with Queen Elizabeth taking her share of the profits from these raids. Of the English raiders, Sir Francis Drake (c. 1540–1596) was the most famous. In 1572, Drake began a series of raids on Spanish treasure in Panama. In his most famous exploit, from 1577 to 1580, Drake sailed in the *Golden Hind* through the Straits of Magellan and along the western coast of South America, carrying out raids as he went. Drake then sailed back to England through the Pacific and Indian Oceans, thus circumnavigating the globe.

The Spanish Armada

Angered by these English raids and frustrated by the failure of plots against Queen Elizabeth, King Philip II decided to take more direct action, launching the Spanish Armada, commanded by the duke of Medina Sidonia (1550–1615), against England in 1588.

Spanish Strategy.   The plan called for the Armada to join forces with a Spanish army of some 33,000 men, commanded by Alessandro Farnese, the duke of Parma (1545–1592), near Dunkirk in the Spanish Netherlands and then to carry out an invasion of

England. The Armada included about 130 ships, carrying 8,000 sailors and 19,000 soldiers.

English Defense.   Against the Armada, the English arrayed a fleet of 197 ships, of which only thirty-four were Royal Navy vessels. Lord Howard of Effingham (1536–1624) commanded the English fleet, with the assistance of Drake, Hawkins, and Sir Martin Frobisher (c. 1535–1594). Most of the English ships were smaller than the Spanish vessels, but they were fast and easily maneuvered. In addition, they were armed with heavier long-range guns.

Defeat of the Spanish Armada.   On July 21, 1588, the Armada entered the English Channel, headed toward Dunkirk. For eight days, the English ships fought the Spanish, aided by a furious storm, which became known as the "Protestant wind." On July 28, the Armada was dispersed and fled to the north, around the tip of Scotland.

The Spanish Armada lost about forty ships, and many of those that made their way back to Spain were unfit for further service. Spanish deaths totaled in the thousands. The English lost no ships and about 100 men.

The defeat of the Spanish Armada dealt a serious blow to Spain's prestige and marked the first step in the long process of Spain's decline as a major power, while it marked England's definitive acquisition of great power status.

Continuing the Spanish War

The defeat of the Spanish Armada did not end the war against Spain, which continued for the remainder of Elizabeth's reign. Although an English counterattack against Spain failed in 1589, the English "sea dogs" continued to harass the Spanish.

The English sent troops to the Netherlands to aid the Dutch rebels in their revolt against Spanish rule. In 1596, they assaulted the Spanish seaport of Cadiz, while King Philip II supported the Irish revolt that began in 1598. The continuing war with Spain and the suppression of the Irish revolt put a heavy strain on Queen Elizabeth's treasury.

The Irish Revolts

The Roman Catholic Irish opposed English efforts both to extend political control over Ireland and to introduce Anglicanism. A revolt broke out in Ireland in 1569, and, with aid from the Spanish, the Irish continued intermittent attacks on the English until 1583.

A more serious revolt broke out in 1598, and Hugh O'Neill, the earl of Tyrone (c. 1547–1616), defeated an English force at the Battle of Blackwater River. Queen Elizabeth I sent an army led by the earl of Essex (1567–1601) to Ireland in 1599, but Essex failed to quell the revolt. Returning to England, Essex supported an ill-conceived plot to overthrow the government. He was executed for treason in February 1601.

In 1601, an English force led by Lord Mountjoy (1563–1606) went to Ireland, where it defeated both the Irish and their Spanish allies. By 1603, Ireland had been subdued.

Colonial Ventures

During Queen Elizabeth I's reign, English efforts to establish colonies in the New World were unsuccessful, although several significant voyages of exploration were undertaken.

Frobisher

From 1576 to 1578, Sir Martin Frobisher made several voyages exploring the coast of northeastern Canada, continuing the search for the Northwest Passage begun by John Cabot almost a century earlier (see Chapter 7).

Gilbert

In 1583, Sir Humphrey Gilbert (c. 1537–1583) sailed to Newfoundland in an unsuccessful effort to establish a colony and to locate the Northwest Passage.

Raleigh and Roanoke Island

In 1585, Sir Walter Raleigh (c. 1552–1618) founded a colony on Roanoke Island on the coast of North Carolina, but the colonists soon returned to England. In 1587, a new group of settlers arrived. For the next several years, the war against Spain required all the ships England had available. When Raleigh was finally able to send a fleet to Roanoke Island in 1590, the commander found the settlement deserted. The fate of the "Lost Colony" has never been determined.

Davis

Between 1585 and 1587, John Davis (c. 1550–1605) made three voyages in the continuing effort to find the Northwest Passage.

From 1591 to 1592, he explored the South Atlantic, sighting the Falkland Islands, and later sailed to the East Indies. Davis's voyages added considerably to geographical knowledge.

Trading Companies

As England's overseas interests increased, new trading companies were established. The Muscovy Company, incorporated in 1555, promoted trade with Russia; the Eastland Company for trade with the Baltic Sea area was established in 1579. The Levant Company, founded in 1592, promoted trade with the eastern Mediterranean, while the important East India Company was established in 1600.

Elizabethan Literature

The reign of Queen Elizabeth I coincided with one of the greatest eras in English literature.

Prose Writers

Lyly

John Lyly (c. 1554–1606) presented a portrait of late sixteenth-century English society in his novel of manners, *Euphues,* which was published in two parts, *The Anatomy of Wit* (1578) and *Euphues and His England* (1580).

Hooker

The theologian Richard Hooker (c. 1554–1600) supported Queen Elizabeth's religious policy in his *Laws of Ecclesiastical Polity.*

Hakluyt

England's overseas activities resulted in the publication, in 1589, of Richard Hakluyt's (c. 1552–1616) *Principal Navigations, Voyages and Discoveries of the English Nation.* This book helped stimulate the growing interest in geography and exploration.

Raleigh

Sir Walter Raleigh wrote a *History of the World* and other prose works, as well as poetry.

Poets and Playwrights

Spenser

Edmund Spenser (c. 1552–1599) was regarded by his contemporaries as the leading poet of the age. The first six books of his unfinished masterpiece, the *Faerie Queen,* were published in 1596. This was a romantic epic, based on an Italian model.

Sidney

Sir Philip Sidney (1554–1586), a prominent figure in the court of Queen Elizabeth, wrote *Astrophel and Stella* (1591), a collection of sonnets, and a treatise on the art of poetry, *The Defence of Poesie* (1595).

Marlowe

Christopher Marlowe (1564–1593), a skilled playwright and poet, produced a number of outstanding works during his brief career. His major dramas include *Tamburlaine the Great, Doctor Faustus,* and *The Jew of Malta.*

Shakespeare

William Shakespeare (1564–1616) wrote lyric poetry but is best known for his dramas, both tragedies and comedies, which were produced on the London stage. Shakespeare's plays, which dealt with the entire range of the human experience, include *The Taming of the Shrew, A Midsummer Night's Dream, The Merchant of Venice, Romeo and Juliet, Julius Caesar, Hamlet, Othello, King Lear, Macbeth,* and *Antony and Cleopatra.*

Jonson

Ben Jonson (1572–1637), a poet and dramatist, was the last major literary figure of the Elizabethan period. Jonson was a student of classical literature, and his plays remind the reader of Greek drama. *Volpone,* his best-known play, was first produced in 1606.

Queen Elizabeth I's moderate religious settlement won the support of the vast majority of her subjects and thus appeared to resolve the religious turmoil that had divided England during the reigns of King Edward VI and Queen Mary. But while the Roman Catholic threat was contained, the Puritan movement continued to gather momen-

tum and in the seventeenth century came to challenge not only the established Church of England but the authority of the monarchy itself.

Recommended Reading

Chamber, E. A. *A Short Life of William Shakespeare* (1935).

Chute, Marchette G. *Ben Jonson of Westminster* (1949).

Chute, Marchette G. *Shakespeare's London* (1949).

Collinson, Patrick. *The Elizabethan Puritan Movement* (1967).

Cowan, Ian B. *The Enigma of Mary Stuart* (1971).

Cowan, Ian B. *The Scottish Reformation: Church and Society in Sixteenth-Century Scotland* (1982).

Donaldson, Gordon. *Scotland: James V to James VII* (1965).

Esler, Anthony. *The Aspiring Mind of the Elizabethan Younger Generation* (1966).

Falls, Cyril B. *Elizabeth's Irish Wars* (1950).

Ferguson, Arthur B. *The Articulate Citizen and the English Renaissance* (1965).

Fraser, Antonia. *Mary Queen of Scots* (1969).

Greaves, Richard L. *Society and Religion in Elizabethan England* (1981).

Greenblatt, Stephen J. *Sir Walter Raleigh: The Renaissance Man and His Roles* (1973).

Haigh, Christopher, ed. *The Reign of Elizabeth I* (1984).

Johnson, Paul. *Elizabeth I: A Study of Power and Intellect* (1974).

Jones, Whitney R. D. *The Mid-Tudor Crisis, 1539–1563* (1973).

Jordan, W. K. *Edward VI: The Threshold of Power* (1970).

Jordan, W. K. *Edward VI: The Young King* (1968).

Lacey, Robert. *Robert, Earl of Essex: An Elizabethan Icarus* (1971).

Loades, D. M. *The Reign of Mary Tudor: Politics, Government, and Religion in England, 1553–58* (1979).

McGrath, Patrick. *Papists and Puritans Under Elizabeth I* (1967).

Mason, A. E. W. *The Life of Francis Drake* (1941).

Mattingly, Garrett. *The Armada* (1962).

Mercer, Eric. *English Art, 1553–1625* (1962).

Neale, J. E. *The Elizabethan House of Commons* (1949).

Neale, J. E. *Queen Elizabeth* (1934).

Parry, J. H. *The Age of Reconnaissance* (1963).

Read, Conyers. *Mr. Secretary Cecil and Queen Elizabeth* (1955).

Rowse, A. L. *The Expansion of England* (1955).

Schenk, Wilhelm. *Reginald Pole: Cardinal of England* (1950).

Smith, Alan G. R. *The Government of Elizabethan England* (1967).

Smith, L. B. *The Elizabethan World* (1967).

Wernham, R. B. *The Making of Elizabethan Foreign Policy, 1558–1603* (1981).

CHAPTER 9

The Seventeenth Century: The Stuarts Versus Parliament

Time Line

1603–1625	Reign of King James I
1605	The Gunpowder Plot results in the execution of Guy Fawkes and other plotters
1611	The King James Version of the Bible is published
1616	James I dismisses Sir Edward Coke, the chief justice
1621	Parliament passes the Great Protestation
1625–1649	Reign of King Charles I
1628	Parliament passes the Petition of Right
1629–1640	Charles I rules England without Parliament

1639	A revolt against Charles I breaks out in Scotland
1640	Charles I calls the Short Parliament into session
	The Long Parliament convenes
1641	The Long Parliament passes the Grand Remonstrance
1642	The Civil War begins
1644	The Cavaliers are defeated at the Battle of Marston Moor
1645	The Cavaliers are defeated at the Battle of Naseby
1646	The Scots take Charles I prisoner
1648	"Pride's Purge" results in the creation of the Rump Parliament
1649	Charles I is executed
1649–1653	Oliver Cromwell heads the Commonwealth
1653	Cromwell becomes lord protector
1658	Cromwell dies and is succeeded by his son, Richard

In early seventeenth-century England, the first two Stuart kings, James I and Charles I, sought to establish an absolute monarchy and to enforce their views on religion. These policies led to a revolt by Parliament, with the support of the Puritans, against Charles I. The English Civil War of the 1640s ended with the victory of Parliament and the execution of the king.

During the period of the Commonwealth and Protectorate, the English, under the leadership of Oliver Cromwell, conducted an unsuccessful experiment in republican government.

King James I (r. 1603–1625)

During the final years of her reign, Queen Elizabeth I had skillfully avoided conflict over two troublesome issues: the precise nature of the relationship between the crown and Parliament and the challenge presented by the Calvinist Puritans to the established Church of England.

Under England's new king, James I, the unresolved problems quickly came to a head. James I was the son of Mary Queen of Scots, a cousin of Elizabeth I, and the first of the Stuart monarchs. He had been King James VI of Scotland and came to the English throne as a foreigner, unfamiliar with English traditions, and he proved to be inept in dealing with powerful men and ticklish problems. To make matters worse, he displayed poor judgment in the selection of his advisers. Until 1612, Robert Cecil, the earl of Salisbury (1563–1612), served as the king's chief minister. Following the death of the experienced and capable Cecil in 1612, James turned to Robert Carr, a Scot who became the earl of Somerset (c. 1587–1645); and, subsequently, James relied on the self-seeking and unpopular George Villiers, who became the duke of Buckingham (1592–1628).

James I and Parliament

Divine Right

James I insisted that he was king by divine right, thereby rejecting the English tradition of parliamentary government. In James's view, the king ruled by the will of God and was responsible only to God. He thus stood above the law, and his subjects had no legitimate right to question or resist his will.

Dismissal of Coke

In 1616, Sir Edward Coke (1552–1634), England's chief justice, insisted that the king was subject to the law, which only the courts had the authority to interpret. In response, James dismissed Coke and extended royal control over the courts. Only Parliament remained to oppose the king.

Parliamentary Opposition to the King

Opposition to the king grew in Parliament. Although the House of Lords, comprising the nobility and the bishops of the Anglican Church, generally supported the king, even here opposition mounted in response to James's more extreme claims.

The House of Commons

While the House of Commons in theory represented the entire country, it was dominated in practice by the merchants, lawyers, and prosperous country gentlemen. They were not radicals, but they were determined to defend what they regarded as Parliament's legitimate role in sharing in the government, and they repudiated the king's claims of divine right. In the early seventeenth century, the House of Commons was predominantly Anglican, but its membership included a growing number of Puritans who desired to "purify" the Anglican Church by eliminating elaborate ceremonies and establishing a representative form of church government to replace the bishops. Because of its control over money bills, the House of Commons became the center of opposition to James I.

The Apology of the Commons (1604)

Rejecting the king's claims to absolute power in 1604, the House of Commons adopted the Apology of the Commons, setting forth "the ancient rights of the subjects of this realm" and insisting that "our privileges and liberties are our right and due inheritance." The House of Commons was asserting its claim to "privileges and liberties" that had, in fact, not been clearly established by past practice, just as the king was demanding power that went beyond the authority exercised by his predecessors.

The Addled Parliament

The conflict between king and Parliament continued. In 1610, when James I asked Parliament for a grant of taxes, Parliament responded by calling on the king to redress grievances. The deadlock ended only with James's dissolution of Parliament in early 1611.

The king's financial situation grew more desperate, and in 1614 he summoned another Parliament. When the king asked for taxes, Parliament once again demanded a redress of its grievances. After two months of fruitless wrangling, James dissolved this so-called Addled Parliament.

Rather than accede to Parliament's demands, James attempted to increase his income without seeking parliamentary approval. He imposed customs duties by proclamation, collected forced loans from his wealthy subjects, and sold titles of nobility, including the new title of baronet.

James I and Religion

James I's religious policies also involved him in conflict with Parliament.

Puritans

Although he had been king of Scotland, James I was an ardent Anglican, rather than a Presbyterian, which was the dominant religion in Scotland. The king distrusted Presbyterianism, regarding its representative system of church government as a threat to royal power. As king of England, James refused to make any concessions to the Puritans who, like the Presbyterians, were Calvinists.

Catholics

James I also ran into trouble over the Catholic issue. At the beginning of his reign, the king relaxed restrictions on Roman Catholics. Then, alarmed by a resurgence of Catholicism in England, he reimposed the restrictions.

The Hampton Court Conference of 1604

Early in his reign, the Puritans presented James with the Millenary Petition, urging him to reform the Anglican Church in accordance with Puritan ideas. James met with the Puritans at the Hampton Court Conference of 1604, where he rejected all of their demands.

The King James Bible

The reign of James I provided one positive accomplishment in religion: the King James Version of the Bible (also known as the Authorized Version), which was published in 1611. The magnificent language of this translation makes it one of the great works of English literature.

The Gunpowder Plot

Several Catholic extremists, including Guy Fawkes (1570–1606), launched a plot to blow up Parliament when it met on November 5, 1605. The government uncovered the Gunpowder Plot before it could be carried out, and the plotters were executed. The plot intensified anti-Catholic feelings in England and strengthened the Puritans' determination to make the Anglican Church more fully Protestant. For many generations, anti-Catholic demonstrations took place in England each year on Guy Fawkes's Day.

Colonial Ventures

Jamestown

The London Company, also known as the Virginia Company, received a charter from James I in 1606 and founded a colony at Jamestown the following year. In 1619, Virginia established the first colonial legislature, patterned after the English Parliament.

Plymouth

In 1620, the Pilgrims, who had crossed the Atlantic on the *Mayflower*, landed at Plymouth on the coast of Massachusetts and established the first permanent English settlement in New England. The Pilgrims were Separatists who had fled from England to the Netherlands in 1607 and 1608. They had originally intended to establish a colony in northern Virginia.

Massachusetts Bay

In 1629, English Puritans established the Massachusetts Bay colony under a charter issued by King Charles I. By 1640, the colony had a population of 40,000. In 1691, the Plymouth colony united with Massachusetts Bay.

West Indies

In the West Indies, Bermuda received a royal charter in 1615. Other important West Indian colonies included Barbados and the Bahamas.

Foreign Affairs

James I's attempt to conduct foreign affairs without consulting Parliament evoked widespread opposition.

Spain

Failed Marriage Alliance.   In 1604, James I ended the war with Spain (see Chapter 8) and began negotiations in an effort to arrange the marriage of his son to a Spanish princess. These negotiations evoked angry anti-Catholic protests in England, but when the Spanish insisted that any children of the marriage be raised as Catholics, James ended the negotiations. He understood his subjects well enough to realize that they would never accept this condition.

Failed Expedition of Raleigh.   In 1617, James permitted Sir Walter Raleigh (c. 1552–1618) to lead an expedition against Spanish colonies in the Caribbean in search of gold. In Guiana, Raleigh became involved in a skirmish resulting in the deaths of several Spaniards. In 1618, he returned to England without any gold. When the Spanish ambassador, Count Gondomar (c. 1567–1626), demanded Raleigh's execution, James acceded to the demand in an effort to placate the angry Spanish government.

Involvement in the Thirty Years' War

In 1618, the Thirty Years' War (1618–1648) broke out in Germany between the Catholics and Protestants. Spain intervened in support of the Catholic cause, and Spanish troops overran the lands of King James I's Calvinist son-in-law Frederick (1596–1632), the elector of the Palatinate in western Germany. James wanted to aid Frederick, and there was considerable popular support for the renewal of the war against Catholic Spain.

The Great Protestation of 1621

In 1621, James summoned Parliament. While the House of Commons backed the war with Spain in principle, it provided the king with less money than he had requested and took advantage of the situation by pressing its grievances against the king.

Asserting its claims, the House of Commons adopted the Great Protestation in 1621, declaring that "the liberties, franchises, privileges, and jurisdictions of Parliament are the ancient and undoubted birthright and inheritance of the subjects of England." Infuriated, James ripped the protest out of the Commons Journal and dissolved Parliament. Without the money, the king was unable to continue his war against Spain.

Failure of Renewed Negotiations with Spain

Gondomar, the Spanish ambassador, now suggested to James that Spain would withdraw from the Palatinate in exchange for an agreement on the marriage alliance that had been discussed earlier. In 1623, Prince Charles and the duke of Buckingham went to Spain, where Catholic priests tried to convert them. They were also told they could not meet the princess until they had promised that concessions would be made to English Catholics. This was a demand they could not meet. Charles and Buckingham returned home as strong supporters of renewing the war against Spain. The king and Parliament now argued about the conduct of the war, with Parliament supporting a naval war, and the king insisting on the necessity of a land war.

Alliance with France

James I now secured an alliance with France. The French would help the English drive the Spanish from the Palatinate, while Prince Charles would marry Henrietta Maria (1609–1669), the sister of France's King Louis XIII. A secret clause required James to grant freedom of worship to English Catholics.

In 1624, England declared war on Spain. James I died the following year.

King Charles I (r. 1625–1649)

King Charles I proved to be even more inflexible and inept than his father had been. Early in his reign, the duke of Buckingham served as his chief adviser. Following Buckingham's assassination in 1628, he turned to Thomas Wentworth, a staunch supporter of royal power, who subsequently became the earl of Strafford (1593–1641).

Relations with Parliament

The antagonism between king and Parliament intensified during the reign of Charles I. When Charles's first Parliament met in 1625, it voted only limited funds to support the war against Spain. The Parliament of 1626 brought further conflict with the king.

The Petition of Right

A dispute developed between Charles I and his brother-in-law, King Louis XIII of France, and war began in late 1627. In 1628, Charles called his third Parliament, requesting money he urgently needed to fight the war.

Taking advantage of the king's need for money, Parliament passed the Petition of Right. Insisting that the king was subject to the law, the Petition of Right provided that the king could not levy taxes without the approval of Parliament, impose forced loans on his subjects, declare martial law in peacetime, imprison citizens without trial, or quarter troops in private homes. Charles was so desperate for money that he agreed to sign the Petition of Right, although he never felt obliged to observe its limitations on his power.

Dissolution of Parliament

In 1629, Sir John Eliot (1592–1632) led an effort in the House of Commons to compel the king to observe the principles set forth in the Petition of Right. Charles responded by having Eliot arrested and dissolving Parliament. Eliot died in the Tower of London. Unable to continue the wars against Spain and France without additional money appropriated by Parliament, Charles I quickly made peace with his enemies.

The Personal Government of Charles I

For eleven years, from 1629 to 1640, Charles I ruled England without Parliament. The king engaged in an incessant search for new sources of income, employing methods that were either illegal or of questionable legality.

Ship Money

A particularly sharp controversy developed over the king's collection of ship money. During past emergencies, even at the time of the Spanish Armada in 1588, ship money had been collected only in the coastal areas. Now, in order to support the Royal Navy in its war against Turkish pirates who were conducting raids in England's home waters, Charles collected ship money throughout the entire kingdom, insisting, against opposition, that it was legitimate to do so since the navy protected the whole country.

Hampden's Case

John Hampden (1594–1643), a country gentleman from the inland county of Buckingham, refused to pay the tax, since Parliament had not approved it. In 1637, Hampden lost his case in court, although five of the twelve judges in the Exchequer Court dared to rule against the king. The episode increased anger at the king's policies.

Religion

Archbishop Laud

Charles I's religious policy also evoked opposition. The king supported the efforts of William Laud (1573–1645), the archbishop of

Canterbury, to enforce strict observance of Anglican doctrine, worship, and church organization and to drive the Puritans from the established church.

Puritans

For their part, the Puritans continued to demand a purification of the Anglican Church. In addition, they feared that Laud's policy might lead to a Catholic revival. This fear was strengthened by what the Puritans regarded as an increase of Catholic influence in the royal court. Charles I's wife, Henrietta Maria, was a Catholic, and laws against Catholics were not being strictly enforced.

Revolt in Scotland

The revolt against Charles I began in Scotland. In 1637, the English government ordered the use of the Anglican *Book of Common Prayer* in the Presbyterian churches of Scotland. In early 1638, thousands of Scots signed the Solemn League and Covenant, pledging to defend their Calvinist religion. The conflict was both religious and political, since Anglicanism was associated with the king's claims to absolute power. In 1639, the Scots rose in revolt.

The Short Parliament

Charles I desperately needed money in order to suppress the Scottish revolt, and he called Parliament into session in April 1640. This Short Parliament, which lasted only three weeks, demanded that the king make concessions before it would vote taxes. In particular, Parliament insisted that the king acknowledge that its approval was necessary for the levying of new taxes and that he agree to make the Church of England more Protestant in character. Charles responded by dissolving Parliament in May.

The Long Parliament

In late August 1640, the Scots defeated Charles I's army at Newburn on the Tyne. In the Treaty of Ripon, signed on October 26, Charles agreed to pay the Scottish army £850 a day until a permanent settlement was reached. The king's need for money was now more desperate than ever, and he once again called Parliament into session.

This Parliament, which met for the first time on November 3, 1640, became the Long Parliament of the English Civil War. Although periodically reduced in size, it was not dissolved until 1653.

Impeachment of Strafford and Laud

The king's opponents, including John Hampden and John Pym (c. 1583-1643) dominated the Long Parliament, and they quickly moved to impeach both the earl of Strafford and Archbishop Laud. Strafford was condemned to death and executed in May 1641, while Laud was executed in 1645, during the Civil War.

Conflict with the King

In other actions, the Long Parliament barred the king from levying taxes without parliamentary approval and abolished the arbitrary courts of the Star Chamber and High Commission. It also passed acts providing that Parliament should meet at least every three years and limiting the king's right to dissolve Parliament.

The Grand Remonstrance

In the Grand Remonstrance, passed in November 1641, the Long Parliament summarized its political and religious grievances against the king. In January 1642, the angry Charles I went to Parliament with several hundred troops, planning to arrest five of its members, including Hampden and Pym. The five had been warned of the king's intentions and escaped.

The Civil War

Outbreak of War

The king left London and went to the north of England, where he was joined by some of his parliamentary supporters. The king's opponents remained in London. The two sides began to raise troops, and the English Civil War broke out in the summer of 1642.

Opposing Sides

Roundheads. During the Civil War, the king's parliamentary opponents, known as Roundheads, dominated London and southeastern England. These opponents included the lawyers and merchants, as well as the country gentry, of the region. Many were Puritans.

Cavaliers. The royalists, known as Cavaliers, controlled the more conservative north and west. The Cavaliers drew their support from the great noble families, ardent Anglicans, and the country gentry and peasants of the area.

Cromwell's Army

In 1643, the Roundhead cause was strengthened by an alliance with the Scots. But even more important for the Roundheads was the creation of an effective army. In July 1644, a Scottish-Roundhead army defeated the Cavaliers in the Battle of Marston Moor. The Ironsides, a force of devoted Puritans led by Oliver Cromwell (1599–1658), played the central role in the Roundhead victory.

Parliament now gave Cromwell the task of organizing and leading the New Model Army, which defeated the Cavaliers at the Battle of Naseby in June 1645. The Scots took Charles I prisoner in May 1646.

The Rump Parliament and the Execution of Charles I

As the Civil War drew to an end, a conflict developed within the Parliament between its more moderate and radical elements. The radicals soon gained the upper hand, and in December 1648, troops commanded by Colonel Thomas Pride (d. 1658) excluded ninety-six moderate Presbyterians from the House of Commons. "Pride's Purge" left some sixty members to comprise what came to be known as the Rump Parliament. The Rump Parliament granted toleration and freedom of public worship to all except Anglicans, Catholics, and Unitarians. It also voted to abolish the monarchy, the House of Lords, and the Anglican Church and ordered that Charles I be tried for treason. The king was executed in January 1649.

The Interregnum

During the eleven-year Interregnum following the execution of King Charles I, England embarked on an experiment in republican government.

The Commonwealth

Under the Commonwealth, from 1649 to 1653, political power was in the hands of a one-house Parliament, while the Council of State conducted the day-to-day affairs of the government.

Cromwell's Religious Policy

Led by Oliver Cromwell, the Commonwealth sought to reestablish order in England. Cromwell imposed restrictions on Anglicans and Roman Catholics, extending toleration only to non-Anglican Protestants (except Quakers) and Jews. An ardent Puritan, he enforced public morality, closing the theaters, prohibiting dancing, and requiring strict observance of the Sabbath.

Ireland

The rebellious Irish proclaimed Charles II, the son of Charles I, as their king. In August 1649, Cromwell landed in Dublin and attacked the rebel strongholds of Drogheda and Wexford, massacring their garrisons. Cromwell and Henry Ireton (1611–1651), who became lord lieutenant of Ireland the following year, devastated Ireland, where about a third of the people either were killed outright or died of starvation. The severity of Cromwell's repression in Ireland earned him the enduring enmity of the Irish.

Scotland

Leaving Ireland in May 1650, Cromwell turned his attention to Scotland, where Charles II had been crowned king. In September, Cromwell defeated Scottish leader David Leslie (d. 1682) in the Battle of Dunbar.

In 1651, Charles II led a Stuart invasion of England, but the invaders were defeated at the Battle of Worcester. For the next nine years, General George Monck (1608–1670) ruled Scotland, although the Scots gained representation in the English Parliament.

Foreign Affairs

Cromwell pursued an aggressive foreign policy designed to promote England's commercial interests.

The Navigation Act of 1651.   Under the terms of the Navigation Act of 1651, goods from Asia, Africa, or America could be imported into England, Ireland, or the English colonies only in English or colonial ships manned by English or colonial crews. The law permitted one exception: Goods might be carried by ships of a country exporting goods that it had produced. The Navigation Act was directed especially at the Dutch, who had been carrying cargo to and from India and the English colonies.

The Dutch War (1652-1654).   Although the Navigation Act did not itself lead to war, some of England's commercial interests favored a showdown with the Dutch, and war broke out in 1652. Both antagonists possessed first-rate navies, and within two years, they fought nine battles. In 1653, the English launched a blockade of the Netherlands, and late in the year, facing starvation, the Dutch sought peace.

Although the terms of the peace treaty signed in 1654 favored the English, the Dutch maintained their large merchant fleet, and the Anglo-Dutch commercial rivalry continued.

War with Spain.   In 1655, the English conquered the Spanish island of Jamaica in the West Indies and captured a Spanish treasure fleet near the seaport of Cadiz the following year. Cromwell's wars and the support of his army proved costly, which led to a decline in his popularity.

The Protectorate

At home, conflict mounted as the lower classes demanded the satisfaction of their economic and social grievances, calling for extending the right to vote to most of the male population and for a redistribution of property. Cromwell now crushed the radicals much as he had earlier defeated the royalists. In April 1653, Cromwell dissolved both the Council of State and the Rump Parliament, replacing them with a new council and a Parliament of 140 members, the so-called Barebone's Parliament. In December 1653, Cromwell dissolved this Parliament. The army leaders drafted a new constitution, the Instrument of Government, which entrusted authority to Cromwell as lord protector. In effect, the Protectorate was one-man rule supported by the army, although Cromwell made several unsuccessful attempts to govern with new parliaments.

The End of the Interregnum

When Cromwell died in September 1658, he was succeeded by his son, Richard (1626-1712), who possessed none of his father's ability and determination. Richard resigned in May 1659, and the army took power. Recognizing the failure of the experiment in republican government, General Monck moved to restore the monarchy.

While the struggle against the first Stuarts, Kings James I and Charles I, resulted in the Civil War and the execution of Charles I in 1649, the eleven-year experiment in republican government failed to provide England with stability in its political and religious life. This failure caused the army leaders to act to restore the monarchy.

Despite England's domestic problems, the English enforced their dominant position in Scotland and Ireland, while in foreign affairs they successfully asserted their interests against the Dutch and the Spanish.

Recommended Reading

Ashley, Maurice. *England in the Seventeenth Century, 1603–1714* (1961).

Ashley, Maurice. *General Monck* (1977).

Ashley, Maurice. *The Greatness of Oliver Cromwell* (1958).

Ashley, Maurice. *The Stuarts in Love* (1963).

Aylmer, G. E. *Rebellion or Revolution? England, 1640–1660* (1986).

Aylmer, G. E. *A Short History of Seventeenth-Century England* (1963).

Bowen, Catherine Drinker. *The Lion and the Throne: The Life and Times of Sir Edward Coke* (1956).

Carlton, Charles. *Archbishop William Laud* (1987).

Carlton, Charles. *Charles I, the Personal Monarch* (1983).

Coward, Barry. *The Stuart Age: A History of England, 1603–1714* (1980).

Donaldson, Gordon. *Scotland: James V to James VII* (1965).

Dow, F. D. *Radicalism in the English Revolution, 1640–1660* (1985).

Fletcher, Anthony. *The Outbreak of the English Civil War* (1981).

Fraser, Antonia. *Cromwell, the Lord Protector* (1973).

Fraser, Antonia. *King James VI of Scotland, I of England* (1975).

Hibbard, Christopher. *Charles I and the Popish Plot* (1983).

Hill, Christopher. *The Century of Revolution, 1603–1714.* (1961).

Hill, Christopher. *God's Englishman: Oliver Cromwell and the English Revolution* (1970).

Hill, Christopher. *The World Turned Upside Down: Radical Ideas During the English Revolution* (1972).

Howat, G. M. D. *Stuart and Cromwellian Foreign Policy* (1974).

Kenyon, J. P. *Stuart England* (1978).

Kishlansky, Mark. *The Rise of the New Model Army* (1979).

Laslett, Peter. *The World We Have Lost* (2nd ed., 1971).

Lee, Maurice, Jr. *Government By Pen: Scotland Under James VI and I* (1980).

Lee, Maurice, Jr. *The Road to Revolution: Scotland Under Charles I, 1625–37* (1985).

Lockyer, Roger. *Buckingham: The Life and Political Career of George Villiers, First Duke of Buckingham, 1592-1628* (1981).

Manning, Brian. *The English People and the English Revolution, 1640–49* (1976).

Notestein, Wallace. *The English People on the Eve of Colonization, 1603-1630* (1954).

Russell, Conrad. *Parliaments and English Politics, 1621-1629* (1979).

Trevor-Roper, H. R. *Archbishop Laud* (2nd ed., 1962).

Wedgwood, C. V. *The King's Peace, 1637-1641* (1955).

Wedgwood, C. V. *The King's War, 1641-1647* (1959).

Wedgwood, C. V. *Oliver Cromwell* (rev. ed., 1973).

Wedgwood, C. V. *Thomas Wentworth, First Earl of Strafford: A Revaluation* (1961).

Wedgwood, C. V. *The Trial of Charles I* (1964).

Woolrych, Austin. *Commonwealth to Protectorate* (1982).

Worden, Blair. *The Rump Parliament, 1648-1653* (1974).

Wrightson, Keith. *English Society, 1580–1680* (1982).

CHAPTER 10

The Seventeenth Century: Restoration and Revolution

Time Line

1660	The restoration of the monarchy
1660–1685	Reign of King Charles II
1661–1665	Parliament passes the Clarendon Code
1665–1667	England fights the Dutch War
1667	John Milton publishes *Paradise Lost*
1670	Charles II signs the Treaty of Dover with King Louis XIV of France
1672	Charles II issues the Declaration of Indulgence
1673	Parliament passes the Test Act

1678	Titus Oates fabricates the Popish Plot
1685–1688	Reign of King James II
1687	James II issues the Declaration of Liberty of Conscience
1688	The Glorious Revolution brings William and Mary to the throne
1689	Parliament passes the Bill of Rights
	Parliament passes the Toleration Act
	England enters the War of the League of Augsburg against France
1690	William III defeats James II and his Irish supporters at the Battle of the Boyne
	John Locke publishes the *Essay Concerning Human Understanding* and the *Second Treatise of Government*
1697	The Treaty of Ryswick ends the War of the League of Augsburg
1701	Parliament passes the Act of Settlement
	The War of the Spanish Succession begins
1702–1714	Reign of Queen Anne
1707	The Act of Union unites England and Scotland to create Great Britain
1709	Dr. Henry Sacheverell is convicted of seditious libel
1713–1714	The Treaty of Utrecht and the Treaty of Baden and Rastatt end the War of the Spanish Succession

The Restoration of 1660 brought King Charles II, the eldest son of King Charles I, to the throne. In the wake of the turmoil of the years after 1649, the Restoration proved popular. The question of the dis-

tribution of power between king and Parliament had not been resolved, however, nor had the conflicts over religion been settled.

These issues quickly came to a head following the accession of King James II in 1685, leading to the Glorious Revolution of 1688 and Parliament's selection of William and Mary as England's new rulers.

While the seventeenth century was an era of political and religious turmoil for England, it was also a time of remarkable achievement in the arts, literature, science, and political thought.

King Charles II (r. 1660–1685)

Following the Stuart Restoration of 1660, King Charles II wisely made no attempt to reestablish royal absolutism and generally avoided conflicts with Parliament, although the king and the leaders of Parliament did not trust one another.

The Clarendon Code

From 1661 to 1665, Parliament passed a series of laws known as the Clarendon Code, named for Charles II's chief adviser, the earl of Clarendon (1609–1674). Reestablishing the Church of England, the Clarendon Code placed restrictions on Roman Catholics and Nonconformists.

The Clarendon Code consisted of four acts.

The Corporation Act

The Corporation Act of 1661 required that all members of city governments receive Holy Communion in the Church of England.

The Act of Uniformity

The Act of Uniformity of 1662 required all clergymen in England and Wales to use the Anglican *Book of Common Prayer* for public worship.

The Conventicle Act

The Conventicle Act of 1664 prohibited Nonconformist religious gatherings of more than five persons.

The Five Mile Act

The Five Mile Act of 1665 barred non-Anglican clergymen from coming within five miles of a city. It proved difficult to enforce the Clarendon Code.

Other Problems

In addition to the religious issue, England faced other problems. In the mid-1660s, two disasters struck London: a severe plague in 1665 and the disastrous fire of 1666. In the latter year, the English suppressed a revolt in Scotland.

Foreign Affairs

The Dutch War

Commercial rivalry with the Dutch, and the English seizure in 1664 of the Dutch colony of New Netherland, which they divided into the colonies of New York and New Jersey, resulted in the outbreak of war in 1665. The Treaty of Breda of July 1667 awarded New York and New Jersey, as well as Delaware, to the English. However, the English returned Surinam in South America to the Dutch and surrendered their claims to the Spice Islands (also known as the Moluccas) in the East Indies.

Relations with King Louis XIV of France

The Triple Alliance.   In 1667, King Louis XIV (r. 1643–1715) moved against the Spanish Netherlands (modern Belgium) in his continuing effort to expand France's borders to the north and northeast. In defense of the balance of power, England and the Netherlands (Holland) joined with Sweden against Louis XIV. Threatened by this Triple Alliance, Louis XIV quickly ended his war with Spain in 1668 and then turned to diplomacy to break up the alliance directed against him.

The Treaty of Dover (1670).   After paying off the Swedes, the French king signed the secret Treaty of Dover in 1670 with Charles II, who agreed to support France against the Dutch in return for annual subsidies from the French. These subsidies reduced Charles II's financial dependence on Parliament.

Alliance with France.   England supported King Louis XIV when he went to war with Holland in 1672. The alliance with the French was unpopular in England, however, and Parliament forced the king to make peace with the Dutch in 1674.

The Catholic Issue

King Charles II's alliance with the French increased fears of an attempt to restore Roman Catholicism in England. These fears were already considerable, since both Charles's wife, Catherine of Braganza (1638–1705), who was the sister of the Portugese king, and Charles's brother, the duke of York, were Catholics.

The Test Act

In 1672, the king issued the Declaration of Indulgence, removing the restrictions imposed on both Nonconformists and Catholics. Parliament forced the king to withdraw the declaration and passed the Test Act of 1673. This law required all officeholders to take oaths of allegiance to and to receive Holy Communion in the Anglican Church. Charles was successful, however, in opposing efforts in Parliament to bar the duke of York from the succession to the throne.

The Popish Plot

In 1678, the revelation of a "Popish Plot," fabricated by Titus Oates (1649–1705), intensified English fears of the Catholics. According to Oates, Catholics had formed a conspiracy to restore Catholicism in England. The testimony of Oates and others led to the execution of thirty-five innocent people.

King James II (r. 1685–1688)

Following Charles II's death in February 1685, his brother, the duke of York, succeeded to the throne as King James II. Shortly after becoming king, James suppressed a revolt led by the duke of Monmouth (1649–1685), an illegitimate son of Charles II. Monmouth was beheaded, and other rebels were severely punished in trials known as the Bloody Assizes.

James II lacked his brother's moderation and understanding of the political realities and attempted both to impose royal absolutism and to promote a restoration of Roman Catholicism. In 1687, the king issued the Declaration of Liberty of Conscience, granting freedom to all religious denominations. While this benefited Nonconformists as well as Catholics, the Protestants believed the declaration favored Roman Catholics. James also defied the law by appointing Catholics to high office.

The Glorious Revolution:
William III and Mary II

In 1688, the birth of a son to James's Catholic second wife, Mary of Este (1658–1718; also known as Mary of Modena), created a crisis, since the king would presumably have a Catholic successor. The leaders of the major political factions in Parliament, the Whigs and the Tories, joined in the Glorious Revolution to drive James from the throne. The Tories were, for the most part, royalists, landowners, and Anglicans and generally opposed the Whigs, who were largely supporters of parliamentary power, merchants, and Nonconformists. While the Tories did not share the Whigs's belief in parliamentary supremacy, they strongly supported the Anglican Church and opposed Catholicism. Some Tories remained loyal to James II and became known as Jacobites (from *Jacobus,* the Latin for James).

The king's opponents offered the crown to the Dutch ruler, William of Orange, the Protestant son-in-law of James II. William accepted the offer and invaded southwestern England in November 1688. The country demonstrated its support for William, and James fled to France in December without abdicating the throne, which Parliament then declared vacant.

The Revolution Settlement

In 1689, Parliament awarded the English crown jointly to William of Orange, who now became King William III (r. 1689–1702), and his wife Mary II (r. 1689–1694), the daughter of James I by his first wife, a Protestant.

The Bill of Rights

Parliament required William and Mary to accept the Bill of Rights of 1689, which established the claims that Parliament had set forth in its long conflict with the Stuarts. The Bill of Rights guaranteed members of Parliament freedom of speech and immunity from prosecution for statements made in parliamentary debate. The king was barred from levying taxes without Parliament's approval, maintaining a standing army in peacetime, and interfering in parliamentary elections. The right to trial by jury was guaranteed, and the king was barred from interfering with jurors. In addition, the Bill of Rights required frequent meetings of Parliament.

The Toleration Act

The Toleration Act, also adopted in 1689, granted some freedom of worship to Nonconformists, but the restrictions on office-holding imposed by the Test Act of 1673 technically remained in effect. After 1689, however, the Test Act was abrogated by Parliament's adoption of legislation legalizing the acts of officials who had not fulfilled the requirements of the Test Act. These officials were usually Nonconformists rather than Roman Catholics. The Test Act was not repealed until 1828, and Roman Catholics did not receive full civil rights until the enactment of Catholic emancipation in 1829.

The Act of Settlement

Following Queen Mary's death in 1694, William III ruled alone until his death in 1702. The crown then passed to Anne, another daughter of King James II. Even before Anne's accession to the throne, it was evident that she would have no heirs, since the last of her thirteen children, the duke of Gloucester, died in 1700. The Act of Settlement of 1701 excluded Catholics from the succession to the throne and provided that if William and Anne died without heirs, the crown would pass to Sophia, the electress of the German state of Hanover, and her descendents. Sophia was a Protestant granddaughter of King James I, the daughter of Frederick, the elector of the Palatinate, and James I's daughter Elizabeth.

Support for the Stuarts in Scotland and Ireland

Scotland

Although Scotland was the home of the Stuarts, many Scots realized that the Calvinist William of Orange would be more sympathetic to Presbyterianism than would the deposed James II. A convention held in Edinburgh agreed to acknowledge William and Mary in return for their pledge not to interfere with the Presbyterian Church. Some Scottish Highlanders, who remained loyal to the Stuarts, rebelled, but when William offered them reasonable terms, most Highland clans accepted them. However, the Macdonalds of Glencoe continued their revolt, which was finally crushed in February 1692.

Ireland

Catholic Ireland remained loyal to James II, the Catholic king. In 1689, with the help of France's King Louis XIV, James landed in Ireland. Gaining the support of Irish Catholics against the Protestants in Ulster (northern Ireland), James laid siege to Londonderry.

Battle of the Boyne (1690).   In 1690, King William III arrived in Ireland at the head of an Anglo-Dutch force and won the support of the Irish Protestants, who became known as Orangemen because of their alliance with William of Orange. James II was defeated at the Battle of the Boyne on July 12, 1690. While James returned to France following his defeat, Irish Catholic resistance continued until 1696. James died in France in 1701.

Punishment of the Irish.   Imposing restrictions on the Irish Catholics, the English barred them from the Irish Parliament, even though Catholics comprised eighty percent of the country's population. In addition, Catholics were not permitted to sit on town councils or juries, to teach in schools, or to serve in the army, and no Catholic was allowed to buy land. Placing restrictions on the Irish economy, the English insisted that Irish woolen textiles could be exported only to England. Furthermore, all Irish imports from the colonies had to pass through England, which raised their price considerably.

Renewed Conflict With King Louis XIV

In the last years of the seventeenth century, England began to play a leading role in Europe's struggle to contain King Louis XIV. In the War of Devolution (1667-1668) and the Dutch War (1672-1678), the French had pushed their borders to the northeast toward the Rhine River, winning several towns along the border of the Spanish Netherlands, as well as the Franche-Comté (the Free County of Burgundy).

The War of the League of Augsburg

In 1686, the Holy Roman Emperor Leopold I (r. 1658-1705) formed a new alliance against the French called the League of Augsburg. In 1688, King Louis XIV sent his army into the Palatinate, beginning the War of the League of Augsburg, also known as the Nine Years' War (1688-1697).

Battle of Beachy Head (1690).   In May 1689, King William III led England into the war against France. In June 1690, the French navy defeated the English and Dutch in the Battle of Beachy Head.

Battle of La Hogue (1692).   In May 1692, as Louis XIV was preparing an invasion of England, the English and Dutch navies inflicted heavy losses on the French fleet in the six-day Battle of La Hogue.

English Victories.   Although the allies now controlled the sea, they suffered setbacks on land in the fighting in the Low Countries from 1692 to 1694. In September 1695, however, the English took the important French fortress of Namur after a three-month siege. In the Mediterranean, the English fleet harassed French commerce. In 1696, the English bombarded Calais, frustrating a French and Jacobite plan to invade England.

The Treaty of Ryswick (1697)

Under the terms of the Treaty of Ryswick, signed in 1697, the French agreed to return all the territory they had taken after 1678, with the exception of the city of Strasbourg on the Rhine. The provision of the treaty requiring the restoration of all colonial conquests to their original holders resulted in the English return of the fortress of Port Royal in Acadia (Nova Scotia) to the French. Agreeing to recognize William III as king of England, Louis XIV abandoned his support of the Jacobite cause.

Queen Anne (r. 1702–1714)

Queen Anne came to the English throne as a staunch supporter of the Anglican Church and the Tories, although she had to include Whigs among her ministers when the Whigs dominated Parliament.

The Act of Union of 1707

Under the terms of the Act of Union of 1707, England and Scotland were joined in a political union known as Great Britain. The act provided Scotland with substantial representation in the British Parliament, as well as guarantees for the established Presbyterian Church of Scotland.

The War of the Spanish Succession

The peace settlement signed with France in 1697 lasted only four years before the outbreak of the War of the Spanish Succession (1701–1714).

Causes of the War

When the childless King Charles II (r. 1665–1700), the last Hapsburg king of Spain, died in 1700, he left the Spanish crown to Philip of Anjou, the grandson of King Louis XIV. The Hapsburg Holy Roman Emperor Leopold I challenged the succession, claiming the Spanish crown for his son, Charles. The stakes were great, since the victor would acquire not only Spain and its possessions in Europe but also Spain's overseas colonies with their vast wealth. The other powers of Europe could not permit France to acquire Spain and its domains and would accept a Bourbon as king of Spain only if he and his heirs were barred from ever holding the French crown as well. England, the Netherlands, and the Holy Roman emperor joined forces to oppose the French.

England's Role in the War

England played a major role in the war against Louis XIV. The great English general, John Churchill, the duke of Marlborough (1650–1722), joined with the Hapsburg commander, Prince Eugene of Savoy (1663–1736), to defeat the French in 1704 at Blenheim in southern Germany and in other battles. In 1704, the English occupied Gibraltar, thereby acquiring an important naval base in the Mediterranean.

The Peace Settlement

Europe

France signed peace treaties with her enemies, except the Hapsburgs, at Utrecht in 1713. The Treaty of Baden and Rastatt of 1714 ended the war with the Hapsburgs. The peace settlement recognized Philip of Anjou as King Philip V (r. 1700–1746) of Spain, but provided that neither he nor his successors could occupy the French throne. The Austrian Hapsburgs were compensated by the acquisition of the Spanish Netherlands and also received Naples, Sardinia, and Milan in Italy. Sicily was awarded to the Italian state of Savoy, which exchanged it in 1720 with the Austrian Hapsburgs for Sardinia. In Germany, the elector of Brandenburg was recognized as king of Prussia.

Colonies

Of more central concern to England, the French lost a number of colonies that the English had taken during the war, including Newfoundland, Acadia (Nova Scotia), and the Hudson Bay area of Canada, although France kept Quebec. The English retained Gibraltar and Minorca and also acquired the *Asiento,* a monopoly on the importation of slaves into Spanish America for thirty years.

Domestic Political Developments

Early in Anne's reign, three individuals exercised great influence on the government. The duke of Marlborough acted as the queen's political and military adviser, while his wife, Sarah Churchill (1660–1744), the duchess of Marlborough, was her closest confidante. Sidney Godolphin (1645–1712), the lord treasurer, provided leadership for the government in Parliament. Both Marlborough and Godolphin were Tories.

Whig Domination

When the Whigs increased their representation in the House of Commons in 1705, they pressured the queen into dismissing several Tory ministers. In 1708, the Whigs increased their majority in the Commons and forced Anne to name additional Whig ministers. Marlborough and Godolphin succeeded in forming an alliance with the Whig leaders and thus were able to continue their leadership role.

The Sacheverell Case.   In 1709, Dr. Henry Sacheverell (1674–1724), a Tory clergyman, preached two sermons attacking the Whig-dominated ministry, criticizing in particular its tolerance of Nonconformists. Convicted of seditious libel, Sacheverell's right to preach was suspended for three years.

Negative public reaction to the Sacheverell prosecution contributed to the success of the Tories in the 1710 election.

The Harley-St. John Tory Cabinet

As the War of the Spanish Succession continued, the Whigs began to lose popular support, and in 1710, the Tories won a majority in the

House of Commons. Robert Harley, who subsequently became the earl of Oxford (1661–1724), served as lord treasurer, while Henry St. John, later Viscount Bolingbroke (1678–1751), was Harley's chief colleague.

Moving to bring the war to a close, the government removed Marlborough as commander, replacing him with the duke of Ormonde (1665–1745). While the House of Commons favored peace negotiations with France, Queen Anne had to create twelve new peers to secure a majority favorable to peace in the House of Lords.

Anti-Whig and Anti-Nonconformist Legislation

The Tory-dominated government pushed through several statutes designed to punish Whigs and Nonconformists.

The Occasional Conformity Act.   The Occasional Conformity Act of 1711 sought to strengthen the ban on office-holding by Nonconformists by prohibiting the practice of Nonconformist office-holders who sought to comply with the requirements of the Test Act by receiving Holy Communion once a year in the Anglican Church.

The Property Qualification Act.   The Property Qualification Act of 1711 required members of the House of Commons to own substantial landed property. This discriminated against Whigs whose wealth was more likely to be based on business rather than land ownership.

The Schism Act.   The Schism Act of 1714 sought to restrict Nonconformist education by requiring that all teachers be licensed by a bishop and attend the Anglican Church.

The Issue of the Succession

Although the Act of Settlement of 1701 had provided that the succession to the English throne would pass to the Hanoverians, many Tories sympathized with the Stuarts. The Tories had tried, without success, to get James, the "Old Pretender" (1688–1766), the son of King James II by his Catholic second wife, to abandon Roman Catholicism.

Although the earl of Oxford (formerly Robert Harley), the lord treasurer, supported the Hanoverians, Viscount Bolingbroke (formerly Henry St. John) persuaded Queen Anne to dismiss Oxford on July 27, 1714. Bolingbroke's own plans for the succession remain unclear, although his contacts with the Old Pretender aroused suspicion.

The duke of Shrewsbury (1660–1718), the leader of the opposition to Bolingbroke, supported the Hanoverian succession. On July 30, the Privy Council urged Queen Anne to make Shrewsbury the lord treasurer, and the dying queen complied with the request.

Following Queen Anne's death, George, the son of Sophia (granddaughter of King James I) and the elector of Hanover, arrived in England in September 1714 to claim his throne.

The Humanities

Art

Anthony Van Dyck

Anthony Van Dyck (1599–1641), an important Flemish artist and pupil of Peter Paul Rubens (1577–1640), first went to England in 1620, where he painted a portrait of King James I. Returning to England in 1632, he became court painter to King Charles I and was knighted. In addition to his portraits, he is known for his religious paintings. Van Dyck's influence appeared in the work of a number of seventeenth-century English painters.

Miniature Painting

During the seventeeth century, and especially during the reign of King Charles II, the painting of miniature portraits flourished in England. Nicholas Hilliard (1537–1619), Samuel Cooper (1609–1672), and Thomas Flatman (1637–1688) were important painters of miniatures.

Architecture

Inigo Jones (1573–1652), a disciple of the Venetian Renaissance architect Andrea Palladio (1508–1580), and Christopher Wren (1632–1723) brought the classical architectural style into England.

Inigo Jones

Inigo Jones built the Banqueting Hall in Whitehall, London, for King James I. This was the first major classical building erected in England, and it introduced a new era in the history of English architecture.

Christopher Wren

The great London fire of 1666 gave Sir Christopher Wren an opportunity to rebuild the city. He designed the new St. Paul's Cathe-

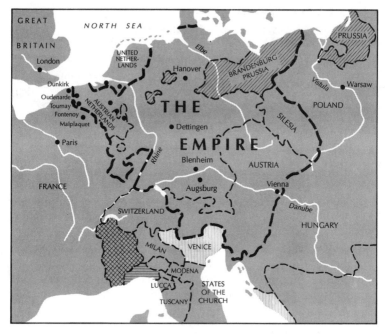

(a) Central Europe (detail)

dral, built between 1675 and 1710, and about fifty other London churches in the classical style.

Music

Opera, which originated in Italy, began to appear in England during the period of the Commonwealth and Protectorate and remained popular during the Restoration.

Henry Purcell (1659–1695) wrote the opera *Dido and Aeneas* (1680) and composed numerous other vocal and orchestral works.

Literature

John Donne

The religious and philosophical poems of John Donne (1572–1631) are regarded as among the finest produced by the English metaphysical poets of the seventeenth century.

(b) **Europe, 1714**

John Milton

The Puritan poet John Milton (1608-1674) was seventeenth-century England's greatest literary figure. His most famous work, the epic poem *Paradise Lost* (1667), is based on the biblical tradition of Satan's revolt against God and the fall of Adam and Eve. *Paradise Regained* (1671), another poem in blank verse, tells of Jesus in the wilderness, overcoming the temptations of Satan. *Samson Agonistes* (1671) is a poetic drama inspired by classical Greek tragedy, although its subject matter is biblical.

John Dryden

Like Milton, John Dryden (1631-1700) was thoroughly familiar with ancient Greek and Roman literature. A poet, dramatist, and critic, Dryden's best-known plays include the comedy *Marriage à la*

Mode (1672) and *All for Love* (1677), a retelling of Shakespeare's *Antony and Cleopatra.*

John Bunyan

A Nonconformist preacher, John Bunyan (1628–1688) published the first part of *The Pilgrim's Progress* in 1678, presenting an allegory of Christian's journey from the City of Destruction to the Celestial City. In the second part, published in 1684, Bunyan described the similar pilgrimage of Christiana, Christian's wife.

Samuel Pepys

An official of the admiralty, Samuel Pepys (1633–1703) published his *Memoirs of the Royal Navy* in 1790 and, at his death, left a diary in code. Deciphered and published in ten volumes in the late nineteenth century, Pepys's diary covering the years from 1660 to 1669 presents a graphic picture of English life during the early Restoration period.

Restoration Drama

The return of the Stuarts to the throne in 1660 brought a reopening of the theaters that the Puritans had closed in 1642 and gave rise to Restoration drama, above all, comedies.

William Wycherley

The Oxford-educated William Wycherley (c. 1640–1716) was recognized for his wit, but he also came to be regarded as the most licentious of the comic dramatists of the Restoration era. His first comedy, *Love in a Wood,* was produced in 1671, but he is best known for his two masterpieces, *The Country Wife* (produced 1674?) and *The Plain Dealer* (produced 1676).

Sir John Vanbrugh

Sir John Vanbrugh's (1664–1726) first play, *The Relapse,* was produced in 1696, while his masterpiece, *The Provoked Wife,* appeared on the stage the following year. An architect as well as a playwright, he designed Blenheim Palace, the home of the duke of Marlborough, and also Castle Howard.

William Congreve

William Congreve's (1670–1729) first comedy, *The Old Bachelor,* was produced in 1693, while *Lost for Love* appeared two years later. His most highly regarded comedy, *The Way of the World,* was produced in 1700. Congreve also wrote one tragedy, *The Mourning Bride,* produced in 1697.

Joseph Addison

The Oxford-educated classical scholar Joseph Addison (1672–1719) wrote essays marked by order, simplicity, and precision, which he published in several leading publications, including the *Tatler,* the *Spectator,* and the *Guardian.* He also wrote a neoclassical tragedy, *Cato* (1713), that became a popular success, as well as a prose comedy, *The Drummer* (1716).

Science and Political Philosophy

Science

England and Scotland made important contributions to the Scientific Revolution that began to gain momentum in Europe during the seventeenth century.

Francis Bacon

Francis Bacon (1561–1626), an attorney and royal official, wrote extensively on history, ethics, and philosophy. While he was not a professional scientist, he did much to promote the inductive method of modern science. Bacon attacked the excessive reverence given to the work of ancient thinkers, including Aristotle. In particular, he challenged Aristotle's dependence on deductive reasoning.

Bacon insisted that valid conclusions about the physical universe could be reached only through the inductive method, which involves experimentation and the systematic collection and analysis of data. Generalizations can then be made on the basis of the collected and analyzed data. If scientists carefully examined the empirical evidence, he believed, they would develop new knowledge that would provide benefits for all of humanity. His major works include *The Advancement of Learning* (1605) and the *Novum Organum* (1620).

William Gilbert

In 1600, William Gilbert (c. 1540–1603), the court physician to Queen Elizabeth I and King James I, described the presence of electric charges in many substances. His work won for him the title of the "Father of Modern Electricity."

Gilbert was also one of the pioneers in the field of geology, the study of the origins, development, and structure of the earth. In *De magnete* (1600), a study of magnetism, Gilbert suggested that the earth operated like a huge magnet.

John Napier

In 1614, John Napier (1550–1617), a Scottish mathematician, published a table of logarithms that provided a simplified method for multiplying and dividing large numbers and for finding square roots.

Using Napier's principle of the logarithm, William Oughtred and Edmund Wingate independently invented the slide rule about 1630.

William Harvey

William Harvey (1578–1657), an English physician educated at the famous university in Padua, Italy, did much to establish the foundations of modern medicine. He was the first to demonstrate the function of the heart and the circulation of the blood, publishing *On the Movement of the Heart and Blood in Animals* in 1628.

Robert Boyle

The title of the "Father of Modern Chemistry" has been bestowed upon Robert Boyle (1627–1691), an Anglo-Irish chemist. He is most famous for Boyle's Law, which states that the volume of a gas under compression is inversely proportional to the amount of pressure. Boyle was the first to make a clear distinction between a chemical element and a chemical compound and to define clearly the nature of a chemical reaction.

Sir Isaac Newton

The work of Nicolaus Copernicus (1473–1543), Johannes Kepler (1571–1630), and Galileo Galilei (1564–1642) established a new view of the universe, based on the heliocentric theory (the idea that the sun stands at the center of the solar system, with the planets revolving around the sun). Their work, however, had left one great unanswered question: What is it that causes the planets, stars, and other heavenly bodies to move in an orderly fashion? Sir Isaac Newton (1642–1727) discovered the answer to this question.

Calculus.   The son of an English farmer, Newton won early recognition for his genius, and he became a professor of mathematics at Cambridge University while he was still in his twenties. Working independently of each other, both Newton and Gottfried Wilhelm von Leibniz (1646–1716), a German philosopher and mathematician, discovered differential and integral calculus.

Law of Gravity.   Newton shared the conviction of other scientists that the physical universe was governed by natural laws. His research convinced him that all of the heavenly bodies moved as they did because of the operation of the law of gravity. In his *Principia Mathematica* (1687), Newton set forth the law of universal gravitation, which provided a mathematical explanation of the operation of gravity everywhere in the universe.

The Royal Society

The Royal Society for Improving Natural Knowledge was founded in 1662. Among its early members were Newton, Boyle, and the architect Christopher Wren.

Political Philosophy

Thomas Hobbes

Thomas Hobbes (1588–1679) advanced a defense of royal authority in his political treatise, the *Leviathan* (1651). In the state of nature, Hobbes believed, the life of human beings was "solitary, poor, nasty, brutish, and short." In order to gain protection, the people joined in a contract, agreeing to submit to the absolute authority of a sovereign.

While Hobbes supported absolutism, he did not accept the theory of divine right, since the sovereign originally acquired his power from the people. Furthermore, Hobbes believed that if the sovereign failed to provide protection to his subjects then their obligation to obedience was ended.

James Harrington

In his *Commonwealth of Oceana* (1656), James Harrington (1611–1677) portrayed an ideal state, a republic where political power would be vested in the hands of the owners of landed property. Harrington's views were less immediately relevant to the political situation of seventeenth-century England than were those of Thomas Hobbes and John Locke.

John Locke

In two works published in 1690, the influential political philosopher John Locke (1632–1704) provided a vigorous defense of the Glorious Revolution of 1688.

Knowledge from Experience.   In his *Essay Concerning Human Understanding,* Locke advanced his theory of the *tabula rasa.* At birth, he argued, every human being's mind is a blank page, and all knowledge comes from experience. Rejecting the doctrine of innate ideas, Locke repudiated the view that human beings were born with a tendency to submit to authority.

Social Contract.   Locke based his *Second Treatise of Government* on the social contract theory. In Locke's view, people had come together in a social contract, creating, by mutual consent, a government to protect their natural rights to life, liberty, and property. The authority of government is thus derived from the consent of the governed. When government fails to protect the people's natural rights and instead interferes with them by attempting to rule absolutely, the people have a right to rebel, as they had done in the Glorious Revolution. Locke supported the creation of a constitutional government that placed limits on the ruler's authority.

Influence of Locke's Ideas.   Locke's doctrine of natural rights influenced many who came after him. Thomas Jefferson, for example, wrote in the American Declaration of Independence of the right to "life, liberty, and the pursuit of happiness."

The long conflict between Parliament and the Stuart monarchs culminated in the Glorious Revolution of 1688. The revolutionary settlement placed restrictions on the power of the crown, establishing a constitutional monarchy, and reaffirmed the position of the Church of England as the country's established church. During the eighteenth century, Parliament clearly established its ascendency over the crown, as its authority continued to increase, while that of the monarchy declined.

In international affairs, England contributed to the effort to contain the expansionist ambitions of King Louis XIV of France and, as a consequence of its efforts, significantly expanded its colonial holdings in the western hemisphere and the Mediterranean.

Recommended Reading

Ashley, Maurice. *The Glorious Revolution of 1688* (1968).

Ashley, Maurice. *James II* (1978).

Bald, R. C. *John Donne: A Life* (1970).

Bell, Walter George. *The Great Fire of London in 1666* (1951).

Bell, Walter George. *The Great Plague in London in 1665* (1951).

Boas, Marie. *Robert Boyle and Seventeenth-Century Chemistry* (1958).

Chandler, David. *Marlborough as Military Commander* (1973).

Churchill, Winston S. *Marlborough, His Life and Times,* 2 vols. (1947).

Clark, George N. *The Later Stuarts, 1660–1714* (2nd ed., 1956).

Cranston, Maurice. *Locke* (1957).

Dickinson, H. T. *Bolingbroke* (1970).

Green, David. *Sarah, Duchess of Marlborough* (1967).

Green, I. M. *The Reestablishment of the Church of England, 1660–1663* (1978).

Gregg, Edward. *Queen Anne* (1980).

Haley, K. D. H. *Charles II* (1966).

Hall, A. R. *The Revolution in Science* (1983).

Hatton, Ragnhild and J. S. Bormley, eds. *William III and Louis XIV* (1968).

Hill, Christopher. *John Milton and the English Revolution* (1977).

Holmes, Geoffrey. *Britain After the Glorious Revolution* (1969).

Holmes, Geoffrey. *British Politics in the Age of Anne* (1967).

Holmes, Geoffrey. *The Trial of Doctor Sacheverell* (1973).

Jacob, Margaret. *The Newtonians and the English Revolution* (1976).

Kenyon, J. P. *The Popish Plot* (1972).

McInnes, Angus. *Robert Harley* (1970).

Millar, Oliver. *English Art, 1625–1714* (1957).

Miller, John. *James II: A Study in Kingship* (1978).

Miller, John. *Popery and Politics in England, 1660–88* (1973).

Ogg, David. *England in the Reign of Charles II* (1955).

Ogg, David. *England in the Reigns of James II and William III* (1955).

Purvery, Margery. *The Royal Society* (1967).

Straka, G. M. *The Revolution of 1688 – Whig Triumph or Palace Revolution?* (1962).

Strong, Roy C. *Van Dyck: Charles I on Horseback* (1972).

Sutherland, James. *English Literature of the Late Seventeenth Century* (1969).

Van der Zee, Henri and Barbara van der Zee. *William and Mary* (1973).

Webster, Charles. *From Paracelsus to Newton: Magic and the Making of Modern Science* (1982).

Westfall, Richard S. *Never at Rest: A Biography of Isaac Newton* (1980).

CHAPTER 11

The Eighteenth Century: The First Hanoverians

Time Line

1714–1727	Reign of King George I
1715	Parliament passes the Riot Act
	The earl of Mar leads a Jacobite uprising in Scotland
1716	Parliament passes the Septennial Act
1719	The Stanhope ministry introduces the Peerage Bill
1720	The South Sea bubble bursts
1721–1742	Robert Walpole serves, in effect, as the first prime minister

1727–1760	Reign of King George II
1733	Walpole's proposal to extend excise taxes evokes opposition
1737	Queen Caroline dies
1744–1754	Henry Pelham serves as prime minister
1745	The Young Pretender launches a Jacobite revolt in Scotland
1757	William Pitt becomes the dominant figure in the government
1760–1820	Reign of King George III
1763	John Wilkes is charged with seditious libel
1770–1782	Lord North serves as prime minister

In the eighteenth century, the monarchy retained considerable authority, although the monarch recognized the need to find ministers who could establish and maintain a cooperative working relationship with Parliament, especially the House of Commons.

The landed aristocracy continued to dominate the country's politics, sharing power with the wealthy merchants, who often married or bought their way into the aristocracy. The first two Hanoverians, Kings George I and George II, maintained close ties with the Whigs, who had supported the Hanoverian succession and had no sympathy with the Jacobite cause, as did some of the Tories. The Whig leaders came primarily from the great landed families and had the support of most of the merchants and Nonconformists.

Of these Whig politicians, Robert Walpole was the most successful, serving as the king's chief minister — in effect, as prime minister — for some twenty years.

King George I (r. 1714–1727)

King George I, the elector of the German state of Hanover, remained interested primarily in German affairs, although he was wise enough not to try to rule his English subjects as an absolute monarch. He never learned English, and never won much in the way of affection from his subjects.

Whig Ministry

Viscount Townshend (1674–1738) and General James Stanhope (1673–1721), who became the earl of Stanhope in 1718, were the most prominent ministers of King George I.

In 1714, the king appointed a ministry led by Townshend, a Whig. The following year, the Whigs won a solid majority in the House of Commons, and many Tories were driven from office.

Jacobite Opposition

Two Tories, Viscount Bolingbroke and the duke of Ormonde (see Chapter 10), fled to France, where they joined the cause of James Edward Stuart, the Old Pretender, the Stuart claimant to the English throne.

The Riot Act (1715)

When some Jacobite demonstrations occurred, the Whig-controlled Parliament passed the Riot Act of 1715, which authorized magistrates to order the dispersal, within an hour, of any assembly of a dozen or more persons who were disturbing the peace. The death penalty could be imposed on any who disobeyed.

"The Fifteen"

Although the Old Pretender and his supporters believed the country stood on the brink of revolution, the only significant Jacobite uprising was a revolt known as "the Fifteen," that began in the Scottish Highlands. Led by the earl of Mar (1675–1732), the revolt broke out in September 1715 (hence the name), but the Jacobite rebels were quickly defeated at Preston in England and Sheriff Muir in Scotland. After the suppression of the revolt, Mar fled to France. The French agreed to end their support for the Jacobite cause, and the Old Pretender had to leave France.

Whig Dominance

Tory support of the Old Pretender further discredited the Tories in England and gave the Whigs an even more decisive hold on power that lasted until 1760. Although the Whigs quarreled among themselves, they continued to dominate the government. If one Whig faction fell from power, another faction was ready to take its place.

The Septennial Act (1716)

In 1716, Parliament passed the Septennial Act, increasing the term of a Parliament from three to seven years. This gave the Whigs four additional years to solidify their hold on power. The Septennial Act remained in effect for almost 200 years, until the passage of the Parliament Act of 1911.

The Stanhope Ministry

In 1717, James Stanhope became the key figure in a new Whig ministry. Townshend and his brother-in-law, Robert Walpole (1676–1745), opposed Stanhope's activist foreign policy (see Chapter 12), which they regarded as dangerous, and they also disagreed with Stanhope on some domestic issues.

While Townshend and Walpole supported Stanhope's successful effort to secure the repeal of the Occasional Conformity Act and the Schism Act, they opposed his attempt to repeal the Corporation Act and the Test Act (see Chapter 10). These two laws remained in effect, and the split in the government led to Townshend's dismissal from the ministry in 1717 and Walpole's resignation the same year.

The Peerage Bill

In 1719, Stanhope introduced the Peerage Bill, restricting the monarch's authority to create new peerages. Its effect would have been to insure the continuance of a Whig majority in the House of Lords.

Walpole led the opposition to the bill, charging that it would make the House of Lords a closed corporation, and Stanhope was compelled to withdraw it.

The South Sea Bubble

In 1711, the South Sea Company received a charter as a joint stock company and soon secured a monopoly on English trade with South America. In early 1720, the company proposed a plan to absorb the national debt and to reduce the interest rate paid by the government. Investors who regarded the company as a state-sponsored venture indulged in a great wave of speculation, which drove up the price of the company's stock.

The bubble burst in September 1720. The value of the South Sea Company's stock collapsed, ruining many investors and provoking a financial and political crisis. A parliamentary investigation revealed high-level corruption, and several members of the cabinet were implicated. Although Stanhope was not among them, he suffered a stroke while defending his innocence before the House of Lords and died in 1721.

The Ministry of Robert Walpole

King George I now turned to Robert Walpole, naming him first lord of the treasury and chancellor of the exchequer in April 1721. From 1721 to 1742, Walpole dominated the government, becoming in effect Great Britain's first prime minister. In exercising his authority, Walpole distributed patronage to his supporters and was ruthless in dealing with his political opponents. His power was further enhanced by the fact that King George I, who spoke no English, seldom attended cabinet meetings, a practice continued by George II.

King George II (r. 1727–1760)

Like his father, King George II was interested primarily in Hanoverian affairs. He disliked his father's ministers and dismissed them, although he soon recalled Walpole, recognizing his need for Walpole's ability as a political manager. Walpole found a staunch ally in Queen Caroline (1683–1737).

Walpole's Economic Policy

Encouragement of Industry and Commerce

Walpole actively sought to promote the expansion of industry and commerce. He reduced or abolished tariffs on imports of raw materials needed by English industry and eliminated export duties on agricultural produce and many manufactured goods. He also opposed the development of manufacturing in the colonies. However, his efforts to combat smuggling proved ineffective.

Reduction of Interest and Taxes

Walpole succeeded in reducing the interest on government loans to four percent, and he also reduced the tax on land, which won for him the support of the country squires who dominated the House of Commons.

The Fall of Walpole

Development of Opposition

Viscount Bolingbroke (see Chapter 10), whom Walpole allowed to return from exile in 1725, became an influential Tory leader and the center of the developing opposition to Walpole. Walpole had earlier forced the Whig leaders John Carteret (1690–1763) and William Pulteney out of the cabinet, and they joined the opposition, as did the duke of Argyll (1682–1761), an influential Scottish nobleman. Walpole's position was further weakened by Townshend's retirement in 1730.

The Excise Tax Issue

Prior to 1733, there were not enough anti-Walpole Whigs to form a new government, but opposition to the prime minister's proposal to levy new excise taxes weakened his position. In 1733, Walpole proposed extending the system of excise taxes, which were already imposed on imported tea, coffee, and chocolate. The new taxes would be levied on tobacco and wine. The proposal evoked strong opposition, and Walpole withdrew the legislation. Walpole's defeat marked the beginning of his decline, and Queen Caroline's death in 1737 deprived him of a powerful ally in dealing with the king.

Young Whigs

Following Walpole's defeat on the excise tax issue, several Whig peers became actively interested in creating a new ministry, and they were joined by a group of younger Whigs, including William Pitt (1708–1778) and George Grenville (1712–1770), known as the "boy patriots."

This opposition group gathered around Frederick, the prince of Wales (1707–1751), who was openly at odds with his father. Leicester House, the prince's London residence, became a meeting place for Walpole's opponents.

Walpole's Resignation

Walpole sought to keep England out of continental wars, believing that they were expensive, threatened England's industry and commerce, and offered an uncertain outcome. The prime minister's opponents favored a bolder foreign policy, and in 1739, he gave way to public pressure and led England into the War of Jenkins's Ear. This conflict served as a prelude to the War of the Austrian Succession that broke out in 1740 (see Chapter 12).

War failed to strengthen Walpole's hand, and the election of 1741 left him with the support of only a small majority in the House of Commons. He resigned in February 1742, accepting a peerage, and died three years later.

Walpole's Successors

Wilmington and Carteret

The earl of Wilmington (d. 1743) succeeded Walpole as first lord of the treasury, although Carteret was the key figure in the new ministry, which included several opposition Whigs and a few Tories, along with several of Walpole's supporters. Carteret, who was now the earl of Granville, encountered increasing opposition because of his conduct of the War of the Austrian Succession. His inability to control the House of Commons led to his fall in 1744.

Henry Pelham

From 1744 to 1754, Henry Pelham (1698–1754) served as prime minister, while his elder brother, the duke of Newcastle (1693–1768), directed foreign affairs and represented Pelham's interests in the House of Lords.

In 1746, King George II attempted to force Pelham out of office. In response to the king's action, the entire cabinet resigned. Unable to form a new cabinet that could control Parliament, the king was forced to recall Pelham.

The Duke of Newcastle

Following Pelham's death in 1754, the duke of Newcastle succeeded to the prime ministership. British defeats in the early stages of the Seven Years' War (see Chapter 12) led to the fall of the Newcastle ministry in 1756.

William Pitt

A new cabinet was formed, led by the duke of Devonshire and William Pitt the Elder, despite King George II's dislike of the latter, who was known as the "Great Commoner." This cabinet failed to secure the support of a parliamentary majority, however, and the king dismissed Pitt in April 1757.

Following several months of political confusion, Newcastle and Pitt formed a coalition in June. Newcastle served as first lord of the treasury, while Pitt led the House of Commons and provided effective direction of England's war effort.

"The Forty-Five"

In July 1745, the Young Pretender, Charles Edward Stuart (1720–1788), the son of the Old Pretender and grandson of King James II, landed in Scotland and, with the support of the Highlanders, launched a new Jacobite revolt. Bonnie Prince Charlie, as the Young Pretender was known, took Edinburgh and defeated a British army at the Battle of Prestonpans in September. The Young Pretender then invaded England, advancing by December as far south as Derby. When the hoped-for English support did not materialize, Bonnie Prince Charlie retreated, evacuating Edinburgh. The duke of Cumberland (1721–1765), King George II's son, took command of the British troops, pushing the Jacobites northward and defeating them decisively at the Battle of Culloden Moor, fought near Inverness in April 1746. Bonnie Prince Charlie escaped to France and subsequently went to Rome, where he died in 1788. The English dealt ruthlessly with the Scots who had supported the revolt, earning for Cumberland the nickname of "the Butcher."

This revolt, known as the "Forty-Five" (from the year), was the last serious attempt to restore the Stuarts to the throne.

Cultural Developments

In 1752, the English replaced the old Julian calendar with the Gregorian calendar, which had been introduced by Pope Gregory XII in 1582. Protestant England had previously been unwilling to adopt a calendar proposed by the pope. In making the transition, the eleven days between September 2 and 14 were omitted.

In 1753, the British Museum was established as a repository for the nation's treasures in science, art, and literature.

King George III (r. 1760–1820)

In 1760, King George III succeeded his grandfather. Unlike the first two Hanoverians, he had been born in England and was interested in English affairs.

King George III's Prime Ministers

During the first decade of his reign, George III ruled in association with seven prime ministers. The king's primary political objectives were to undermine the Whig oligarchy and to weaken the cabinet system that placed limits on his authority. Using bribery and patronage, the king developed during the 1760s a party of "King's Friends," which resulted in the return to power of the Tories for the first time since 1714.

Fall of the Newcastle-Pitt Ministry

By the time of the accession of King George III, opposition to William Pitt the Elder had increased considerably. While some of his opponents objected to the mounting cost of the war, others were jealous of his prestige and power and had been antagonized by his domineering personality. The new king did not care for his grandfather's ministers and joined the ranks of Pitt's critics. In 1761, Pitt resigned, and Newcastle resigned the following year.

The Earl of Bute (1762–1763)

Following the fall of the Newcastle-Pitt ministry, the earl of Bute (1713–1792), an influential Scottish peer who had been the king's tutor, became prime minister. As a royal favorite and a Scot, Bute was already unpopular with Parliament, and his unpopularity mounted when he forced through Parliament an excise tax on cider. Facing increasing opposition and tired of political wrangling, Bute resigned in April 1763.

George Grenville (1763–1765)

George Grenville (1712–1770), a Whig, put a parliamentary majority together by forming a political alliance with the duke of Bedford (1710–1771) and his so-called Bloomsbury Gang. An efficient administrator, Grenville sought to restrict access to the king and to control all the patronage of the crown. Resentful of Grenville's efforts to concentrate power in his own hands, the king dismissed him in 1765.

The Marquess of Rockingham (1765-1766)

The marquess of Rockingham (1730–1782) was a member of the "Old Whig" faction. The new cabinet won parliamentary repeal of the Stamp Act (see Chapter 12) but could not maintain unity among the Whigs in Parliament, particularly after Pitt refused to support the cabinet.

William Pitt, the Earl of Chatham (1766-1768)

William Pitt the Elder, who had accepted a peerage and was now the earl of Chatham, headed a coalition of Whigs, Tories, and King's Friends. Suffering from poor physical and mental health, he could not control his colleagues in the cabinet.

The Duke of Grafton (1768-1770)

After Pitt suffered a mental breakdown, the duke of Grafton (1735–1811) became prime minister, quickly proving to be an ineffective leader. One positive accomplishment of his tenure in office was the creation of a new cabinet post, that of secretary of state for the colonies.

Lord North (1770-1782)

With the Tory Lord North (1732–1792), King George III finally found a prime minister to his liking. North and his cabinet were subservient to the king, and the prime minister proved to be an effective manager of the House of Commons, using a combination of skill and patronage to construct a solid majority of Tories and King's Friends. That, together with the support of George III, enabled him to remain in office for twelve years.

Lord North's misfortune was that he had to confront the problem of the American Revolution (see Chapter 12). He fell from power following the defeat of Lord Cornwallis at Yorktown.

The Wilkes Case

In 1763, John Wilkes (1727–1797) published an attack on the cabinet and the king in his newspaper, the *North Briton.* King George III resented any criticism of his negotiations with France to end the Seven Years' War (see Chapter 12). Prime Minister Grenville issued a general warrant for the arrest, on charges of seditious libel, of everyone involved in the publication of the offending issue of the *North Briton.*

Wilkes contended that general warrants were illegal and claimed immunity as a member of Parliament. Nevertheless, the House of Commons expelled him in January 1764, and he fled to France. Returning to England in 1768, he won the support of the London mob with the cry of "Wilkes and Liberty." On four occasions, the voters of Middlesex elected him to the House of Commons, and on four occasions the House of Commons refused to seat him. He was not allowed to take his seat until 1774. In the Commons, he supported the cause of the American colonists and parliamentary reform. Although Wilkes was a demagogue, he became a symbol of opposition to tyranny.

Literature

Eighteenth-century English men of letters often found inspiration in the literary achievements of the ancient Greeks and Romans, and the early decades of the century came to be known as the Augustan Age, recalling the Roman Empire when it was at its height in the time of the Emperor Augustus.

Alexander Pope

Alexander Pope (1688–1744) is generally recognized as England's greatest eighteenth-century poet. He is known for his translations into English of Homer's *Iliad* (1720) and *Odyssey* (1725–1726), as well as for his original works. *The Rape of the Lock* (1714) is a mock-heroic poem poking fun at the fashionable society of the time. In a more serious vein, his *Essay on Criticism* (1711), written in heroic couplets, sets forth critical standards and tastes, while his *Essay on Man* (1734) is a summary, in poetic form, of eighteenth-century philosophical ideas.

Daniel Defoe

England also produced several noted novelists. Daniel Defoe (1659–1731) wrote *Robinson Crusoe* (1719), which some regard as the first true novel in English. *Robinson Crusoe* is the story of a man who meets the challenge of surviving on a desert island while maintaining his human integrity. Another Defoe novel, *Moll Flanders* (1722), is the tale through her own eyes of a London prostitute and thief.

Jonathan Swift

The Irish-born Jonathan Swift (1667–1745) is best known for *Gulliver's Travels* (1726), a biting political and social satire. Written in four parts, it is the story of Lemuel Gulliver's journey to Lilliput — a land of tiny inhabitants whose small size makes their pompous activities especially ridiculous — and to other mythical lands. Above all, *Gulliver's Travels* expresses Swift's contempt for the vices and follies of his fellow human beings.

Samuel Richardson

Samuel Richardson (1689–1761) wrote the two-volume novel *Pamela, or Virtue Rewarded* (1740), the tale of a virtuous household servant who escapes the lecherous advances of her employer's son. He later wrote two additional volumes, as well as a novel in seven volumes, *Clarissa Harlowe* (1747–1748), the tragic story of a young woman who runs off with the man who becomes her seducer. While Richardson was an immensely popular writer in his own time, his novels are regarded today as excessively sentimental.

Henry Fielding

A novelist and dramatist, Henry Fielding (1707–1754) is best known for *Tom Jones* (1749), a cheerful and often bawdy account of the wild adventures of its foundling hero.

Dr. Samuel Johnson

Dr. Samuel Johnson (1709–1784), who published his famous dictionary in 1755, was the dominant figure in English letters in the mid-eighteenth century, although he was more a critic than a creative artist. He was the leading figure in the Literary Club founded in 1764. The club included many prominent figures of the age, including James Boswell, Johnson's biographer; the portrait painter Sir Joshua Reynolds; the statesman Edmund Burke; the economist

Adam Smith; and such literary figures as Richard Brinsley Sheridan, Oliver Goldsmith, and Edward Gibbon.

Oliver Goldsmith

Oliver Goldsmith (c. 1730–1774), an Anglo-Irish essayist, poet, and dramatist, is known for his nostalgic pastoral poem, *The Deserted Village* (1770); for his lively comedies, *The Good-natur'd Man* (1768) and *She Stoops to Conquer* (1773); and for his only novel, *The Vicar of Wakefield* (1766).

Edward Gibbon

The historian Edward Gibbon (1737–1794) gained fame for his panoramic and polished *History of the Decline and Fall of the Roman Empire* (6 vols., 1776–1788).

Richard Brinsley Sheridan

Richard Brinsley Sheridan (1751–1816), the manager of London's famed Drury Lane Theatre, wrote witty comedies, including *The Rivals* (1775), featuring the character of Mrs. Malaprop, and *The School for Scandal* (1777).

Art

The eighteenth century was the great age of English portraiture.

Sir Joshua Reynolds

Sir Joshua Reynolds (1723–1792) produced over 2000 historical paintings and portraits. In 1768, he became the first president of the Royal Academy.

Thomas Gainsborough

Thomas Gainsborough (1727–1788) painted both portraits and landscapes. One of his most famous works is the *Blue Boy*. A founding member of the Royal Academy, Gainsborough was a successful rival of Reynolds for commissions and royal favor.

George Romney

George Romney (1734–1802) studied art in Italy and then became a portrait painter in London, where his popularity came to rival that of Reynolds. His portraits of women are particularly noteworthy.

William Hogarth

While William Hogarth (1697–1764) was a painter, he is better known as an engraver whose satirical work often depicted the seamy side of English life.

Music

John Gay

Opera was popular in eighteenth-century England. *The Beggar's Opera,* composed by John Gay (1685–1732) and first produced in 1728, was particularly successful. A satirical tale of highwaymen and thieves, it ridiculed the corruption of contemporary society in general and the government in particular.

George Frederick Handel

George Frederick Handel (1685–1759), a German-born composer, made his home in England beginning in 1712. Handel wrote close to fifty operas and developed the oratorio, a musical drama performed in concert form. The most famous of his more than thirty oratorios, *Messiah,* received its first performance in Dublin in 1742. Handel composed his well-known orchestral *Water Music* (1717) for King George I. Among his other well-known compositions is the *Music for the Royal Fireworks* (1749).

Religion

During the eighteenth century, the Church of England became increasingly formalistic and lacking in spiritual fervor. In response, John Wesley (1703–1791), an Anglican priest, founded the Methodist movement. Opposing the formalism of the established church, Methodism emphasized the development of personal piety, evangelism, and salvation through faith in Jesus Christ alone. The Methodists also worked to reduce social evils, campaigning against alcohol and the slave trade. John Wesley, his brother Charles (1707–1788), and other Methodist leaders, including George Whitefield (1714–1770) and Francis Asbury (1745–1816), won many converts in England and America. While Methodism began as a reform movement within the Church of England, it had become a separate denomination by the end of the eighteenth century.

After acceding to the throne in 1760, King George III attempted to shift the balance of political power away from the House of Commons, seeking to develop a party of King's Friends in Parliament and to make the cabinet ministers instruments of his will. Although he achieved a partial success, the authority of the House of Commons continued to grow over the course of the eighteenth century, as cabinets came increasingly to depend on the Commons for support. Robert Walpole owed his long tenure as the country's first real prime minister to his ability to manage the House of Commons, and the success or failure of the prime ministers who followed him would be measured primarily in terms of their ability to secure and maintain the support of a majority of the House of Commons.

Recommended Reading

Ayling, Stanley. *The Elder Pitt, Earl of Chatham* (1976).

Ayling, Stanley. *George the Third* (1972).

Bate, W. Jackson. *Samuel Johnson* (1977).

Black, Jeremy, ed. *Britain in the Age of Walpole* (1985).

Carswell, John. *The South Sea Bubble* (1960).

Colley, Linda. *In Defiance of Oligarchy: The Tory Party, 1714–60* (1982).

Foord, Archibald S. *His Majesty's Opposition, 1714–1830* (1964).

Hatton, Ragnhild. *George I: Elector and King* (1978).

Humphreys, A. R. *The Augustan World: Society, Thought, and Letters in Eighteenth-Century England* (1954).

Kelch, Ray. *Newcastle: A Duke Without Money* (1974).

Kemp, Betty. *Sir Robert Walpole* (1976).

Kramnick, Isaac. *Bolingbroke and His Circle* (1968).

Kronenberger, Louis. *The Extraordinary Mr. Wilkes* (1974).

Lang, Paul Henry. *George Frederick Handel* (1970).

Lawson, Philip. *George Grenville: A Political Life* (1984).

Mack, Maynard. *Alexander Pope* (1986).

Marshall, Dorothy. *Eighteenth-Century England, 1714–1783* (2nd ed., 1975).

Moody, T. W. and W. E. Vaughan, eds. *Eighteenth-Century Ireland, 1691–1800* (1986).

Namier, L. B. *The Structure of Politics at the Accession of George III,* 2 vols. (2nd ed., 1967).

O'Gorman, Frank. *The Emergence of the British Two-Party System, 1760–1832* (1982).

Owen, John B. *The Rise of the Pelhams* (1957).

Pares, Richard. *King George III and the Politicians* (1953).

Paulson, Ronald. *Emblem and Expression: Meaning in English Art of the Eighteenth Century* (1975).

Plumb, John H. *England in the Eighteenth Century* (1963).

Porter, R. *English Society in the Eighteenth Century* (1982).

Reitan, E. A., ed. *George III: Tyrant or Constitutional Monarch* (1964).

Semmel, Bernard. *The Methodist Revolution* (1974).

Speck, W. A. *The Butcher: The Duke of Cumberland and the Suppression of the '45* (1981).

Speck, W. A. *Society and Literature in England, 1700–60* (1984).

Thomas, Peter D. G. *Lord North* (1975).

Waterhouse, Ellis. *Painting in Britain, 1530–1790* (4th ed., 1978).

Watson, J. Steven. *The Reign of George III, 1760–1815* (1960).

Wilkes, John W. *A Whig in Power: The Political Career of Henry Pelham* (1964).

Williams, Basil. *The Whig Supremacy, 1714–1760* (2nd ed., 1962).

CHAPTER 12

The Eighteenth Century: Empire and Politics

Time Line

1718	Austria, France, and the Netherlands join Great Britain in the Quadruple Alliance
1739	The War of Jenkins's Ear begins
1740–1748	The War of the Austrian Succession
1748	The Peace of Aix-la-Chapelle ends the War of the Austrian Succession
1756	The diplomatic revolution occurs, as Prussia forms an alliance with Great Britain while Austria becomes allied with France
1756–1763	The Seven Years' War

1757	Robert Clive's forces defeat the French in the Battle of Plassey
1758	American colonists take Fort Duquesne in western Pennsylvania
1763	The Treaty of Paris ends the Seven Years' War
1765	Parliament passes the Stamp Act
1773	Colonial protesters stage the Boston Tea Party
1774	Parliament passes the Quebec Act and the Intolerable Acts
1775	The American Revolution begins
1776	The Continental Congress approves the Declaration of Independence
1777	The Americans defeat General John Burgoyne's army at Saratoga
1778	France enters the war in support of the Americans
1781	The Americans defeat Lord Cornwallis at Yorktown
1782	The Renunciation Act makes the Irish Parliament independent of the British Parliament
1783	The Treaty of Paris confirms the independence of the thirteen former colonies as the United States
	William Pitt the Younger becomes prime minister
1784	Parliament passes the India Act, establishing dual control by the British government and the East India Company
1791	An act of Parliament divides Quebec into Upper and Lower Canada

The peace settlement of 1713–1714, which ended the War of the Spanish Succession, brought only an armistice in the conflict between Great Britain and France. During the eighteenth century, in the War of the Austrian Succession and the Seven Years' War, the

British supported their continental allies in the effort to maintain the European balance of power. Victory in the Seven Years' War resulted in the British acquisition of a number of French possessions in the western hemisphere, including Canada. In Asia, Great Britain replaced France as the dominant power in India. In the American Revolution, however, the thirteen British colonies along the eastern seaboard of North America made good their claim to independence.

Following the American Revolution, the British confronted some serious domestic issues, including demands for reform, problems in Ireland, and problems elsewhere in the empire, such as in India and in Canada. The appointment of William Pitt the Younger as prime minister at the end of 1783 marked the emergence of a political leader who would leave a powerful mark on his country and Europe.

Great Power Rivalries in the Early Eighteenth Century

The Quadruple Alliance

The treaties signed in 1713–1714 concluding the War of the Spanish Succession brought only a temporary cessation in a long period of warfare among the European powers. In an effort to maintain peace, Great Britain made an alliance with Austria in 1716 and signed a treaty with France the same year and with the Netherlands in 1717.

Believing that the peace settlement of 1713–1714 had made Austria too powerful in Italy, Spain attacked the Austrians in Italy. In 1718, the Quadruple Alliance of Great Britain, Austria, France, and the Netherlands went to war in an effort to restrain the Spanish. The French invaded northeastern Spain, while the British destroyed a Spanish fleet in the Mediterranean. The war ended in 1720, and the following year, Spain joined the Quadruple Alliance.

The War of the Polish Succession (1733–1735)

This alliance remained in effect until 1733, when the War of the Polish Succession broke out. French efforts to install their candidate on the Polish throne encountered the opposition of Austria and Russia.

Prime Minister Robert Walpole (1676–1745) resisted pressure from the Austrians, King George II, and much of the British public and refused to enter the war. Walpole then helped arrange the peace settlement of 1735, which recognized Augustus III (r. 1735–1763), the Austro-Russian choice, as Poland's king.

The War of Jenkins's Ear

In 1739, war broke out between Great Britain and Spain. The conflict quickly became a wider war between Great Britain and the French and Spanish Bourbons. This conflict continued, with interruptions, until the final defeat of Napoleon I in 1815. This "Second Hundred Years' War" had, in fact, begun in the late seventeenth century, during the time of King Louis XIV.

Causes of the War

The issue in 1739 involved a dispute over British trade with the Spanish colonies in America. The *Asiento* privilege, awarded to Great Britain by the Treaty of Utrecht of 1713 (see Chapter 10), gave the British a monopoly of the slave trade in the Spanish colonies, as well as the right to send one ship a year to Spanish America for other trade. In an effort to expand their trade, British sea captains engaged in smuggling, which evoked a firm response from the Spanish. In 1738, one of these sea captains, Robert Jenkins, displayed his ear to the House of Commons, claiming that it had been cut off by the Spanish at Havana in 1731.

First Phase of the War

The Whigs in Parliament, who represented British commercial interests, called for war with Spain. Despite Prime Minister Robert Walpole's efforts to restrain anti-Spanish sentiment among his fellow Whigs, Great Britain declared war in October 1739. France soon entered the war in support of Spain.

Early in the war, the British seized Porto Bello in the West Indies from the Spanish, but further expeditions to the West Indies accomplished little.

The War of the Austrian Succession (1740–1748)

The War of Jenkins's Ear quickly became part of a general European war that began in the wake of the efforts of Prussia's new king,

Frederick the Great (r. 1740–1786), to take Silesia from Maria Theresa (r. 1740–1780) of Austria.

During the War of the Austrian Succession, Prussia, France, Spain, Bavaria, and Saxony fought Austria, Great Britain, and the Netherlands.

The Continental War

Intervention of Frederick the Great

In 1742, the anti-Austrian alliance collapsed when Prussia concluded a separate peace with Austria. Maria Theresa agreed to recognize Prussia's acquisition of Silesia. Then, when Austria began to win battles over her other enemies, Frederick the Great feared that Maria Theresa might attempt to regain Silesia and so he reentered the war. After compelling the Austrians once again to recognize his conquest of Silesia, Frederick dropped out of the war in December 1745.

British Participation

While the British provided financial assistance to Austria, they had little impact on the war on the continent, although in 1743, King George II led an army into battle against the French. The last English monarch to command troops in the field, he defeated the French in the Battle of Dettingen. Two years later, the British were defeated at Fortenoy in Flanders.

The Colonial War

For the most part, the British focused their attention on the colonial war against France.

North America and the West Indies

In North America, the Anglo-French conflict was known as King George's War. The French used their stronghold at Louisburg, at the mouth of the St. Lawrence River, as a base of operations for assaults on Nova Scotia and Massachusetts. In 1745, British troops and the Massachusetts militia counterattacked, capturing Louisburg. British ships could now sail up the St. Lawrence River and threaten Quebec. To the south, in the West Indies, British naval action disrupted France's profitable trade with her sugar islands.

India

The British navy also disrupted French trade in the Indian Ocean. In retaliation, Joseph François Dupleix (1697–1763), the governor of the French East India Company, took the British trading station at Madras in India in 1746.

The Peace of Aix-la-Chapelle (1748)

Territorial Adjustments

The War of the Austrian Succession ended in 1748 when the exhausted antagonists signed the Peace of Aix-la-Chapelle. The peace settlement attempted to restore the balance of power that had been established after the War of the Spanish Succession. Although Prussia retained Silesia, all other conquests, both in Europe and overseas, were restored to their former owners. In the New World, France regained Louisburg, while in India, Madras was returned to the British East India Company. In addition, Spain renewed the *Asiento* agreement with Great Britain.

Dynastic Recognitions

The peace settlement recognized Maria Theresa's right to inherit the Hapsburg domains and confirmed her husband, Francis I (r. 1745–1765), as Holy Roman emperor. The settlement also recognized the rights of the House of Hanover, the British royal family, to its lands in northern Germany.

Continued Colonial Unrest

While the Peace of Aix-la-Chapelle confirmed the emergence of Prussia as a European great power, it did not provide an enduring resolution of the colonial conflict between Great Britain and France. In the years after 1748, clashes between American and French settlers occurred in northern New England and the Ohio River valley, while in India, the French and British East India Companies continued their conflict by supporting rival Indian princes.

The Diplomatic Revolution

As an uneasy peace prevailed in the years after 1748, a diplomatic revolution took place in Europe. Fearing a conflict between

Russia and Prussia for control of the Baltic Sea and Poland, Prussia's King Frederick the Great decided to seek an alliance with the British. Under the terms of the Convention of Westminster, signed in January 1756, Frederick promised Great Britain that he would not move against Hanover, the German kingdom ruled by the English monarch.

The Austrians, for their part, hoped to retake Silesia from the Prussians. Seeking a more effective military ally than Great Britain, they concluded an alliance with France in May 1756, ending for a time the traditional rivalry between France and the Hapsburgs. The Russians soon joined the Franco-Austrian alliance.

As a result of the diplomatic revolution, Great Britain and Prussia faced Austria, France, and Russia. Despite this reversal of alliances, the basic antagonisms remained: Prussia versus Austria and Great Britain versus France.

The Seven Years' War (1756–1763)

Like the earlier War of the Austrian Succession, the Seven Years' War involved both a continental war and a colonial conflict.

The War on the Continent

The continental war began in August 1756, when Frederick the Great of Prussia invaded Austria's ally, the kingdom of Saxony. Frederick believed he was fighting a preventive war, attacking before his enemies could move against him. Confronting the powerful alliance of Austria, France, Russia, and Saxony, Frederick faced the greatest crisis of his career and suffered defeat in several battles.

British Support for Prussia

While the British could provide no direct military assistance to their Prussian ally, they did contribute substantial financial support. By strengthening Prussia, the British hoped to divert France's resources away from the colonial war overseas. Frederick also benefited from France's inability to fight both a continental and a colonial war simultaneously.

The Treaty of Hubertusburg (1763)

The Treaty of Hubertusburg, signed in February 1763, confirmed Prussia's possession of Silesia.

The Colonial War

In the colonial war against Great Britain, King Louis XV (r. 1715–1774) of France won the support of Spain's Bourbon King Ferdinand VI (r. 1746–1759).

British Losses

At first, the war went badly for the British. They quickly lost the Mediterranean island of Minorca, while in North America, where the war was known as the French and Indian War, they failed in their attempt to take Louisburg. In addition, the British lost Fort Oswego on Lake Ontario.

The Black Hole of Calcutta

In India, the Anglo-French struggle resulted in a notorious event: The princely ruler of Bengal, an ally of the French, imprisoned 146 British captives in a small room. By morning, only 23 had survived what became known as the Black Hole of Calcutta.

William Pitt the Elder

The British finally found the war leader they needed in the person of William Pitt the Elder (see Chapter 11). From 1757 to 1761, Pitt's war ministry secured loans from London bankers to help pay the cost of the war, provided increased financial assistance to Frederick the Great, and replaced incompetent military and naval commanders.

British Victories

Naval Successes. The British benefited from their control of the sea. They raided the coasts of France, capturing the port of Cherbourg in Normandy and destroying its forts. In 1759, Admiral Edward Hawke (1705–1781) defeated the French at Quiberon Bay off the coast of Brittany, nearly destroying the French Atlantic fleet and ending the threat of a French invasion of the British Isles. The same year, Admiral Edward Boscawen (1711–1761) smashed the French Mediterranean fleet in Lagos Bay on the coast of West Africa. The British then seized the French West African colonies of Senegal and Goree.

While the British were able to maintain their profitable trade, their naval action reduced French commerce by about 80 percent in the period from 1755 to 1760. With their inadequate navy, the French could not provide adequate supplies and reinforcements to their colonies.

India.   The tide in the colonial war began to turn in Britain's favor. In India, the British punished France's ally, Surajah Dowlah, the ruler of Bengal, for the Black Hole of Calcutta. In June 1757, an army of 3000 Indian and British troops, commanded by Robert Clive (1725-1774), defeated Surajah Dowlah's army of 50,000 men in the Battle of Plassey. In 1760, Sir Eyre Coote defeated the French fleet commanded by the Comte de Lally (1702-1766) at Wandewash.

West Indies and North America.   In the West Indies, the British seized the major French sugar islands, including Guadaloupe. In North America, the American colonists took Fort Duquesne in western Pennsylvania in November 1758, renaming it first Fort Pitt and then Pittsburgh in honor of William Pitt. The colonists also seized Fort Oswego and Fort Frontenac on Lake Ontario. Further to the north, General James Wolfe (1727-1759) took Louisburg in July 1758 and then advanced up the St. Lawrence River. In September 1759, both Wolfe and the French commander, Lieutenant General Louis Joseph Montcalm (1712-1759), were killed on the Plains of Abraham as the British moved to take Quebec. Montreal fell to the British in September 1760.

War with Spain

In 1762, Great Britain went to war against Spain, fearing Spanish intervention in support of France. The British occupied Havana, the capital of Cuba, and an expedition dispatched from India took Manila in the Philippines.

The Treaty of Paris (1763)

British Acquisitions from France

The great colonial conflict ended with the British winning a decisive victory over France. Under the terms of the Treaty of Paris, signed in February 1763, the British acquired French Canada and the land between the Appalachian Mountains and the Mississippi River.

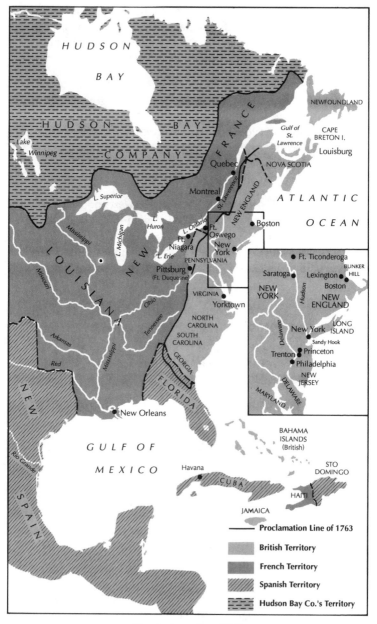

North America, 1754

Little was left of the French empire in the New World. The French retained a few islands in the West Indies, including Martinique and Guadaloupe, as well as the islands of St. Pierre and Miquelon off the coast of Canada. The French also held fishing rights off Newfoundland. In India, the British also established their dominance, although French trading stations remained at Pondichéry and Chandernagor. In West Africa, the British retained Senegal.

Settlement with Spain

From Spain, France's ally, the British received Florida, including a strip of land along the Gulf of Mexico extending westward to the Mississippi River. Having acquired Florida, the British returned Havana and Manila to the Spanish. As compensation for the Spanish loss of Florida, France turned over to Spain the city of New Orleans and the Louisiana territory west of the Mississippi River.

The American Revolution (1775–1783)

The Origins of the Revolution

While the Seven Years' War resulted in a considerable expansion of the British Empire, Great Britain would soon lose an important part of that empire: the thirteen colonies along the Atlantic seaboard of North America.

Colonists' Desire to Expand

The British conquest of French Canada had eliminated the American colonists' fear of French aggression, thereby reducing their need for British protection. At the same time, the colonists objected to a royal proclamation issued in October 1763, prohibiting them from establishing settlements in the newly acquired lands west of the Appalachian Mountains. While the British sought to avoid conflict with the Indians of the area, the colonists wanted to be free to exploit the new lands.

Objections to British Economic Interference

A number of other factors contributed to the growing conflict between the American colonists and Great Britain. The Seven Years' War had left the British with a substantial national debt, and the British government also had to bear the continuing costs of protecting the frontier in America. The colonists objected both to new taxes levied by the British and to Britain's mercantilist policies (see Chapter 14), which placed restrictions on trade conducted by the colonists.

The Stamp Act

The Stamp Act of 1765 required that revenue stamps be placed on legal documents, newspapers, playing cards, and other items. The income was to be used mainly to cover the cost of maintaining troops in the colonies. In October 1765, protesting colonists held the Stamp Act Congress in New York, which proclaimed the famous doctrine of "no taxation without representation." In 1766, the British Parliament repealed the Stamp Act but insisted in the Declaratory Act that it possessed the authority to legislate for the colonies.

Other Tariffs and
the Boston Tea Party

The Sugar Act of 1764 imposed tariffs on the importation of sugar and molasses, and in 1767 the British imposed tariffs on tea, paint, lead, and paper. The colonists' protests led to the repeal of the tariffs in 1770, with the exception of the tariff on tea, which the British retained as a symbol of Parliament's right to levy taxes in the colonies. In December 1773, a group of protesters staged the Boston Tea Party, assaulting three ships of the British East India Company in Boston harbor and dumping chests of tea overboard.

The Intolerable Acts

In 1774, as punishment for the destruction of British property, Parliament passed the Coercive Acts, known to the colonists as the Intolerable Acts. These acts closed the port of Boston to commerce, reorganized the colonial government of Massachusetts, authorized the quartering of troops in private homes, and provided that persons accused of capital crimes could be removed from Massachusetts for trial.

The Quebec Act

Parliament also angered the colonists by adopting the Quebec Act of 1774, which joined the lands in the Ohio River valley with

Canada, subjecting them to direct British rule. The colonists regarded this as a further effort to prevent their movement into the lands west of the Appalachians.

Committees of Correspondence and the Continental Congress

In March 1773, Virginia established a Committee of Correspondence to keep in touch with the situation and attitudes in other colonies. By February 1774, similar committees had been established in all of the colonies, with the exception of Pennsylvania.

In September 1774, the first Continental Congress assembled in Philadelphia.

The Struggle for Independence

The American Revolution began at Lexington and Concord, Massachusetts, in April 1775. In June, General George Washington (1732–1799) became commander-in-chief of the Continental army.

British forces commanded by General Thomas Gage (1721–1787) evacuated Boston in March 1776, but the colonists failed in their effort to conquer Canada during the winter of 1775–1776.

The Declaration of Independence

Although the early stages of the war proved indecisive, the Continental Congress declared American independence in July 1776.

Early Battles

As the war intensified, General William Howe (1729–1814) replaced Gage as the British commander in America. In August 1776, Howe defeated Washington in the Battle of Long Island. In September, the British occupied New York, which became the main British base. During the winter of 1776–1777, Washington's army rallied, defeating the British in New Jersey at Trenton in December 1776 and at Princeton in January 1777.

The Battle of Saratoga (1777)

During 1777, the British sought to divide the colonies by taking control of the area running north along the Hudson River and Lake Champlain in New York. General John Burgoyne (1722–1792) advanced southward from Canada, planning to join forces with Howe, who was to move up the Hudson. However, Howe had occupied Philadelphia and delayed his advance. In October, the colonists defeated Burgoyne's army at Saratoga, New York, in a battle that marked the turning point in the war.

American Alliances

In February 1778, the colonists concluded an alliance with France. In 1779, Spain entered the war against Great Britain, and the Netherlands went to war against the British in 1780. As the war broadened, the British lost Minorca in the Mediterranean, most of Florida, two islands in the Caribbean, and trading stations on the African coast. British fear of a French invasion forced them to keep troops at home that otherwise could have been sent to reinforce their army in America.

The Battle of Yorktown

In 1778, General Henry Clinton (c. 1738–1795) replaced Howe as the British commander in America, and the theater of operations shifted to the southern colonies. During the summer of 1781, Lord Cornwallis (1738–1805) moved from the Carolinas to Yorktown, Virginia, hoping that supplies could reach him by sea. In September, a French fleet commanded by Admiral François de Grasse (1722–1788) defeated the British in the Battle of Chesapeake Bay, thereby preventing reinforcements from reaching Cornwallis. In October, Cornwallis lost the Battle of Yorktown to a combined American and French army.

Impact on the British Government

After news of Cornwallis's defeat at Yorktown reached London, Parliament adopted a resolution in early 1782 calling for an end of the war in America. Recognizing the failure of both the British war effort in America and King George III's attempt to dominate Parliament, Lord North resigned as prime minister.

The Marquess of Rockingham, a Whig, returned to the prime ministership (see Chapter 11) and began peace negotiations.

Peace Treaties

The Treaty of Versailles (1783)

Territorial Changes.   Under the terms of the Treaty of Versailles of 1783, which the British signed with France and Spain, the French regained the islands of St. Pierre and Miquelon, as well as the islands of Tobago and St. Lucia in the West Indies. The French also recovered Senegal in West Africa and their trading stations on the coast of India. Spain acquired Florida and the Mediterranean island of Minorca and returned the Bahamas to Great Britain.

Effects on France.   While the French had supported the American cause in order to gain revenge for losses suffered to the British in the Seven Years' War, the cost of the war put further strains on French finances and thus contributed to the problems of the French monarchy that culminated in the French Revolution of 1789.

The Treaty of Paris (1783)

In the Treaty of Paris, signed in September 1783, the British formally recognized the independence of the thirteen colonies as the United States of America. The boundaries of the new United States were set at the Great Lakes, the Mississippi River, and the northern border of Florida. The Americans also acquired fishing rights off Newfoundland.

British Politics
in the Late Eighteenth Century

Beginning of Parliamentary Reform

Demands for Correction of Abuses

During the years of the American Revolution, demands for parliamentary reform had been mounting. In the late eighteenth century, Parliament was not truly representative of the people. Not only was the right to vote for members of the House of Commons restricted, but population shifts had resulted in the creation of many rotten boroughs (towns with very small populations whose voters could readily be bribed or otherwise influenced) and pocket boroughs (towns whose representatives in the House of Commons were selected by noble landowners).

In 1776, John Wilkes (see Chapter 11) had introduced a bill for parliamentary reform in the House of Commons, but it failed to receive serious consideration.

Economical Reform Acts

In 1780, the House of Commons adopted a resolution proposed by John Dunning (1731–1783) seeking to curtail the Crown's ability to influence Parliament. In 1782, the Rockingham Whigs passed two Economical Reform Bills that reduced the number of sinecures (positions requiring little or no work) that the government could award its followers in the House of Commons. This substantially lessened the ability of the Crown and the cabinet to distribute bribes to members of Parliament. However, a proposal for the reapportionment of seats in the House of Commons failed to win approval.

The Gordon Riots

The late eighteenth century also witnessed a resurgence of anti-Roman Catholic sentiment in England. In 1779, Lord George Gordon (1751–1793) became the leader of the Protestant Association that had been created to agitate for the repeal of the Catholic Relief Act of 1778. This act had relieved English Catholics of restrictions on the inheritance and purchase of land.

On June 2, 1780, Gordon led a large crowd to present a petition to Parliament. What began as a peaceful demonstration quickly turned into a riot that devastated London for a week. Some 800 people were killed or injured. Although twenty-one rioters were executed, Gordon won acquittal.

End of the Rockingham Ministry

Whig Factions

The cabinet headed by the Marquess of Rockingham (see p. 198), which was weakened by its initiation of negotiations with the Americans soon after it came to power in early 1782, was further undermined by a conflict between the earl of Shelburne, Rockingham's ally, and Charles James Fox (1749–1806), the leader of the young Whigs. When the Whigs split into two factions, King George III sought to take advantage of the dispute.

Defection of Fox

Following Rockingham's death, Fox resigned from the cabinet in July 1782, refusing to serve under Shelburne, the new prime minister.

Fox now formed an alliance with the Tory Lord North, whom he had earlier bitterly opposed.

The Fox-North Ministry

In April 1783, Shelburne was defeated in Parliament. Much to the king's displeasure, Fox and North now established a new ministry, with the duke of Portland (1738–1809) serving as prime minister. George III regarded North as a traitor and strongly disliked Fox, regarding him as the most dangerous of the Whig leaders and believing that his debauchery was a bad influence on the Prince of Wales (later King George IV).

When Fox proposed a reform of the East India Company, the king used his personal influence to secure the bill's defeat in the House of Lords. This defeat gave the king an excuse to dismiss the ministry in December 1783.

The Ministry of William Pitt the Younger

William Pitt the Younger (1759–1806), the leader of the resurgent Tories, now became prime minister at the age of twenty-five. He remained the leading figure in British politics and government until his death in 1806.

Attaining a Parliamentary Majority

While Pitt was acceptable to the king, he initially lacked the backing of a majority in Parliament. With the king's support, he survived a series of defeats in the House of Commons while he gradually reduced the Fox-North majority. The election of 1784 gave Pitt a working majority in the Commons, and the king created new peers to break the Whigs' hold on the House of Lords. The long supremacy of the Whigs came to an end, and an era of Tory domination of British political life began.

In 1787–1788, the temporary insanity of King George III presented a threat to Pitt. If the Prince of Wales became regent, Pitt feared, he would name his friend, Charles James Fox, to the prime ministership. When the king suddenly regained his sanity, the threat was removed.

Financial Reforms

The American Revolution had almost doubled Britain's national debt and threatened the government's credit. Pitt's budgets from

1784 to 1787 brought much-needed reforms of state finances and served to increase public confidence. The prime minister established an auditing commission to supervise government finances. In addition, he simplified the complicated system of tax collection and reformed and reduced tariffs, thereby discouraging smuggling, which was no longer profitable. Increases in revenue soon led to budgetary surpluses, and in 1786, Pitt created a sinking fund whose interest was used to pay off the public debt.

Pitt also strove to reduce the mercantilist restrictions on foreign trade. In 1786, the British signed a reciprocal trade treaty with France, providing for mutual reductions of tariffs on many imports. This treaty marked the first step on Britain's road to a free-trade policy.

Other Reform Efforts

During the 1780s, Pitt sought to win approval of other reforms.

In 1785, the prime minister proposed a bill for the redistribution of seats in the House of Commons. Pitt's bill would have abolished some thirty-five rotten boroughs and assigned the seats to the counties and to boroughs with large populations. When the bill was defeated, Pitt abandoned the issue, since he did not want to endanger his majority by antagonizing Parliament unduly.

Pitt also failed in his efforts to secure the repeal of restrictions on the political rights of Nonconformists and Roman Catholics.

Abolition of the Slave Trade

In the Sommersett Case of 1772, the earl of Mansfield (1705–1793), the lord chief justice, ruled that a slave brought to England by a West Indies planter was automatically free, since the law did not permit slavery in Great Britain. British opponents of slavery now began a campaign to end the slave trade and slavery itself throughout the British Empire. In the House of Commons, William Wilberforce (1759–1833), Pitt's political ally, led the effort.

In 1787, a group of emancipated slaves from the West Indies was settled in Sierra Leone in West Africa, but the issue remained unresolved.

Although Pitt endorsed bills for the abolition of the slave trade, he did not work actively for their passage. In 1807, after Pitt's death, Parliament abolished the slave trade. This was the only significant reform to win parliamentary approval during the years of conflict with France.

Ireland

During the eighteenth century, the Irish continued their long struggle against Poynings's Acts of 1494 that prevented the election of a free Irish Parliament (see Chapter 7).

Although Parliament voted in 1780 to allow Ireland to trade freely with the West Indies and Europe, Ireland's fundamental grievances remained. In 1782, when the Rockingham ministry came to power, Henry Grattan (1746–1820) secured the repeal of Poynings's Acts. The following year, Fox and North won parliamentary approval of the Renunciation Act, which made the Irish Parliament and courts independent of the British Parliament. Nevertheless, the Irish executive was still to be appointed from London, and friction continued.

India

The British triumph over the French in India (see p. 195) had converted the East India Company from merely a large trading company into the dominant power in the Indian subcontinent. Governors named by the company ruled at Madras, Calcutta, and Bombay without any clearly defined responsibility to the British government.

Following an investigation of the East India Company's activities by the House of Commons, Lord North won approval of the Regulating Act of 1773, which established a British governor general who was responsible to a resident council of four members appointed by Parliament. Nevertheless, the company's power was left largely intact.

Warren Hastings

Warren Hastings (1732–1818) was the first governor-general under the Regulating Act. He strengthened the East India Company's dominant position by waging a successful war against Indian princes who were backed by the French. Despite his achievements, Hastings was criticized for his arbitrary methods and the high cost of his administration. Accused of misgoverning India, Hastings was summoned home in 1785 to face impeachment charges. The trial, with a number of postponements, lasted for seven years, from 1788 to 1795. While Hastings was eventually acquitted, the trial convinced Parliament of the need for Great Britain to assume greater responsibility for India if it intended to maintain its dominant position there.

The India Act of 1784

Pitt won parliamentary approval of the India Act of 1784, which established dual control of India by the British government and the East India Company. While the government assumed overall direction of political and military affairs in India, the company retained control of trade, as well as the authority to appoint all officials, except the governor general. However, a new Board of Control, based in London and headed by a secretary of state, supervised the administration of India and had the authority to remove officials appointed by the company. The system established by the 1784 act remained in effect until the Indian Mutiny of 1858 (see Chapter 17).

During the governorships of Lord Cornwallis, who served from 1786 to 1793, and Richard Wellesley (1760–1842), whose term lasted from 1798 to 1805, pro-French elements were defeated and India enjoyed efficient government.

Colonial Policy

Canada

The Quebec Act

Although the British took control of Canada at the end of the Seven Years' War (see p. 193), the country remained overwhelmingly French in population. The Quebec Act of 1774 (see pp. 196–197) recognized French law and the Roman Catholic religion and extended the boundaries of Quebec far to the southwest in an effort to provide greater protection to both the Indians and fur traders.

Division into Two Provinces

During and after the American Revolution, some 40,000 Loyalists fled the United States and took refuge in Canada, where they quickly became unhappy with the political and religious provisions of the Quebec Act.

In 1791, an act of Parliament divided Quebec into Upper and Lower Canada (present-day Ontario and Quebec, respectively), with the Loyalists dominant in Upper Canada, and the French settlers in Lower Canada. Each province had its own lieutenant governor, an appointed upper house, an elected representative assembly, and freedom of religion.

Australia

In 1769, Captain James Cook (1728-1779) discovered Australia, and two decades later, in 1788, the first 750 British settlers, most of whom were convicts, established Sydney. In the eighteenth century, few questioned the practice of transporting convicts, and for many convicts themselves, being transported to Australia was better than being confined to a British prison. By the time the practice was ended in 1832, some 170,000 convicts had been transported to Australia.

Foreign Affairs

Alliance with the Netherlands and Prussia

While Pitt focused his attention primarily on domestic issues and imperial issues, he did act to end Britain's diplomatic isolation by forming the Triple Alliance of 1788 with the Netherlands and Prussia. This alliance was designed to block French efforts to expand their influence in the Netherlands.

The Near East

Pitt also opposed Russia's expansionist policy in the Near East at the expense of the Ottoman Empire. In 1791, however, Parliament refused to allow Pitt to intervene directly in the region. However, Pitt's efforts laid the foundation for the future British policy of supporting the Turks against Russian expansionism.

Spain

In 1791, Spain threatened the British settlement at Nootka Sound on Vancouver Island, which the Spanish claimed by right of discovery. Pitt was prepared to go to war to defend Britain's position, but the Spanish abandoned their claim when it became clear that events in France would prevent the French monarchy from coming to the aid of its fellow Bourbons in Spain.

Although the British defeat in the American Revolution is often seen as marking the end of the First British Empire, Great Britain's gains at the expense of France during the eighteenth century left the

British in possession of a substantial empire. Nevertheless, the loss of the thirteen American colonies caused many in Great Britain to question the value of overseas possessions. As a result, the British displayed relatively little interest in colonial expansion during the early nineteenth century.

In the late eighteenth century, the British confronted colonial problems in India and Canada and, closer to home, in Ireland. In domestic affairs, movements for parliamentary reform and for the abolition of the slave trade gained momentum. But as the eighteenth century drew to a close, the greatest challenge to Great Britain was posed by the revolution in France.

Recommended Reading

Alden, John R. *The American Revolution, 1775–1783* (1954).

Black, Jeremy. *British Foreign Policy in the Age of Walpole* (1985).

Cannon, John. *The Fox-North Coalition* (1971).

Christie, Ian. *Crisis of Empire: Great Britain and the American Colonies, 1754–1783* (1966).

Christie, Ian and Benjamin W. Labaree. *Empire or Independence, 1760–1776* (1976).

Derry, John. *Charles James Fox* (1972).

Derry, John. *English Politics and the American Revolution* (1976).

Donoughue, Bernard. *British Politics and the American Revolution: The Path to War, 1773–1775* (1964).

Dorn, Walter L. *Competition for Empire, 1740–1763* (1940).

Ehrman, John. *The Younger Pitt: The Years of Acclaim* (1969).

Ehrman, John. *The Younger Pitt: The Reluctant Transition* (1983).

Furneaux, Robin. *William Wilberforce* (1974).

Gipson, Lawrence H. *The British Empire Before the American Revolution*, 15 vols. (1958–1970).

Hargrove, Richard J. *General John Burgoyne* (1983).

Hibbert, Christopher. *King Mob: The Story of Lord George Gordon and the Riots of 1780* (1958).

Horn, D. B. *Great Britain and Europe in the Eighteenth Century* (1967).

Jarrett, Derek. *Pitt the Younger* (1974).

Jones, J. R. *Britain and the World, 1649–1815* (1980).

Liss, Peggy. *Atlantic Empires: The Network of Trade and Revolution, 1713–1826* (1983).

McKay, Derek and H. M. Scott. *The Rise of the Great Powers, 1648–1815* (1983).

Mackesy, Piers. *The War for America, 1775–1783* (1965).

Marshall, P. J. *Problems of Empire: Britain and India, 1757–1813* (1968).

Namier, L. B. *England in the Age of the American Revolution* (2nd ed., 1961).

Parry, J. H. *Trade and Dominion: The European Overseas Empires in the Eighteenth Century* (1971).

Ritcheson, Charles R. *British Politics and the American Revolution* (1954).

Roberts, Penfield. *The Quest for Security, 1715–1740* (1947).

Sutherland, Lucy. *The East India Company in Eighteenth Century Politics* (1952).

Thomas, P. D. G. *British Politics and the Stamp Act Crisis* (1975).

Tucker, Robert W. and David C. Hendrickson. *The Fall of the First British Empire* (1982).

Wallace, Willard M. *Appeal to Arms: A Military History of the American Revolution* (1951).

Ward, Christopher. *The War of the Revolution*, 2 vols. (1965).

Willcox, William B. *Portrait of a General: Sir Henry Clinton in the War of Independence* (1964).

CHAPTER 13

Great Britain, the French Revolution, and Napoleon

Time Line

1789	The French Revolution begins
1790	Edmund Burke publishes *Reflections on the Revolution in France*
1792	France declares war on Austria; Prussia enters the war on Austria's side
1792–1797	The War of the First Coalition is fought
1793	The French revolutionaries execute King Louis XVI
	War breaks out between Great Britain and France
1795	Parliament passes the Treasonable and Seditious Practices Act and the Seditious Assemblies Act

1797	Austria makes peace with France; Great Britain continues fighting without allies
	The British navy defeats the French and their allies at Cape St. Vincent and Camperdown
1798	Lord Nelson defeats the French navy in the Battle of the Nile
1799	Napoleon Bonaparte seizes power in France
1799–1800	The Combination Acts outlaw trade unions
1799–1801	The War of the Second Coalition is fought
1800	The Act of Union of 1800 abolishes the Irish Parliament and provides for Irish representation in the British Parliament
1802	Great Britain and France sign the Treaty of Amiens
1805–1807	The War of the Third Coalition is fought
1805	Lord Nelson defeats the French and Spanish fleets at Trafalgar
	Austria signs the Treaty of Pressburg with France
1806	William Pitt the Younger dies; the Ministry of All the Talents is formed
	Napoleon initiates the Continental System
1807	Prussia and Russia sign the Treaties of Tilsit with France
	Parliament abolishes the slave trade
	France invades Portugal and Spain
1812	The earl of Liverpool becomes prime minister
	Napoleon invades Russia
1812–1814	Great Britain and the United States fight the War of 1812
1813	Napoleon is defeated in the Battle of the Nations

1814	Napoleon abdicates
	The Treaty of Ghent ends the War of 1812
1814–1815	The Congress of Vienna meets
1815	Napoleon regains power
	Napoleon is defeated at Waterloo
	The Quadruple Alliance is signed

*The outbreak of the French Revolution in 1789 initiated a genera-
tion of warfare in Europe. When revolutionary France executed its
king, advanced into the Low Countries, and threatened British control of the English Channel, Great Britain went to war against
France in 1793. The conflict lasted, with brief intervals of peace, for
over twenty years.*

*At home, the French Revolution raised fears of radicalism and
effectively ended British movements for reform.*

The French Revolution

The Estates General

In July 1788, as the French government faced bankruptcy, King
Louis XVI (r. 1774–1792) decided to summon into session the
Estates General, a consultative assembly that had held its last meeting in 1614. The Estates General represented the three legally defined
classes (estates). The First Estate consisted of the clergy, while the
nobility comprised the Second Estate. The Third Estate included all
who were not clergy or nobility, primarily the middle class (the
bourgeoisie), the peasants, and the urban workers.

The National Assembly

The Estates General held its first meeting at Versailles in early
May 1789. On June 17, the increasingly rebellious Third Estate
defied the king and proclaimed itself to be the National Assembly.
In the Tennis Court Oath, the members of the National Assembly
vowed that they would not disband until they had given France a con-

stitution. A number of liberal aristocrats and a large part of the First Estate, especially parish priests, joined the National Assembly.

With the support of the Paris mob, the National Assembly succeeded in imposing its will on the king.

Declaration of the Rights of Man

In August 1789, the National Assembly approved the Declaration of the Rights of Man, proclaiming that all men were "born and remain free and equal in rights." More specifically, the declaration provided for freedom of speech and of the press, freedom of assembly and the right to petition the government, freedom of religion, and freedom from arbitrary arrest and imprisonment.

The Civil Constitution of the Clergy

In November 1789, in an attempt to deal with the financial crisis faced by the French state, the National Assembly confiscated the land owned by the Roman Catholic Church. The National Assembly then issued paper money, known as *assignats,* using the confiscated land as security. The *assignats* declined rapidly in value, however, and the government's financial problems continued.

Deprived of its land, the church lost its major source of income, and the French government now assumed the obligation of paying the salaries of the clergy.

The National Assembly proceeded to reorganize the administration of the church, adopting the Civil Constitution of the Clergy in July 1790. Bishops and priests would be elected by the people, and members of the clergy were required to swear an oath of allegiance to support the new arrangement. Over half the clergy refused to do so. These non-jurors, as they were called from the French word *jurer* ("to swear"), became bitter opponents of the revolution, as did many faithful Catholic laypeople.

The Constitution of 1791

In September 1791, King Louis XVI reluctantly accepted the constitution drafted by the National Assembly. This Constitution of 1791 established a limited monarchy with separation of powers between the executive, legislative, and judicial branches. The king and his ministers constituted the executive, but their authority was limited by a one-house parliament, the Legislative Assembly, which was indirectly elected by adult males who met a property qualification.

The National Assembly now gave way to the newly elected Legislative Assembly, which held its first meeting in October 1791.

Beginning of the War of the First Coalition

The Legislative Assembly confronted a threat from foreign powers. Having declared their readiness to intervene in France if necessary to protect the French royal family and safeguard the monarchy, Austria and Prussia concluded an alliance in February 1792.

The Legislative Assembly responded by declaring war on Austria on April 20, 1792. The War of the First Coalition (1792–1797) quickly got under way, as Prussia entered the war on Austria's side. Within a year, France was at war with most of Europe, including Great Britain. The war continued, with a few interruptions, until the final defeat of Napoleon Bonaparte (1769–1821) in 1815.

Early in the war, France suffered some setbacks, and the revolution moved in a more radical direction. In August 1792, the Legislative Assembly voted to depose the king and called for elections for a National Convention that would draft a constitution for a French republic.

The National Convention

On September 20, 1792, the French army turned back a Prussian attack at Valmy in northern France. The following day, the National Convention held its first meeting. Proclaiming France a republic, the National Convention ruled the country for the next three years.

Execution of King Louis XVI

In December, the National Convention found King Louis XVI guilty of conspiracy against the liberty of the people and the security of the state. The king was executed on January 21, 1793. The queen, Marie Antoinette, was guillotined the following October.

British Reaction to the French Revolution

The British initially sought to remain uninvolved as France sank into revolution, and as late as 1792, William Pitt predicted that there would be fifteen years of peace.

Pro-Revolution Sentiment

Many in Great Britain, including Charles James Fox (1749–1806) and the poet William Wordsworth (1770–1850), in fact welcomed the events in France, comparing the French Revolution to the Glorious Revolution of 1688 and regarding the French establishment of a constitutional monarchy in 1791 as an attempt to imitate the British example.

Renewed Demands for Parliamentary Reform

Encouraged by developments in France, the British movement for parliamentary reform revived, as old societies renewed their activities and new ones were established. Among them were the Society of Friends of the People and the London Corresponding Society, founded in 1792 to promote universal manhood suffrage.

Conservative Opposition

Others were more skeptical. In his pamphlet, *Reflections on the Revolution in France,* published in October 1790, Edmund Burke (1729–1797) warned that the ideas of the French Revolution threatened the fundamental order and values of Western society. Burke and many other conservative Whigs soon joined forces with Pitt and the Tories, leaving Fox at the head of an increasingly smaller and ineffectual opposition.

When the French Revolution moved in a more radical direction and the French sought to foment revolution elsewhere in Europe, British opinion became more hostile to France, and British reformers came to be viewed as little more than would-be revolutionaries. While Pitt had earlier supported reform efforts, the fear of radicalism and revolution pushed him in an increasingly reactionary direction.

Entry into the War of the First Coalition

Following the execution of King Louis XVI, Great Britain broke diplomatic relations with France, which responded by declaring war on February 1, 1793. Great Britain now joined Austria, Prussia, Spain, and Sardinia in the War of the First Coalition against France. Pitt hoped that the British could once again achieve victory by providing financial aid to their continental allies and using their navy against the French empire, as his father's government had done during the Seven Years' War (see Chapter 12). In early 1793, a small

British army joined with the Prussians to push France out of the Austrian Netherlands (Belgium).

The French Reign of Terror

In addition to suffering military reverses, the National Convention faced mounting domestic opposition. In March 1793, a major revolt broke out in the region of the Vendée, southwest of Paris.

In an effort to combat the crisis, in April 1793, the National Convention established the Committee of Public Safety, which exercised dictatorial authority. Within a few months, the radical Jacobins, led by Maximilien Robespierre (1758–1794), gained control of the Committee of Public Safety and, from the summer of 1793 to the summer of 1794, carried out the Reign of Terror, designed to root out counterrevolutionaries and suspected counterrevolutionaries. The Reign of Terror ultimately claimed some 16,000 victims.

French Military Victories

In August 1793, Lazare Carnot (1753–1823), the member of the Committee of Public Safety in charge of military affairs, ordered a *levée en masse,* the conscription of able-bodied men into the armies of the revolution. During 1793–1794, the French armies succeeded in defending the country against invasion. Then, during 1794–1795, they occupied the Low Countries, the Rhineland in Western Germany, Switzerland, Savoy, and part of Spain. The treaties of Basel, signed in March and June 1795, ended the war against Prussia and Spain, respectively, although France remained at war with the Austrians and the British.

In 1796, a French army commanded by the young general Napoleon Bonaparte invaded Italy, defeated the Austrians and Sardinians, and occupied large areas of the country. Under the terms of the Treaty of Campo Formio, signed with the Austrians in October 1797, France annexed the Austrian Netherlands (Belgium). The treaty ended the War of the First Coalition against France, although Great Britain continued fighting without allies.

The Thermidorean Reaction and the Directory

During early 1794, opposition mounted to Robespierre and his Reign of Terror. On July 27, 1794 (9 Thermidor according to the new revolutionary calendar), a group of conspirators arrested Robespierre; he was beheaded the following day. A number of others who were responsible for the Reign of Terror were also executed. Power passed to the wealthy middle class, and an element of stability was restored to French national life.

The National Convention prepared a new constitution, the Constitution of 1795, which created a new two-house parliament and vested executive authority in the Directory of five members. The National Convention was dissolved on October 26, 1795, and the new government of the Directory took office.

Repression in Great Britain

The war with France brought an intensifying repression to Great Britain. In fact, even before the British went to war, a proclamation issued in 1792 warned that authors of seditious writings would be subject to prosecution.

In 1794, the Habeas Corpus Act was suspended in certain cases. The spirit of repression led to the passage in 1795 of the Treasonable and Seditious Practices Act and the Seditious Assemblies Act. The first act broadened the definition of treason to include speaking and writing, as well as acting, against the government, while the second banned public meetings without the approval of a magistrate. With the exception of Fox and a small group of his ardent supporters, opposition to the government was silenced.

Fear of radicalism also resulted in the adoption of the Combination Acts of 1799 and 1800, which outlawed trade unions.

Britain's War Against France

Acquisition of Dutch Colonies

Despite the French victory in the War of the First Coalition, the British had achieved some successes. Following the French occupation of the Netherlands, the British seized several Dutch colonies, including the Cape of Good Hope, the island of Ceylon off the southeast coast of India, and several islands in the Dutch East Indies.

Threat to Ireland

Elsewhere, the outlook for the British was less positive. Although the Royal Navy continued to dominate the English Channel, the threat of a French invasion of Ireland mounted. In fact, only a violent storm prevented a French landing in Ireland in 1797.

Domestic Problems

That same year, mutinies broke out in the British navy at Spithead and in the North Sea, protesting food, living conditions, the mistreatment of sailors, and the system of promotions. Although these mutinies further lowered morale in the navy, they also resulted in much-needed reforms.

At home, the British experienced food shortages, and the Bank of England had to suspend cash payments in order to prevent a run on the bank.

British Naval Victories

Nevertheless, before the end of 1797, the British began to regain their confidence. In July 1797, the British Mediterranean fleet defeated a combined French-Spanish fleet at Cape St. Vincent, and in October, the North Sea fleet defeated a combined French-Dutch force at Camperdown. These British naval victories ended French hopes of invading England.

Napoleon's Egyptian Campaign

In 1798, Napoleon invaded Egypt, hoping to threaten Britain's commercial interests in the Mediterranean and, ultimately, to restore French domination over India.

In August 1798, a British fleet, commanded by Lord Horatio Nelson (1758–1805), destroyed a French fleet at Abukir Bay, near Alexandria. This British victory in the Battle of the Nile stranded the French army in Egypt. In early 1799, Napoleon invaded Syria, but the Turks, aided by the British navy, checked the French advance. Leaving his army in Egypt, Napoleon returned to France. The setback in Egypt did little to injure his prestige or popularity.

Napoleon's Seizure of Power

Organizing a conspiracy against the ineffectual government of the Directory, Napoleon seized power in early November 1799. Napoleon then directed the drafting of a new constitution, the Constitution of 1799, which established the regime known as the Consulate. As first consul, Napoleon was in effect France's dictator.

In 1804, Napoleon had himself proclaimed emperor of the French.

The Struggle Against Napoleon

The War of the Second Coalition

In late 1798, while Napoleon was still in Egypt, Russia formed a new alliance with Great Britain. Austria, Portugal, Naples, and the Ottoman Empire soon joined, beginning the War of the Second Coalition (1799–1801) against France. The Austrians, aided by British subsidies, drove the French out of northern Italy and advanced into Switzerland.

Napoleon's Defeat of Austria

Following his seizure of power, Napoleon took the offensive against France's enemies. In June 1800, he defeated the Austrians at Marengo in northwestern Italy and, later in the year, defeated them again at Hohenlinden in Bavaria. In February 1801, Austria dropped out of the war, signing the Treaty of Lunéville.

The League of Armed Neutrality

The French persuaded Tsar Paul I (r. 1796–1801) of Russia to abandon the Second Coalition, and the Russians now turned against Britain by assuming the leadership of the League of Armed Neutrality of Northern Powers, which also included Prussia, Sweden, and Denmark. The League was designed to counter British efforts to prevent the shipment of goods to France.

Britain's Warfare

Once again, the British stood alone in the war. In the spring of 1801, Lord Nelson destroyed the Danish fleet at Copenhagen and moved into the Baltic Sea to confront the Russians. Alexander I (r. 1801–1825), Russia's new tsar, wanted peace, and without Russian support, the league disintegrated. Thus the Baltic Sea, as well as the Mediterranean, remained open to the British. Also during 1801, the British forced the French armies in Egypt to surrender. Nevertheless, Great Britain was in no position to wage war effectively against France without allies.

The Treaty of Amiens

In March 1802, France and Great Britain signed the Treaty of Amiens, which proved to be only a truce in the long conflict between

Napoleon and his implacable British foe. Under the terms of the treaty, France kept almost all of its conquests in Europe, while the British were required to return the French colonies they had taken, including the island of Malta in the central Mediterranean. France's allies, the Netherlands and Spain, were required respectively to recognize British possession of Ceylon and the West Indies island of Trinidad.

Ireland

The success of the American colonists in their struggle for independence and the outbreak of the French Revolution encouraged the Irish in their opposition to British rule.

Some reforms had recently come to Ireland. Irish Nonconformists were no longer bound by the Test Act (see Chapter 10), while Catholics were permitted to lease land for ninety-nine years. Nevertheless, acts of the Irish Parliament remained subject to British approval, and the Irish had numerous long-standing political, economic, and religious grievances against the British.

The Society of United Irishmen, founded in 1791 and headed by Wolfe Tone (1763–1798), a Belfast lawyer, called for Irish independence. The Defenders, a more radical group, favored the use of violence, if necessary, in its campaign for economic reforms and for the abolition of tithes levied on Catholics for the support of the Anglican Church of Ireland.

Mounting pressure resulted in further reforms. In 1793, Irish Catholics acquired the right to vote, but they were still not permitted to serve in the Irish Parliament, and other Irish grievances remained unsatisfied.

Tone called on revolutionary France for assistance, but French efforts to invade Ireland failed. When a revolt broke out in 1798, the British quickly suppressed it.

The Act of Union of 1800

The unrest in Ireland convinced William Pitt of the need for changes in the relationship between Great Britain and Ireland, and he secured the adoption by both Parliaments of the Act of Union of 1800. The Irish Parliament was initially reluctant to vote in favor of its own dissolution, but Pitt overcame this reluctance with generous distributions of money, pensions, and peerages. In addition, he indicated his readiness to support Catholic emancipation, which would allow Irish Catholics to sit in the British Parliament, and to abolish the tithes.

The Act of Union provided for the abolition of the Irish Parliament and for Irish representation in the British Parliament with thirty-two peers in the House of Lords and one hundred members in the House of Commons. In addition, free trade between Ireland and Great Britain was instituted.

Pitt's Resignation

Following the passage of the Act of Union, Pitt proposed his bill for Catholic emancipation. King George III strongly opposed this legislation. Having lost the support of the king, Pitt resigned the prime ministership in early 1801. Henry Addington (1757–1844), who later became Viscount Sidmouth, replaced him.

The War of the Third Coalition

Fearing that Napoleon was preparing for further conquests, the British refused to abandon their control of Malta, despite the terms of the Treaty of Amiens. In 1803, Great Britain renewed the war against France.

Faced with the threat of a French invasion, the British recalled Pitt to the prime ministership in 1804. Pitt took the lead in forming a new coalition against Napoleon, with Austria and Russia as Britain's chief allies in the War of the Third Coalition (1805–1807). Prussia remained neutral at the outset. Despite substantial British subsidies, this Third Coalition was no more successful than its predecessors.

Napoleon's Victory at Ulm

Napoleon quickly advanced into Germany, beginning a great march of conquest across Europe. On October 17, 1805, he defeated the Austrians at Ulm, located on the Danube in southern Germany.

British Naval Victory at Trafalgar

Before Napoleon could launch his planned invasion of England, he had to end Britain's control of the English Channel. On October 21, 1805, four days after Napoleon's victory at Ulm, the French suffered a major naval defeat. Lord Nelson's British fleet smashed the combined French and Spanish navies near Cape Trafalgar off the southwest coast of Spain in what proved to be the last major naval engagement to be fought by sailing ships. Although Nelson died in the battle, the victory at Trafalgar was the greatest British naval triumph since the defeat of the Spanish Armada in 1588. The victory eliminated French naval power for the balance of the war, and Napoleon had to suspend his plans for the invasion of England.

French Victories on Land

On land, however, Napoleon's victories continued. Moving east from Ulm, he defeated a combined Austrian and Russian army at Austerlitz, north of Vienna, on December 2, 1805. Austria dropped out of the war, signing the Treaty of Pressburg at the end of December.

In July 1806, Napoleon organized a number of German states into a French satellite state known as the Confederation of the Rhine. This new state provided a buffer for France against both Austria and Prussia. In August 1806, Napoleon ordered the dissolution of the Holy Roman Empire.

Napoleon's actions in Germany brought Prussia into the war against France. On October 14, 1806, however, Napoleon defeated the Prussians at Jena in central Germany, while on the same day, another French army defeated a Prussian force at Auerstädt, not far from Jena.

The Treaties of Tilsit

During the spring of 1807, Napoleon moved into East Prussia, defeating the Russians at Friedland on June 13. The emperor then met with Tsar Alexander I of Russia and King Frederick William III (r. 1797–1840) of Prussia. The rulers agreed on the terms of the Treaties of Tilsit, thus ending the War of the Third Coalition.

Prussia lost about half of its territory, ceding some to Saxony and some to the newly created French satellite state, the Grand Duchy of Warsaw. Prussia was also required to pay an indemnity.

In return for a promise to support France in its struggle against Great Britain, the Russians gained a free hand to deal as they wished with the Ottoman Empire.

British Politics After 1806

On January 2, 1806, William Pitt died. While it proved difficult to replace him, the British did not waver in their determination to continue their resistance to Napoleon.

Whig Cabinet

During the next six years, a series of prime ministers held office in fairly rapid succession. Following Pitt's death, King George III agreed reluctantly to the formation of a Whig-dominated coalition cabinet, known as the Ministry of All the Talents. Lord William Grenville (1759–1834) served as prime minister, while Charles James Fox was foreign secretary. Before his death later in 1806, Fox introduced a bill for the abolition of the slave trade (see Chapter 12).

Tory Cabinets

When the Whigs attempted to remove restrictions that prevented Catholics from holding military commissions, they were forced out of the cabinet. A series of Tory cabinets followed. In 1807, the duke of Portland became prime minister. He was succeeded in 1809 by Spencer Perceval (1762–1812), who held office until he was assassinated by a maniac in 1812. Then the earl of Liverpool (1770–1828) became prime minister, beginning a remarkably long tenure that lasted until 1827.

The Continental System

Unable to defeat the British militarily, Napoleon devised the Continental System in an effort to destroy the British economically.

The Berlin Decree (1806)

In the Berlin Decree of November 1806, the French emperor proclaimed the establishment of a blockade of the British Isles, prohibited neutrals subject to French influence from trading with the British, and authorized French privateers to attack British and neutral ships sailing from British ports.

The British responded with an order-in-council forbidding neutrals to trade with France or her allies and to observe the Berlin Decree. Those who disobeyed would be subject to the seizure of their ships and cargoes. A second order-in-council permitted neutral ships to sail to a French port after securing a license at a British port.

The Milan Decree (1807)

In the Milan Decree of December 1807, Napoleon declared that any ship sailing to or from a British port was a lawful prize.

Effects of the Continental System

In practice, the Continental System proved virtually impossible to enforce. Smuggling was widespread, and even the French violated the rules of trade. Nevertheless, trade between Great Britain and the continent dropped off considerably.

The Peninsular War

In late 1807, French troops moved into Portugal, which had failed to support the Continental System. To keep their lines of supply and communication open, the French also occupied Spain. In early 1808, Napoleon deposed Spain's Bourbon dynasty and installed his older brother Joseph (1768–1844) as king of Spain.

When the Spanish people rose up in revolt against French domination, the British sent troops to Spain to support the insurgents. The British expeditionary force was commanded, first, by Sir John Moore (1761–1809), who was killed in 1809, and then by Sir Arthur Wellesley (1769–1852), who later became the duke of Wellington. Possessing naval superiority, the British could reinforce their troops with ease.

The British expeditionary force gradually freed Portugal from French domination and helped the Spanish guerrillas keep some 300,000 French troops tied down in Spain. Continuing until 1814, the Peninsular War created a serious drain on France's military resources and served to encourage Napoleon's enemies elsewhere in Europe.

The War of 1812

Causes of the War

Following the Anglo-French declarations of war in 1793, President George Washington (1732–1799) declared American neutrality, although many Americans favored an alliance with the French, who had aided the American struggle for independence from Great Britain. The United States traded extensively with both Great Britain and France and, during the Napoleonic wars, became caught in the crossfire between the Continental System and the British orders-in-council. As a result of Britain's command of the sea, however, the British were in a better position to interfere with American shipping. On a number of occasions, they seized both British deserters and American seamen.

This interference, combined with the expansionist ambitions of American "War Hawks" who hoped to annex Canada, led to an American declaration of war against the British in June 1812.

Course of the War

During the War of 1812, the British repulsed poorly prepared American efforts to conquer Canada, and in 1814, a British force captured and burned much of Washington, D.C., including the Capitol and the White House. However, in January 1815, Andrew Jackson succeeded in defeating a second British army at New Orleans, where news had not arrived that peace had been made two weeks earlier.

At sea, Admiral Oliver Hazard Perry (1785–1819) established American control of Lake Erie, while in the Atlantic, American privateers seriously damaged British commerce before the British imposed an effective blockade of the American coast.

The Treaty of Ghent

Neither side won a clear-cut victory in the war, and the Treaty of Ghent of December 1814 restored peace on the basis of the prewar territorial status quo. While the British did not formally agree to cease their interference with American shipping, they did so in practice. Disputes over boundaries and fishing rights were to be resolved through arbitration by joint commissions. The Rush-Bagot Convention of 1817 established the American-Canadian frontier and provided for the virtual naval disarmament of the Great Lakes. This accord led to an enduring peace between the United States and Canada.

Napoleon's Russian Campaign

The Russians became increasingly dissatisfied with their position of subordination to France and with the French unwillingness to allow them as much of a free hand in dealing with the Ottoman Empire as they had expected. For his part, Napoleon was angered at Russia's violations of the Continental System (opening Russian ports to British shipping). The deterioration of Franco-Russian relations led to Napoleon's decision to go to war.

Invasion of Russia

For his Russian campaign of 1812, the French emperor assembled a Grand Army of some 600,000 men, one of history's largest armies.

In late June 1812, the Grand Army crossed the Niemen River and entered Russia. The Russians continued to retreat, trading space for time and destroying food supplies to keep them from falling into the hands of the invader. In September, the Russians engaged the French at the Battle of Borodino, some 75 miles west of Moscow. Both sides suffered heavy casualties, and Napoleon failed to win a decisive victory over the Russians.

On September 14, the Grand Army entered Moscow. Napoleon remained in the city for five weeks, hoping that Tsar Alexander I would admit defeat and sue for peace. The tsar refused to do so.

French Retreat

On October 19, Napoleon's retreat from Moscow began. Aided by the onset of winter, the Russians harassed the retreating French. Little of the Grand Army was left when the survivors regrouped near the Russian border in mid-December. Napoleon had already left his troops to return to Paris to raise a new army.

The Fall of Napoleon

Viscount Castlereagh (1769–1822), the British foreign secretary, took the lead in forming a new coalition against Napoleon. In October 1813, the Russian, Prussian, and Austrian armies joined to defeat Napoleon in the Battle of the Nations, fought near Leipzig in central Germany. Napoleon retreated across the Rhine River back into France.

While a British army, commanded by the duke of Wellington, moved across the Pyrenees from Spain into southern France, Russian, Prussian, and Austrian forces invaded France from Germany. On March 31, 1814, the allied armies entered Paris.

On April 11, Napoleon abdicated at Fontainebleau. The allies allowed him to retain his title and gave him the island of Elba, located in the Mediterranean Sea off the west coast of Italy, on condition that he promise never to leave. The allies restored the Bourbon dynasty to the French throne with Louis XVIII (r. 1814–1824), a younger brother of Louis XVI, as king.

The Hundred Days

In early 1815, Napoleon left Elba and, on March 1, landed on the Mediterranean coast of France with a small force. The restored Bourbon monarchy enjoyed little popular support, and the French army remained loyal to Napoleon. Troops sent out to apprehend him joined him instead. On March 20, Napoleon entered Paris in triumph, and the period of the Hundred Days began.

The Battle of Waterloo

Once again, the British, Russians, Prussians, and Austrians prepared for war. Napoleon decided to attack the allies in Belgium. At Waterloo on June 18, 1815, a British army commanded by the duke of Wellington and a Prussian army commanded by Field Marshal Gebhard von Blücher (1742–1819) defeated Napoleon.

Following the Battle of Waterloo, the allies sent Napoleon into his final exile on the remote island of Saint Helena in the South Atlantic, where he remained until his death in 1821.

Peace Treaties with France

The First Treaty of Paris (1814)

In the first Treaty of Paris, signed in May 1814, the allies offered France lenient terms. France lost all of its conquests of the revolutionary and Napoleonic periods but was permitted to retain its frontiers of 1792. France regained almost all of its colonies and was not required to pay an indemnity.

The Second Treaty of Paris (1815)

However, following Napoleon's return to power during the Hundred Days and his defeat at Waterloo, the allies imposed harsher terms on France in the second Treaty of Paris of November 1815. France was reduced to the borders of 1790. The French were required to pay an indemnity of 700 million francs to the allies and to accept an allied military occupation of seventeen French forts for five years.

The Congress of Vienna

The other details of the peace settlement were determined by an international congress. The statesmen who met in this Congress of Vienna in 1814–1815 sought to reestablish a conservative order in Europe following the years of upheaval and war brought about by the French Revolution and Napoleon.

Europe, 1815

Although a number of small states were represented, the four great powers that had joined to defeat Napoleon — Great Britain, Austria, Prussia, and Russia — made the major decisions.

The Major Statesmen at Vienna

Metternich (Austria)

Prince Klemens von Metternich (1773–1859), the Austrian foreign minister, acted as host for the Congress of Vienna. Metternich was firmly committed to the principles of conservatism, regarding the new ideas of liberalism and nationalism as a threat to the survival of the Austrian Empire. He hoped the major powers would cooperate to maintain the conservative order in Europe.

Castlereagh (Britain)

Viscount Castlereagh, the British foreign secretary from 1812 to 1822, generally shared Metternich's conservative views and strongly supported efforts to restore the balance of power so that no one country could attempt to dominate Europe, as France had done.

Alexander I (Russia)

Tsar Alexander I of Russia (r. 1801–1825) was in general agreement with his colleagues, although he also pushed for substantial territorial acquisitions, especially in Poland.

Hardenberg (Prussia)

Prussia's representative, Prince Karl von Hardenberg (1750–1822), shared his colleagues' belief that the great powers should collaborate to maintain European peace and stability.

Talleyrand (France)

Charles-Maurice de Talleyrand (1754–1838), the foreign minister in the government of France's king, Louis XVIII, found himself in the difficult position of representing the interests of his defeated country. He did this with skill and aplomb.

The Principle of Legitimacy

Bourbon Restorations

As a servant of the Bourbon king of France, Talleyrand was an ardent advocate of the principle of legitimacy: the idea that rulers and frontiers should be restored as they had existed prior to the wars of the French Revolution and Napoleon. Not only was the legitimate Bourbon ruler restored to the French throne, but Talleyrand's influence also led to the decision to restore Bourbons to the thrones of Spain and the Kingdom of the Two Sicilies. Legitimate rulers were also restored to their thrones in several other Italian states.

The German Confederation

In Germany, however, the principle of legitimacy was ignored. The statesmen at Vienna had little desire to create the old Holy Roman Empire, which Napoleon had abolished in 1806, or to restore the more than 300 states it had comprised. Instead, the Congress of Vienna created thirty-nine German states, loosely joined in a new German Confederation.

The Territorial Settlement

In reaching a territorial settlement, the statesmen at Vienna were influenced by the principle of compensation, the idea that if one power made gains, the other powers should be compensated.

Russia

Tsar Alexander I acquired additional Polish territory, although not as much as he had initially demanded, and also retained Finland, which he had taken from Sweden in 1809. As compensation, Sweden retained Norway, which it had seized from Denmark, Napoleon's ally.

Prussia

In addition to acquiring two-fifths of the German kingdom of Saxony, which had supported Napoleon, Prussia gained Swedish Pomerania, along the shores of the Baltic Sea, and territory in the Rhineland in western Germany. Possession of the Rhineland brought Prussian power to the border of France to serve as a check on possible future French aggression.

The Netherlands and Sardinia-Piedmont

The Netherlands acquired the Austrian Netherlands (Belgium). The enlarged Kingdom of the Netherlands, bordering on France, would also serve as a check against any future French aggression. For the same reason, the northern Italian state of Sardinia-Piedmont was strengthened by the acquisition of the republic of Genoa.

Austria

As compensation for its loss of Belgium, Austria acquired the northern Italian provinces of Lombardy and Venetia, which strengthened Austrian control over Italian affairs. In addition to dominating Italy, Austria, the largest of the German states, dominated the German Confederation. Metternich was thus able to impose his repressive policies on the German states, just as he did in Italy.

Great Britain

Territorial Gains.   The British, whose interests lay primarily outside of Europe, gained a number of valuable colonial possessions. They retained the Cape of Good Hope at the southern tip of Africa and the island of Ceylon off the southeastern coast of India, which they had occupied during the Napoleonic wars. In the West Indies, they acquired several islands, including Trinidad, Tobago, and St. Lucia. The British also gained permanent possession of several other strategically located islands, including Helgoland in the North Sea, Malta in the Mediterranean, and Mauritius and the Seychelles Islands in the Indian Ocean.

Postwar Depression.   Although the British made important imperial gains, Great Britain emerged from the wars of the French Revolution and Napoleon with a huge national debt and experienced a severe postwar economic depression that lasted until 1820.

The Holy Alliance

In September 1815, the rulers of Russia, Prussia, and Austria signed the Holy Alliance, proposed by Tsar Alexander I. The three rulers pledged to observe Christian principles in both domestic and international affairs. While most of Europe's rulers ultimately signed the Holy Alliance, the British refused to have anything to do with it. Castlereagh dismissed it as "a sublime piece of mysticism and nonsense."

The Quadruple Alliance

The Quadruple Alliance, signed by Great Britain, Austria, Prussia, and Russia in November 1815, was of greater importance. The four powers agreed to maintain the alliance that had defeated Napoleon and to meet periodically to discuss issues of mutual concern. This accord laid the basis for the Concert of Europe, the effort of the great powers to resolve international issues by consultation and agreement. In 1818, France rejoined the ranks of the great powers, and the Quadruple Alliance became the Quintuple Alliance.

While Prime Minister William Pitt proved to be a determined war leader during most of Britain's long struggle against revolutionary and Napoleonic France, Foreign Secretary Castlereagh ultimately represented his country's interests at the Congress of Vienna, striving to reestablish a balance of power on the European continent and acquiring some important additions for Britain's maritime empire. Despite the allied victory over France, the fear of revolution that had led to repressive policies during the war years continued to influence the British government in the postwar era.

Recommended Reading

Bartlett, J. C. *Castlereagh* (1967).

Bryant, Arthur. *The Years of Endurance, 1793–1802* (1942).

Bryant, Arthur. *The Years of Victory, 1802–1812* (1945).

Bryant, Arthur. *The Age of Elegance, 1812–1822* (1950).

Cone, Carl B. *Burke and the Nature of Politics,* 2 vols. (1957–1964).

Cone, Carl B. *The English Jacobins* (1968).

Cookson, J. E. *The Friends of Peace: Anti-War Liberalism in England, 1793–1815* (1982).

Derry, John W. *Castlereagh* (1976).

Ehrman, John. *The Younger Pitt: The Years of Acclaim* (1969).

Ehrman, John. *The Younger Pitt: The Reluctant Transition* (1983).

Emsley, Clive. *British Society and the French Wars, 1793–1815* (1979).

Gatres, David. *The Spanish Ulcer: A History of the Peninsular War* (1986).

Glover, Michael. *Wellington as Military Commander* (1968).

Glover, Richard. *Britain at Bay: Defense Against Bonaparte, 1803–14* (1973).

Glover, Richard. *Peninsular Preparation: The Reform of the British Army, 1795–1809* (1963).

Goodwin, Albert. *The Friends of Liberty: The English Democratic Movement in the Age of the French Revolution* (1979).

Jarrett, Derek. *Pitt the Younger* (1974).

Longford, Elizabeth. *Wellington: The Years of the Sword* (1969).

Mackesy, Piers. *The War in the Mediterranean, 1803–1810* (1957).

Mackesy, Piers. *War Without Victory: The Downfall of Pitt, 1799–1802* (1984).

Marcus, G, J. *The Age of Nelson: The Royal Navy, 1793–1815* (1971).

Sherwig, John M. *Guineas and Gunpowder: British Foreign Aid in the Wars with France, 1793–1815* (1969).

Webster, Charles K. *The Foreign Policy of Castlereagh, 1812–1815* (1931).

Ziegler, Philip. *Addington: A Life of Henry Addington, First Viscount Sidmouth* (1965).

CHAPTER 14

The Agricultural and Industrial Revolutions

Time Line

1712	The Newcomen steam engine is used to pump water from a coal mine
1733	John Kay invents the flying shuttle
1764	James Hargreaves invents the spinning jenny
1769	Richard Arkwright patents the water frame
	James Watt patents a more efficient version of the Newcomen steam engine
1776	Adam Smith publishes *The Wealth of Nations*
1779	Samuel Crompton perfects the spinning mule

1784	Arthur Young establishes the *Annals of Agriculture*
1785	Edmund Cartwright patents a power loom
1789	Jeremy Bentham publishes *Principles of Morals and Legislation*
1793	The British government establishes the Board of Agriculture
	Eli Whitney invents the cotton gin
1798	Thomas Robert Malthus publishes *An Essay on the Principle of Population*
1807	Robert Fulton's steamboat, the *Clermont,* goes into service on the Hudson River
1817	David Ricardo publishes *The Principles of Political Economy and Taxation*
1826	Robert Owen establishes the socialist community of New Harmony, Indiana
1830	George Stephenson's locomotive, the *Rocket,* operates successfully on the Liverpool to Manchester railroad
1840	Samuel Cunard begins regular transatlantic steamship passenger service
	Great Britain inaugurates the penny post
1844	Samuel F. B. Morse sends a telegraph message from Washington to Baltimore
1848	John Stuart Mill publishes the first edition of *Principles of Political Economy*
1856	Henry Bessemer develops the Bessemer converter
1859	John Stuart Mill publishes *On Liberty*
1866	The Siemens brothers develop the open hearth process of steelmaking
	Cyrus Field lays the first successful transatlantic cable

The agricultural and industrial revolutions brought immense changes to the economy of Great Britain, Europe, and, ultimately, the world.

During the eighteenth and nineteenth centuries, the pace of the agricultural revolution quickened. The development of scientific agriculture, the introduction of new crops, the enclosure of agricultural land, and increasing mechanization expanded agricultural production and ended the specter of famine. Fewer farm workers were needed to produce food for Britain's growing population, and surplus agricultural labor migrated to the new industrial towns to find employment in the factories.

The industrial revolution, which began in Great Britain in the late eighteenth century, involved a number of elements, including the invention of power-driven machinery, the introduction of the factory system, and advances in the production of coal and iron and, eventually, steel. In addition, the expansion of banking and credit facilities and the broader application of the principle of limited liability to business organization helped promote the process of industrialization. The industrial revolution was both accompanied and encouraged by contemporaneous revolutions in transportation and communications.

The age of the agricultural and industrial revolutions also witnessed the emergence of new ideas about how the economy operated and how it should operate.

The Agricultural Revolution

The industrial revolution was preceded and accompanied by a revolution in agriculture, in which Great Britain led the way, as it would later do in the industrial revolution.

The Development of Scientific Agriculture

During the seventeenth and eighteenth centuries, science and technology were increasingly applied to British agriculture. Marshlands were drained, new agricultural implements were introduced, and agricultural reformers urged the practice of crop rotation and other improved farming methods.

In the seventeenth century, Dutch engineers, drawing on the experience they had gained in their homeland redeeming land from the sea, drained marshlands in England, making them suitable for cultivation.

Influence of Tull and Townshend

Improved plows were introduced, and, around 1700, Jethro Tull (1674–1741) developed a device which planted seeds in neat rows. Tull's horse-drawn seed drill replaced the less efficient method of scattering the seed.

Viscount Townshend (1725–1767), an aristocrat and statesman, urged Britain's farmers to plant turnips and clover, which would both nourish the soil and provide food for livestock during the winter months. The increased cultivation of turnips and clover ended the need for the mass slaughter of livestock at the onset of winter, and fresh meat gradually replaced salted meat in the British diet during the winter months. Townshend was such a fervent promoter of turnips that he gained the nickname "Turnip Townshend."

Townshend also experimented with a four-course crop rotation: the consecutive planting of wheat, turnips, barley or oats, and clover or rye. This rotation system eliminated the need to allow one field to lie fallow each year.

Advances in Livestock and Agricultural Techniques

Later in the eighteenth century, Robert Bakewell (1725–1795) introduced the scientific breeding of cattle and sheep. The records of the Smithfield Market in London reveal that the average weight of cattle and sheep sold more than doubled between 1710 and 1795.

Arthur Young (1741–1820) became an effective publicist for the new methods of scientific agriculture, founding the periodical *Annals of Agriculture* in 1784.

In 1793, the British government established the Board of Agriculture to promote the scientific and technological advances in farming, and Young became its first head. Even King George III became interested in the new agriculture, establishing a model farm on the grounds of his castle at Windsor, outside of London.

New Crops

Scientific and technological advances in agriculture were accompanied by the introduction of new crops, in addition to turnips and clover. The potato, which originated in the Western Hemisphere, had become the basic foodstuff of Ireland by the mid-eighteenth century, although many continental Europeans continued to believe that potatoes were poisonous. French farmers, in fact, did not raise potatoes or turnips on an extensive scale until well into the nineteenth century. During the eighteenth century, peas and new varieties of beans were introduced into Great Britain from the Netherlands. Other new vegetables included artichokes, asparagus, and cauliflower, while wealthy men began to grow oranges, lemons, and figs in greenhouses.

In the late eighteenth century, King Frederick the Great of Prussia sent agents to Great Britain to learn more about British accomplishments in scientific agriculture, and he urged Prussian farmers to plant potatoes and turnips. Nevertheless, British advances in agriculture won only gradual acceptance on the European continent.

The Enclosure Movement

The agricultural revolution in Great Britain was accompanied by an intensification of the enclosure movement, which had begun during the sixteenth century. Enclosure involved the efforts of landowning aristocrats and country gentry to enclose common land by building fences and stone walls and planting hedges, thereby ending the medieval practice of providing free access to grazing lands and woodlands. During the eighteenth century, Parliament passed hundreds of enclosure acts. As a result, by the early years of the nineteenth century, almost all of England's agriculturally useful land had been enclosed. While peasants were supposed to receive their fair share of the enclosed land, in practice they were often cheated.

The enclosure movement resulted in an increase in the number of large and medium-sized farms, as well as an increase in the production of food and other agricultural products. At the same time, many peasants were reduced to the status of impoverished farm laborers. A growing number of these displaced peasants migrated to the industrial towns to find employment in factories.

The Industrial Revolution

Although the precise reasons for Great Britain's leadership in the industrial revolution cannot be fully explained, a number of elements helped make that role possible. First of all, Great Britain possessed ample resources of coal and iron, which were basic necessities for modern industry. In addition, British merchants had become wealthy as a consequence of their activities during the commercial revolution and thus had capital available for investment in the new industries. The British could also apply their mercantile experience to selling the products of their industries in the world market. Furthermore, the British government adopted policies designed to promote the interests of the country's merchants and industrialists.

The Cotton Textile Industry

The British cotton textile industry, centered in the area of Lancashire and its major industrial town, Manchester, was the first to experience the application of power-driven machinery on a wide scale.

Invention of Machinery

Kay.   In 1733, John Kay (1704–1764), a Lancashire weaver, invented the flying shuttle, which enabled one weaver, rather than two, to operate a loom. While Kay's invention encountered angry opposition from weavers who feared losing their jobs, the flying shuttle won increasing acceptance in the cotton textile industry.

Hargreaves.   In the mid-1760s, James Hargreaves (d. 1778) invented a spinning machine which he called the spinning jenny, in honor of his wife. Although the spinning jenny made it possible for a single worker to spin a number of threads simultaneously, the thread produced was relatively weak.

Arkwright.   The water frame, patented by Richard Arkwright (1732–1792) in 1769, produced a stronger thread, although it was coarser than that made by the spinning jenny.

Crompton.   In 1779, Samuel Crompton (1753–1827) perfected a spinning machine called the mule, which combined the best features of the spinning jenny and the water frame and produced thread that was both fine and strong.

Cartwright.   The first power loom was patented by Edmund Cartwright (1743–1823) in 1785.

Whitney.   As the new textile machinery was placed in wider use, the demand for raw cotton increased. The problem of removing the seeds from the cotton, however, made it difficult to meet the demand. Then, in 1793, the American Eli Whitney (1765–1825) invented the cotton gin, an effective device for removing the seeds from the cotton fiber. The American South increasingly became a land of cotton, meeting about three-quarters of the total British demand for raw cotton.

Improved Manufacturing Methods.   The cotton textile industry benefited from other inventions as well. Mechanical engineers studied the techniques used by watchmakers and developed precision parts that increased the operational efficiency of the new machines. The next step involved the development of standardized, interchangeable parts for industrial machinery. Eli Whitney, who operated an arms factory in Connecticut, made important contributions to this development.

In the 1780s, a rolling press was introduced for the printing of textiles, replacing the hand-operated plates that had been used previously.

Growth of the Textile Industry

As a result of the application of technology, the British cotton textile industry experienced explosive growth.

In 1796, Great Britain manufactured 21 million yards of cotton cloth, while in 1830, 347 million yards were produced. In monetary terms, the value of cotton textiles exported from Great Britain totaled £355,000 in 1781. By 1801, exports had increased to £7,000,000, and by 1841, to £32,400,000.

The expansion of the cotton textile industry was also reflected in the importation of raw cotton and in the number of power looms in use. In 1761, the British imported 4 million pounds of raw cotton. By 1800, the amount had grown to 56 million pounds, and by 1815, to 100 million pounds. In 1813, there were 2400 power looms in operation in Great Britain, and the number grew to 12,150 in 1820. Then an improved power loom was developed, and by 1829, some 45,500 power looms were in use. By 1833, the number had grown to 85,000.

The Factory System

The introduction of larger and more complex industrial machinery gradually resulted in the construction of factories, which replaced small workshops and cottage-based industries. During the period from 1760 to 1830, the number of workers in the British cotton textile industry grew from about 40,000 to more than 800,000. The majority of these workers were employed in large and medium-sized textile mills.

In England, some workers blamed machine industry for their low wages and unemployment. Between 1811 and 1816, angry mobs of workers assaulted factories and smashed machines. The Luddites, as they were known, were named for Ned Ludd, who had destroyed machinery a generation earlier.

Development of the Steam Engine

The invention and perfection of the steam engine provided a dependable and efficient source of power for the new industrial machinery.

Savery and Newcomen

About 1700, Thomas Savery, an English inventor, built a practical steam pump. A few years later, Thomas Newcomen (1663–1729) built a steam engine that was first used in 1712 to pump water from a coal mine. Although it was wasteful of fuel, the Newcomen steam engine met a need, and by 1760 about 100 Newcomen engines were operating in Great Britain.

Watt

In 1769, James Watt (1736–1819) patented a more efficient version of the Newcomen engine. Watt's steam engine required substantially less fuel.

Increased Use of Steam

While most of the early steam engines were used to pump water, by 1800 some 300 steam engines powered machinery in cotton textile mills and other factories. The use of the steam engine made possible the development of industry in towns that were not located along rivers.

Coal, Iron, and Steel

The interrelationship among the steam engine, coal mining, and iron production was a central aspect of the early industrial revolution.

Coal

The steam engine was used not only to pump water out of coal mines but also to power ventilating fans which pushed fresh air into the mines, making it possible for the miners to work longer hours underground. Coal mining also benefited from the invention of the safety lamp, in which an oil flame burned behind a metal screen, reducing the risk from dangerous gases in the mines. These technological innovations led to a tremendous increase in British coal production, from 16 million tons in 1816 to some 65 million tons in 1856.

Iron

The increased production of coal provided the fuel needed to power the growing number of steam engines. These steam engines, in turn, also were applied to the production of iron. The steam engine was as essential part of the blast furnace, which produced a purer and stronger iron, called pig iron. This stronger iron, in turn, made possible the manufacture of more efficient steam engines.

An important innovation in iron production came in 1784 with the development by Henry Cort (1740–1800) of a new type of blast furnace, known as the "puddling process." The iron produced in this process was tougher, more malleable, and less expensive than the iron that had been available previously.

In 1740, Great Britain produced only 17,000 tons of pig iron. By 1788, the production of pig iron had increased to 60,000 tons, and by 1796, to 125,000 tons. In 1806, pig iron production reached 256,000 tons and then increased to almost 1.4 million tons in 1840.

Steel

Even the best quality of iron lacked the strength and flexibility of steel, which is iron whose carbon content has been reduced by a process of intense heating. In the early nineteenth century, it was possible to manufacture steel, but to do so required a costly process which was economically justifiable only in special circumstances. In Great Britain, small steel mills operated in Birmingham and Sheffield.

Bessemer.   In 1856 , Henry Bessemer (1813–1898), an English inventor, developed the Bessemer converter, the first efficient method for the mass production of steel.

Siemens.   A decade later, in 1866, William Siemens (1823–1883), a German-born inventor living in England, and his brother, Ernst Werner von Siemens (1816–1892), developed the open hearth process of steelmaking. As a result of these inventions, the steel industry experienced a rapid growth. In the period from 1865 to 1880, the worldwide production of steel grew by 1000 percent.

The Revolution in Transportation

Canals and Roads

The revolution in transportation began with the construction of canals and improvements in road construction.

Canal Construction

In 1761, the duke of Bridgewater completed the construction of one of England's first canals. Running 11 miles, this canal brought coal from the duke's mines in Worsley to Manchester. By 1830, England had a canal network of more than 4000 miles, while canal mileage in Scotland and Wales totaled about 500. Extensive canal systems were built in Europe and America, as well, until the construction of railroads made the digging of additional canals unnecessary.

Improved Roads

Thomas Telford (1757–1834), a Scottish engineer, improved road building in England and Scotland by using a base of large stones with a surface of compacted layers of small stones. About 1815, John McAdam (1756–1836), another Scotsman, developed a durable road surface made of crushed stones cemented by stone dust and water. These macadam roads, as they were known, represented a marked improvement over the dirt roads then generally in use.

Railroads

The development of the steam engine and improvements in the quality of iron led to the invention of railroads.

For several generations, horse-drawn carts, operating on wooden rails, had been used to move coal and iron. During the eighteenth century, iron replaced wood for both the rails and the wheels of the carts.

Trevithick

The next step was to develop a steam-powered locomotive to pull the carts. In 1803, Richard Trevithick (1771–1833) demonstrated his steam locomotive in the streets of London, and the following year, Trevithick's locomotive was used to pull a coal train. However, this locomotive proved expensive to operate.

Stephenson

George Stephenson (1781–1848), another British inventor, was the first to develop an economically successful locomotive. In 1825, a Stephenson locomotive was put into operation on the world's first real railroad, running some 40 miles from the coal fields around Darlington in northern England to the port of Stockton. In 1830, Stephenson's famous locomotive, the *Rocket,* demonstrated its speed on the new Liverpool-to-Manchester railway, running 12 miles in 53 minutes.

Expansion of Railroads

A great boom in railroad construction began. By 1842, British railway mileage totaled 1857. By 1846, the mileage had increased to 3036, and by 1850, to 6621.

Steamships

River Transportation

Steam power was also applied to water transportation. In 1807, Robert Fulton (1765–1815), an American, introduced the first economically successful steamship, the *Clermont,* on the Hudson River in New York state. In 1812, Henry Bell, a Scotsman, demonstrated his steamboat on the River Clyde.

Ocean Crossings

In 1816, the first steamship crossed the English Channel, and three years later the *Savannah,* an American sailing ship equipped with auxiliary steam power, crossed the Atlantic in 29 days. In 1833, the *Royal William,* a Canadian vessel, became the first ship powered entirely by steam to cross the Atlantic, in a voyage taking 20 days.

Passenger and Freight Service

In 1839, the Peninsula and Orient (P & O) Line established regular steamship service from England to Egypt to meet ships of the East India Company coming up the Red Sea. The following year, Samuel Cunard (1787–1865), a Canadian, inaugurated regular passenger service by steamship from the English port of Liverpool to Boston. The marine steam engine was still relatively inefficient, and the coal required for the voyage occupied about half the available space on the ship. While the cost of transporting passengers by steamship could be justified economically, freight continued to be carried by sailing ship. By the 1860s, however, a more efficient marine steam engine had been developed, and the screw propeller replaced the paddle wheel. Steam ships soon operated on the seaways of the world, and the era of the great sailing ships came to an end.

The Revolution in Communications

Innovations introduced during the nineteenth century made rapid communication possible for the first time in human history.

The Telegraph

In 1836, Samuel F. B. Morse (1791–1872), an American, invented the telegraph; eight years later, in 1844, he sent a message from Washington to Baltimore. In 1851, the first successful submarine telegraph cable was laid beneath the English Channel from Dover to Calais, linking Great Britain with the continent. In 1866, soon after the end of the American Civil War, Cyrus Field (1819–1892), an American, laid the first successful transatlantic cable joining the United States and Great Britain.

Mail Delivery

In 1840, Great Britain introduced the penny post, creating the first modern postal system. The Universal Postal Union was established in 1874 to regulate the international delivery of mail.

Banking, Credit, and Business Organization

Banking and Credit

During the industrial revolution, there was a great expansion of banking and credit as private banks lent increasing amounts of capital to assist the expansion of industry.

Limited Liability

The joint stock principle, which had earlier been applied to trading companies, soon began to be used for banks and industrial enterprises. Joint stock companies operated on the basis of limited liability. Investors purchased shares of stock in the company, thereby becoming part owners. The investors would share in the profits, if any, in proportion to the amount of stock owned. In the event the enterprise failed, the investors were liable only for the amount they had invested. Creditors of a bankrupt enterprise could not demand additional payments from them. By reducing the investors' risks, the principle of limited liability encouraged investment in new and untried ventures.

Population Growth and Distribution

During the eighteenth and nineteenth centuries, Great Britain experienced a substantial population growth.

In the period from 1700 to 1830, Britain's population increased from about 7 million to over 16 million. The greatest population growth occurred in northern England, where the cotton textile industry was centered. The population of Lancashire increased by some 800 percent, while the city of Manchester, which became a symbol of industrialization, grew from a population of some 5000 in 1700 to 200,000 in 1830 and 400,000 in 1850. Other major English industrial towns, including Birmingham and Leeds, experienced a similar growth.

The Human Cost of Industrialization

While industrialization promoted the prosperity and wealth of both nations and individuals, the human cost was considerable. During the early stages of the industrial revolution, men, women, and children—many of them under ten years old—worked 12 to 18 hours a day for very low wages in unsafe and unhealthy factories. The workers and their families lived in crowded slums, without adequate sewage facilities, a safe water supply, educational opportunities, or access to health care.

Liberalism

At the heart of the ideology of liberalism was the belief in individualism and individual freedom. In the economic realm, this liberal belief expressed itself in the doctrine of laissez-faire, which repudiated the prevailing economic theory and practice known as mercantilism. The mercantilists, who emphasized trade rather than production, sought to establish and maintain a favorable balance of trade in order to increase the nation's supply of gold and silver. To accomplish this objective, they advocated government regulation of economic activity.

The economists who championed the doctrine of laissez-faire are known as the classical economists.

Adam Smith

The first major advocate of laissez-faire in the English-speaking world was Adam Smith (1723–1790), a Scottish professor at the University of Glasgow. In *The Wealth of Nations* (1776), Smith insisted that a nation's wealth did not depend on its holdings of precious metals but consisted instead of the useful goods being produced. He argued that government attempts to regulate the economy, as the mercantilists had been doing, interfered with the operation of the natural laws that governed the operation of the economy. Government should abandon these policies of interference and restrict itself to the role of a passive policeman, preserving order and protecting private property. Each individual should be free to pursue economic self-interest. This pursuit of self-interest, Smith believed, would promote the wealth and prosperity of society as a whole.

Thomas Malthus and David Ricardo

The work of Thomas Malthus (1766–1834) and David Ricardo (1772–1823) brought a further development of laissez-faire doctrine. Malthus and Ricardo viewed the economic world with much less optimism than did Adam Smith. They believed that while the misery of the workers might be regretted, it was the unavoidable result of the operation of the natural economic laws of population and wages.

Malthus on Population

In *An Essay on the Principle of Population* (1798), Malthus contended that the population was increasing in a geometric ratio, while the food supply was increasing only in an arithmetic ratio. The inevitable result of population outstripping the food supply would be misery for most of humanity. Some slowing of population growth might result from war, famine, and disease. Malthus believed, however, that "moral restraint"—postponing marriage and practicing chastity until marriage—would serve as the most effective way of limiting population growth.

Ricardo on Wages

Influenced by Malthus's work, Ricardo set forth what came to be known as the Iron Law of Wages. In *The Principles of Political Economy and Taxation* (1817), he argued that wages would tend to hover around the subsistence level. In Ricardo's view, labor should be regarded like any other commodity, whose price fluctuated in accordance with supply and demand. If the supply of labor was less than the demand for it, wages would increase. When wages rose above the subsistence level, workers would be encouraged to have more children, thereby enlarging the labor supply. In turn, if the supply of labor exceeded the demand for it, wages would decrease, causing workers to have fewer children, thus reducing the labor supply. Ricardo concluded that it was useless to raise wages in an effort to improve workers' lives, since higher wages would serve only to encourage them to have more children, thereby increasing the labor supply and forcing wages down once again.

Jeremy Bentham

Some liberals came to question the strict laissez-faire doctrine of the classical economists. Although Jeremy Bentham (1748–1832) believed in the fundamental validity of laissez-faire, he argued that in some instances the government should not be merely a passive policeman but should intervene on behalf of the disadvantaged.

Bentham developed the doctrine of utilitarianism, also known as philosophic radicalism, in his *Principles of Morals and Legislation* (1789) and many other writings. Central to this doctrine was the belief that every human practice and institution should be evaluated in terms of its utility, which Bentham defined as the amount of happiness it provides. In turn, he defined happiness as the presence of pleasure and the absence of pain.

For the most part, Bentham believed, the government could assure happiness (the most pleasure and the least pain) for the greatest number of people by permitting them the maximum possible amount of individual freedom. If, however, the pains suffered by the many exceeded the pleasures enjoyed by the few, then the government could justifiably intervene to redress the balance. In this way, Bentham began to develop the ideas that ultimately led to the creation of the twentieth-century welfare state.

John Stuart Mill

The thought of John Stuart Mill (1806–1873) represented a further evolution of liberal doctrine away from the doctrine of laissez-faire. Mill shared the liberals' belief in individual freedom, a belief he expressed in his eloquent essay *On Liberty* (1859). He was ahead of his time in advocating women's rights, including the right to vote, in *The Subjection of Women* (1869).

In his *Principles of Political Economy,* published in 1848 and in several subsequent editions, Mill expressed growing disagreement with the views of the classical economists. Concerned about economic and social injustice, he contended that society could and should exercise some control over the distribution of wealth. He believed that workers should have the freedom to form labor unions to promote their interests and that the government should adopt laws to restrict child labor and to protect women workers. He endorsed the establishment of universal suffrage, which would give workers a degree of influence over the actions of government. He also called for the creation of a system of state-supported elementary education, as well as the enactment of income and inheritance taxes to place limits on the concentration of wealth.

Socialism

While John Stuart Mill and some other liberals advocated a redistribution of wealth to benefit the disadvantaged, the socialists called for a fundamental change in the nature of property ownership itself. They denounced the capitalist system for its promotion of greed and injustice and urged that private ownership of the means of production, and perhaps also of the means of distribution, should be replaced by some form of community or state ownership. This social ownership of property, the socialists argued, would ensure that property would serve the interests of all the people, rather than the interests of a few profit-seekers. The socialists also believed that people were — or could be educated to be — cooperative, rather than ruthlessly competitive and that they should work together to promote their mutual well-being.

While the socialists agreed on these general principles, socialist thinkers offered a variety of proposals outlining their conceptions of what a socialist society would be like and how it could be brought into being.

Utopian Socialism: Robert Owen

The socialist thinkers of the early nineteenth century are known collectively as Utopian Socialists. Robert Owen (1771–1858) was one of the first Utopian Socialists to gain wide attention.

After achieving an early success in the cotton textile industry, in 1799 Owen acquired part ownership of several textile mills at New Lanark in Scotland. He improved the conditions of health and safety in the mills, increased the workers' wages and reduced their hours, and provided them with decent housing. No children under the age of eleven were employed in the mills, and schooling was provided for the workers' children. Owen made a substantial profit, thereby demonstrating that successful industrial capitalism did not require the exploitation of labor.

Owen's great dream, however, was to establish a socialist community. Selling his interest in the New Lanark mills, he went to America, where he bought land in Indiana. In 1826, he established his community of New Harmony, where people would share both the ownership of property and the fruits of their labor. Within a few years, New Harmony failed. Owen returned to England and devoted the remaining years of his life to other reform projects, including the establishment of a national labor union and the promotion of the cooperative movement.

Christian Socialism

Some economic and social reformers found their inspiration in the teachings of the Christian religion. In the mid-nineteenth century, the

Christian Socialist movement developed in the Church of England. The Christian Socialists did not propose a specific ideology but instead advocated reforms, motivated by the Christian spirit of brotherly love, to benefit industrial workers and other disadvantaged groups.

Frederick Denison Maurice

Frederick Denison Maurice (1805–1872), an Anglican priest and professor at Cambridge University, emerged as a major spokesman for Christian Socialism. In addition to promoting economic and social reform, he sought to advance educational opportunities for women and factory workers. These efforts led to the establishment of Queen's College for women in 1848 and the Working Men's College in 1854.

Charles Kingsley

Charles Kingsley (1819–1875), another Anglican priest and professor at Cambridge, served as chaplain to Queen Victoria. Kingsley denounced the evils of industrial capitalism in several novels, including *Alton Locke* (1850) and *Yeast* (1851).

The influence of the agricultural and industrial revolutions spread gradually beyond Great Britain to the rest of Europe and North America and, ultimately, to other regions of the world. Over the course of a few generations, these revolutions brought greater material changes to the lives of human beings than had occurred during all of recorded history up to that time.

While the agricultural and industrial revolutions were producing vast changes in the economies of Great Britain and the world, liberal and socialist thinkers were advancing new ideas about the relationship between government and society, on the one hand, and the operation of the economy, on the other. These ideas, which emerged in the final years of the eighteenth century and the first years of the nineteenth, have continued to exert a powerful influence on economic theory and practice.

Recommended Reading

Ashton, Thomas S. *The Industrial Revolution, 1760–1830* (rev. ed., 1964).

Ashton, Thomas S. *Iron and Steel in the Industrial Revolution* (3rd ed., 1963).

Briggs, Asa. *The Power of Steam* (1982).

Chambers, J. D. *The Workshop of the World: British Economic History from 1820 to 1880* (1961).

Chambers, J. D. and G. E. Mingay. *The Agricultural Revolution, 1750–1880* (1966).

Checkland, S. G. *The Rise of Industrial Society in England, 1815–1885* (1965).

Crafts, N. F. R. *British Economic Growth During the Industrial Revolution* (1985).

Deane, Phyllis. *The First Industrial Revolution* (2nd ed., 1979).

Hadfield, Charles. *British Canals* (1950).

Harrison, John F. C. *Quest for the New Moral World: Robert Owen and the Owenites in Britain and America* (1969).

Heilbroner, Robert L. *The Worldly Philosophers* (5th ed., 1980).

Henderson, W. O. *Britain and Industrial Europe, 1750–1870* (3rd ed., 1972).

Hobsbawm, E. J. *Industry and Empire: The Making of Modern English Society, 1750 to the Present Day* (1968).

Landes, David S. *The Unbound Prometheus: Technological Change and Industrial Development in Western Europe from 1750 to the Present* (1969).

Laslett, Peter. *The World We Have Lost: England Before the Industrial Age* (1965).

Letwin, S. H. *The Pursuit of Certainty: David Hume, Jeremy Bentham, John Stuart Mill, Beatrice Webb* (1965).

Mathias, Peter. *The First Industrial Nation: An Economic History of Britain, 1700–1914* (2nd ed., 1983).

Mitchell, B. R. *Economic Development of the British Coal Industry, 1800–1914* (1984).

Morris, R. J. and John Langton, eds. *Atlas of Industrializing Britain* (1986).

O'Brien, Patrick and Caglar Keyder. *Economic Growth in Britain and France, 1780–1914: Two Paths to the Twentieth Century* (1978).

Robbins, Michael. *The Railway Age* (1962).

Salaman, Radcliffe. *The History and Social Influence of the Potato* (rev. ed., 1985).

Taylor, George Rogers. *The Transportation Revolution, 1815–1860* (1951).

Taylor, P. A. M., ed. *The Industrial Revolution in Britain: Triumph or Disaster?* (2nd ed., 1970).

Thomas, Malcolm I. *The Luddites* (1970).

Turner, Michael. *Enclosures in Britain, 1750–1830* (1984).

Wrigley, E. A. and R. S. Schofield. *The Population History of England, 1541–1871: A Reconstruction* (1982).

CHAPTER 15

Reaction and Reform in the Early Nineteenth Century

Time Line

1798	William Wordsworth and Samuel Taylor Coleridge publish *Lyrical Ballads*
1812–1827	Lord Liverpool, a Tory, serves as prime minister
1812–1822	Viscount Castlereagh serves as foreign secretary
1817	Parliament passes the Coercion Acts
1819	The Peterloo Massacre takes place in Manchester
	Parliament passes the repressive Six Acts
1819–1824	Lord Byron publishes *Don Juan*

1820	Percy Bysshe Shelley publishes *Prometheus Unbound*
	Sir Walter Scott publishes *Ivanhoe*
1820–1830	Reign of King George IV
1820	The Cato Street Conspiracy is revealed
1828	Parliament repeals the Test Act
1829	Parliament enacts Catholic emancipation
1830	Great Britain, France, and Russia formally recognize Greek independence
	Great Britain supports Belgian independence
1830–1837	Reign of King William IV
1830–1834	Earl Grey, a Whig, serves as prime minister
1830–1841	Lord Palmerston serves as foreign secretary
1832	Parliament passes the Reform Bill of 1832
1833	Parliament passes a Factory Act
	Slavery is abolished in the British Empire
1834	Parliament enacts a new Poor Law
1835–1841	Lord Melbourne, a Whig, serves as prime minister
1837–1901	Reign of Queen Victoria
1839	The People's Charter is presented to Parliament for the first time
	The Anti-Corn Law League is established
	Great Britain and the other major powers pledge to guarantee the independence and permanent neutrality of Belgium
1841–1846	Sir Robert Peel, a Tory, serves as prime minister
1846	Parliament repeals the Corn Laws
	Great Britain and the United States resolve the Oregon boundary dispute

1846–1852	Lord John Russell, a Whig, serves as prime minister
1846–1851	Lord Palmerston serves as foreign secretary
1850	Lord Palmerston asserts British power in the Don Pacifico affair
1852	The first Conservative Derby-Disraeli ministry holds office
1852–1855	Lord Aberdeen, a Peelite, serves as prime minister
1853–1856	Great Britain and France support the Ottoman Empire in the Crimean War against Russia
1855–1858	Lord Palmerston, a Whig, heads his first ministry
1858–1859	The second Derby-Disraeli ministry holds office
1859–1865	Lord Palmerston heads his second ministry
1861–1865	Great Britain remains neutral during the American Civil War

In the early nineteenth century, reactionary rule gradually gave way to a movement for reform. Religious restrictions were eliminated, the criminal code was modified, and slavery was abolished throughout the British Empire. The most important reform of these years, however, was the Reform Bill of 1832, which redistributed seats in the House of Commons and granted the right to vote to most adult middle-class males. Nevertheless, the British ruling classes rejected the demands of the Chartist movement for full political democracy. In the area of trade policy, the British moved toward the adoption of free trade.

In foreign affairs, Great Britain refused to align itself with the conservative continental powers that advocated intervention in countries whose governments were threatened by revolution. Instead, the British recognized the independence of the Latin American states, Greece, and Belgium. Great Britain also acted to defend the Ottoman Empire against Russian encroachment. Its growing power generally enabled Great Britain to assert its influence in international affairs.

In literature, art, and intellectual life, the Romantic movement flourished during the early nineteenth century, which proved to be an era of particular accomplishment.

Reactionary Rule After 1815

For several years after 1815, the British ruling classes lived in fear of revolution. The country experienced a postwar economic depression, and mounting unemployment resulted in widespread hardship and unrest. Discharged soldiers and sailors swelled the ranks of the unemployed.

The Liverpool Cabinet

The earl of Liverpool (1770–1828), a Tory, served as prime minister from 1812 to 1827, heading a cabinet that initially opposed demands for reform and sought to repress expressions of discontent.

Expressions of Dissent

Of the many advocates of reform, William Cobbett (c. 1763 – 1835) won the greatest response from the masses. A fierce opponent of the reactionary government and the aristocrats who dominated it, Cobbett began the publication of his newspaper, the *Political Register,* in 1802.

In December 1816, violence erupted during a reform meeting in Spa Fields, London. Parliament responded by passing the Coercion Acts of 1817, which temporarily suspended habeas corpus and tightened existing laws restricting seditious meetings.

In 1817, unemployed workers, known as the Blanketeers, planned a protest march from Manchester to London. The leaders of the march were arrested.

The Peterloo Massacre

More serious violence occurred in August 1819, when troops fired on a large crowd which had gathered at St. Peter's Fields in Manchester to hear a speech on parliamentary reform by the radical agitator, Henry Hunt (1773–1835). Eleven people were killed, and several hundred wounded. The affair became known as the Peterloo Massacre, in ironic contrast with the British victory over Napoleon at Waterloo in 1815.

The Six Acts

Following the Peterloo Massacre, Parliament adopted the Six Acts in December 1819. This repressive legislation prohibited unauthorized military training, restricted the freedoms of speech and assembly and other civil liberties, increased taxes on newspapers and fines for seditious libel, expanded the right of the police to search private homes, and provided for the speedy trial and harsh punishment of offenders against public order.

King George IV

In 1810, when King George III lapsed into permanent insanity, the Prince of Wales became regent. In January 1820, following the king's death, the prince regent succeeded to the throne as George IV (r. 1820–1830).

The Cato Street Conspiracy

In February 1820, the government uncovered a plot to assassinate the entire cabinet. The leaders of the Cato Street Conspiracy, as the plot became known, were arrested and tried, and four were executed. Whether a serious revolutionary movement existed in Great Britain is impossible to determine. It is evident, however, that the reactionary government was widely unpopular.

Tory Reform in the 1820s

Although Lord Liverpool remained prime minister until 1827, a younger group of Tory leaders gradually began to push for a program of moderate reform.

Criminal Codes

Robert Peel (1788–1850), who served as home secretary from 1822 to 1827, won parliamentary approval for a reform of the criminal codes, reducing the number of capital crimes from over 200 to about 100. Peel also reorganized the London police, who came to be known as "bobbies" in his honor.

Trade

William Huskisson (1770–1830), the president of the Board of Trade from 1823 to 1827, moved away from mercantilist regulation in the direction of free trade. He persuaded Parliament to allow British goods to be carried by foreign ships and to reduce tariffs on a number of imports.

Labor

In 1824, Parliament repealed the Combination Acts of 1799 and 1800, which had made both labor unions and strikes illegal. A new law passed in 1825, however, reimposed the ban on strikes.

Religion

Some religious restrictions were removed. In 1828, Parliament repealed the Test and Corporations Acts, which had been enacted in the late seventeenth century (see Chapter 10). These acts barred Nonconformists from public office, although they had not been enforced for some years.

In 1829, a campaign led by Daniel O'Connell (1775–1847), an Irish attorney and founder of the Catholic Association, achieved success when Parliament passed Catholic emancipation, extending to Roman Catholics the right to hold public office. Restrictions on office-holding by Jews remained in effect for several more years.

The Reform Act of 1832

In the early nineteenth century, the British Parliament was far from democratic and not representative of the population. The House of Lords consisted of the hereditary nobility and the bishops of the Church of England. In addition, from time to time the king invoked his right to create new peers (noblemen), who acquired the right to sit in the House of Lords. The House of Lords could block the adoption of legislation passed by the House of Commons.

The House of Commons consisted mainly of prosperous country gentlemen (the gentry) and wealthy business and professional men. They received no salaries. Only a small percentage of the adult male population was able to meet the property qualifications for voters.

Many members of the House of Commons represented rotten boroughs or pocket boroughs (see Chapter 12). The new industrial towns, especially those of the English Midlands, were either completely without representation in the House of Commons or seriously underrepresented.

Agitation for parliamentary reform had begun in the late eighteenth century. While it had made little headway in the face of conservative opposition, it gradually won increased popular support.

Whig Support of Reform

From 1828 to 1830, the duke of Wellington (1769–1852) served as prime minister. While the victor of Waterloo was a great national hero, he was a reactionary Tory in his politics and had no sympathy for reform. In 1830, however, the Tories lost the general election to the Whigs.

In 1831, the new Whig prime minister, Earl Grey (1764–1845), won the approval of the House of Commons for a parliamentary reform bill, but the Lords rejected it. When the Commons passed a second reform bill the same year, the Lords rejected it once again. Grey now appealed to the new king, William IV (r. 1830–1837), who promised to create enough new Whig peers to assure the Lords' passage of a reform bill.

The threat sufficed. In 1832, the House of Lords approved the third reform bill passed by the House of Commons.

Provisions of the Bill

Redistribution of Parliament Seats

The Reform Bill of 1832 deprived fifty-six rotten and pocket boroughs of their 111 seats in the House of Commons, while thirty-two other small boroughs each lost one of their two members. The 143 available seats were then redistributed, with 65 seats assigned to boroughs that had been either underrepresented or without any representation at all. Another 65 seats went to English counties, while 5 were assigned to Ireland and 8 to Scotland.

Extension of Suffrage

In addition to this redistribution of seats in the House of Commons, the reform Bill of 1832 extended the right to vote to all householders in the boroughs who paid £10 a year in rent. The right to vote was also broadened in the counties.

In essence, adult male members of the middle class gained voting rights. In a population of almost 17 million, there were now close to 800,000 voters, some 250,000 more than before the bill's adoption. Property qualifications continued to bar most workers from voting. Nevertheless, the Reform Bill of 1832 represented the beginning of a decisive shift in political power from the landed aristocracy to the middle class.

Other Reforms

Abolition of Slavery

In 1833, Parliament abolished slavery throughout the British Empire. This represented a victory for the abolitionists led by William Wilberforce (see Chapter 12) and the Anti-Slavery Society, which had been founded in 1823.

Limitations on Work by Women and Children

Factory Acts of 1816 and 1833

The Factory Act of 1816 sought to restrict child labor in the cotton textile industry, but it proved ineffective because it lacked enforcement provisions. In 1833, Parliament passed another Factory Act placing restrictions on child labor in the textile industry. Children under the age of nine could not be employed in textile mills, while those between the ages of nine and thirteen could not work for more than nine hours a day and were to receive two hours of schooling daily. Work by children between the ages of thirteen and eighteen was limited to twelve hours a day. The act provided for a system of inspectors to make certain that the law was being observed.

Mines Act of 1842

The Mines Act of 1842 prohibited the employment in mines of women and girls and of boys under the age of ten. (The age was raised to twelve in 1860.)

Factory Acts of 1844 and 1847

The Factory Act of 1844 limited the workday of children to six-and-a-half hours and of women to twelve hours, while the Factory Act of 1847 reduced the workday for women and for persons aged thirteen to eighteen to ten hours.

The Poor Law

In 1834, Parliament adopted a controversial new Poor Law. Under its terms, the sick and elderly poor would continue to receive relief payments, while workhouses were established for the poor who were physically able to work. The principle behind the workhouses was the belief that the able-bodied poor were lazy and that if they were made as uncomfortable as possible, they would be more willing to find employment.

Municipal Councils

The Municipal Corporations Act of 1835 established a system of elected councils to govern most cities and towns. Similar acts were also adopted for Scotland (1833) and Ireland (1840).

Political Trends

Lord Melbourne

Earl Grey's resignation in July 1834 was followed by a period of political uncertainty that persisted until Viscount Melbourne (1779–1848), a Whig, became prime minister in 1835. Lord Melbourne proved to be an effective political manager and, for the next six years, until 1841, he governed Great Britain in partnership with Lord John Russell (1792–1878), the leader of the House of Commons. A supporter of aristocratic government, Melbourne opposed further parliamentary reform and the repeal of the Corn Laws (see pp. 261–262).

Queen Victoria

When King William IV died in 1837, he was succeeded by his niece, the eighteen-year-old Victoria (r. 1837–1901), whose reign proved to be the longest in English history. In 1840, Victoria married Albert of Saxe-Coburg-Gotha (1819–1861), a German prince. His untimely death in 1861 left her disconsolate.

Separation of Hanover

British monarchs since King George I in the early eighteenth century had also ruled the German state of Hanover, although the two countries remained separate. When Victoria succeeded to the British throne, her uncle became king of Hanover, because the traditional Salic Law observed there barred women from the succession.

The Chartist Movement

The People's Charter

Following the adoption of the Reform Bill of 1832, agitation developed for further parliamentary reform. In 1838, a group of working class leaders drew up the People's Charter, which contained six demands:

1. Universal manhood suffrage.

2. The secret ballot instead of voting in public meetings.

3. The abolition of property requirements for members of the House of Commons.

4. The payment of salaries to members of the House of Commons.

5. The creation of equal electoral districts: that is, members of the House of Commons should represent approximately the same number of people.

6. Annual elections for the House of Commons.

Chartist Agitation

The Chartists (people who supported the People's Charter) won support among many intellectual reformers, as well as from urban workers. In 1839, the Chartists presented to Parliament a petition setting forth their demands. However, the British middle classes were not yet prepared to share political power with the masses, and Parliament ignored the petition.

Chartist agitation continued under the leadership of Feargus O'Connor (1794–1855), who published a Chartist newspaper, *The Northern Star*. Although Parliament also ignored Chartist petitions presented in 1842 and 1848, all the demands of the Chartists were ultimately enacted except for annual elections for the House of Commons.

The Repeal of the Corn Laws

The campaign for the repeal of the Corn Laws (the tariff on wheat and other grains) provided powerful evidence of the increased political power of the British middle class.

In 1815, Parliament had revised the Corn Laws, increasing the tariff. While this provided the great landowners with a protected market for their crops, it also led to higher prices for bread. In the mid-1820s, Parliament further revised the Corn Laws by adopting a sliding scale of tariffs. When the price of wheat declined, the tariff would be increased and vice versa. This concession, however, did not satisfy the advocates of repeal of the Corn Laws.

The Anti-Corn Law League

The Anti-Corn Law League, which was established in 1839, campaigned for the repeal of the Corn Laws and, more broadly, for the introduction of free trade. The leaders of the Anti-Corn Law League included the prominent industrialists Richard Cobden (1804–1865) and John Bright (1811–1889).

The Anti-Corn Law League argued that reducing the price of food would improve the workers' standard of living, while reducing the cost of raw materials would increase the profits of industry. In addition, low food prices would make it easier for the industrialists to pay their workers lower wages.

Peel's Economic Program

Sir Robert Peel, the Tory prime minister from 1841 to 1846, believed in the laissez-faire doctrine (see Chapter 14) and thus favored free trade in principle. However, as the leader of the Tories, who were coming to be known as the Conservatives, he felt obliged to support the interests of the landowners who formed the backbone of his party.

Peel's budget of 1842 called for reductions in the tariff on grain imports but did not repeal it. Peel also removed tariffs on some manufactured goods and reduced the tariffs on others. The prime minister introduced an income tax, and his 1845 budget abolished export duties and reduced tariffs on additional imports.

Irish Famine

During the winter of 1845–1846, a severe famine struck Ireland following a failure of the potato crop. Starvation and diseases such as typhus and cholera took the lives of some 700,000 people. Hundreds of thousands of survivors emigrated, with many finding new homes in the United States.

Establishment of Free Trade

The Irish famine demonstrated the need for lower food prices, and in 1846 Peel won parliamentary approval for the repeal of the Corn Laws. Peel's support of repeal split the Conservatives, and Peel himself lost the prime ministership in 1846.

The repeal of the Corn Laws was a victory for Britain's urban dwellers, who for the first time comprised a majority of the population. In the following years, the British eliminated the remaining tariffs, establishing a free trade policy.

Politics After Peel

After Peel's fall from the prime ministership, Great Britain entered a period of political uncertainty, as neither the Conservatives (formerly the Tories) or the Whigs could command a clear majority in the House of Commons. The Peelites, loyal to their leader's memory, split from the Conservatives, while the Whigs were divided into conservative Whigs, led by Lord John Russell and Viscount Palmerston, and the Radicals, under the leadership of Cobden and Bright, who urged further reform.

For the next two decades, from the mid-1840s to the mid-1860s, most governments were formed by uneasy alliances of conservative Whigs and Peelites, with two brief interludes of Conservative government.

Lord John Russell

From 1846 to 1852, Lord John Russell, a Whig, served as prime minister.

The Russell cabinet had to confront unrest in Ireland that resulted from the Irish famine. A Coercion Act, designed to suppress discontent, and the distribution of free food failed to quell disorders. In 1848, the radical leaders of the Young Ireland movement planned a revolt, which was prevented by the timely arrest of its leaders. While calm was gradually restored in Ireland, Irish grievances persisted.

The First Derby-Disraeli Ministry

In 1852, the earl of Derby (1799–1869), a Conservative, held the prime ministership for ten months. Benjamin Disraeli (1804–1881) served as chancellor of the exchequer and leader in the House of Commons.

The Earl of Aberdeen

Lord Aberdeen (1784–1860), a Peelite, became prime minister in 1852, heading a Whig-Peelite coalition. William E. Gladstone (1809–1898) served as chancellor of the exchequer.

Although Aberdeen was generally successful in domestic affairs, he failed to prevent Lord Palmerston and others in his government from involving Great Britain in the Crimean War (see pp. 269–270). Failures in the Crimean campaign and the unpopularity of the war led to Aberdeen's fall in 1855.

Viscount Palmerston's First Ministry

From 1855 to 1858, Lord Palmerston (1784–1865), a Whig, headed his first ministry, providing Great Britain with effective leadership in the Crimean War.

The Second Derby-Disraeli Ministry

In 1858, the Conservatives returned to power with the second Derby-Disraeli ministry. Failing to win the support of the Peelites, the cabinet had the support of only a minority in the House of Commons and fell in 1859.

Lord Palmerston's Second Ministry

In 1859, Palmerston became prime minister for the second time, serving until his death in 1865. The Whigs, Peelites, and Radicals now joined to form the Liberal Party. Gladstone once again held office as chancellor of the exchequer.

Foreign Affairs:
Castlereagh and Canning

Both Viscount Castlereagh (1769–1822), who served as foreign secretary from 1812 to 1822, and George Canning (1770–1827), foreign secretary from 1822 to 1827, proved to be both active and successful in that office.

The Concert of Europe

In the years after 1815, the European great powers hoped that their collaboration in the Concert of Europe would lead to the preservation of the balance of power and of the conservative order established at the Congress of Vienna (see Chapter 13). While Castlereagh, who had represented Great Britain in Vienna, shared the continental powers' fears of liberalism, he opposed intervention in the domestic affairs of other countries.

The Congress of Aix-la-Chapelle

In 1818, meeting in the Congress of Aix-la-Chapelle, the members of the Quadruple Alliance agreed to permit France to rejoin the ranks of the great powers, thus converting the Quadruple Alliance into the Quintuple Alliance.

When Tsar Alexander I (r. 1801–1825) of Russia proposed that the great powers should act, when necessary, to support existing governments and frontiers in Europe, Castlereagh rejected the proposal, marking the first break in the post-1815 accord among the major powers.

The Congresses of Troppau and Laibach

In 1820, revolutions broke out in Spain and the Kingdom of the Two Sicilies. In both countries, army rebels forced the monarchs to become constitutional rulers. These revolutions were high on the agendas of the Congresses of Troppau and Laibach in 1820–1821.

Troppau. In the Protocol of Troppau, Russia, Prussia, and Austria asserted their right to intervene in other countries to oppose revolutions. Once again, Castlereagh objected to this interventionist policy.

Laibach. The breach between the British and the three conservative powers widened at the Congress of Laibach, which authorized Austria to suppress the revolution in the Kingdom of the Two Sicilies, which it did in 1821.

The Congress of Verona

In 1822, the last Concert of Europe congress, the Congress of Verona, authorized France to intervene to overthrow the revolution in Spain. George Canning, who became foreign secretary following Castlereagh's suicide in 1822, continued Britain's opposition to the policy of intervention. This opposition, in effect, resulted in Britain's withdrawal from the Quintuple Alliance.

Latin American Independence

British Opposition to Intervention

British opposition to intervention made it impossible for the conservative powers of Europe to suppress the revolts against Spanish rule in Latin America because they could not act effectively without the support of Britain's naval power. The British opposed intervention both because of principle and because they did not want any interference with their profitable trade with Latin America. Canning proposed that Great Britain and the United States join in a declaration against any European intervention in the Western Hemisphere.

The Monroe Doctrine

The United States, however, preferred to act independently. In the Monroe Doctrine, issued by President James Monroe (1758–1831) in December 1823, the United States announced its opposition to intervention and any further colonization by the European powers in the Western Hemisphere. The British endorsed the Monroe Doctrine, and in 1824, they recognized the governments of the independent Latin American republics, including Brazil, which had been a Portuguese possession.

Greek Independence

The British traditionally sought to prevent any Russian advance into the eastern Mediterranean and the Near East, and thus they opposed Russian encroachments against the Ottoman Empire. However, during the 1820s, the British cooperated with the Russians in support of the Greek struggle for independence from the Turks. British intervention could help the Greeks win their independence, while a British presence in the region would place restraints on the Russians.

The Greek revolt against the Turks began in 1821, and often brutal fighting continued for several years. By 1825, the Turks had almost crushed the revolt.

In Great Britain and elsewhere in Western Europe, sympathy for the Greeks mounted, in large part because of a sentimental regard for the contribution of the ancient Greeks to the development of Western civilization. The Russians, for their part, saw the conflict in Greece as an opportunity for them to make gains at Turkish expense.

The Treaty of London (1827)

In the Treaty of London of 1827, Great Britain, France, and Russia agreed to demand that the Ottoman Empire recognize Greek independence and to use force, if necessary, to end the fighting. When efforts at negotiation failed, an allied fleet defeated a Turkish and Egyptian force at Navarino in October 1827.

The Treaty of Adrianople (1829)

In 1828, Russia declared war on Turkey, and Russian forces advanced into the Turkish-controlled Danubian Provinces of Moldavia and Wallachia (modern Romania). Under the terms of the Treaty of Adrianople of 1829, the Danubian Provinces gained autonomy, as did Serbia, which the Turks had also ruled. Russia acquired Turkish territory at the mouth of the Danube River and in the Caucasus on the eastern coast of the Black Sea. The Turks also agreed to permit Russia, France, and Great Britain to determine the future of Greece.

The Treaty of London (1830)

In the Treaty of London of 1830, Great Britain, France, and Russia formally recognized Greek independence.

Foreign Affairs: Palmerston

Lord Palmerston was Britain's third great foreign secretary of the early nineteenth century. He first gained that office in 1830, when the Whig Earl Grey (see p. 257) became prime minister. From 1841 to 1846, during the prime ministership of Sir Robert Peel, Palmerston was in opposition, but he again served as foreign secretary from 1846 to 1851, in the cabinet of Lord John Russell. As prime minister from 1855 to 1858 and from 1859 until his death in 1865, Palmerston focused his attention on foreign affairs.

Belgian Independence

Palmerston supported the successful Belgian effort to win independence from the Netherlands. The revolt against Dutch rule began in August 1830, and in November, a national congress declared Belgium's independence.

Under the terms of the Convention of 1839, Great Britain, France, Austria, Prussia, and Russia agreed to guarantee Belgium's independence and permanent neutrality.

The Near East

In 1832, Mehemet Ali, the pasha of Egypt, defeated the Ottoman Empire and occupied Syria. When the Ottoman sultan signed a defensive alliance with Russia, British suspicions were aroused.

Then, in 1839, the conflict between Mehemet Ali and the sultan was resumed. When France supported Mehemet Ali's claim to Syria, Palmerston succeeded in getting the other major European powers to put pressure on the pasha to evacuate Syria. This action served both to reduce the threat of Russian encroachments on Turkey and to keep French influence out of Egypt.

China

Palmerston also pursued an activist policy in East Asia, fighting the Opium War against China in the early 1840s. This war resulted in the British acquisition of Hong Kong (see Chapter 17).

The United States

During the prime ministership of Sir Robert Peel from 1841 to 1846, Lord Aberdeen served as foreign secretary. While Aberdeen was less of an activist than Palmerston, he succeeded in easing strained relations with the United States.

The Webster-Ashburton Treaty

The Webster-Ashburton Treaty of 1842 resolved a dispute over the boundary between New Brunswick and the American state of Maine.

The Oregon Boundary

In 1846, an Anglo-American agreement established the northern boundary of the Oregon Territory at the 49th parallel. Thus the boundary established in the Rush-Bagot Agreement of 1818 (see Chapter 13) to apply to the Great Lakes region was extended to the Pacific Ocean. Great Britain retained possession of all of Vancouver Island.

The Clayton-Bulwer Treaty

Following Palmerston's return to the foreign ministry, Great Britain and the United States signed the Clayton-Bulwer Treaty of 1850, agreeing on joint Anglo-American construction and operation of any canal built in Central America.

The Revolutions of 1848

Palmerston endorsed the unsuccessful liberal and national revolutions that swept much of Europe in 1848 and condemned the repressive policies of the conservative regimes in restoring their authority. Great Britain became a refuge for political exiles, including the Hungarian Louis Kossuth (1802–1894) and the Italian Giuseppe Mazzini (1805–1872).

The Don Pacifico Affair

The Don Pacifico Affair of 1850 serves as a striking symbol of Palmerston's activist foreign policy.

David Pacifico, a Portuguese Jew, had become a British subject while living at Gibraltar. He later moved to Greece, where a mob in Athens destroyed his house.

Don Pacifico called on the British foreign office to support his claim against the Greek government for compensation. When the Greeks failed to respond satisfactorily to diplomatic appeals, Palmerston ordered the Royal Navy to seize Greek ships. Faced with this threat, the Greek government hastened to acknowledge its responsibility.

Palmerston's impetuous action evoked considerable criticism, and the House of Lords voted to censure the foreign secretary. When a vote of no confidence was sought in the House of Commons, Palmerston successfully defended himself by advancing the dramatic argument that a British subject anywhere should be able to depend on the protection of the British government, just as a Roman citizen could claim his government's support by declaring *"civis Romanus sum"* ("I am a Roman citizen").

The Crimean War (1853–1856)

Russia's continuing pressure on the declining Ottoman Empire and in particular, Russia's claims to be the protector of the Orthodox Christian subjects of the Ottoman sultan led to the outbreak of the Crimean War. In July 1853, the Russians occupied the Danubian Provinces of Moldavia and Wallachia, and in October the Turks responded by declaring war. Great Britain joined with France in declaring war on Russia in March 1854. Sardinia-Piedmont soon joined the allies. Although they had no quarrel with Russia, the Piedmontese sought to curry support among the British and French in their efforts to unite Italy (see p. 270). Prussia and Austria remained neutral.

British and French Intervention

Motives for Intervention.   The British and French intervened in the war primarily because they wanted to block any further expansion of Russian power and especially to prevent Russia from acquiring control of the Turkish Straits, which would give the Russians access to the eastern Mediterranean. Napoleon III (r. 1852–1870), the French emperor, also believed that an activist foreign policy would increase domestic political support for his regime.

Sebastopol.   During the war, the allies concentrated on efforts to take the Russian fortress at Sebastopol in the Crimea. The siege of Sebastopol included the famous and tragic charge of the light brigade at Balaclava in late October 1854. Here British cavalry units charged recklessly into a natural amphitheater where they were mowed down by cannon fire on three sides. Of the 700 who began the

the action, only 195 survived. Following a siege of eleven months, Sebastopol fell to the allies in September 1855.

Impetus to British Reforms.   For the British, the Crimean War had two important long-term consequences. The heroic work in the Crimea of nurse Florence Nightingale (1820–1910) led to the establishment of the British Red Cross, while the poor performance of the British army resulted in a program of army reform.

The Treaty of Paris

Under the terms of the Treaty of Paris, signed in March 1856, Russia was compelled to return southern Bessarabia and the mouth of the Danube to the Turks. In the so-called Black Sea Clauses, the Russians accepted the neutralization of the Black Sea, agreeing not to maintain any navy or coastal fortifications in the area. The Russians also renounced their claim to be the protector of Orthodox Christians in the Ottoman Empire. (In 1870, when the attention of Europe was distracted by the Franco-German War, the Russians unilaterally abrogated the Black Sea Clauses.)

Italian Unification

The British sympathized with the efforts of Camillo Cavour (1810–1861), the prime minister of Sardinia-Piedmont, to unite Italy. In May 1860, ships of the Royal Navy supported the landing of Giuseppe Garibaldi (1807–1882) and his Red Shirts in Sicily. Garibaldi's action resulted in the overthrow of the Bourbon monarchy in the Kingdom of the Two Sicilies and southern Italy's inclusion in the new Kingdom of Italy, which was proclaimed in March 1861.

The American Civil War (1861–1865)

When the American Civil War broke out in 1861, Great Britain declared its neutrality, although the upper classes generally sympathized with the Confederacy. The loss of American cotton injured Britain's textile industry, and on several occasions, the cabinet considered recognizing Confederate independence. President Abraham Lincoln's Emancipation Proclamation of 1863 and Union victories on the battlefield put an end to that possibility.

Wartime Incidents

Two incidents during the war strained relations between Great Britain and the United States although war between the two countries did not result.

The Trent.   In November 1861, a United States cruiser stopped a British ship, the *Trent,* and seized two Confederate diplomats, James M. Mason and John Slidell, who were traveling to London and Paris, respectively. The British cabinet responded to this violation of neutral rights with a strong note of protest. The Americans released Mason and Slidell with an apology.

The Alabama.   During the war, British shipyards constructed several Confederate cruisers, which were used to raid Union shipping. The most famous of these ships was the *Alabama,* built in Liverpool in 1861–1862. The United States government protested this construction and in late 1863, the British decided not to make additional raiders available to the Confederacy.

Romanticism

During the early nineteenth century, the movement known as romanticism influenced literature, the arts, and thought in Great Britain, as it did elsewhere in Europe. While romanticism was a complex and diverse phenomenon, romantic writers, artists, and thinkers were united in reaction against what they regarded as the eighteenth-century Enlightenment's excessive emphasis on the supremacy of reason in human affairs. Instead, the romantics emphasized feelings and emotions, faith and intuition, and imagination and spontaneity. In their literary and artistic activity, the romantics rebelled against the formalism of eighteenth-century classicism and the rigid rules that classicism applied to the creative process.

The romantics also manifested a reverence for the past and an awareness of the emotional ties that joined the present with the past and gave a sense of meaning and stability to society and its institutions. In particular, many romantics had a fascination with the culture of the Middle Ages, an age of faith, which stood in contrast to the eighteenth-century age of reason.

Literature

William Wordsworth and Samuel Taylor Coleridge

The Romantic era was a great age for English poetry. In 1798, William Wordsworth (1770-1850) and Samuel Taylor Coleridge (1772-1834) published *Lyrical Ballads,* the first major work of English romantic literature. The volume contained Wordsworth's poem "Tintern Abbey."

While Wordsworth found inspiration in nature, Coleridge was fascinated by the mystical and exotic. "The Rime of the Ancient Mariner," a somber tale of a sailor burdened by a curse after killing an albatross, was his major contribution to *Lyrical Ballads.* Coleridge expressed the same fascination in his later poems, including "Christabel" and "Kubla Khan."

Lord Byron, Percy Bysshe Shelley, and John Keats

During their short lives, three other English romantic poets — Lord Byron (1788-1824), Percy Bysshe Shelley (1792-1822), and John Keats (1795-1821) — gave free reign to the expression of their emotions. Byron and Shelley were ardent advocates of political liberty, and Byron died in Greece, where he had gone to help the Greeks fight for independence from the Turks. Perhaps the most popular of England's romantic poets, Byron is best known for *Childe Harold's Pilgrimage* (1812-1818), *The Prisoner of Chillon* (1816), and his masterpiece, *Don Juan* (1819-1824).

One of Shelley's most important works, *Prometheus Unbound* (1820), was inspired by *Prometheus Bound,* by the ancient Greek playwright Aeschylus. In Shelley's poem, Prometheus, who represents what is good and creative in humanity, is locked in struggle with Jupiter, the symbol of tyranny and evil.

Keats wrote some of the most beautiful romantic poetry in the English language, including "The Eve of St. Agnes," "Ode to a Nightingale," and "Ode on a Grecian Urn," all published in 1820.

William Blake

William Blake (1757-1827) was an accomplished painter and engraver in addition to being a poet. He demonstrated his imaginative, sensitive, and mystical genius in such poems as "The Lamb," "The Tiger," and "The Mental Traveler."

Sir Walter Scott

Sir Walter Scott (1771–1832) holds a preeminent position among romantic British novelists. Inspired by a fascination with the Middle Ages and his native Scotland, he wrote more than thirty historical novels. *Ivanhoe* (1820), his best-known novel, is set in the twelfth century, the time of King Richard the Lionhearted and the Crusades.

Painting

The nineteenth century was the great age of English romantic landscape painting. John Constable (1776–1837) and J. M. W. Turner (1775–1851) are the best known of this genre.

Architecture

Architecture during the romantic period was dominated by the neoclassical and neo-Gothic styles, as well as by a fascination with the exotic. Inspired by ancient Greek and Roman architecture, the neoclassical style had won acceptance in the eighteenth century and remained popular in the romantic era. Romantic architects, reflecting the fascination with the Middle Ages that was characteristic of romanticism, promoted a revival of Gothic architecture. Following a fire in 1834, the reconstruction of the British Houses of Parliament in the neo-Gothic style began in 1840.

Other architects found their inspiration in the more exotic styles of the Orient, ranging from the Middle East and Persia to China. The Royal Pavilion in the seaside town of Brighton, built for Britain's prince regent, later King George IV, is a memorable example of this style.

The Oxford Movement

In the early nineteenth century, the romantics' emphasis on the mystical and supernatural led to a revival of traditional religious belief. In England, a group of Anglicans, known as the Oxford Movement, reasserted Catholic elements in the faith and practice of the Church of England. The Oxford Movement proved influential in the development of Anglo-Catholicism within the English church, although some of its leaders, including John Henry Newman (1801–1890), ultimately became converts to Roman Catholicism.

Historians

The romantics' sense of an organic union between the present and the past led to the writing of romantic national histories, which emphasized the uniqueness of a people's development and their historical mission. Thomas Babington Macauley (1800–1859) was a prominent English romantic historian. His major work, *The History of England from the Accession of James the Second* (5 vols., 1849–1861), reflected his Whig and Protestant bias.

During the early nineteenth century, the British succeeded in averting possible revolution by carrying out a program of gradual reform. The most important of the reform measures, the Reform Bill of 1832, marked a decisive step in the shift of political power from the landed aristocracy to the middle class. This transition made possible the repeal of the Corn Laws in 1846 and the subsequent adoption of free trade. While Parliament ignored the demands of the Chartists for full political democracy, the impetus for reform continued. In foreign affairs, the British pursued an independent and activist policy.

Recommended Reading

Beales, Derek. *From Castlereagh to Gladstone, 1815–1885* (1969).

Bourne, Kenneth. *The Foreign Policy of Victorian England, 1830–1902* (1970).

Briggs, Asa. *The Age of Improvement, 1783–1802* (1959).

Briggs, Asa, ed. *Chartist Studies* (1974).

Brock, Michael. *The Great Reform Act* (1973).

Clark, G. Kitson. *The Making of Victorian England* (1962).

Derry, John W. *Castlereagh* (1976).

Derry, John W. *A Short History of Nineteenth-Century England* (1963).

Dixon, Peter. *George Canning: Politician and Statesman* (1976).

Gash, Norman. *Aristocracy and People: Britain, 1815–1865* (1979).

Gash, Norman. *Lord Liverpool* (1984).

Gash, Norman. *Peel* (1976).

Gooch, Brison D., ed. *The Origins of the Crimean War* (1969).

Hayes, Paul. *The Nineteenth Century, 1814–1880* (1975).

Hibbert, Christopher. *George IV, Regent and King, 1811–1830* (1974).

Krein, David F. *The Last Palmerston Government* (1978).

Longford, Elizabeth. *Queen Victoria: Born to Succeed* (1965).

Longford, Elizabeth. *Wellington: Pillar of State* (1973).

McCord, Norman. *The Anti-Corn Law League, 1838–1846* (1958).

O'Ferrall, Fergus. *Catholic Emancipation: Daniel O'Connell and the Birth of Irish Democracy, 1820–30* (1986).

Prest, John. *Lord John Russell* (1972).

Quennell, Peter. *Romantic England: Writing and Painting, 1717–1851* (1970).

Read, Donald. *Cobden and Bright: A Victorian Political Partnership* (1967).

Rich, Norman. *Why the Crimean War? A Cautionary Tale* (1985).

Ridley, Jasper. *Lord Palmerston* (1970).

Smith, Robert A. *Late Georgian and Regency England, 1760–1837* (1984).

Thompson, Dorothy. *The Chartists* (1986).

Thomson, David. *England in the Nineteenth Century, 1815–1914* (1950).

Woodham Smith, C. V. *The Great Hunger: Ireland, 1845–1849* (1962).

Woodham Smith, C. V. *The Reason Why* (1954).

Woodward, E. L. *The Age of Reform, 1815–1870* (2nd ed., 1962).

Young, G. M. *Victorian England: Portrait of an Age* (2nd ed., 1953).

Ziegler, Philip. *King William IV* (1973).

Ziegler, Philip. *Melbourne* (1976).

CHAPTER 16

The Age of Disraeli and Gladstone

Time Line

1874–1880	Benjamin Disraeli serves as prime minister
1875	Parliament adopts the Public Health Act
	Parliament passes the Artisans' Dwellings Act
1876	Queen Victoria becomes empress of India
1878	Parliament enacts the Factory and Workshops Act
	The Congress of Berlin restricts Russia's advance in the Balkans
1880–1885	Gladstone heads his second ministry
1881	Parliament adopts the Irish Land Act of 1881
1883	The Fabian Society is established
1884	Parliament passes the Reform Bill of 1884
1885–1886	Lord Salisbury heads his first ministry
1886	Gladstone heads his third ministry
	The House of Commons rejects a Home Rule Bill
1886–1892	Lord Salisbury heads his second ministry
1892–1894	Gladstone heads his fourth ministry
1893	The House of Lords rejects a Home Rule Bill
1894–1895	Lord Rosebery serves as prime minister
1895–1902	Lord Salisbury heads his third ministry
1897	Parliament adopts the Workmen's Compensation Act
1900	The Labor Representation Committee is established
1901	Great Britain and the United States sign the Hay-Pauncefote Treaty
1901	The House of Lords issues the Taff Vale Decision
1901–1910	Reign of King Edward VII
1902–1905	Arthur James Balfour serves as prime minister

| 1902 | Parliament passes the Education Act of 1902 |
| 1903 | Joseph Chamberlain proposes an imperial preferential tariff |

The death of Lord Palmerston in 1865 introduced a new era in British politics. For the next two decades, a new generation of political leaders dominated public life, with Benjamin Disraeli at the helm of the Conservative Party and William E. Gladstone heading the Liberals.

The Reform Bill of 1867, enacted by Disraeli and the Conservatives, worked to the immediate benefit of Gladstone and the Liberals; however, Disraeli's program of Tory Democracy soon won mass support for the Conservatives among the enlarged electorate. Thus, the tradition of liberal reform that had begun in the 1820s was advanced further by both major parties.

In the mid-1880s, Gladstone's commitment to the cause of Irish Home Rule split the Liberals. This split led to two decades of Conservative domination, broken only by Gladstone's brief fourth ministry in the mid-1890s.

The Reform Bill of 1867

Gladstone and Disraeli

Following Lord Palmerston's death in October 1865 at the age of eighty, Lord John Russell once again became prime minister. But William E. Gladstone (1809–1898) was the Liberals' real leader.

The situation of the Conservatives was similar. While the earl of Derby remained the titular head of the party, Benjamin Disraeli (1804–1881) was emerging as the Conservatives' leader.

The Reform Act of 1867

For several years, the campaign for a further reform of the House of Commons had been gaining momentum.

Passage of the Bill

In 1866, Gladstone introduced a bill to extend the right to vote to some categories of urban workers. The proposal encountered heavy opposition in the House of Commons, from both the Conservatives and some of Gladstone's fellow Liberals, and it failed to win approval.

Later in 1866, a new Derby-Disraeli cabinet took office. Disraeli saw an opportunity for the Conservatives to profit from the passage of a Reform Bill and succeeded in pushing through the Reform Bill of 1867.

Provisions of the Bill

Redistribution of Seats in Parliament.   The Reform Bill of 1867 redistributed some seats in the House of Commons. A few small boroughs lost their representatives, while towns with fewer than 10,000 inhabitants were allowed only one seat.

Extension of Franchise.   More important, however, was the extension of the right to vote to most of Great Britain's urban workers. The right to vote in the counties was also extended, although farm laborers were not enfranchised. The electorate was more than doubled, to about 2 million.

Gladstone's Great Ministry 1868–1874

In February 1868, Derby retired, and Disraeli became prime minister. He served only briefly, however, because the parliamentary elections of 1868 resulted in a Liberal victory. From 1868 to 1874, Gladstone served as prime minister, heading what came to be known as his Great Ministry.

Ireland

In 1865, the British had suppressed the Fenian Rebellion in Ireland. (The Fenians, a secret revolutionary organization, had been established in 1858 by Irish-Americans. Its purpose was to achieve Ireland's independence.) The crushing of this revolt, however, did not solve the Irish problem, and Gladstone set out to tackle this difficult issue.

Disestablishment of the Church of Ireland

In 1869, Parliament voted to disestablish the Anglican Church of Ireland. Since ninety percent of the Irish were Roman Catholics, it was not reasonable to continue to compel them to support what they regarded as an alien church.

The Irish Land Act of 1870

The Irish Land Act, passed by Parliament in 1870, required landlords to compensate their tenants for improvements they had made on the property when they were evicted for no fault of their own. However, the act did not protect tenants from rent increases or from eviction if they could not afford to pay exorbitant rents. The land issue thus remained high on the list of Irish grievances.

The Education Act of 1870

The Education Act of 1870 created, for the first time, a national system of elementary education.

Provisions

The country was divided into school districts with local school boards. These boards were authorized to build and operate public schools wherever the voluntary schools conducted by Anglicans and Nonconformists did not meet the district's needs. The cost of these new schools would be covered by grants from the government, local taxes, and fees. These fees could be waived for poor children. (In 1880, elementary school attendance became compulsory, and in 1891, all fees were abolished.)

Religious Instruction

The 1870 act also provided more state aid for voluntary schools, where religious instruction would not be subject to restrictions. In the new public schools, however, religious instruction would be nondenominational and could be scheduled only at the beginning or end of the school day. This schedule would facilitate nonattendance by children whose parents did not wish them to receive religious instruction in school.

Effect on Literacy

The Education Act of 1870 had a powerful impact. In 1869, only about one-half of elementary school-age children actually attended school, and in 1870, male illiteracy was nearly twenty percent. By the end of the century, it had decreased to less than two percent.

Civil Service Reform

An executive order issued in 1870 provided for filling almost all positions in the civil service on the basis of competitive examination. Merit thus replaced favoritism in appointment to government posts, with the notable exception of the Foreign Office.

Reform of the Army

The Gladstone government ended the practice of army officers buying their commissions. In addition, the reform of the army reduced the size of the standing army, introduced short-term enlistments of six years instead of twelve, and established an effective reserve force.

The Ballot Act of 1872

The Ballot Act of 1872 introduced the use of the secret ballot in British elections.

Judicial Reform

The Judicature Act of 1873 reorganized and reformed Great Britain's complex court system, establishing three levels of courts similar to the court system in the United States: a court of original jurisdiction, an appellate court, and a supreme court.

The act created the Court of High Justice with three divisions (Chancery; King's Bench; and Admiralty, Probate, and Divorce) to serve as a court of original jurisdiction in both civil and criminal cases. In civil cases, appeals could be made to the Court of Appeal, also established by the Judicature Act, and in certain instances to the House of Lords, which remained Britain's highest court. In criminal cases, appeals based on writ of error initially went directly to the House of Lords, but a subsequent law created a new court to hear appeals of criminal cases.

Other Reforms

In 1869, imprisonment for debt was abolished.

All religious restrictions imposed on students and fellows at the once Anglican-dominated universities of Oxford and Cambridge were removed in 1871.

Other legislation adopted in 1871 reaffirmed the right of workers to organize unions by nullifying a recent court decision (*Hornby v. Close*) that a trade union was an association acting in restraint of trade and was thus illegal. Although the ban on strikes was repealed (see Chapter 15), the prohibition on picketing remained.

The adoption of the Licensing Act of 1872, restricting the sale of alcohol, reflected the influence of the temperance movement in the Liberal Party.

While Gladstone and the Liberals enacted a substantial program of reform, the party maintained its laissez-faire tradition and opposed direct state intervention in economic affairs.

Foreign Affairs

The Franco-German War of 1870–1871

Great Britain remained neutral in the Franco-German War of 1870–1871 that brought about the unification of Germany. The new German Empire now became the most powerful state on the European continent.

Russian Abrogation of the Black Sea Clauses

While Europe's attention was distracted by the Franco-German War, the Russians unilaterally abrogated the Black Sea Clauses of the Treaty of Paris of 1856 (see Chapter 15).

A great-power conference held in London confirmed the Russians' action. While the British were not prepared to fight to preserve the neutralization of the Black Sea, they remained concerned both about Russian encroachments on the Ottoman Empire and about Russian advances in Central Asia in the direction of Afghanistan, which presented a potential threat to India (see Chapter 17).

Anglo-American Relations

British sympathy for the Confederate cause during the American Civil War had strained Anglo-American relations (see Chapter 15). The most serious issue, resulting from lax British enforcement of their neutrality laws, involved the construction in British shipyards of cruisers for the Confederacy. These ships, the most famous of which was the *Alabama,* preyed on Union shipping.

The United States government demanded compensation from the British for the damage caused by these cruisers. For several years, however, the dispute over the so-called *Alabama* Claims remained unresolved.

Settlement of the Alabama *Claims.*   The Treaty of Washington of 1871 settled this and several other Anglo-American disputes. The British acknowledged their partisan behavior during the Civil War and agreed that the *Alabama* claims should be submitted to an international tribunal. Meeting in Geneva, Switzerland in 1872, the arbitration panel awarded the United States $15.5 million.

Property and Fishing Claims.   Another provision of the Treaty of Washington led to an award of $2 million to Great Britain for property lost by British subjects during the Civil War. The treaty also provided for a new definition of the fishing rights of American fishermen in the North Atlantic off the shores of Newfoundland, and an arbitration panel awarded $5.5 million to Great Britain in settlement of claims resulting from previous American fishing in these waters.

The settlement of these disputes by peaceful means was important in establishing an improved relationship between the United States and Great Britain.

Disraeli and Tory Democracy
1874–1880

In the parliamentary elections of 1874, the Conservatives won their first clear majority in the House of Commons since 1841. Disraeli, the Conservative leader, became prime minister.

Formulation of Tory Democracy

Disraeli had set forth the Conservative program in a series of speeches, most notably the famous Crystal Palace speech of 1872. While the Conservatives were committed to maintaining both the country's historic institutions, including the monarchy and the established church, and the British Empire, Disraeli also endorsed what came to be known as Tory Democracy: the Conservative Party's support of extensive economic and social reforms to benefit British workers.

The Public Health Act of 1875

The Public Health Act of 1875 strengthened and codified earlier legislation relating to urban water, sewage, and drainage.

The Artisans' Dwellings Act of 1875

The Artisans' Dwellings Act of 1875 authorized local governments to initiate programs of slum clearance and public housing.

Labor Legislation

The Trade Union Act of 1875 repealed the prohibition of peaceful picketing in labor disputes. Collective bargaining between labor and management was legalized.

The Factory and Workshops Act of 1878 revised and codified earlier legislation relating to hours of work and conditions of labor.

Imperial Policy

Disraeli, a staunch imperialist, pursued an active policy in Egypt, South Africa, and India (see Chapter 17). In 1876, he persuaded Parliament to give Queen Victoria the title of empress of India. The same year, the queen bestowed a peerage on Disraeli, who became the earl of Beaconsfield.

The Balkan Crisis in Foreign Affairs

Revolts Against the Turks

In 1875, the Balkan provinces of Bosnia and Herzegovina rebelled against Turkish misrule. The following year, the revolt spread to Bulgaria, Montenegro, and Serbia. Turkish efforts to suppress the Bulgarian revolt were marked by extreme atrocities, which evoked a strong reaction throughout Europe.

In Great Britain, the pressure of public opinion forced Disraeli to call on the Turks to end their brutality and introduce reforms. The Turks rejected this demand, confident that the European great powers would be unable to cooperate to enforce their will on the Ottoman Empire.

Disraeli believed that it was not desirable for Great Britain to act against the Ottoman Empire, since this policy would aid the Russians in their effort to drive into the eastern Mediterranean and Near East. Gladstone strongly criticized Disraeli's position on humanitarian grounds, and his pamphlet on the Turkish atrocities, *Bulgarian Horrors,* quickly sold over 200,000 copies.

The Treaty of San Stefano (1878)

Sultan Abdul Hamid II (r. 1876–1909) continued to resist the pressure of foreign powers to introduce reforms. In 1877, Russia went to war against the Ottoman Empire and in March 1878 imposed the Treaty of San Stefano on the Turks. This treaty established the independence of Serbia, Montenegro, and Romania and granted autonomy to a large Bulgaria, including most of Macedonia with access to the Aegean Sea. Bulgaria would, in effect, be dominated by Russia. The treaty also awarded Batum and Kars and other Turkish lands in the Caucasus to Russia.

Threat of Anglo-Russian War

The Treaty of San Stefano marked a substantial advance of Russian power at the expense of the Turks. Disraeli protested the treaty and called for an international congress to consider its terms, while Parliament increased appropriations for armaments. The British also sent units of their fleet to the Turkish Straits, which joined the Aegean and Black seas, and they threatened war against Russia.

The Congress of Berlin

In an effort to prevent a major war, Otto von Bismarck (1815–1898), the German chancellor, presented himself as an "honest broker" and invited the great powers to send representatives to a meeting in Berlin.

The Treaty of Berlin (1878).   The Congress of Berlin replaced the Treaty of San Stefano with a new treaty, the Treaty of Berlin of 1878. This treaty confirmed the independence of Serbia, Montenegro, and Romania, as well as the Russian acquisition of Batum and Kars. However, the size of Bulgaria was reduced. The northern area, Bulgaria proper, would be autonomous. To the south, Eastern Rumelia would be semiautonomous. Further to the south, the Turks would retain full sovereignty over Macedonia, including the access to the Aegean that the Treaty of San Stefano had awarded to Bulgaria. (Eastern Rumelia united with Bulgaria in 1885, but the Turks continued to hold Macedonia.)

As compensation for the increase of Russian influence in the Balkans, Austria received the right to occupy and administer the Turkish provinces of Bosnia and Herzegovina, although the Austrians were not to annex them. The British gained the right to occupy the island of Cyprus, a valuable base for the defense of the eastern Mediterranean and the Suez Canal.

Effects of the Treaty.   The Balkan crisis thus ended peacefully. Russian expansionism had been contained, and the British had advanced their interests in the eastern Mediterranean. Disraeli stood at the height of his popularity.

Gladstone's Second Ministry 1880-1885

The Midlothian Campaign

In his famous Midlothian campaign of 1879–1880, named for the Scottish constituency of that name, Gladstone denounced Disraeli and the Conservatives for their activist foreign and imperial policies.

The Midlothian campaign helped the Liberals regain power. In the parliamentary elections of 1880, the Liberals won 347 seats in the House of Commons to 240 for the Conservatives and 65 for the Irish Nationalists. Gladstone became prime minister for the second time. Although he sought to pursue a less active imperial policy than Disraeli had, the British extended their control over Egypt in 1882 (see Chapter 17).

Ireland

Gladstone remained committed to the effort to resolve the Irish problem. Since the Act of Union of 1800, the British Parliament had ruled Ireland directly. The 100 Irish members of Parliament had little influence, except when the Liberals or Conservatives needed their votes.

Beginning of the Campaign for Home Rule

In 1871, the Irish Home Government Association, later called the Home Rule League, was established to agitate for the right of the Irish themselves to govern Ireland in its domestic affairs. In the 1880 parliamentary elections, advocates of Home Rule won 60 of the 100 Irish seats in Parliament. Charles Stewart Parnell (1846–1891), a Protestant Irish landowner, was the leader of the advocates of Home Rule (known as the Irish Nationalists) in the House of Commons.

The Irish Land Act of 1881

In 1880, the Irish potato crop failed, causing hardship for many Irish tenant farmers. Those who could not afford to pay their rent were often evicted by English landlords. The Irish Land League urged tenant resistance to eviction, and acts of violence increased.

The Irish Land Act of 1881 overcame some of the deficiencies of the 1871 law by enacting the demand of the Irish Land League for the "three F's:" fixity of tenure, free sale of tenants' interests to other tenants, and fair rent, to be decided by the courts.

The Phoenix Park Murders

In May 1882, Lord Frederick Cavendish (1836–1882), the new chief secretary for Ireland, and Thomas Burke, the undersecretary, were murdered in Phoenix Park, Dublin, by a Fenian gang known as the Invincibles.

Ulster's Opposition to Home Rule

Although a tough new Prevention of Crimes Act reduced disorders in Ireland, it remained evident that the southern Irish were determined to secure Home Rule.

However, the six counties of northern Ireland, known as Ulster, were predominantly Protestant. The Ulsterites, fearing domination by the Roman Catholics of the south, desired to maintain the union with Great Britain. These Irish Unionists, as they were known, had strong British support, and the issue of Irish Home Rule remained deadlocked.

Parliamentary Reform

The Reform Bill of 1884

The Reform Bill of 1884 gave the right to vote to agricultural laborers. The electorate was increased by about 2.5 million, and now virtually all of Great Britain's adult males who owned or rented property had the right to vote.

The Redistribution of Seats Act of 1885

The Redistribution of Seats Act of 1885 increased the membership of the House of Commons to 670 and established, with a few exceptions, a system of single-member constituencies with approximately equal populations.

Lord Salisbury's First Ministry, 1885

In June 1885, Gladstone's government was defeated on a budgetary issue, and the prime minister resigned. The marquess of Salisbury (1830–1903), who had succeeded Disraeli as the leader of the Conservative Party, became prime minister, heading a short-lived caretaker government.

Gladstone's Third Ministry, 1886

The Liberals won 335 seats in the House of Commons in the parliamentary elections of December 1885 to the 249 won by the Conservatives, and Gladstone again became prime minister.

Endorsement of Home Rule

The Irish Nationalists, with 86 seats, held the balance of power between the two major parties. Gladstone endorsed Home Rule, and Parnell and the Irish Nationalists agreed to support the Liberal leader's third ministry (1886).

The Fight Over the Home Rule Bill

Gladstone proposed a Home Rule Bill, calling for an end to the union of Great Britain and Ireland and the establishment of an Irish Parliament. Ninety-three Liberals, including John Bright (1811–1889) and Joseph Chamberlain (1836–1914), opposed their party leader.

The opponents of Home Rule warned that the Irish Catholics would oppress the Protestant minority in Ireland. "Home Rule means Rome Rule," they insisted. In Protestant Ulster, Lord Randolph Churchill (1849–1894) stirred up opposition to Home Rule. "Ulster will fight and Ulster will be right," was the cry. In June 1886, the House of Commons defeated Gladstone's Home Rule Bill by a vote of 343 to 313.

Split in the Liberal Party

The issue split the Liberals. Most of those who became Liberal Unionists, including Chamberlain, eventually joined the Conservatives. This division kept the Liberals out of office, except for one brief interlude, for the next twenty years.

Lord Salisbury's Second Ministry
1886–1892

In the parliamentary elections of 1886, the Conservatives and their Liberal Unionist allies triumphed over the Liberals and the Irish Nationalists. Lord Salisbury, the Conservatives' leader, became prime minister.

Reforms

The County Council Act of 1888

The County Council Act of 1888 (sometimes called the Local Government Act) restructured government in the counties by transferring authority from the justices of the peace to elected county councils. The justices of the peace retained their judicial functions.

The Technical Instruction Act of 1889

The Technical Instruction Act of 1889 empowered the local school boards to operate schools for technical education in addition to elementary schools.

Ireland

Ireland remained a central problem for the new Conservative government. Arthur James Balfour (1848–1930), Salisbury's nephew, served as secretary of state for Ireland and won adoption in 1887 of a severe Crimes Act in an effort to control violence in Ireland.

Land Reform

Balfour also expanded the program begun by the Ashbourne Act of 1885 to assist Irish tenants in buying land from their landlords. By 1912, some £75 million in loans had been made, and tenants had bought almost 7 million acres of land.

Parnell

While Balfour's policy improved the life of Ireland's farmers, the Irish Nationalists remained determined to secure Home Rule. The Nationalist cause, however, was weakened by the problems of their leader, Parnell.

In 1887, Parnell was charged with involvement in the Phoenix Park murders (see p. 287). He was cleared of these charges, but in

1890, he was named a corespondent in a divorce action, accused of committing adultery with a Mrs. O'Shea. This scandal undermined his effectiveness as the leader of the Irish Nationalists. Parnell died in 1891.

Redmond

The Irish Nationalists remained divided between Parnell's supporters and opponents until John Redmond (1856–1918) emerged as their new leader at the end of the decade.

The Liberals in Power, 1892–1895

Gladstone's Fourth Ministry, 1892–1894

Coalition of Liberals and Irish Nationalists

In the 1892 parliamentary elections, the Liberals and Irish Nationalists won a majority of seats in the House of Commons, and Gladstone became prime minister for the fourth time, at the age of 83.

Defeat of Irish Home Rule

Although the Liberals' Newcastle Program promised extensive reforms, Gladstone decided to give priority to a new Irish Home Rule Bill. While the House of Commons approved the bill, the House of Lords rejected it in September 1893 by a vote of 419 to 41.

Lord Rosebery's Government 1894–1895

In March 1894, Gladstone gave up his leadership of the Liberal Party and the prime ministership at the age of 85. The earl of Rosebery (1847–1929) succeeded him in both positions. This government proved to be weak, and Rosebery resigned in June 1895. The brief interlude of Liberal government in an era of Conservative domination ended.

Lord Salisbury's Third Ministry 1895-1902

In the parliamentary elections of 1895, the Conservatives and the Liberal Unionists triumphed, with the Conservatives winning 340 seats in the House of Commons and their allies winning 71. The Liberals gained 177 seats, while their Irish Nationalist partners won 82. Lord Salisbury, the Conservative leader, once again became prime minister, the last member of the House of Lords to hold that position. Under Salisbury's leadership, the Conservative–Liberal Unionist partnership also won the elections held in 1900.

The Workmen's Compensation Act of 1897

While the Salisbury government focused its attention on foreign and imperial problems (see below and Chapter 17), it had some accomplishments in domestic policy to its credit, most notably the Workmen's Compensation Act of 1897. This act created a system of insurance for workers who suffered job-related injuries. At first, the act applied only to railroad and factory workers and miners, but in 1900 it was extended to cover agricultural workers.

Relations with the United States

The Venezuelan Boundary Dispute

For some years, a boundary dispute had simmered between Venezuela and Great Britain, which ruled the neighboring colony of British Guiana. By 1895, the discovery of gold in the disputed territory raised the prospect of British action against Venezuela.

The United States, anxious to assert its power in inter-American affairs, intervened in the dispute. Richard Olney (1835–1917), the secretary of state in the administration of President Grover Cleveland (1837–1908), invoked and expanded the Monroe Doctrine. The United States, Olney asserted, was "practically sovereign on this continent," and he demanded that the British agree to submit the dispute with Venezuela to arbitration.

The British flatly rejected both Olney's broad interpretation of the Monroe Doctrine and the demand for arbitration. This response angered American opinion, and some Americans went so far as to advocate war against Great Britain.

The British did not want a conflict with the United States and bowed to the American demand for arbitration. The arbitration tribunal awarded most of the territory in question to British Guiana.

Although tension between London and Washington had run high, the peaceful resolution of the conflict contributed to an improvement in Anglo-American relations.

The Panama Canal

In the early years of the twentieth century, the United States set out to build an American-controlled canal in Panama. Before the United States could undertake such a project, however, it was necessary to cancel the Clayton-Bulwer Treaty of 1850, which had provided for joint Anglo-American construction and operation of a Central American canal (see Chapter 15). The Hay-Pauncefote Treaty of 1901 ended this agreement, enabling the United States to proceed on its own. The Americans promised to maintain the neutrality of the canal and agreed that it would be open to ships of all nations on equal terms.

King Edward VII

In 1901, the death of Queen Victoria brought an end to a reign of 63 years, the longest in English history. Victoria was succeeded by her son, the Prince of Wales, who became King Edward VII (r. 1901–1910).

The Balfour Ministry, 1902–1905

Following Salisbury's retirement in 1902, Balfour became prime minister.

The Education Act of 1902

The Education Act of 1902, the most important achievement of Balfour's government, reorganized the national system of education that had been established by the 1870 act. The local school boards authorized by that act were abolished. Henceforth the borough and county councils would supervise education in elementary schools, including both the schools established by the school boards under the terms of the Education Act of 1870 and the voluntary schools. The 1902 act also contained provisions regarding technical education and secondary schools. For the first time, the operation of secondary schools was recognized as a proper function of government.

The Licensing Act of 1904

The Licensing Act of 1904 reflected the increasing influence of the temperance movement. The law reduced the number of places licensed to sell alcoholic beverages and provided that the proceeds from the alcohol tax would be used to compensate those who thereby lost their licenses.

Joseph Chamberlain and the Imperial Preferential Tariff

In 1903, Joseph Chamberlain, who served as colonial secretary in the Salisbury and Balfour ministries, challenged the British tradition of free trade with a dramatic proposal for the introduction of an imperial preferential tariff. While high tariffs would be imposed on imports from outside the British Empire, preferential tariffs would be established for the dominions and colonies. Closer economic ties would strengthen the empire, Chamberlain argued, while the British treasury would benefit from increased tariff revenues. Furthermore, British manufacturers would have guaranteed markets for their industrial products, while the dominions and colonies would have a secure market for their raw materials and food.

Chamberlain's proposal caused a split in the Conservative Party, and the Balfour ministry resigned in December 1905. The Liberals now returned to power.

Emergence of the Labor Party

Early Labor Representation in the House of Commons

During the late nineteenth century, the idea emerged that Britain's industrial workers should establish their own political party to represent their interests more effectively in Parliament.

As early as 1874, two officials of the Miners' Union won election to the House of Commons, where they were regarded as left-wing Liberals. By 1885, there were twelve labor representatives in the Commons who voted with the Liberals.

In 1892, three representatives of the new Independent Labor Party, led by Keir Hardie (1856–1915), won seats in the House of Commons.

Although all three were defeated in 1895, ten labor representatives aligned with the Liberals won seats that year.

The Fabian Society

In 1883, the Fabian Society was established. Taking its name from Fabius Cunctator, a Roman general who pursued a waiting policy in his war against Hannibal, the Carthaginian commander, the Fabian Society advocated a gradual, evolutionary development of a socialist economy and society. The leaders of the Fabian Society included Sidney Webb (1859–1947) and Beatrice Webb (1858–1943), the writer H. G. Wells (1866–1946), the playwright George Bernard Shaw (1856–1950), and Ramsay MacDonald, who became Britain's first Labor prime minister in 1924 (see Chapter 20). At first, many Fabians maintained ties with the Liberal Party.

Growth of Trade Unions

During the late nineteenth century, Britain's trade unions experienced a substantial growth. In the early 1870s, union membership numbered about 400,000. By 1900, it had increased to over 2 million. As the unions grew in size, their interest in political activism increased.

The Labor Representation Committee

In 1900, a meeting of representatives of the Trades Union Congress, Keir Hardie's Independent Labor Party, the Fabian Society, and the Marxist Social Democratic Federation, founded by H. M. Hyndman (1842–1921) in 1884, decided to establish the Labor Representation Committee.

Fifteen candidates sponsored by the Labor Representation Committee ran for seats in the House of Commons in 1900, and two were elected.

The Taff Vale Decision

In 1901, the House of Lords, acting in its judicial capacity as the country's highest court of appeals, ruled that a railroad workers' union should pay damages to the Taff Vale Railway Company to compensate it for losses suffered as the result of a strike. By depriving unions of their most powerful weapon, this decision gave them a strong incentive to increase political activity.

Labor's Political Success in 1906

In 1906, twenty-nine members of the new Labor Party won seats in the House of Commons, along with twenty-four Labor members who had ties to the Liberals. These fifty-three labor members agreed to support the new Liberal government because of its commitment to a program of economic and social reform.

During the late nineteenth century, under both Liberal and Conservative leadership, Great Britain achieved a remarkable record of gradual reform. The extension of the right to vote established close to universal manhood suffrage, and the state assumed an expanding role in education. The civil service, the army, and the judicial system also experienced reform, while the government became more active in urban sanitation, slum clearance, and housing construction. Nevertheless, working class discontent persisted, resulting in the establishment of the Labor Party at the turn of the century.

Although the Church of Ireland was disestablished and the hardships of the Irish peasants were eased, the failure to enact Home Rule left Great Britain with an enduring Irish problem.

In foreign affairs, the British continued to oppose Russian expansion toward the eastern Mediterranean and the Near East. The improvement of relations with the United States laid the foundations for what would become a relationship of the utmost importance in the new century.

Recommended Reading

Ausubel, Herman. *The Late Victorians* (1957).

Beckett, J. C. *The Making of Modern Ireland, 1603–1923* (3rd ed., 1966).

Blake, Robert. *The Conservative Party from Peel to Thatcher* (1985).

Blake, Robert. *Disraeli* (1966).

Clark, G. Kitson. *An Expanding Society: Britain, 1830–1900* (1967).

Cook, Chris. *A Short History of the Liberal Party* (1978).

Curtis, L. P. *Coercion and Conciliation in Ireland, 1880–1892* (1963).

Ensor, R. C. K. *England, 1870–1914* (1936).

Hamer, D. A. *Liberal Politics in the Age of Gladstone and Rosebery* (1972).

Judd, Denis. *Radical Joe* (1977).

Kee, Robert. *The Green Flag: A History of Irish Nationalism* (1972).

Kennedy, Aubrey Leo. *Salisbury, 1830–1903: Portrait of a Statesman* (1953).

Lyons, F. S. L. *Charles Stewart Parnell* (1977).

Lyons, F. S. L. *Ireland Since the Famine* (2nd ed., 1973).

McCaffrey, Lawrence J. *The Irish Question, 1800–1922* (1968).

Magnus, Sir Philip. *Gladstone* (1954).

Marsh, Peter. *The Discipline of Popular Government: Lord Salisbury's Domestic Statecraft, 1881–1902* (1978).

Matthew, H. C. G. *Gladstone, 1809–1874* (1986).

Millman, Richard. *Britain and the Eastern Question, 1875–1878* (1979).

Morgan, Kenneth O. *Keir Hardie: Radical and Socialist* (1975).

O'Brien, C. C. *Parnell and His Party, 1880–1890* (1957).

Pelling, Henry. *A History of British Trade Unionism* (3rd ed., 1976).

Pelling, Henry. *The Origins of the Labour Party, 1880–1900* (2nd ed., 1966).

Pelling, Henry. *A Short History of the Labour Party* (6th ed., 1978).

Perkins, Bradford. *The Great Rapprochement: England and the United States, 1895–1914* (1968).

Pugh, Martin. *The Making of Modern British Politics, 1867–1939* (1982).

Read, D. *England, 1868–1914* (1979).

Shannon, R. T. *Gladstone and the Bulgarian Agitation of 1876* (2nd ed., 1975).

Smith, Francis B. *The Making of the Second Reform Bill* (1966).

Smith, Paul. *Disraelian Conservatism and Social Reform* (1967).

Swartz, Marvin. *The Politics of British Foreign Policy in the Era of Disraeli and Gladstone* (1985).

Young, Kenneth. *Arthur James Balfour* (1963).

CHAPTER 17

The British Empire in the Nineteenth Century

Time Line

1835–1837	The Great Trek results in the establishment of the Orange Free State and the Transvaal in South Africa
1839	Lord Durham presents his report on Canada
1842	Great Britain acquires Hong Kong
1857	The Indian Mutiny challenges British rule in India
1858	The India Act establishes the British government's direct control over India
1867	The British North America Act creates the Dominion of Canada

1875	Prime Minister Disraeli buys about forty-four percent of the shares in the Suez Canal Company
1881	The British East Africa Company is chartered
1882	The British establish their control over Egypt
1886	The Royal Niger Company is founded
	Great Britain acquires Burma
1895	The Jameson Raid fails to establish British control over the Transvaal
1898	Anglo-French rivalry in the Sudan results in the Fashoda Crisis
1899–1902	The Boer War results in the British conquest of the Orange Free State and the Transvaal
1901	Australia gains dominion status
1902	The Anglo-Japanese Alliance is signed
1907	New Zealand acquires dominion status
1909	The Morley-Minto reforms for India are enacted
1910	The Union of South Africa becomes a dominion

Although the British had created a substantial empire in the eighteenth century, during the early nineteenth century they demonstrated little enthusiasm for further expansion. This attitude was understandable. Only a few years earlier, the thirteen British colonies along the Atlantic seaboard of North America had rebelled against British rule and had gained their independence. The American Revolution suggested that the acquisition of colonies was ultimately an unproductive activity. British opponents of colonial expansion, known as the Little Englanders, insisted that their government should focus its attention on domestic affairs and not seek additional overseas possessions.

A new era in British imperialism, in particular, and in European imperialism, more generally, opened in the 1870s, as the major powers began to expand their existing holdings and to acquire new possessions in Africa and Asia.

The British Empire
in the Early Nineteenth Century

While the British did not pursue an active imperialist policy in the early nineteenth century, they did maintain and consolidate their existing possessions.

The Western Hemisphere

In the Western Hemisphere, the British ruled Canada, a number of islands in the West Indies, British Honduras in Central America, and British Guiana in South America.

Canada

In the early nineteenth century, British North America consisted of predominantly French Lower Canada (later Quebec); predominantly British Upper Canada (later Ontario); the three Maritime Provinces of Nova Scotia, New Brunswick, and Prince Edward Island; and Newfoundland.

Revolts.   Growing discontent with British rule resulted in the outbreak of two revolts in 1837, led by William Lyon Mackenzie (1795–1861) in Upper Canada and Louis Joseph Papineau (1786–1871), a French-Canadian, in Lower Canada. The Canadian rebels demanded the establishment of a responsible government where executive authority would be exercised by Canadian ministers responsible to a Canadian legislature. The governor general, the crown's representative in Canada, would have limited powers, similar to those of the monarch in Great Britain.

The Durham Report.   Troubled by the events in Canada, Lord Melbourne (1779–1848), the prime minister, sent the earl of Durham (1792–1840) to Canada as high commissioner.

In January 1839, Durham presented his report, entitled *Report on the Affairs of British North America.* Warning of "two races warring in the bosom of a single nation," he recommended the joining of Upper and Lower Canada, in the hope that the English-speaking and French-speaking Canadians would ultimately become one people. This process would be aided by immigration that would ultimately create an English-speaking majority.

Lord Durham also recommended that Canada should be granted responsible government in its domestic affairs, although such matters as foreign affairs, defense, and commercial policy should remain under British control.

The Act of Union.   In July 1840, Parliament accepted Lord Durham's recommendation in the Act of Union, which united the two provinces. However, Durham's hoped-for fusion of the two language groups did not occur.

"Responsible Government".   For several years, the precise meaning and extent of "responsible government" remained uncertain. In April 1849, Lord Elgin (1811-1863), Canada's governor general and Lord Durham's son-in-law, signed the Rebellion Losses Bill, which provided compensation to those who had suffered losses in the 1837 revolt. Although the British government and the Canadian Tories both opposed this legislation, it had been enacted by the Canadian legislature. In signing the bill, Elgin established an important precedent for Canadian self-government.

The British North America Act of 1867.   In 1867, Parliament passed the British North America Act, which created a British-style parliamentary government for what was now the Dominion of Canada. Initially, the new dominion was a federal union of four provinces: Ontario, Quebec, Nova Scotia, and New Brunswick. In 1871, British Columbia and Manitoba joined the federation, while Prince Edward Island entered in 1873. The provinces of Alberta and Saskatchewan were added in 1905. Newfoundland became Canada's tenth province in 1949.

Africa

The British had acquired the Cape of Good Hope during the Napoleonic wars, and they also controlled a number of trading stations along Africa's coasts. During the 1820s, British settlers moved into the Cape Colony, where friction soon developed between them and the Boers, the descendants of Dutch colonists who had settled at the Cape during the seventeenth century. In the Great Trek of 1835-1837, the Boers moved northward into the interior, where they established two independent republics: the Orange Free State and the Transvaal. The British recognized the virtual independence of the Transvaal in 1852 and of the Orange Free State in 1854.

In 1843, the British took control of Natal, to the east of Cape Colony, which had originally been founded by the Boers.

Asia

India

The British had defeated France in the Seven Years' War (1756–1763), gaining control over India, which was administered by an uneasy partnership of the East India Company and the British government. During the first half of the nineteenth century, the British extended and consolidated their control over India, and acts of Parliament adopted in 1813, 1833, and 1853 reduced the authority of the East India Company.

Princely States.   The marquess of Dalhousie (1812–1860), who served as governor general from 1847 to 1856, established the doctrine of lapse, which provided for British assumption of direct control of princely states whose rulers died without immediate heirs.

The Indian Mutiny.   The people of India increasingly resented the imposition of British laws and customs. By 1857, there were about 46,000 British troops in India, serving with some 233,000 Indian soldiers, known as *sepoys*. The British had introduced the use of a new cartridge wrapped in paper and greased with mutton fat. A rumor spread among Hindu troops that the grease came from sacred cows, while Moslem soldiers believed that it came from unclean pigs. There were other rumors, as well, including one to the effect that the British intended to force the Indians to adopt Christianity.

In May 1857, the Indian Mutiny (also known as the Sepoy Rebellion) broke out. In this dramatic uprising, Indian troops of the Bengal army seized Delhi, the traditional capital, and the revolt quickly spread through the valley of the Ganges River. The British suppressed the revolt with little difficulty.

The India Act of 1858.   In the aftermath of the Indian Mutiny, the British ended the system of dual control by the government and the East India Company that had been established by the India Act of 1784 (see Chapter 12). Under the terms of the India Act of 1858, the British government established its direct control over India, which would now be governed by a viceroy responsible to the secretary of state for India.

The British renounced the doctrine of lapse, and Indians would now be eligible for subordinate positions in the Indian civil service.

India increasingly became the most valuable of Britain's overseas possessions, coming to be known as "the jewel in the crown." In 1876, the Conservative prime minister Benjamin Disraeli, an ardent imperialist, arranged for Queen Victoria to be proclaimed empress of India (see Chapter 16).

China

Since the late seventeenth century, the British had developed significant commercial relations with China despite the Chinese hostility to foreigners. Until 1833, the East India Company controlled British trade with China. When the company's charter was renewed, its monopoly on the sale of Indian-grown opium was ended, and other British merchants now entered the opium trade with China.

The First Opium War, 1839–1842.   In 1839, the Chinese government began a campaign to end the importation of opium, seizing opium in Canton and quarreling with the British over the trial of British subjects in Chinese courts. The British went to war in order to enforce their will on China. In the Treaty of Nanking, which ended the Opium War in 1842, the British annexed Hong Kong and compelled the Chinese to open Canton, Shanghai, and three other ports to foreign trade. In addition, the Chinese were required to pay an indemnity, grant diplomatic status to British representatives in China, and extend rights of extraterritoriality (exemption from China's legal jurisdiction) to most foreigners.

The Second Opium War, 1856–1858.   During the next several years, the Chinese sought to restrict the concessions they had made, while British merchants sought an expanded access to the Chinese market. From 1856 to 1858, the Second Opium War was fought. Under the terms of the Treaty of Tientsin of 1858, the Chinese agreed to open the Yangtze River and five additional ports to foreign trade. China also agreed to permit the establishment of a permanent British embassy in Peking, the Chinese capital, and to establish a Chinese embassy in London. In addition, the Chinese promised to protect Christians in China.

The South Pacific

In the South Pacific, British possessions included Australia and New Zealand, which attracted many settlers from Great Britain and Ireland.

Worldwide Outposts

The British also controlled a number of key strategic points around the world: Gibraltar at the western entrance to the Mediterranean Sea, the island of Malta in the central Mediterranean, Aden at the southern end of the Red Sea, and Ceylon off the southeastern coast of India. In 1819, Sir Stamford Raffles gained the great port of Singapore at the southern tip of the Malay Peninsula for the British. During the next several decades, the British pushed northward into the Malay Peninsula. In 1867, Singapore, Penang, and Malacca became a crown colony known as Straits Settlements.

Renewed Interest in Imperial Expansion

During the 1870s, the European powers developed a new interest in overseas expansion. In Great Britain, as well as in France, Germany, and Italy, the expansion of existing possessions and the acquisition of new colonies became an object of government policy and won wide and often enthusiastic public support.

Motives for Imperialism

A number of factors contributed to the drive for empire in the final decades of the nineteenth century.

National Rivalries

Political and psychological factors were particularly significant. During the late nineteenth century, competition among states for power and prestige intensified. One power would often move to acquire a colony before one of its rivals had an opportunity to do so. While colonization offered a means to increase a country's military and economic power in relation to that of its rivals, the idea also came to be widely accepted that the possession of colonies was a sign of national greatness and vitality. Conversely, the failure to acquire colonies came to be regarded as a sign of national decadence.

Religious and Humanitarian Motives

Religious and humanitarian motives also encouraged imperialist policies. During the late nineteenth century, there was a great upsurge in Christian missionary activity by both Protestants and Roman Catholics. These Christian missionaries not only sought to follow the command of Jesus Christ to go forth into the world and make disciples of all nations but also believed in their mission to bring the advantages of European civilization to less advanced people.

The story of Dr. David Livingstone (1813–1873), a Scottish missionary, provides a good example of the joining of religious and humanitarian motives. Livingstone spent close to thirty years exploring Central Africa and gathering evidence on the activities of African and Arab slave traders. He and his supporters in the British antislavery movement believed the British government should act to eliminate this slave trade. People motivated by such religious and humanitarian impulses generally expected their governments to protect them. This protection led to an expansion of the political and military control exercised by European states in Africa and Asia.

Economic Motives

Economic motives also helped promote the growth of imperialism, though the influence of economic factors has often been exaggerated. The growth of European industry led to demands for new sources of raw materials, as well as to a need for new markets for the products of industry. Furthermore, those who had accumulated fortunes from the profits of industry were often seeking new opportunities for the investment of their surplus capital. Other parties also had economic motives for supporting imperialist policies, among them shipping companies and the manufacturers of munitions and other goods required by imperialist ventures.

Hobson and Lenin.   Two early analysts of imperialism, J. A. Hobson (1858–1940), a British socialist, and V. I. Lenin (1870–1924), the leader of the Russian Bolsheviks, emphasized the importance of economic factors. In *Imperialism: A Study* (1902), Hobson argued that great financiers, who desired to increase their wealth through overseas investments, were the power behind imperialist policies.

These financiers manipulated public opinion to win broad popular support for expansion, and they used their political influence to induce governments to acquire colonies.

In *Imperialism: The Last Stage of Capitalism* (1916), Lenin contended that capitalism must continually expand in order to survive. Once capitalist investment has saturated the domestic market, the capitalists are forced to seek overseas outlets for investment. When capitalism can expand no further, he insisted, it will collapse as a consequence of its internal contradictions.

Criticism of Economic Motives.   Though economic factors undeniably played a role in late-nineteenth-century imperialism, it is important to stress that they were by no means the only factors, nor the most important ones. While some colonies possessed rich resources of raw materials, others had few or even none. Colonies inhabited by the impoverished peoples of Africa and Asia did not provide a sizable market for the products of European industry. And, while some colonies offered substantial opportunities for investment, others did not. In the race for colonies, Great Britain and the other imperial powers appeared more interested simply in the acquisition of territory than they did in the specific economic advantages that might be gained thereby.

British Imperialism in Africa

The Scramble for Africa

In the 1870s, the European powers began a race to acquire colonial possessions in Africa. By the first years of the twentieth century, virtually all of the continent had been partitioned among the imperial states.

France

In North Africa, the French, who had established their domination over Algeria in the 1830s, acquired Tunisia and, by the early twentieth century, Morocco as well. To the south, the French gained extensive holdings, establishing a group of colonies in French West Africa and French Equatorial Africa. In addition, in East Africa, France acquired part of Somaliland, as well as the island of Madagascar.

Germany

The Germans established colonies in Southwest Africa, Togoland and the Cameroons in West Africa, and German East Africa.

Italy

Italy occupied Eritrea and part of Somaliland in West Africa, but the Italian attempt in the mid-1890s to seize Ethiopia failed. Shortly before the outbreak of World War I in 1914, the Italians acquired Tripoli in North Africa.

Belgium

King Leopold II (r. 1865–1909) of Belgium carved out a private domain in the basin of the Congo River. This personal empire was organized as the Congo Free State in 1885 and in 1908 was acquired by the Belgian government, becoming the Belgian Congo.

Portugal

The Portuguese, who had been the first Europeans to arrive in sub-Saharan Africa in the late fifteenth century, expanded their holdings in Angola and Mozambique.

Great Britain

Great Britain also established a substantial empire in Africa, second in size only to that of France.

Egypt

Purchase of Suez Canal Shares

In 1875, Prime Minister Benjamin Disraeli (1804–1881), acting initially on his own responsibility, bought 177,000 shares – about forty-four percent of the total – in the Suez Canal Company from Egypt's ruler, Khedive Ismail (r. 1863–1879). The remaining shares were divided among several powers. The purchase pleased British imperialists, who regarded the Suez Canal, which had been built by a French company and opened in 1869, as an essential link between Great Britain and India.

Extension of British Control

The khedive had accumulated an enormous debt, borrowing heavily from European bankers who demanded repayment. The sale of his Suez Canal shares provided him with only temporary financial relief, however, and at the end of the decade, the British and French established their joint control over Egypt's finances.

Egyptian resentment of foreign intervention grew. In 1881, a revolt broke out against both the foreigners and the weak Khedive Tewfik (r. 1879–1892), Ismail's successor. When the French declined to join the British in intervening in Egypt, Great Britain acted alone in 1882. Although Prime Minister William E. Gladstone (1809–1898) declared that British troops would be withdrawn when order was restored, this did not happen. Egypt's government had collapsed, and it was apparent that if the British were to withdraw, some other power would probably intervene.

Lord Cromer's Administration

Egypt became, in effect, a British protectorate. Sir Evelyn Baring, Lord Cromer (1841–1917), who dominated Egypt from 1883 to 1907, provided efficient government and carried out important financial, educational, and other reforms.

South Africa

The Transvaal

Prime Minister Disraeli also pursued an active imperialist policy in South Africa, and in 1877, the British proclaimed the annexation of the Transvaal.

Gladstone, the leader of the Liberal Party, condemned the annexation, but he took no action when he succeeded Disraeli as prime minister in 1880. A Boer revolt began in December 1880, and in February 1881, the Boers defeated a small British force at Majuba Hill. Despite public pressure for firm British counteraction, Gladstone recognized the virtual independence of the Transvaal under British suzerainty.

In the Convention of London, signed in 1884, the British abandoned their claim to suzerainty although they insisted that the Transvaal's foreign affairs should remain subject to British control.

The Zulu War

Also in South Africa, the Zulus, an indigenous African people, resented the influx of Europeans into their traditional lands. Increasing tension led to the hard-fought Zulu War of 1879, which ended with a decisive British victory.

Cecil Rhodes

During the 1880s, Cecil Rhodes (1853–1902) became the central figure in British imperialist activity in South Africa. Rhodes had made a fortune in diamonds, which had been discovered at Kimberley in the Cape Colony in 1869. His great dream was the creation of a belt of British African possessions reaching from the Cape of Good Hope in the south to Egypt in the north. Rhodes hoped that someday a railroad would link the Cape with Cairo; however, the link was established by a telegraph line joining Capetown and Cairo that went into operation in 1892.

In 1889, Rhodes founded the British South Africa Company, which established Southern and Northern Rhodesia. The British also secured control of Bechuanaland and Nyasaland.

The Jameson Raid

Boer-British Hostility. In 1886, gold was discovered in the Boer republic of the Transvaal. As prospectors moved in, tension mounted between the Boers and the British. The Boer farmers resented the British intruders, while British settlers complained that they were the victims of discrimination. In 1895, Dr. Leander S. Jameson (1853–1917) led an unsuccessful raid into the Transvaal.

The Jameson Raid convinced President Paul Kruger (1825–1904) of the Transvaal that Rhodes, who had become prime minister of Cape Colony in 1890, was plotting to take over the Transvaal and its sister Boer republic, the Orange Free State.

German Involvement. Emperor William II (r. 1888–1918) of Germany sent an 1896 New Year's telegram to Kruger, congratulating him on his success in turning back the Jameson Raid "without appealing to the help of friendly powers." The British greatly resented this interference, and the Kruger Telegram contributed to a further deterioration of Anglo-German relations (see Chapter 19).

Milner's Negotiations. In the aftermath of the Jameson Raid, Rhodes resigned his prime ministership. Sir Alfred Milner (1854–1925), the British high commissioner in South Africa, began a series of negotiations with Kruger over the grievances of foreigners ("Uitlanders") in the Transvaal, but these talks proved fruitless.

The Boer War

Tension between the British and the Boer republics continued to mount, and in October 1899, the Transvaal demanded the removal of British troops from its frontier within forty-eight hours. When the British did not comply, the Transvaal and the Orange Free State invaded Natal and Cape Colony.

During the first phase of the Boer War, from October 1899 to February 1900, the Boers achieved some success, besieging the British at Ladysmith, Kimberley, and Mafeking.

British Victory. The British reinforced their army in South Africa and tightened their blockade of the two Boer republics. During the war's second phase, from February to September 1900, British forces took the offensive under the command of Lord Roberts (1832–1914) and Lord Kitchener (1850–1916). In March 1900, Roberts seized Bloemfontein, the capital of the Orange Free State. He took Pretoria, the Transvaal's capital, in May.

The Treaty of Vereeniging (1902). Although the British proclaimed the annexation of the Boer republics, guerrilla war continued during the third phase of the conflict from September 1900 to May 1902.

In the Treaty of Vereeniging of May 1902 the British offered lenient peace terms to the Boers. They could continue to use their language, Afrikaans, in the schools and law courts. The British promised that representative government for the Boers would be established and provided financial support for a program of rehabilitation. In 1906, the Transvaal gained self-government with Louis Botha (1862–1919), a former Boer general, serving as prime minister. Another former Boer general, Christian de Wet (1854–1922), became prime minister of the Orange Free State when it acquired self-government in 1908.

The Union of South Africa

In 1910, the British united Cape Colony, Natal, the Transvaal, and the Orange Free State to form the Union of South Africa, a self-governing dominion. General Botha became its first prime minister.

West and East African Possessions

West Africa

In West Africa, the British expanded their old trading stations into full-scale colonies, including Gambia, Sierra Leone, the Gold

Coast, and Nigeria, where the expansion of British control was directed by the Royal Niger Company, founded in 1886.

East Africa

In East Africa, the British East Africa Company, chartered in 1881, acquired British East Africa (1888), later known as Kenya, and Uganda (1894). The British also acquired part of Somaliland (1884). In 1890, the British gained Zanzibar from the Germans in return for the small North Sea island of Heligoland.

The Anglo-French Conflict Over the Sudan

The Sudan, located to the south of Egypt, became the object of a serious Anglo-French dispute in 1898.

Gordon's Expedition

In the early 1880s, a revolt, led by a Moslem religious leader known as the Mahdi, broke out among the Arabs of the Sudan, which was nominally an Egyptian province. The British decided to abandon the Sudan. In 1884, a British and Egyptian force commanded by General Charles Gordon (1833–1885) marched up the Nile River toward the Sudan's capital of Khartoum from its base in Egypt with the mission of directing the evacuation of Egyptian personnel from the country. While women and children were evacuated, Gordon remained in Khartoum, hoping to regain control of the situation. After a ten-month siege, the Mahdi's troops took the city in January 1885, massacring Gordon and his troops. The remaining British forces in the Sudan were removed, and the British did not renew their efforts to extend their control over the Sudan for more than a decade.

The Fashoda Crisis

In 1896, an Anglo-Egyptian force commanded by Lord Kitchener advanced into the Sudan. After winning several battles, Kitchener decisively defeated the Mahdi's followers, the dervishes, at Omdurman in early September 1898. A few days later, at Fashoda on the Nile, Kitchener encountered a French force under the command of Major Jean Baptiste Marchand (1863–1934), who had moved into the Sudan from French Equatorial Africa.

During the ensuing Fashoda Crisis, tension ran high between London and Paris, and for a time, war threatened. The crisis eased when the French decided to yield to the British. This decision represented an important step toward the improvement of France's relations with Great Britain, which culminated in the 1904 Entente Cordiale (see Chapter 19).

British Imperialism in Asia

India

The British provinces in India included about half of the country's territory and eighty percent of its population. The rest of India was divided into princely states that were bound by treaty to British India. During the late nineteenth century, Indian nationalism began to develop, with the emergence of two major movements, one Hindu and the other Moslem. In 1885, the Hindu-led Indian National Congress was established. Although the British were able to take advantage of Indian religious divisions in maintaining their control over the country, anti-British feeling continued to increase.

Indian Council Act of 1894

In an effort to conciliate the Indians, the British began to afford them more opportunities to serve in the government. The Indian Council Act of 1894, for example, provided for the election of Indian minorities to the provincial legislative councils.

Morley-Minto Reforms

Under the leadership of Viscount Morley (1838–1923), the secretary of state for India, and Lord Minto (1845–1915), the viceroy, these opportunities were increased. In 1909, the Liberal government adopted the Morley-Minto reforms, particularly the Indian Council Act of 1909, which provided for elected Indian majorities on the provincial legislative councils. The right to vote was restricted to educated Indians who, the British believed, understood the nature of self-government. Despite British concessions, Indian nationalism continued to develop.

Afghanistan

Although India remained firmly under the control of Great Britain in the late nineteenth century, the British were concerned about

Growth of the British Empire

Russian advances into Central Asia, north of India. The interests of Great Britain and Russia collided in Afghanistan, where tension ran high for a number of years.

War of 1878–1880

During Disraeli's prime ministership, the British began the Afghan War of 1878–1880, sending troops into the country to enforce their will. In 1880, after Gladstone assumed office, the Afghans agreed to a treaty allowing the British to control Afghan-

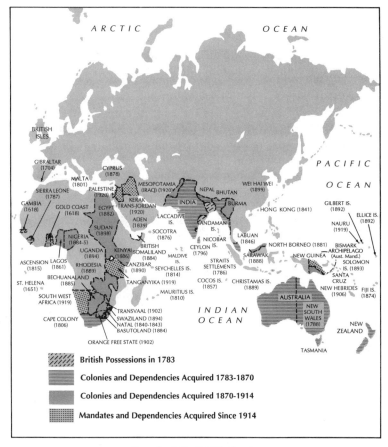

ARCTIC   OCEAN

BRITISH
ISLES

PACIFIC

OCEAN

GIBRALTAR
(1704)
CYPRUS
(1878)
MALTA
(1801)
PALESTINE
(1920)
MESOPOTAMIA
(IRAQ) (1920)
NEPAL BHUTAN
WEI HAI WEI
(1899)
SIERRA LEONE
(1787)
KERAK
EGYPT TRANS-JORDAN
(1882)   (1920)
INDIA
BURMA
HONG KONG (1841)
GILBERT IS.
(1892)
GAMBIA
(1618)
GOLD COAST
(1618)
LACCADIVE
IS.
ELLICE IS.
(1892)
ADEN
(1839)
ANDAMAN
IS.
NAURU
(1919)
SUDAN
(1898)
SOCOTRA
(1876)
CEYLON IS.
(1796)
LABUAN
(1846)
NORTH BORNEO (1881)
BISMARK
ARCHIPELAGO
(Aust. Mand.)
NIGERIA
(1884-5)
NICOBAR
UGANDA
(1894)
KENYA
(1886)
BRITISH
SOMALILAND
(1884)
MALDIVE
IS.
SOLOMON
IS. (1893)
ASCENSION
(1815)
LAGOS
(1861)
RHODESIA
(1889)
ZANZIBAR
(1890)
SEYCHELLES IS.
(1814)
STRAITS
SETTLEMENTS
(1786)
SARAWAK
(1888)
NEW GUINEA
SANTA
CRUZ
ST. HELENA
(1651)
BECHUANALAND
(1885)
TANGANYIKA (1919)
COCOS IS.
(1857)
CHRISTAMAS IS.
(1889)
NEW HEBRIDES
(1906)
FIJI IS.
(1874)
SOUTH WEST
AFRICA (1919)
MAURITIUS IS.
(1810)
INDIAN
OCEAN
AUSTRALIA
NEW
SOUTH
WALES
(1788)
CAPE COLONY
(1806)
TRANSVAAL (1902)
SWAZILAND (1894)
NATAL (1840-1843)
BASUTOLAND (1884)
NEW
ZEALAND
ORANGE FREE STATE (1902)
TASMANIA

British Possessions in 1783

Colonies and Dependencies Acquired 1783-1870

Colonies and Dependencies Acquired 1870-1914

Mandates and Dependencies Acquired Since 1914

Growth of the British Empire

istan's foreign relations in return for a British subsidy and protection against Russian encroachments.

Russian Withdrawal

In 1885, however, Russian troops occupied Penjdeh on the border of Afghanistan. While the immediate crisis ended when the Russians agreed to arbitration, Anglo-Russian interests continued to clash in Afghanistan. In 1907, the issue was resolved when the Russians agreed to withdraw from Afghanistan (see Chapter 19).

Southeast Asia

Burma

To the east of India, the British responded to France's moves into Indochina by annexing Burma in 1886.

Siam

As the French expanded their Indochinese empire and the British moved into Burma, the possibility of conflict developed between the two major imperial powers. In 1896, however, Great Britain and France agreed to maintain Siam (present-day Thailand) as an independent buffer state.

The Malay Peninsula

Further to the south, the British increased their control over the Malay Peninsula, where they had established their presence in the eighteenth century.

New Guinea and Borneo

Great Britain and Germany agreed to partition New Guinea, north of Australia, in 1884, while the British and Dutch partitioned Borneo in the East Indies in 1891.

The South Pacific

In 1901, the six self-governing colonies in Australia—New South Wales, Victoria, Queensland, Tasmania, South Australia, and West Australia—were joined in a federation to form the new Dominion of Australia.

New Zealand acquired substantial rights of self-government in 1853 and gained dominion status in 1907.

China

During the late nineteenth century, the British retained a sizable interest in China, which conducted about seventy percent of its foreign trade with Great Britain.

The Sino-Japanese War of 1894–1895

A new era in imperialism in China began with Japan's victory in the Sino-Japanese War of 1894–1895. Under the terms of the Treaty of Shimonoseki of 1895, the Chinese ceded the island of Formosa (Taiwan) to Japan. In addition, the Chinese recognized the independence of Korea, which would now be open to Japanese penetration. China also granted the Japanese a lease to the strategic Liaotung Peninsula in southern Manchuria, including Port Arthur. Manchuria, too, would be open to Japanese penetration.

Russia, Germany, and France, fearing the advance of Japanese power in China, intervened, forcing Japan to agree to a nullification of Korean independence and the lease to the Liaotung Peninsula. Great Britain refused to support this intervention.

Gains by European Powers

The Germans, Russians, and French soon moved to take advantage of Japan's setback. In 1898, the Germans acquired a lease to the port of Kiaochow on China's Shantung Peninsula, while the Russians secured a lease to the Liaotung Peninsula, as well as the right to build railroads in Manchuria. The French took control of the port of Kwangchow in southern China.

British Reaction

Concerned about these European encroachments on China, the British sought to protect their interests by securing control of Kowloon, adjacent to Hong Kong, and the port of Weihaiwei, near Germany's holdings in the Shantung Peninsula. The British also supported the American effort to secure a great power agreement to maintain an open door in China. This Open Door policy, advanced by John Hay (1838–1905), the American secretary of state, in his notes of 1899 and 1900, would give all countries equal status in their commercial dealings in China.

The Anglo-Japanese Alliance of 1902

The British remained particularly suspicious about Russian intentions, and in 1902, they signed a defensive alliance with Japan. Under the terms of the Anglo-Japanese Alliance, in the event of an attack on one signatory by a third power, the other signatory would remain neutral. If, however, either signatory was attacked by two or more powers, the other signatory would intervene to support its ally. This alliance represented a significant departure from the traditional British reluctance to make specific international commitments in peacetime.

The Russo-Japanese War of 1904–1905

Russian expansion into Manchuria and indications that Russia planned to advance into Korea, as well, angered the Japanese, who went to war against Russia in 1904. The Russo-Japanese War of 1904–1905 resulted in a Russian defeat. Under the terms of the Treaty of Portsmouth of 1905, Japan acquired the lease to the Liaotung Peninsula. While northern Manchuria remained a Russian sphere of influence, the Japanese established their dominance in southern Manchuria. Russia ceded to Japan the southern half of Sakhalin Island. In addition, Korea was now open to Japanese penetration, and Japan annexed Korea in 1910.

The British were pleased with the victory of their Japanese ally, which effectively contained Russian expansionism in East Asia.

During the late nineteenth century, the British added to their existing possessions in Africa, creating a sizable empire. In Asia, the British government assumed direct control of India, displacing the East India Company. In addition, the British increased their holdings in Southeast Asia and expanded their commercial interests in China.

While creating the largest empire in world history, the British extended rights of self-government in the colonies of European settlement, creating the dominions of Canada, Australia, New Zealand, and the Union of South Africa.

British imperialism resulted in conflicts with both France and Russia. In Africa, Anglo-French rivalry in the Sudan led to the Fashoda crisis of 1898, while in Asia, the British were concerned about French advances in Southeast Asia and Russian pressure on Afghanistan, as well as Russian encroachments on China. However, the British resolved their differences with both the French and the Russians (see Chapter 19), and when World War I broke out in 1914, the British were allies of their former imperial antagonists.

Recommended Reading

Beloff, Max. *Imperial Sunset,* vol. I, *Britain's Liberal Empire, 1897–1921* (1969).

Carrington, C. E. *The British Overseas: Exploits of a Nation of Shopkeepers* (2nd ed., 1968).

Eldridge, C. C. *England's Mission: The Imperial Idea in the Age of Gladstone and Disraeli, 1868–1880* (1973).

Eldridge, C. C. *Victorian Imperialism* (1978).

Flint, John. *Cecil Rhodes* (1974).

Gifford, Prosser and William Roger Lewis, eds. *Britain and Germany in Africa: Imperial Rivalry and Colonial Rule* (1971).

Gifford, Prosser and William Roger Lewis, eds. *France and Britain in Africa: Imperial Rivalry and Colonial Rule* (1971).

Headrick, Daniel R. *The Tools of Empire: Technology and European Imperialism in the Nineteenth Century* (1981).

Hibbert, Christopher. *The Great Mutiny: India 1857* (1978).

Hutchins, Francis. *The Illusion of Permanence: British Imperialism in India* (1967).

Hyam, Ronald. *Britain's Imperial Century, 1815–1914: A Study of Empire and Expansion* (1976).

Lewis, Martin D. *The British in India: Imperialism or Trusteeship?* (1962).

Lloyd, T. O. *The British Empire, 1558–1983* (1984).

Lowe, C. J. *The Reluctant Imperialists, 1870–1902* (1968).

Lowe, Peter. *Britain in the Far East: A Survey from 1819 to the Present* (1981).

Magnus, Sir Philip. *Kitchener: Portrait of an Imperialist* (1958).

Metcalf, Thomas. *The Aftermath of Revolt: India, 1857–1870* (1965).

Moorhouse, Geoffrey. *India Britannica* (1983).

Porter, Bernard. *The Lion's Share: A Short History of British Imperialism, 1850–1970* (2nd ed., 1984).

Robinson, Ronald, John Gallager, and Alice Denny. *Africa and the Victorians* (1961).

Schreuder, D. M. *The Scramble for Southern Africa, 1877–1895* (1980).

Wheatcroft, Geoffrey. *The Randlords: The Men Who Made South Africa* (1985).

Winks, Robin, ed. *British Imperialism: Gold, God, and Glory* (1963).

Woodcock, George. *The British in the Far East* (1969).

Woodruff, Philip. *The Men Who Ruled India,* 2 vols. (1954).

CHAPTER 18

The Triumph of Liberalism

Time Line

1903	The Women's Social and Political Union begins its campaign for women's suffrage
1905–1908	Henry Campbell-Bannerman, a Liberal, serves as prime minister
1906	The Liberals win the parliamentary election
	Parliament passes the Workmen's Compensation Act and the Trade Disputes Bill
1908	The Old Age Pensions Act is adopted
	Herbert Asquith, a Liberal, becomes prime minister
1909	Parliament passes the Labor Exchanges Act, the Trade Boards Act, and the House and Town Planning Act

	David Lloyd George proposes the "People's Budget"
1910–1936	Reign of King George V
1910	The Liberals lose their majority in the House of Commons but remain in power with Irish Nationalist and Labor support
1911	The Parliament Act trims the powers of the House of Lords
	Parliament adopts the National Insurance Act of 1911
	Railroad and transport workers go on strike
1912	The strike movement continues with a walk-out of coal miners
1913	Parliament passes a Minimum Wage Law
1914	The Irish Home Rule Act becomes law
	The railroad and transport workers and the coal miners plan a general strike for September

The Liberal government that took office in 1905 enacted a broad program of socioeconomic and political reforms. The system of workmen's compensation was expanded, and programs of old age pensions, health insurance, and unemployment insurance were instituted. The "People's Budget" of 1909 shifted more of the tax burden onto the shoulders of the wealthy, while the Parliament Act of 1911 sharply reduced the power of the House of Lords.

While the nineteenth century — in historic terms, the period from the end of the Napoleonic Wars in 1815 to the beginning of World War I in 1914 — was a time of reform as well as of imperial expansion, it was also an era of considerable intellectual achievement for Great Britain. In science, Charles Darwin launched a revolution in biology, while the writers of the Victorian and post-Victorian periods built upon the achievements of their predecessors of the Romantic movement of the early nineteenth century.

The New Liberal Government

The Elections of 1906

Henry Campbell-Bannerman (1836–1908), the Liberal who succeeded Balfour in the prime ministership in December 1905 (see Chapter 16), led his party into the parliamentary elections of 1906. The Liberals triumphed, winning 401 seats to the 157 seats won by the Conservatives and Liberal Unionists, 83 by the Irish Nationalists, and 29 by the new Labor Party.

During its two decades out of power, with the brief exception of the Gladstone-Rosebery ministries of the mid-1890s, a new Liberal Party had taken shape, abandoning its earlier doctrinaire commitment to laissez-faire principles and embracing a powerful philosophy of reform.

The Campbell-Bannerman Ministry

Campbell-Bannerman remained prime minister, with Herbert Asquith (1852–1928) as his chancellor of the exchequer. David Lloyd George (1863–1945) served as president of the Board of Trade. A third future prime minister, Winston Churchill (1874–1965), was undersecretary of state for the colonies. Churchill had earlier been a Conservative, but he broke with his party in 1905 and joined the Liberals.

Liberal Reforms, 1906–1909

The Workmen's Compensation Act of 1906

The Workmen's Compensation Act of 1906 expanded both the coverage and benefits established by earlier legislation. The new act covered almost 6 million workers, providing them with benefits in the event they suffered a job-related injury.

The Trade Disputes Bill of 1906

The Trade Disputes Bill of 1906 nullified the Taff Vale Decision of 1901 by providing that a labor union could not be held liable for damages caused by a strike (see Chapter 16).

The Education Bill of 1906

The Education Bill of 1906 reflected the powerful influence of the Nonconformists in the Liberal Party. Noting that Britain's voluntary schools, which were largely sponsored by religious groups, received substantial tax support, the Nonconformists argued that there should be no religious tests for teachers in these schools.

The Education Bill of 1906 contained this provision and also provided that religious education in the voluntary schools should be nondenominational. Although the bill encountered strong opposition from the Church of England, which conducted many of the nation's voluntary schools, it won passage in the House of Commons.

However, the House of Lords blocked the bill, leaving the Education Act of 1902 unchanged (see Chapter 16).

The Plural Voting Bill

The House of Lords also rejected the Plural Voting Bill, which would have barred individuals who owned property in more than one constituency from voting in more than one place.

The Old Age Pensions Act of 1908

The House of Lords came close to rejecting the Old Age Pensions Act of 1908, which provided small benefits for retirees over the age of seventy who had only very limited incomes from other sources. However, the act was passed.

The Asquith Ministry

In April 1908, Campbell-Bannerman retired because of failing health, and Asquith succeeded to the prime ministership. Lloyd George became chancellor of the exchequer, and Churchill moved up to become president of the Board of Trade.

Labor and Housing Legislation

In 1905, Parliament had established a commission to study poverty and poor relief. Acting on the information provided by the commission's forty-volume report, Parliament adopted several pieces of legislation in 1909.

The Labor Exchanges Act

The Labor Exchanges Act established 350 labor exchanges to provide information on job opportunities to workers seeking employment.

The Trade Boards Act

The Trade Boards Act established a number of trade boards, composed of representatives of the government, employers, and workers, to establish minimum wages and maximum hours for certain specified trades that employed unskilled or semi-skilled workers.

The House and Town Planning Act

The House and Town Planning Act consolidated and extended earlier legislation relating to urban housing. Landlords could now be held legally responsible for the condition of their rental property, and the construction of back-to-back houses was prohibited. The act also increased state financial assistance to municipal authorities for programs of slum clearance and housing construction.

Lloyd George's "People's Budget"

The cost of social reforms and the program of naval expansion resulting from the German decision to build a high seas fleet (see Chapter 19) necessitated a substantial tax increase. In a budget presented in April 1909, David Lloyd George, the chancellor of the exchequer, proposed a bold redistribution of national income by placing the heaviest burden of taxation on the landowners and capitalists. Promoting this budget as a "People's Budget," Lloyd George called for higher income tax rates for the wealthy and increases in the tax on large inheritances (death duties). In addition, new taxes would be levied on all increases in the value of urban land and on undeveloped land that was being held in anticipation of an increase in value. Furthermore, taxes on tobacco and alcohol would be raised.

On November 5, 1909, the House of Commons passed the budget by a vote of 349 to 149.

Rejection of Budget by the House of Lords

The People's Budget required the wealthy to pay the bulk of the government's increased expenditures, and the aristocrats were among the country's wealthiest people. On November 30, 1909, the Lords rejected the budget by a vote of 300 to 75.

The House of Lords had blocked other legislation proposed by the Liberal government, but the budget was in a different category. Traditionally, financial matters were reserved to the House of Commons, and more specifically, the House of Lords could not initiate or amend any money bills. The Lords' rejection of the budget thus precipitated a political crisis.

The Election of January 1910

Prime Minister Asquith called for a parliamentary election on the issue. In this election, held in January 1910, the Liberals lost their majority in the House of Commons. The Liberals won 275 seats to 273 for the Conservatives, 82 for the Irish Nationalists, and 40 for the Labor Party. With the support of the Irish Nationalists and Labor, the Asquith government was able to remain in power.

Passage of the Budget

The House of Commons once again passed the People's Budget, and this time the House of Lords accepted it with only brief debate and without a formal vote.

King George V

On May 7, 1910, King Edward VII died. He was succeeded by his son, who became King George V (r. 1910–1936).

Restrictions on the House of Lords

Acceptance of the budget by the House of Lords did not prevent the Asquith government from seeking to restrict the Lords' powers.

The Parliament Bill of 1910

Under the terms of a Parliament Bill proposed in 1910, the House of Lords could not block the passage of any money bill for more than one month. Furthermore, the bill provided that the House of Lords could not prevent the adoption of other legislation if the House of Commons passed it in three successive sessions in a period of not less than two years after its first introduction. Another provision limited the term of Parliament to five years instead of seven.

Efforts to achieve a compromise settlement failed, and the House of Lords defeated the Parliament Bill.

The Election of December 1910

Asquith called for a new election, and in December 1910, for the second time that year, a new House of Commons was elected. The results differed little from those of the January election. The Liberals won 272 seats, as did the Conservatives, with the Irish Nationalists winning 84 and the Laborites 42.

The Parliament Act of 1911

In February 1911, the House of Commons passed the Parliament Bill. Confronted with the likelihood that the Lords would once again reject it, King George V agreed to create about 500 Liberal peers to assure the bill's passage by the upper house. Faced with this threat, the Lords relented. With most of the Conservative peers absent when the vote was taken, the House of Lords adopted the Parliament Act in August 1911 by a vote of 131 to 114.

By weakening the power of the aristocratic House of Lords, the Parliament Act of 1911 represented another step towards the creation of full political democracy in Great Britain.

Other Reforms of the Liberal Government

Salaries for Members of the House of Commons

In the Osborne Case of 1909, the House of Lords had prohibited unions from using their funds to pay Labor members of the House of Commons. Since most of these Labor members came from the working class, they were deprived of income while serving in Parliament.

Legislation adopted in 1911 provided for the payment of salaries of £400 a year to members of the House of Commons. Thus, all of the demands of the People's Charter of 1839 (see Chapter 15) had been enacted, with the exception of annual elections for the House of Commons.

The National Insurance Act of 1911

Health Insurance

The National Insurance Act of 1911 established a program of compulsory health insurance, supported by contributions by the government, employers, and workers, for all workers earning less than £160 a year. Some 14 million people, about one-third of the country's population, were covered by this legislation, which provided the basis for the establishment of the National Health Service in 1948 (see Chapter 22).

Unemployment Compensation

In addition, the National Insurance Act established a system of unemployment insurance, which was also supported by contributions by the government, employers, and workers. Initially, only about 2.25 million workers, in such trades as construction, shipbuilding, vehicle-building, and engineering, were covered. They were entitled to a weekly payment of seven shillings for a maximum of fifteen weeks a year in the event of unemployment.

The Trade Disputes Act of 1913

The Trade Disputes Act of 1913 provided that the country's shop workers, who were for the most part not unionized and often exploited, be given a half day off each week in addition to Sunday.

The act also nullified the judgment in the Osborne Case by authorizing labor unions to collect money for political purposes if their members approved and if the funds were placed in a separate account.

Pre-War Crises

On the eve of the outbreak of World War I in the summer of 1914, Great Britain faced three crises: the suffragette movement, mounting labor unrest, and Ireland.

The Suffragette Movement

In 1903, the Women's Social and Political Union (WSPU) was established under the leadership of Emmeline Pankhurst (1857–1928) and her two daughters, Christabel (1880–1958) and Sylvia (1882–

1960). In their drive to secure the right to vote for women, the suffragettes engaged in militant and often violent tactics. Imprisoned suffragettes began hunger strikes, while one suffragette, Emily Davison, threw herself at the foot of the horses at the Derby and was killed. Despite the mounting pressure for women's suffrage, Parliament took no action on the issue prior to 1914.

Labor Unrest

Increase in Union Membership

Despite the reforms of the Liberal government, the hardships and discontents of Britain's workers persisted and labor unrest intensified. Although wages had increased, inflation led to a decline in the workers' purchasing power. By 1910, Britain's union membership exceeded 4 million.

Strikes

In 1911, the epidemic of strikes began with a walkout of railroad and transport workers. Close to a million workers walked off their jobs, and 10 million working days were lost as a result of strikes.

The strike movement continued during 1912, as some 1.5 million coal miners left the pits. The strike by the miners and other workers resulted in the loss of almost 40 million working days during the year.

The passage of a minimum wage law in 1912 did little to ease the unrest, although strikes tapered off during 1913. Labor unrest intensified once again during the first half of 1914, when 937 strikes occurred and 40 million working days were lost. The miners and the railroad and transport workers planned a great general strike for September 1914 to demand "a living wage" for all workers. However, Britain went to war in August, and the general strike did not take place.

Ireland

In April 1912, Prime Minister Asquith kept his promise and introduced a new Irish Home Rule Bill. Under its terms, a two-house Irish Parliament would be established in Dublin with full control over domestic affairs. Some forty-two Irish members would continue to sit in the British Parliament.

Although the Irish Nationalists, led by John Redmond (1856–1918), endorsed the bill, it evoked powerful opposition from the

Protestants of Ulster, led by Sir Edward Carson (1854–1935). In September 1912, some 500,000 Ulsterites signed the Solemn League and Covenant pledging their determination to resist Home Rule.

The Home Rule Act of 1914

The House of Commons passed Asquith's Home Rule Bill twice, in January and July 1913, and the House of Lords rejected it twice.

In Ireland, the threat of civil war loomed. The Ulsterites armed themselves, forming the Volunteer Army, while the Irish Nationalist Volunteers took shape in the south.

In May 1914, the House of Commons passed the Home Rule Bill a third time. Under the terms of the Parliament Act of 1911, it would now become law without its adoption by the House of Lords. In an effort to avert bloodshed, Carson and Redmond met at Buckingham Palace in July 1914, but they failed to reach any agreement.

Postponement of Home Rule

Civil war in Ireland was averted only by the outbreak of the First World War. While the Home Rule Act became law in September 1914, Parliament adopted a Suspensory Act, providing that Home Rule would not take effect until the end of the European conflict. In fact, the Home Rule Act of 1914 never went into effect and was replaced by the Home Rule Act of 1920 (see Chapter 20).

Science and Literature in the Mid- and Late Nineteenth Century

Darwinism

Developments in biology during the nineteenth century had a powerful impact on Western thought. Charles Darwin (1809–1882), a British scientist who was fascinated by the world of plants and animals, advanced his theory of biological evolution.

Theory of Evolution

In *On the Origin of Species* (1859), Darwin repudiated the theory of the special creation of each species, contending instead that all existing forms of life had evolved out of earlier forms. He also argued that life involves a constant struggle for existence, in which, as a result of a process of natural selection, the fittest survive. The organisms that survive because of their favorable characteristics then pass these characteristics on to subsequent generations. In time, an entirely new organism evolves. In *The Descent of Man* (1871), Darwin applied the concept of evolution to human beings.

Scientists accepted the fundamental validity of the theory of evolution, although some of Darwin's particular conclusions were subsequently disproved.

Thomas Huxley and the Cult of Science

Thomas Huxley (1825–1895), a British biologist, became a fervent advocate of the theory of evolution. His attacks on religious leaders who rejected the theory won him the nickname of "Darwin's Bulldog."

For Huxley and those who thought as he did, science appeared to be revealing all of the secrets of the universe. Through their understanding and application of science, human beings could continue their march of progress.

Herbert Spencer and Social Darwinism

In his *Synthetic Philosophy* (10 vols., 1860–1896), the British thinker Herbert Spencer (1820-1903) sought to apply Darwin's theory of evolution to virtually every aspect of human society. He contended that in human society, just as in nature, life involves a struggle for existence as a result of which the fittest survive. This doctrine of Social Darwinism provided support for the economic doctrine of laissez-faire, which emphasized free competition and opposed state intervention in the economy.

Poetry

Alfred, Lord Tennyson

Alfred, Lord Tennyson (1809–1892), who became poet laureate in 1850, was the most popular of the Victorian poets. Much of his work was marked by the romantic sentimentality that had such a strong appeal to the nineteenth-century literary audience. In *Poems* (1842), Tennyson expressed his doubts in a materialistic age and his hope for the discovery of an abiding faith. He is also known for his elegy *In Memoriam* (1850) and *Idylls of the King,* published between 1859 and 1885, which reflected Tennyson's fascination with the Middle Ages in his retelling of the story of the legendary King Arthur and the knights of the Round Table.

Robert Browning

Robert Browning (1812–1889) wrote verse dramas and dramatic monologues, including "My Last Duchess" (1842). *The Ring and the Book,* generally regarded as his masterpiece, was published in four volumes in 1868 and 1869.

Elizabeth Barrett Browning

After a romantic courtship, Elizabeth Barrett Browning (1806–1861) married Robert Browning in 1846. Her major work, *Sonnets from the Portuguese,* was inspired by her own love story.

Matthew Arnold

The poetry of Matthew Arnold (1822–1888) was less sentimental than that of many of his Victorian contemporaries, and modern readers relate readily to his mood of stoic resignation. His best-known poem is "Dover Beach."

Dante Gabriel Rossetti and Christina Rossetti

Dante Gabriel Rossetti (1828–1882) and his sister, Christina (1830–1894), were among the founders of the Pre-Raphaelite Brotherhood, a group of poets and painters who found inspiration for their work in the Middle Ages. Dante, a poet and painter, is best known for his poem "The Blessed Damozel," written when he was nineteen. Much of Christina's poetry was religious in nature.

Algernon Charles Swinburne

Algernon Charles Swinburne (1837–1909) manifested a spirit of revolt against Victorian mores in his poetry and poetic dramas. As a consequence, his work was often attacked as immoral and anti-Christian.

Rudyard Kipling

In both his poetry and prose, Rudyard Kipling (1856–1936) glorified British imperialism, especially in India, his birthplace. His early poems were published in *Departmental Ditties* (1886) and *Barrack-Room Ballads* (1892). His best-known poems include "The White

Man's Burden," "Mandalay," and "Gunga Din," as well as "Recessional" (1897), which was written to commemorate the diamond jubilee of Queen Victoria's accession to the throne but expresses a warning against imperialistic pride.

Kipling also wrote popular children's stories, including *The Jungle Book* (1894), *Kim* (1901), and *Just So Stories* (1902). He was England's first winner of the Nobel Prize for literature, which he received in 1907.

Fiction

William Makepeace Thackeray

In his novel *Vanity Fair* (1848), William Makepeace Thackeray (1811–1863) presented a fascinating portrayal of upper-middle-class London society at the beginning of the nineteenth century. His other well-known novels include the partly autobiographical *Pendennis* (1850) and *Henry Esmond* (1852), set in the eighteenth century.

Charles Dickens

In such novels as *Oliver Twist* (1838), *A Christmas Carol* (1843), *David Copperfield* (1850), *A Tale of Two Cities* (1859), and *Great Expectations* (1861), Charles Dickens (1812–1870) demonstrated elements of both Romanticism and Realism. He was critical of the bourgeoisie, whose influence was increasing in British life, and he also portrayed the hardships endured by the urban workers during the first generations of the industrial revolution.

George Eliot

Mary Ann Evans, who wrote under the pseudonym George Eliot (1819–1880), in such novels as *The Mill on the Floss* (1860) and *Silas Marner* (1861) focused on the moral choices that individuals must make.

Benjamin Disraeli

The Conservative Party leader and prime minister Benjamin Disraeli (1804–1881) turned a cynical eye on England's social classes in such novels as *Vivian Gray* (1826), *Coningsby* (1844), and *Sybil* (1845). Writing fiction also provided him with a vehicle for the expression of his political views.

Charlotte Brontë and Emily Brontë

Charlotte Brontë (1816–1855) is best known for her novel *Jane Eyre* (1847), the dramatic story of its heroine, a governess who eventually marries her master.

Emily Brontë (1818–1848) wrote *Wuthering Heights* (1847). Set in Yorkshire, the novel deals with the human condition by telling the story of the relationships among members of two families, the Earnshaws and the Lintons, and Heathcliff, a foundling and interloper.

Anthony Trollope

In *Barchester Towers* (1857) and other volumes in the series of Barsetshire novels, Anthony Trollope (1815–1882) depicted life in the cathedral towns of southern England. In his later novels, including *Phineas Finn* (1869) and *The Prime Minister* (1876), he turned his attention to urban society and politics.

Thomas Hardy

Thomas Hardy (1840–1928) wrote powerful realistic novels. In such works as *The Return of the Native* (1878), *The Mayor of Casterbridge* (1886), *Tess of the D'Urbervilles* (1891), and *Jude the Obscure* (1895), he expressed the view that human beings are ultimately the victims of fate.

Robert Louis Stevenson

Robert Louis Stevenson (1850–1894), a Scot, is best known for his adventure stories, including *Treasure Island* (1883), *Kidnapped* (1886), and *The Strange Case of Dr. Jekyll and Mr. Hyde* (1886). He also wrote *A Child's Garden of Verses* (1885).

Joseph Conrad

The Polish-born Joseph Conrad (1857–1924) wrote of the sea, society, and politics in such works as *Lord Jim* (1900), *Heart of Darkness* (1902), *The Secret Agent* (1907), and *Under Western Eyes* (1911).

H. G. Wells

H. G. Wells (1866–1946), a leader of the Fabian Society (see Chapter 15), won a sizable audience for his science fiction, including *The Time Machine* (1895) and *The War of the Worlds* (1898). Following World War I, *The Outline of History* (1920) gained a wide readership, as did the futuristic novel *The Shape of Things to Come* (1933).

Arthur Conan Doyle

Arthur Conan Doyle (1859–1930) created the detective hero, Sherlock Holmes, in *A Study in Scarlet* (1887). He was knighted in 1902.

Drama

Oscar Wilde

Born in Dublin, Oscar Wilde (1854–1900) became a leading figure in the Aesthetic Movement that emphasized art for art's sake. He is known for his clever social comedies, including *Lady Windermere's Fan* (1892) and *The Importance of Being Earnest* (1895). He also wrote a horror novel, *The Picture of Dorian Gray* (1891).

William Butler Yeats

The leading figure in the Irish literary renaissance, William Butler Yeats (1865–1939) was both a playwright and poet. He was a founder of Dublin's Abbey Theatre, for which he wrote many plays.

George Bernard Shaw

George Bernard Shaw (1856–1950), who was also Irish-born, won popularity for a number of witty plays, including *Man and Superman* (1905) and *Pygmalion* (1913). *Saint Joan* (1923) was among Shaw's successful plays produced in the 1920s. He won the Nobel Prize for literature in 1925.

The Liberal governments headed by prime ministers Henry Campbell-Bannerman and Herbert Asquith produced a series of notable socioeconomic and political reforms. Nevertheless, as World War I approached, the militant suffragette movement, intensifying labor unrest, and what appeared to be the insoluble Irish problem confronted the government with disturbing challenges. It seemed that the country's commitment to moderation, gradualism, and a sense of fair play was being abandoned by many in favor of militancy and violence.

Recommended Reading

Bernstein, George L. *Liberalism and Liberal Politics in Edwardian England* (1986).

Brent, Peter. *Charles Darwin: A Man of Enlarged Curiosity* (1981).

Bruce, Maurice. *The Coming of the Welfare State* (4th ed., 1968).

Dangerfield, George. *The Strange Death of Liberal England* (1935).

Fulford, Roger. *Votes for Women* (1957).

Gilbert, Bentley B. *David Lloyd George: A Political Life* (1987).

Grigg, John. *Lloyd George,* 3 vols. (1973–1985).

Harrison, Brian. *Separate Spheres: Opposition to Women's Suffrage in Britain* (1978).

Irvine, William. *Apes, Angels, and Victorians: The Story of Darwin, Huxley, and Evolution* (1955).

Jenkins, Roy. *Asquith: Portrait of a Man and an Era* (1964).

Kynaston, David. *King Labour: The British Working Class, 1850–1914* (1976).

Lloyd, T. O. *Empire to Welfare State: English History, 1906–1985* (3rd ed., 1986).

Mackenzie, Norman and Jeanne Mackenzie. *Dickens: A Life* (1979).

Meacham, Standish. *A Life Apart: The English Working Class, 1890–1914* (1977).

Morgan, David. *Suffragists and Liberals: The Politics of Woman Suffrage in England* (1975).

O'Day, Alan, ed. *The Edwardian Age: Conflict and Stability, 1900–1914* (1979).

Phillips, Gregory D. *The Diehards: Aristocratic Society and Politics in Edwardian England* (1979).

Read, Donald. *Edwardian England, 1901–1915: Society and Politics* (1972).

Rosen, Andrew. *Rise Up, Women! The Militant Campaign of the Women's Social and Political Union, 1903–1914* (1974).

Rowland, Peter. *The Last Liberal Governments, 1905–1915,* 2 vols. (1968–1971).

Thompson, Paul. *The Edwardians: The Remaking of British Society* (1975).

Wilson, John. *CB: A Life of Sir Henry Campbell-Bannerman* (1973).

CHAPTER 19

Great Britain and the First World War

Time Line

1904	Great Britain and France form the Entente Cordiale
1905	Germany provokes the First Moroccan Crisis
	Great Britain and France initiate military conversations
1906	Great Britain launches the *Dreadnought*
1907	The Anglo-Russian Entente is formed
1908	Austria's annexation of Bosnia and Herzegovina leads to the Bosnian Crisis
1911	Germany provokes the Second Moroccan Crisis
1912–1913	The Balkan Wars are fought
1914	Archduke Francis Ferdinand is assassinated at Sarajevo
	World War I breaks out in Europe
	The British Expeditionary Force is sent to France
	The Germans fail to take Paris; trench warfare begins in France
1915	The British launch an invasion of the Gallipoli Peninsula
	Germany's campaign of unrestricted submarine warfare results in the sinking of the *Lusitania*
	Prime Minister Herbert Asquith forms a coalition
1916	The German offensive at Verdun and the Allied offensive on the Somme fail to produce breakthroughs
	The British and German fleets fight the Battle of Jutland
	Prime Minister Asquith resigns; David Lloyd George forms a new coalition government
	The British suppress the Easter Rebellion in Ireland

1917	The United States enters the war on the Allied side
1918	The German offensive in France fails to achieve a breakthrough
	A French, British, and American counterattack drives the Germans back
	Germany agrees to an armistice

With its achievement of unification in 1871, Germany suddenly became the most powerful state on the European continent. From 1871 to 1890, Otto von Bismarck, the Prussian minister-president who had led Germany to unity, served as the country's chancellor. Bismarck made Germany the center of continental diplomacy, arranging alliances and alignments with Austria, Russia, and Italy.

After 1890, the diplomatic center of gravity began to shift in the direction of France, which concluded an alliance with Russia in 1894.

During the late nineteenth century, Great Britain stood apart from these continental entanglements. In 1902, however, the British abandoned their traditional aversion to peacetime alliances by signing an accord with Japan. The British then reached diplomatic understandings with France in 1904 and Russia in 1907. As Britain's relations with Germany deteriorated, the British drew closer to France, in particular, and when war began in the summer of 1914, Great Britain entered the conflict as an ally of France and Russia.

The European Alliance System

Bismarck's Diplomatic Objectives

After forging the German Empire under Prussian domination during the Franco-German War of 1870–1871, Chancellor Otto von Bismarck (1815–1898) had two major foreign policy objectives. First, he sought to isolate France so the French could not wage a war of revenge against Germany. In the 1871 peace treaty, the Germans had annexed the border provinces of Alsace and Lorraine, and the French remained resentful over this loss. Second, Bismarck desired to maintain close relations with Austria-Hungary and Russia.

The Three Emperors' League (1872)

Bismarck's efforts achieved their first success in the formation of the Three Emperors' League in 1872. Germany's Emperor William I (r. 1871–1888), Austria's Emperor Francis Joseph (r. 1848–1916), and Russia's Tsar Alexander II (r. 1855–1881) pledged to cooperate to preserve peace and the status quo.

The Dual Alliance (1879)

Austro-Russian rivalry in the Balkans presented a serious threat to Bismarck's efforts to maintain Germany's ties with both Austria and Russia, and the Three Emperors' League collapsed during the Balkan crisis of the late 1870s (see Chapter 16).

In 1879, Bismarck concluded a defensive alliance with Austria. This Dual Alliance remained the foundation of Germany's international commitments.

Revival of the Three Emperors' League (1881)

Bismarck hoped to restore the close relationship between Germany and Russia. In 1881, his efforts succeeded with the reestablishment of the Three Emperors' League. This association of the German, Austrian, and Russian rulers remained fragile, however, as a result of continuing Austro-Russian conflict in the Balkans.

The Triple Alliance (1882)

In 1882, Italy joined Germany and Austria in a defensive alliance, the Triple Alliance. Bismarck now had ties with Italy as well as with Austria and Russia. In addition, Germany remained on good terms with Great Britain, although the British, adhering to their traditional "splendid isolation" from continental entanglements, had no direct part in the alliance system.

The Reinsurance Treaty (1887)

Continued Austro-Russian tension in the Balkans led to the Russian decision in 1887 not to renew the Three Emperors' League. However, the Russians wanted to maintain their ties with Germany, and the two powers signed the Reinsurance Treaty of 1887.

German Diplomacy After Bismarck

While Bismarck's creation of these alliances and alignments served to isolate France, balancing commitments to both Austria and Russia required great skill. In 1890, Germany's new emperor, William II (r. 1888–1918) dismissed Bismarck. The same year, the Germans decided not to renew the Reinsurance Treaty with Russia. The Germans believed that breaking the tie with Russia would pose no threat to Germany's interests since autocratic Russia and revolutionary, republican France were so ideologically antagonistic that an alliance between them was inconceivable. This belief proved to be mistaken.

The Franco-Russian Alliance (1894)

In the early 1890s, a diplomatic revolution began as long-isolated France and newly isolated Russia began to draw together.

Although the Russians were strongly hostile to France's radical tradition, the two countries improved their relations following the lapse of the Reinsurance Treaty. In 1894, the Franco-Russian Alliance was signed. At the time, the alliance seemed directed primarily against Great Britain, the rival of France in Africa and of both France and Russia in Asia (see Chapter 17).

British Diplomacy at the
Turn of the Century

Deterioration of Anglo-German Relations

Belligerence of William II

Although Anglo-German relations had been cordial during Bismarck's tenure as German chancellor, William II's often belligerent quest for greater world importance, what the Germans called "a place in the sun," resulted in increasing tension in the Anglo-German relationship.

In 1891 and again in 1899, William II visited England, where his boorish behavior irritated both his grandmother, Queen Victoria (r. 1837–1901), and his uncle, the Prince of Wales, who became King Edward VII (r. 1901–1910). William II's telegram of support to President Paul Kruger of the Transvaal in 1896 angered the British, as did rumors of possible German intervention in the Boer War which broke out in 1899 (see Chapter 17).

Failure of Moves toward Alliance

However, in the late 1890s, the British remained more antagonistic to France and Russia than they were to Germany and, in fact, sought to conclude a defensive alliance with Germany. When Joseph Chamberlain (1836–1914) proposed such an alliance, however, the Germans declined, fearing that ties with Britain would involve them in Britain's imperial disputes with Russia or France. In 1902, the British and Germans once again discussed the possibility of an alliance. The Germans wanted the British to join the Triple Alliance, which they refused to do.

The Anglo-Japanese Alliance (1902)

During the Boer War, widespread international hostility to Great Britain convinced the British that isolation was dangerous. The first step in Britain's abandonment of isolation came in 1902, with the signing of the Anglo-Japanese alliance. This alliance reflected Britain's concerns about Russian expansion in East Asia and especially the possibility that Russia might secure French support (see Chapter 17).

The Anglo-French Entente (1904)

French Fear of Germany

Although colonial disputes led to tension in Anglo-French relations, the French sought to improve that relationship, believing that Germany, rather than Great Britain, posed the greater threat to France. The French withdrawal from the Sudan in 1898 marked the beginning of a reorientation of French policy (see Chapter 17).

Settlement of Anglo-French Differences

Lord Lansdowne (1845–1927), the pro-French foreign secretary in the Balfour cabinet, arranged for a visit of King Edward VII to Paris in 1903. A few months later the French president paid a return visit to London. Anglo-French negotiations followed and led to the conclusion of the Entente Cordiale in 1904. This diplomatic understanding dealt with colonial issues. The French recognized British dominance in Egypt (see Chapter 17), while the British agreed to support French claims to Morocco. The British and French also settled other differences in Africa and Asia and resolved a long-standing dispute about fishing rights in the North Atlantic off Newfoundland.

The First Moroccan Crisis (1905)

Intervention of William II

Germany's Emperor William II and his chancellor, Prince Bernhard von Bülow (1849–1929), believed that French ambitions in Morocco offered them an opportunity to improve their diplomatic position. In March 1905, William II paid an unexpected visit to the Moroccan city of Tangier, where he declared that Germany had interests in Morocco and spoke in support of Moroccan independence. The Germans expected that Russia, which was being defeated by Japan in the Russo-Japanese War (see Chapter 17), could not assist France, and they hoped that Britain would give France only token support at best. If these things happened, France's ties with Russia and Great Britain would be weakened.

The Algeciras Conference (1906)

The Germans continued to believe that the Moroccan crisis would weaken the French alliance system, and they pressed for an international conference to consider the status of Morocco. The conference met in early 1906 at Algeciras in southern Spain, near Gibraltar.

At Algeciras the Germans found themselves virtually isolated, securing only the support of Austria. Great Britain and Russia both backed France, as did Italy, even though Italy was still technically allied with Germany and Austria. France was now in a strong position to proceed with the establishment of its protectorate over Morocco.

Germany's belligerent attitude during the First Moroccan Crisis created an unfavorable impression and resulted in strengthening, rather than weakening, the French alliance system.

The Anglo-Russian Entente (1907)

Japan's victory in the Russo-Japanese War weakened Russia, France's ally and Britain's imperial antagonist. With their concern about Russian expansionism reduced, the British responded to French urging to seek a resolution of their differences with Russia.

The Anglo-Russian Entente of 1907 settled imperial disputes concerning Persia, Afghanistan, and Tibet. Persia was divided into three spheres of influence, a Russian sphere in the north and a British sphere in the south, while central Persia would be a neutral zone, open to both powers. The Russians acknowledged Britain's predominant position in Afghanistan and agreed to deal with the Afghans only through the British. Both countries promised to respect the territorial integrity of Tibet. With these differences resolved, Britain and Russia could seek to collaborate in European affairs.

The Two Alliance Systems

The Anglo-Russian Entente completed the process of establishing the Triple Entente of France, Great Britain, and Russia. The Triple Entente faced the Triple Alliance of Germany, Austria, and Italy. The two power blocs were not as evenly balanced as that would suggest, however. As the Algeciras Conference had demonstrated, Italy was less than completely faithful to its alliance partners. In the years since Bismarck's dismissal in 1890, the diplomatic balance of power in Europe had shifted dramatically in France's favor. Austria was Germany's only reliable ally, and the Germans began to complain about being encircled by an iron ring.

Anglo-German Naval Rivalry

In the late 1890s, Germany began the construction of a high seas fleet under the direction of Admiral Alfred von Tirpitz (1849–1930). The British regarded Germany's naval construction as a threat to their predominance on the seas and a serious Anglo-German naval rivalry gradually developed.

Battleships

In 1906, the British launched a large new battleship, the *Dreadnought*. Equipped with more heavy guns than previous battleships, the *Dreadnought* represented a revolution in ship construction. While the British planned to build two more ships of this class in

1908, the Germans began the construction of four, and Admiral Tirpitz planned to build four more in 1909. In response, Prime Minister Herbert Asquith (1852–1928) proposed that the British begin the construction of four additional "dreadnoughts" in 1909 and four others in 1910, if necessary. By 1914, the number of British dreadnoughts in service increased to eighteen, while the number of German dreadnoughts grew to thirteen.

Fleet Dispositions

In 1912, Richard Haldane (1856–1928), the British secretary of state for war, went to Berlin in an unsuccessful effort to secure German agreement on a mutual slow-down of naval construction.

As the Anglo-German naval race intensified, the British began in 1912 to concentrate their fleet in the North Sea, thereby reducing their naval strength in the Mediterranean. In turn, the French shifted units of their fleet from the North Sea to the Mediterranean.

Anglo-French Military Conversations

At the time of the First Moroccan Crisis, Sir Edward Grey (1862–1933), the foreign secretary, responded favorably to a French request that Anglo-French military conversations take place regarding the possibility of cooperation in the event of a German attack on France. Continuing for several years, these conversations resulted in the development of a plan for rushing 100,000 British troops to France within twelve days after the outbreak of war.

The nature of the Anglo-French Entente was thus gradually changed. Although the British might assert that Great Britain had no specific commitments to support France in the event of a German attack, it could be argued that the British had made a moral commitment to the French. The concentration of the French fleet in the Mediterranean left the Royal Navy to defend France's North Sea and Atlantic coast, which would otherwise be unprotected, while the military conversations at least implied a British intention to come to France's aid in the event of war. The Entente Cordiale of 1904 had come close to being converted into a full alliance.

International Crises, 1908-1914

A series of international crises beginning in 1908 increased tension and uncertainty in Europe and led to the outbreak of war in 1914. With Austria as its only reliable ally, Germany could no longer seek to restrain Austria's activities in the Balkans as it had in the past. This increased the possibility that a crisis in the Balkans could escalate, thereby endangering the peace of Europe.

The Bosnian Crisis (1908)

In October 1908, Austria annexed the Balkan provinces of Bosnia and Herzegovina, which the Austrians had occupied and administered under the terms of the Treaty of Berlin of 1878 (see Chapter 16). The Austrian action infuriated the Russians.

As the crisis mounted, Germany gave Austria its full support. In the spring of 1909, the threat of war with both Austria and Germany forced the Russians to back down and accept the annexation. The Bosnian Crisis thus ended with Russia's humiliation. The Russians were determined not to yield again in the Balkans for fear of losing all influence there.

The Second Moroccan Crisis (1911)

German Intervention

In 1911, Germany renewed its objections to the establishment of a French protectorate over Morocco. The Germans sent a warship, the *Panther,* to Agadir, a seaport on Morocco's Atlantic coast, ostensibly to protect German interests. In fact, the Germans were putting pressure on the French to make concessions elsewhere in Africa. Tension eased when the French agreed to cede some 100,000 square miles of mostly desert land in the French Congo to Germany in return for German recognition of the French position in Morocco.

Lloyd George's Warning

Once again, Germany's belligerent diplomacy caused alarm. David Lloyd George (1863-1945), the chancellor of the Exchequer, made a famous speech at London's Mansion House, warning that when Great Britain's interests were involved, she should not be treated "as if she were of no account in the cabinet of nations" because "peace at that price would be a humiliation intolerable for a great country like ours to endure."

The Balkan Wars (1912–1913)

The First Balkan War

Under Russian patronage, Bulgaria, Serbia, Montenegro, and Greece had formed the Balkan League. In 1912, the Balkan League went to war against the Ottoman Empire. As a consequence of the First Balkan War, the Turks lost all their territory in Europe except for the area immediately adjacent to the Turkish Straits.

The Second Balkan War

Disputes among the victors then led to the outbreak of the Second Balkan War in 1913. Serbia, Montenegro, Greece, Romania, and the Ottoman Empire joined to defeat Bulgaria. While Serbia and Greece gained most of Macedonia, Bulgaria was forced to cede territory to Romania and the Ottoman Empire. The Balkan Wars thus resulted in the weakening of Bulgaria, which was pro-Austrian, and the strengthening of Serbia, which was anti-Austrian. However, Austrian diplomatic intervention had resulted in the creation of an independent Albania, which deprived Serbia of access to the Adriatic Sea.

The Sarajevo Crisis (1914)

The crises in the Balkans had been serious and the situation remained dangerous. Russia's ambitions in the Balkans and the Turkish Straits had been frustrated, while Austro-Serbian relations were becoming increasingly antagonistic. The Russians felt compelled to support Serbia more fully in the future, while the Germans believed it was essential to back Austria, their only reliable ally.

On June 28, 1914, the final crisis began at Sarajevo, the capital of the Austrian province of Bosnia. A South Slav nationalist, Gavrilo Princip (1895–1918), assassinated Archduke Francis Ferdinand (1863–1914), the heir to the Austro-Hungarian throne, and his wife. Although the Serbian government was not directly involved, some Serbian officials were aware of the plot but took no action either to prevent its execution or to warn the Austrians.

The Outbreak of War

Convinced that the Serbian government bore ultimate responsibility for the assassination, Austria was determined to settle accounts with Serbia, which had been encouraging nationalist unrest among South Slavs within Austria's borders. The Austrians hoped to wage a limited war against Serbia and dispatched a stern ultimatum to the Serbian government on July 23. While Serbia did not accept all of Austria's demands, the reply was moderate enough to warrant further negotiations. However, determined to press forward against Serbia, the Austrians declared war on July 28.

The German "Blank Check"

Germany had earlier indicated its readiness to support Austria fully, issuing the so-called "blank check" to the Austrian government. Instead of trying to restrain the Austrians, the Germans appeared to be encouraging them to move against Serbia, whatever the risk of a general war might be.

Declarations of War

It was impossible for the Russians to accept another setback in the Balkans, and they were determined to back Serbia. On July 30, Tsar Nicholas II (r. 1894–1917) ordered a general mobilization of his armies. Germany responded by sending Russia an ultimatum, demanding an end to Russian mobilization. When the Russians refused, Germany declared war on Russia on August 1. The Germans asked the French government about its intentions and received a vague reply. On August 3, Germany declared war on France.

The Schlieffen Plan

The German general staff had established a plan for fighting a war on two fronts against both Russia and France. Assuming that Russia would mobilize slowly, this Schlieffen Plan called for a massive assault on France. When the French had been defeated, the Germans would then turn against Russia. The success of the Schlieffen Plan depended not only on rapid German mobilization but also on a speedy defeat of France. The Germans calculated that this objective could most readily be achieved by invading France by way of

Belgium, even though this would involve a violation of Belgian neutrality, which the European powers had guaranteed by the Convention of 1839 (see Chapter 15).

British Declaration of War

The British government and people had been surprised by the rapid turn of events. Although the French and the Russians urged the British to make a firm commitment to support them in the war, the cabinet remained divided.

The British government asked the French and the Germans if they intended to respect Belgian neutrality. The French reply was affirmative, while the German response was evasive. On the afternoon of August 3, Sir Edward Grey spoke to the House of Commons. He declared that the cabinet had agreed that the Royal Navy would defend the northern coast of France. Furthermore, while the military conversations with France did not impose a binding commitment on Great Britain to come to France's aid, he explained, the British had a moral obligation to do so. The House of Commons expressed its strong support of the government's position.

Following Germany's assault on Belgium, the British dispatched an ultimatum to Berlin on August 4, demanding a German withdrawal. When the time limit expired late in the evening of the same day, Great Britain went to war. Foreign Secretary Grey uttered an epitaph for the age that had ended: "The lamps are going out all over Europe; we shall not see them lit again in our lifetime."

The War in the West
1914–1917

While the Germans hoped that a push against France by way of Belgium would achieve a quick victory in the West, General Helmuth von Moltke (1848–1916), the German chief of staff, weakened his drive by sending some of his troops to Lorraine, to counter a French offensive, while other German forces were dispatched to East Prussia to meet an unexpected Russian advance. These diversions of troops slowed down the German advance through Belgium into northern France.

The First Battle of the Marne

Although the British Expeditionary Force (BEF) of some 100,000 men, commanded by Sir John French (1852-1925), arrived too late to help Belgium, it did support the French in the First Battle of the Marne.

At the end of August, the Battle of the Frontiers resulted in a major German defeat of the French. A few days later, on September 5, 1914, the Germans crossed the Marne River at a point about 12 miles from Paris, but they lacked the strength to push on and take the French capital. General Joseph Joffre (1852-1931), the French commander, then launched a counterattack, and the First Battle of the Marne ended with the French turning back the German threat to Paris. Following the battle, the Germans named General Erich von Falkenhayn (1861-1922) to replace Moltke.

The Race to the Sea

During the autumn of 1914, the British helped keep the French channel ports, including Calais and Boulogne, from falling into German hands. If the Germans had won this race to the sea, Britain's ability to send men and equipment to the fighting front in France would have been severely handicapped.

Stalemate in the West

The Germans' hopes of winning a quick victory over France had been dashed. The front in France now became stalemated, with the Germans controlling most of Belgium and a large section of northern France. The two sides dug trenches, which they protected with barbed wire and concrete pill boxes.

Trench warfare continued in France for the better part of four years, with neither side being able to make a decisive breakthrough. Each side launched offensives, but the machine guns of the defenders mowed down the advancing infantrymen.

The War During 1915

In the Second Battle of Ypres, fought in the spring of 1915, the Germans used chlorine gas for the first time in an unsuccessful attempt to score a breakthrough against the Allies.

Unsuccessful British offensives during the year included those of Neuve-Chapelle in March and Festubert in May. In the Battle of Loos in September, the British suffered heavy casualties without making any major inroads against the Germans. In December 1915, Sir Douglas Haig (1861–1928) replaced Sir John French as commander of the BEF.

The Battle of Verdun (1916)

In February 1916, the Germans massed their armies and artillery in an assault on the French stronghold of Verdun. Failing to take Verdun, the Germans moved to the defensive in July, and the battle continued until December. By that point, the French had stabilized the front much as it had been at the beginning of the year. At Verdun, the French suffered some 540,000 casualties, while German losses exceeded 430,000. The battle became a lethal symbol of the horrors of trench warfare.

The Battle of the Somme (1916)

In July 1916, the British and French launched a great offensive on the Somme River, with the British suffering 60,000 casualties on the first day of fighting alone. Along the 30-mile Somme front, the Allies achieved a maximum advance of only 7 miles. By the time the battle ended in November, British casualties totaled 410,000, while the French suffered 200,000 casualties. German casualties have been estimated at 650,000. During the Battle of the Somme, the British used tanks for the first time. But, like heavy artillery and poison gas, tanks failed to produce a decisive breakthrough.

In August 1916, while the Battle of the Somme was under way, the Germans removed Falkenhayn as their commander in the West. General Paul von Hindenburg (1847–1934) succeeded Falkenhayn, with General Erich Ludendorff (1865–1937) as his chief of staff. In December, the French replaced Joffre with General Robert Nivelle (1856–1924).

The War During 1917

In early 1917, the Germans established new defenses at the Hindenburg Line. In April, the so-called Nivelle offensive in the Aisne failed, with the French suffering extraordinarily high casualties. Mutinies broke out in the French army in May, leading to the dismissal of Nivelle, who was replaced with General Henri Philippe Pétain (1856–1951), who had commanded the French at Verdun.

The war-weariness of the French required the British to assume greater responsibility for the war in France. British offensives at Passchendale (near the coast of Flanders) and Cambrai proved both indecisive and costly.

After more than three years of fighting, neither the Allied nor the German armies had made any real gains, and both sides had suffered tremendous casualties.

The Italian Front, 1915–1917

The Treaty of London (1915)

Although still technically allied with Germany and Austria under the terms of the Triple Alliance, Italy remained neutral when the war began. In an effort to win Italy's support, the Allies agreed to the secret Treaty of London of 1915, promising the Italians Austrian and Turkish territory, as well as colonies in Africa. In May 1915, Italy entered the war on the Allied side.

The Battle of Caporetto

Italy was unsuccessful in its war against Austria, and in the fall of 1917, the Austrians inflicted a humiliating defeat on the Italians in the Battle of Caporetto. The British and French had to rush troops in to help the Italians stabilize the front at the Piave River, a few miles north of Venice.

The Eastern Front, 1914–1918

German Victories in East Prussia

When the war began in the summer of 1914, the Russians succeeded in mobilizing more rapidly than the Germans had expected. Two Russian armies invaded East Prussia, but the Germans defeated them at the Battle of Tannenberg at the end of August and the Battle of the Masurian Lakes in early September.

The War in the East, 1914–1916

German Advance

The Russians initially scored some successes at the expense of the Austrians. In order to relieve the pressure on their allies, the Germans pushed toward Warsaw in Russian Poland. By the end of 1914, the Russians held almost all of Galicia (Austrian Poland), while the Germans occupied about one-quarter of Russian Poland. Russia was already in poor condition, with ammunition and military equipment in short supply. Russia's industry was inadequate to meet the country's military needs.

The German advance against Russia continued during 1915. By the end of the year, the Germans occupied most of Russian Poland and Lithuania. While the Russian offensives against the Austrians in Galicia achieved some success during 1915, they remained indecisive.

Failure of Russian Offensive

In June 1916, the Russians began a great offensive in Galicia, but the Germans rushed in fifteen divisions to reinforce the Austrians and halt the Russian advance. The Russians suffered about 1 million casualties in the offensive, whose failure left the Russian army seriously demoralized.

Romania

Prior to the Russian setback, Romania entered the war on the Allied side in August 1916. By January 1917, however, Austrian and German forces had defeated and occupied Romania.

Bulgaria

Bulgaria entered the war on Germany's side in October 1915. Bulgaria had been at odds with Serbia since the Second Balkan War in 1913 and hoped to square accounts. Bulgarian forces helped Germany and Austria crush Serbia at the end of 1915.

Defeat of Russia

By the end of 1916, the Germans had, in effect, defeated Russia, and the Russian revolutions of 1917 ended any possibility that the Russians might continue fighting. The Treaty of Brest-Litovsk, signed with the Bolshevik government in March 1918, ended the war between Russia and the Central Powers (Germany and its allies).

The Gallipoli Campaign

In November 1914, the Ottoman Empire entered the war on the side of the Central Powers, thereby closing to the Allies the Turkish Straits that join the Black and Aegean seas. The Western Allies were thus unable to ship vital war supplies to the faltering Russians.

British Attempt to Open Straits

Winston Churchill (1874–1965), the British first lord of the admiralty, pushed for a campaign to open the Straits. If this effort succeeded, aid could be sent to the Russians, and the Allied position in the Balkans would be strengthened.

Defeat of British Expeditionary Force

In April 1915, the British launched an amphibious invasion of the Gallipoli Peninsula at the southern end of the Dardanelles. However, the operation failed as a result of errors in its planning and execution. In January 1916, the British withdrew, having suffered the loss of 100,000 lives.

The War in the Middle East

With the Turkish Straits closed to Allied shipping, the British hoped to open a route to Russia through Turkish-ruled Mesopotamia. In 1916, the Turks defeated the British at Kut-el-Amara, about 100 miles south of Baghdad. In March 1917, however, the British seized Baghdad and soon took control of most of Mesopotamia (present-day Iraq).

Under the leadership of Colonel T. E. Lawrence (1888–1925), known as Lawrence of Arabia, the British succeeded in stirring up revolts among the Arab subjects of the Turks. In 1917, General Edmund Allenby (1861–1936) invaded Turkish-ruled Palestine, capturing Jerusalem in December.

The War at Sea

Germany's much-vaunted high seas fleet had little impact on the Allies during World War I. Their submarines, on the other hand, posed a serious threat.

Early British Naval Victories

Early in the war, the British succeeded in hunting down Germany's scattered cruisers. The *Emden* was destroyed in the Indian Ocean in November 1914. A squadron commanded by Admiral Graf Spee (1861–1914), including the *Scharnhorst* and *Gneisenau,* raced across the Pacific and around Cape Horn, only to be destroyed by a British squadron off the Falkland Islands in the South Atlantic in early December.

The Battle of Jutland

During the afternoon and evening of May 31, 1916, the British Grand Fleet battled the German fleet at the Battle of Jutland in the North Sea, off the coast of Denmark. Although the British possessed superiority in the engagement, with twenty-eight battleships and nine battle cruisers versus sixteen battleships and five battle cruisers for the Germans, Sir John Jellicoe (1859–1935), the British commander, acted with great caution. The German fleet, commanded by Admiral Scheer, inflicted substantially greater damage on the British than it suffered, but the battle proved indecisive. The Germans failed to break the British blockade, while the British failed to open the Baltic Sea route to Russia. Following the battle, however, the German surface fleet limited its activities to the Baltic Sea and therefore ceased to present any threat to the Allies.

Submarine Warfare

The German submarine fleet presented a more substantial threat. In February 1915, in an effort to starve out the British, the Germans declared a submarine blockade of the British Isles. In May, off the Irish coast, a German U-boat sank the British passenger liner *Lusitania,* which was unarmed but carried munitions, with the loss of 139 American lives. Vigorous American protests caused the Germans to reduce their submarine campaign.

During 1916, however, many German leaders urged the renewal of a campaign of unrestricted submarine warfare in an attempt to knock Great Britain out of the war. On February 1, 1917, the campaign began. The Germans were taking a calculated risk, hoping that the British would be forced out of the war before the United States could bring its power to bear in Europe.

The United States Declaration of War

On February 26, 1917, the British liner *Laconia* was sunk without warning; two Americans died in the sinking. On March 1, the British revealed the Zimmermann Telegram, which British intelligence agents had intercepted earlier. In this dispatch, the Germans proposed an alliance with Mexico, promising to restore Texas, New Mexico, and Arizona to the Mexicans. American antagonism toward Germany mounted.

By April 1917, British losses as a result of Germany's campaign of unrestricted submarine warfare reached the huge monthly total of 875,000 tons of shipping. The British had only a six weeks' supply of grain, although British convoys gradually reduced the submarine threat.

The United States declared war on Germany in early April, but American forces were not present in large numbers on the front in France until almost a year later.

The End of the War

The Germans' 1918 Offensive

In March 1918, the Germans launched a massive offensive in France in a final, desperate effort to win the war. The British rushed in reinforcements, and some 2 million American troops began to arrive in France. In April, the Allies established a unified command, headed by French general Marshal Ferdinand Foch (1851–1929). The Germans scored some impressive advances and by the end of May reached a point less than 40 miles from Paris, but the Allies halted the enemy's push in the Second Battle of the Marne.

The Allied Counteroffensive

In mid-July 1918, the French, British, and American armies began a counterattack that marked the beginning of the long offensive that ended the war. The Germans began to retreat along a broad front. On August 8, 1918, the Black Day of the German army, British tanks scored a major breakthrough of the Hindenburg Line near Amiens. Five days later, on August 13, General Ludendorff told Emperor William II that the war was lost.

Armistice

On September 30, Bulgaria signed an armistice. Turkey capitulated to the Allies on October 30, and Austria gave up on November 3. The armistice with Germany was signed in the forest of Compiègne in northern France at 5 A.M. on November 11, 1918, to go into effect at 11 A.M.

Manpower and Casualties

During 1914 and 1915, the British depended on voluntary enlistments to meet their military manpower needs, but it became increasingly apparent that conscription would be necessary. Under the terms of the Military Service Act, adopted in January 1916, all unmarried men between the ages of eighteen and forty-one became liable for military service. Conscription was later expanded to include all men between the ages of eighteen and fifty.

By the autumn of 1918, the British had mobilized a total of almost 8.7 million into their armed forces. Some 5.7 million came from the United Kingdom, while India provided 1.1 million. Some 640,000 Canadians had been mobilized, while there were close to 420,000 Australians, 220,000 New Zealanders, and 135,000 South Africans.

British war dead totaled 947,000, while over 2 million were wounded. In comparison, France's war dead numbered 1.4 million, while Germany's totaled 1.8 million. The United States counted 130,000 war dead.

The Home Front

Coalition Government

By the spring of 1915, the military failure in France brought mounting criticism of Prime Minister Asquith's government, especially of Lord Kitchener (1850–1916), who was both secretary of state for war and the commander-in-chief. Also contributing to the criticism was the evident failure of the Gallipoli campaign. Admiral Sir John Fisher (1841–1920), the first sea lord, had favored an assault on Germany's Baltic coast and opposed the Gallipoli invasion, the pet project of Winston Churchill, the first lord of the admiralty.

Responding to the government's critics, Asquith created a twenty-two member coalition cabinet, composed of twelve Liberals, eight Conservatives (including Andrew Bonar Law, the Conservative leader; Arthur Balfour, a former prime minister; Lord Curzon; and Sir Edward Carson), one Laborite (Arthur Henderson, the party leader), and Lord Kitchener. David Lloyd George, the chancellor of the exchequer, became head of a new Ministry of Munitions, which was established to overcome the shortage of artillery shells.

In June 1916, when Kitchener was drowned at sea, Lloyd George became secretary of state for war.

The Lloyd George Government

In late 1916, a new round of criticism charged Prime Minister Asquith with a lack of vigor and decisiveness in leading the war effort. Lloyd George, Asquith's fellow Liberal, joined the critics. In December 1916, Asquith resigned. He had served longer than any prime minister since Lord Liverpool in the early nineteenth century (see Chapter 15).

Split in Liberal Party

Asquith was bitter over what he regarded as Lloyd George's betrayal, and the Liberal Party now became divided between Asquith's followers and supporters of Lloyd George. This split contributed to the party's decline.

The War Cabinet

Lloyd George now became prime minister, establishing a small War Cabinet of five members: himself, the only Liberal; the Conservatives Bonar Law, Sir Alfred Milner, and Curzon; and the Laborite Henderson. The War Cabinet was occasionally expanded into an Imperial War Cabinet, including the prime ministers of the dominions, a representative from India, and the secretary of state for colonies.

Wartime Regulation

As the war continued, the government extended its control over Britain's national life. A series of Defense of the Realm Acts (DORA) increased state regulation of the economy, while the submarine threat led to the establishment of new ministries of Food, Blockade, Pensions, and Labor. In early 1918, food rationing was introduced.

Inflation and National Debt

During the war, prices increased by an average annual rate of twenty-seven percent until the end of 1917, when price and wage controls were imposed. The cost of the war increased the national debt to some £7 billion, but it would have been higher if the government had not increased taxes considerably.

Women

As increasing numbers of men entered the armed services, women became more numerous in the domestic labor force. The number of women employed in industry grew by about 800,000 during the war, while some 100,000 additional women found jobs in transport and 250,000 in agriculture. About 200,000 women found employment in government offices, while 400,000 secured jobs in private offices. Several hundred thousand more became retail salespersons.

Although employers generally paid women workers about half the wages earned by men doing the same jobs, women workers gained greater freedom since they were earning money of their own. Furthermore, the large number of women in the labor force helped promote a change of male attitudes on the controversial subject of women's suffrage.

Ireland

By the time of World War I, the old Irish Nationalist Party of Parnell and Redmond (see Chapter 16) was being replaced by a more radical movement, Sinn Fein (Gaelic for "We Ourselves"). Rather than Home Rule, Sinn Fein demanded the establishment of an independent Irish Republic including all of Ireland.

In the Easter Rebellion of 1916, the Sinn Feiners and Irish Volunteers rose in revolt. While the British crushed the uprising after a week of often bitter fighting, the Easter Rebellion served as a reminder that not only had Irish nationalism not subsided but it had taken on a more radical character.

During the First World War, British support of France had made possible French survival in the face of the German onslaught, and the British made powerful contributions to the eventual Allied victory. But the war had imposed a heavy burden on the British people, for whom it was an exhausting and often horrifying experience. Although Prime Minister Lloyd George held out the hope of better things to come, of "a country fit for heroes to live in," the cost of the war had been high, and it seriously weakened Britain's position as a world power.

Recommended Reading

Adams, R. J. Q. *Arms and the Wizard: Lloyd George and the Ministry of Munitions* (1978).

Beckett, Ian F. W. and Keith Simpson. *A Nation in Arms: A Social Study of the British Army in the First World War* (1985).

Bennett, Geoffrey. *The Battle of Jutland* (1964).

Falls, Cyril. *The Great War, 1914–1918* (1959).

Guinn, Paul. *British Strategy and Politics, 1914–1918* (1965).

Hazlehurst, Cameron. *Politicians at War, July 1914 to May 1915* (1971).

Higgins, Trumbull. *Winston Churchill and the Dardanelles* (1963).

Kennedy, Paul. *The Rise of Anglo-German Antagonism, 1860–1914* (1980).

Lafore, Laurence. *The Long Fuse: An Interpretation of the Origins of World War I* (1965).

Marwick, Arthur. *The Deluge: British Society and the First World War* (1966).

Marwick, Arthur. *Women at War, 1914–1918* (1977).

Monger, George W. *The End of Isolation: British Foreign Policy, 1900–1907* (1963).

Moorehead, Alan. *Gallipoli* (1956).

Padfield, Peter. *The Great Naval Race: The Anglo-German Naval Rivalry, 1900–1914* (1974).

Pitt, Barrie. *1918: The Last Act* (1963).

Robbins, Keith. *Sir Edward Grey* (1971).

Rolo, P. J. V. *The Entente Cordiale: The Origins and Negotiations of the Anglo-French Agreements of 8 April 1904* (1969).

Rowland, Peter. *David Lloyd George: A Biography* (1975).

Steiner, Zara S. *Britain and the Origins of the First World War* (1978).

Taylor, A. J. P. *English History, 1914–1945* (1965).

Taylor, A. J. P. *The First World War: An Illustrated History* (1963).

Tuchman, Barbara. *The Guns of August* (1962).

Williams, John. *The Other Battleground: The Home Fronts—Britain, France and Germany, 1914–1918* (1972).

Williamson, S. R., Jr. *The Politics of Grand Strategy: Britain and France Prepare for War, 1904–1914* (1969).

Wilson, Trevor. *The Myriad Faces of War: Britain and the Great War, 1914–1918* (1986).

Winter, J. M. *The Great War and the British People* (1986).

Wolff, Leon. *In Flanders Fields: The 1917 Campaign* (1958).

CHAPTER 20

The Age of Baldwin
and MacDonald

Time Line

1918	Women over the age of thirty acquire the right to vote
	The Education Act establishes compulsory elementary school attendance
	Prime Minister David Lloyd George's coalition wins the Coupon Election
1919	Lloyd George heads the British delegation at the Paris Peace Conference
1921	The Irish Free State is established
1922–1923	Andrew Bonar Law, a Conservative, serves as prime minister

1922	Great Britain recognizes Egyptian independence
1923	Stanley Baldwin, a Conservative, succeeds Bonar Law
1924	Ramsay MacDonald heads Great Britain's first Labor government
	Great Britain recognizes the Soviet Union
1924–1929	Baldwin heads his second ministry
1925	Great Britain acts as a guarantor of the Locarno Pact
	Great Britain returns to the gold standard
1926	The Imperial Conference defines dominion status
	A general strike confronts Great Britain with its greatest crisis of the 1920s
1928	Women receive the right to vote on the same basis as men
1929–1931	MacDonald heads his second ministry
1930	The Great Depression hits Great Britain
1931–1935	MacDonald heads the National Government
1931	Great Britain abandons the gold standard
1932	Eamon de Valera becomes head of the government of the Irish Free State
1935–1937	Baldwin heads his third ministry
1935	The Government of India Act fails to establish dominion status for India
1936	King George V dies
	King Edward VIII abdicates; George VI begins his reign
1937–1940	Neville Chamberlain, a Conservative, serves as prime minister

The interwar era began with the prime ministership of David Lloyd George and ended with that of Neville Chamberlain. However, Stanley Baldwin and Ramsay MacDonald, the leaders of the Conservative and Labor parties respectively, were the leading figures in British politics during the 1920s and 1930s.

Following the First World War, Great Britain confronted serious economic problems, which became even more intense during the depression decade of the 1930s.

Despite these economic problems, British politics remained generally stable. The most significant political development was the decline of the Liberal Party and the emergence of Labor as one of the major parties in the British two-party system. This political shift served to make the Conservatives the predominant party for most of the interwar years.

The British confronted continuing problems in Ireland. In the Empire, demands for independence mounted in Egypt and India, while the dominions called for greater rights of self-government.

Postwar Britain

The war had been an exhausting experience, both physically and psychologically, for the British people. The loss of over 900,000 people in the war was a profound shock for Great Britain and deprived the country of an important segment of its male population.

The war had been costly in economic and financial terms, as well. British economic prosperity depended on foreign trade, but the war had disrupted Britain's trade links, which could not easily be reconstructed in a disorganized world. The national debt had increased by about 1000 percent, and British finances were under a severe strain. Industry, which had been mobilized for the war, had to be reconverted to peacetime production. Jobs had to be found for discharged veterans, and labor leaders demanded economic and social reform.

1918 Domestic Reforms

Suffrage

The Representation of the People Act, adopted in 1918, granted the right to vote to women over the age of thirty and extended male voting rights by abolishing virtually all property qualifications.

Education

The Education Act of 1918 made elementary education compulsory for all children between the ages of five and fourteen.

The 1918 Elections

Soon after the signing of the armistice in November 1918, the Labor Party pulled out of the wartime coalition government headed by Prime Minister David Lloyd George (1863–1945), and the prime minister was unable to make peace with the Liberals who followed Herbert Asquith (1852–1928), his predecessor (see Chapter 19). Lloyd George thus formed an alliance with the Conservatives for the parliamentary elections of December 1918.

The "Coupon"

The candidates who supported this coalition received an endorsement signed by both Lloyd George and Andrew Bonar Law (1858–1923), the Conservative leader. Asquith called this endorsement a "coupon," and the election came to be known as the "Coupon Election."

Results

During the campaign, Lloyd George called for a new mandate to strengthen his position at the coming peace conference. The coalition won an overwhelming victory, gaining 484 seats in the House of Commons. Of these, the Conservatives held 338, while the Lloyd George Liberals won 136. Labor held 59 seats, and the Asquith Liberals held 26.

The Peace Settlement

Lloyd George, Wilson, and Clemenceau

During the 1918 election campaign, Lloyd George had taken a strong anti-German position, demanding harsh peace terms. However, during the Paris Peace Conference, which began its deliberations in January 1919, the prime minister found himself in the position of a mediator between Woodrow Wilson (1856–1924), the American president, and Georges Clemenceau (1841–1929), the French premier.

Wilson advocated a peace based on principles of justice. In the Fourteen Points, which Wilson had presented in January 1918, he called for open diplomacy, freedom of the seas, free trade, a reduction of armaments, and self-determination for the subject peoples of the German, Austrian, and Ottoman empires. In the fourteenth point, Wilson endorsed the creation of a League of Nations, which became the central part of his vision of the postwar world.

While Wilson sought what he had earlier termed a "peace without victory," Clemenceau was determined to gain security for France against a possible future resurgence of German power, and he demanded substantial reparations from Germany to pay for the reconstruction of war-ravaged northern France.

The Treaty of Versailles

The Paris Peace Conference produced five treaties for Germany, Austria, Hungary, Bulgaria, and Turkey. The most important was the Treaty of Versailles, the peace settlement with Germany, which was signed in June 1919. At the insistence of President Wilson, the Covenant of the League of Nations was included in the Treaty of Versailles and the other treaties.

The Treaty of Versailles restored the provinces of Alsace and Lorraine to France and provided for the permanent demilitarization of the Rhineland, the area of western Germany bordering on France. In addition, the Rhineland would be occupied by Allied troops for fifteen years. In the East, the newly recreated Poland received a large section of eastern Germany, most notably the Polish Corridor. This strip of land gave Poland access to the Baltic Sea and also separated the province of East Prussia from the rest of Germany. The Germans greatly resented this as they resented the Allies' decision to make a free city of the German-inhabited port city of Danzig, at the head of the Polish Corridor. Other provisions of the treaty imposed restrictions on the German armed forces, forced Germany to accept responsibility for causing the war, and required the Germans to pay reparations.

Although the Germans denounced the Treaty of Versailles as excessively harsh, the influence of Lloyd George and Wilson made its terms less severe than Clemenceau desired.

Criticism of the Treaty of Versailles

John Maynard Keynes (1883–1943), an economist who served as an adviser to the British delegation in Paris, criticized the reparations provisions of the Treaty of Versailles in *The Economic Consequences of the Peace,* published in 1919. Excessive reparations would not only impose a heavy burden on Germany's economy and finances, he insisted, but would also endanger the recovery and stability of the European economy, of which Germany's economy was a vital part.

Keynes's argument caused many educated Britons to become more sympathetic to German complaints about the peace treaty, while the French maintained a hard-line attitude toward Germany. This division between the two major wartime Allies made it difficult for them to cooperate either in maintaining the peace settlement or in promoting the development of political and economic stability in Europe.

The Mandate System

The Treaty of Versailles deprived Germany of its colonies in Africa and the Pacific and assigned them as mandates to the allies. The mandate system was designed to protect the indigenous populations and to prepare them for independence, but in practice the system proved to be little more than disguised annexation.

Africa.   In Africa, the Union of South Africa acquired German Southwest Africa, while German East Africa passed to Great Britain, which renamed the region Tanganyika. The British divided the German colonies of Togoland and the Cameroons with France.

The Pacific.   Germany's island colonies in the North Pacific went to Japan, while Australia acquired northeastern New Guinea. New Zealand gained German Samoa.

The Middle East.   Under the terms of the Treaty of Sèvres, Turkey lost its Arab lands in the Middle East. Great Britain acquired Palestine, Transjordan, and Iraq as mandates, while Syria and Lebanon became French mandates.

The Postwar Economy

During 1919 and 1920, Great Britain enjoyed a brief postwar economic boom. Rationing was ended, wartime controls over the economy were removed, and demobilized military personnel found employment with little difficulty.

Territorial Settlements, 1919–1926

Housing

In order to help meet the need for more housing, the Lloyd George government sponsored a housing act passed in 1919 that provided government subsidies for the construction of 200,000 units of housing over the next four years. While the program was insufficient to meet the country's housing needs, it did establish an important precedent in expanding the role of government in housing.

Economic Downturn

During late 1920, an economic downturn began. At year's end, the number of unemployed reached 700,000. By March 1921, the number had risen to over 2 million, more than ten percent of the work force.

Unemployment Insurance

Attempting to cope with the recession, the Lloyd George government secured the passage of the Unemployment Insurance Acts of 1920 and 1922, which increased unemployment insurance payments (the dole) and extended the coverage of the law originally passed in 1911 to include virtually all workers.

Tariffs and Trade

The Safeguarding of Industries Act, passed in June 1921, imposed a tariff on some imports. This act represented a significant departure from Great Britain's traditional policy of free trade. The government also negotiated a trade treaty with Soviet Russia, which failed to produce much improvement in Britain's depressed foreign trade.

Despite the government's efforts, the recession persisted and deepened, especially in Britain's basic industries: coal, iron, steel, textiles, and shipbuilding.

The Coal Miners' Strike of 1921

The British coal-mining industry, one of the country's oldest and most outmoded, was deeply troubled in the postwar era. In 1919, the government averted a miners' strike by retaining controls over the industry and attempting to placate the miners with wage increases. This policy served only to postpone trouble.

In 1921, after the economy had begun to sink into recession, the coal miners began an unsuccessful strike. The mine operators remained firm in the face of the miners' demands and forced the union to accept a wage reduction.

Persistence of the Recession

As a result of a number of factors, including British complacency and increased foreign competition, Great Britain failed to regain its position of leadership in world trade. Economic problems persisted, and between 1921 and 1930 unemployment averaged in the range of ten to twelve percent.

Foreign Affairs

The Washington Conference of 1921–1922

At the Washington Conference of 1921–1922, Great Britain agreed to abandon its traditional naval superiority in order to avoid a costly naval arms race with the United States and Japan. The Five Power Treaty of 1922 limited capital ships (battleships) to a tonnage ratio of 5:5:3 for Great Britain, the United States, and Japan and 1.75:1.75 for France and Italy. While this treaty slowed down the naval race, it did not place any limits on lesser categories of ships.

Great Britain also gave up its 1902 alliance with Japan (see Chapter 17), which was replaced by the Four Power Treaty of 1922, in which Great Britain, the United States, France, and Japan promised to maintain the status quo in the Pacific.

The Chanak Crisis and the Treaty of Lausanne (1923)

In Turkey following World War I, a nationalist revolution led by Mustapha Kemal, known as Kemal Ataturk (1881–1938), challenged and ultimately overthrew the government of the Ottoman sultan. Ataturk's forces pushed the Greeks out of the area of Smyrna in Anatolia, on the Asian side of the Turkish Straits, which they had been awarded by the peace treaty with Turkey. Ataturk also threatened a small British force that had been stationed at Chanak along the Dardanelles.

While Lloyd George supported the Greeks, many Conservatives in his coalition favored the Turks and, above all, opposed British involvement in the Greek-Turkish conflict. The Chanak crisis was finally resolved in 1923 with the negotiation of the Treaty of Lausanne, a new peace treaty with Turkey, that left the Turks in control of the disputed area.

Politics During the 1920s

End of the Lloyd George Coalition

The deepening recession cost Lloyd George much of his popularity, while the prime minister's often heavy-handed manner and his pro-Greek position in the Chanak crisis led to an erosion of Conservative support. In October 1922, the Conservatives withdrew from the coalition. Lloyd George resigned and Andrew Bonar Law, the Conservative leader, became prime minister.

The 1922 Elections

Parliamentary elections in November gave the Conservatives solid control of the House of Commons. A split in the Liberal Party between the factions led by Lloyd George and Asquith helped the Labor Party become for the first time the second largest party in the House of Commons. The Conservatives won 347 seats in the new House of Commons, and labor held 142 seats. The Asquith Liberals won 60 seats, while 57 seats went to the Lloyd George Liberals.

The First Baldwin Government, 1923–1924

In May 1923, Bonar Law left the prime ministership for reasons of health. He was succeeded by Stanley Baldwin (1867–1947), who became the most important Conservative leader of the interwar period, although his first term as prime minister proved brief, lasting only until January 1924.

Baldwin decided that it was necessary to enact a broad program of tariffs to protect British industry from foreign competition. Although the Conservatives supported Baldwin's call for an end to free trade, the proposal encountered strong opposition from Labor and the Liberals. The intense controversy caused Baldwin to decide to call an election on that issue.

The First Labor Government, 1924

The 1923 Elections

In the parliamentary elections of December 1923, the Conservatives lost their majority in the House of Commons, although they remained the largest party. The Conservatives won 258 seats, while Labor held 191. The Liberals, who had reunited in defense of free trade, won 158 seats and held the balance of power.

The MacDonald Cabinet

Ramsay MacDonald (1866–1937), the leader of the Labor Party, took office as prime minister in January 1924, heading a minority government that depended on the support of the Liberals in the House of Commons. This first Labor government in British history lasted less than a year, resigning in November.

Although the Laborites, like the Conservatives before them, failed to find a solution to the problem of unemployment, they did liberalize unemployment insurance and expand the government's role in providing housing for Britain's workers.

The German Question

The Ruhr Occupation.   During the early 1920s, Anglo-French differences regarding Germany persisted. In January 1923, after the Germans had fallen behind in their reparations payments, the French occupied the industrial Ruhr valley in western Germany. The British opposed the French action, believing that a German economic recovery would create a market for their exports.

The Dawes Plan.   In 1924, MacDonald and his foreign secretary, Arthur Henderson (1863–1935), helped ease the Ruhr crisis and secure French agreement to the Dawes Plan, which provided for lower reparations payments over a longer period of time, without reducing Germany's total reparations obligation. The Dawes Plan also provided for foreign loans to assist Germany's economic recovery. The following year, the French withdrew from the Ruhr.

Relations with Soviet Russia

MacDonald extended full diplomatic recognition to the Soviet Union in February 1924, hoping that increased trade with Russia would help promote British economic recovery. In August, a new trade treaty was signed with the Soviets, and there was talk of a British loan to Russia. This stimulated opposition among the Conservatives and Liberals. When the Liberals refused to support MacDonald, he was forced to resign. A new election was called for October 1924, the second election within a year.

The 1924 Elections

The publication of the so-called "Zinoviev Letter" by the London *Daily Mail* hurt MacDonald's campaign. This letter, purportedly written by Grigori Zinoviev (1883–1936), the head of the Communist International, urged Britain's Communists to work harder on behalf of the proletarian revolution. Neither MacDonald personally nor his

Labor Party was sympathetic to Communism, but they had endorsed closer relations with the Soviet Union. The election resulted in a major victory for the Conservatives, who won 415 seats in the House of Commons to 152 for Labor. The Liberals won only 42 seats.

The Second Baldwin Government
1924–1929

Stanley Baldwin began his second term as prime minister at the end of 1924 and remained in office for the next five years, until 1929.

Foreign Affairs

Soviet Russia.   Great Britain repudiated MacDonald's trade treaty with the Soviet Union and severed diplomatic relations in 1927, following charges of Soviet espionage. While a British raid on the headquarters of Arcos, the Soviet trading company in London, did not produce evidence of espionage, relations were not resumed until 1929.

The Locarno Pact.   In an effort to promote stability in continental affairs, Austen Chamberlain (1863–1937), Baldwin's foreign secretary, worked with his German and French counterparts, Gustav Stresemann (1878–1929) and Aristide Briand (1862–1932). In the Locarno Pact of 1925, Germany and France agreed to recognize the permanence of their frontiers, while Great Britain and Italy acted as guarantors of this commitment. Germany also pledged to maintain the demilitarization of the Rhineland, which had been imposed by the Treaty of Versailles. Germany's entry into the League of Nations in 1926 symbolized the improved climate of international relations.

The Young Plan.   The Young Plan of 1929 further eased the conflict over reparations, and in 1930, the Allies ended their occupation of the Rhineland five years ahead of schedule.

The Kellogg-Briand Pact of 1928.   The signing of the Kellogg-Briand Pact of 1928, officially known as the Pact of Paris, suggested to many the dawning of a new age of international harmony. Some sixty countries, including Great Britain, ultimately signed the pact, which bore the names of the American secretary of state and the French foreign minister. The signatories pledged to renounce war as an instrument of national policy. Events would soon demonstrate how little this noble renunciation meant.

The Economy

The country's major problems involved the continuing economic and financial downturn, rather than foreign affairs. Unemployment remained high, although some recovery had occurred by 1925. Winston Churchill (1874–1965), who had become a Conservative and now served as chancellor of the exchequer, returned Britain to the gold standard in May 1925, with the value of the pound set at $4.36. The pound was overvalued, resulting in a further decline in foreign trade.

The General Strike of 1926

The general strike of 1926 confronted Baldwin's government with its greatest domestic crisis. Britain's coal mining industry remained depressed, labor-management conflict in the industry had intensified, and government commissions appointed to study the industry's problems had found no acceptable solutions.

Baldwin appointed yet another commission, this one headed by Sir Herbert Samuel (1870–1963). Although the Samuel Commission proposed a number of reforms to reorganize the coal industry, they were rejected by both management and labor.

In early May 1926, the coal miners went on strike. The Trades Union Congress (TUC) then called a general strike in sympathy with the miners. For nine days, beginning on May 4, most of Britain's organized workers walked off their jobs. The workers expected the government to give way to their demands, but Baldwin stood firm. In the face of public opposition and volunteer replacements for strikers, the general strike quickly collapsed. The coal miners ultimately returned to work on terms set by the mine owners.

The Trade Disputes Act of 1927 outlawed both general and sympathy strikes.

Social Legislation

The Baldwin government secured the enactment of several important pieces of social legislation. The Widows, Orphans, and Old Age Pensions Act of 1925 expanded the program originally enacted in 1911, while the Unemployment Insurance Act of 1927 reduced both contributions and benefits, while extending the period during which benefits could be paid. The Local Government Act of 1929 reorganized the county councils and reformed the old Poor Law system by assigning the responsibility for the care of the poor to the counties. In addition, the Baldwin government built on the work of its predecessors by constructing some 400,000 units of housing. Much of this program was pushed through Parliament by Neville Chamberlain (1869–1940), Austen's half-brother, who served as minister of health.

Voting Rights

The Representation of the People Act of 1928 extended the right to vote to women on equal terms with men by reducing the voting age for women from thirty to twenty-one.

The 1929 Elections

In 1929, the Conservatives lost their majority in the House of Commons, largely because of dissatisfaction with Baldwin's economic policies. For the first time in British history, the Labor Party held the largest number of seats, but, as in 1924, it was not a majority. Labor won 287 seats to 261 for the Conservatives and 59 for the Liberals, whose decline to the status of a minor third party continued.

The Second MacDonald Government 1929–1931

In June 1929, MacDonald returned to the prime ministership, heading a minority Labor government with the support of the Liberals. His policies from 1929 to 1931 did not differ markedly from those of his Conservative predecessor, although he did reestablish diplomatic relations with the Soviet Union.

The Depression

By 1930, the effects of the world depression were evident in Great Britain, whose economy was especially vulnerable because of its dependence on world trade. When MacDonald took office, there were 1.2 million unemployed. By March 1930, the number had increased to 1.6 million and by December 1930 to 2.5 million.

The May Report

As the depression deepened, not only did unemployment continue to increase, but government tax revenues fell. In a report issued in July 1931, a committee of financial experts headed by Sir George May predicted a deficit of £120 million and warned of an impending financial crisis. The May Report called for a tax increase and urged drastic reductions in government expenditures, especially a cut in the dole (unemployment benefits).

This proposal infuriated much of MacDonald's own Labor Party, and the cabinet was deeply divided on the issue.

MacDonald and the National Government

Formation of the National Government

In August 1931, MacDonald resigned the prime ministership but quickly returned to office at the head of a coalition known as the National Government. King George V (r. 1910–1936) played an active role in forming this coalition, which had the backing of the Conservatives, some Liberals, and a few Laborites who supported MacDonald. The cabinet included four Laborites, four Conservatives, and two Liberals. The bulk of the Labor Party angrily rejected the National Government and went into opposition.

The 1931 Elections

In the parliamentary elections of October 1931, the National Government won an overwhelming majority of 556 seats in the House of Commons, with some 472 held by the Conservatives. The Liberals won 68 seats and the National Laborites 13. The opposition Labor Party held only 56 seats. While MacDonald continued to hold the prime ministership, Stanley Baldwin, the Conservative leader, was the dominant figure in the National Government.

Economic Retrenchment

Pursuing a policy of retrenchment, the National Government increased taxes in an effort to make up for the loss of revenue caused by the depression and cut government spending in order to avoid a budget deficit. Interest rates were lowered, and Britain abandoned the gold standard. The British pound fell in value from $4.86 to $3.49. Devaluation failed to stimulate exports significantly, while the decrease in the pound's value wounded British pride.

In an effort to provide a protected domestic market for British industry, protective tariffs were imposed on imports in February 1932. This marked a definitive end to Britain's traditional free trade policy. An Imperial Economic Conference met in Ottawa to establish a system of preferential tariffs within the British Empire.

Uneven Economic Recovery

During the early 1930s, British unemployment fell from 3 million at the end of 1932 to 2 million at the end of 1934 and to 1.6 million at the end of 1936. However, economic recovery was uneven. New light industry, the building trades, and the armaments industry showed more improvement than did coal mining, heavy industry, textiles, and shipbuilding, which had once been the backbone of Great Britain's industrial might.

The Unemployment Act of 1934 consolidated the insurance and relief systems, while the Special Areas Act of 1934 began an effort to move unemployed workers to more prosperous areas. These were limited measures, and the government generally refrained from active intervention in the economy.

Communism and Fascism

Despite Great Britain's serious economic problems, extremist movements attracted relatively few supporters. Communism won some converts, particularly among intellectuals who believed in the necessity of a radical restructuring of the country's political, economic, and social order. The British Union of Fascists, led by Sir Oswald Mosley (1896–1980), also gained only modest support.

Return of Conservative Government

The Third Baldwin Government
1935–1937

In May 1935, the British people celebrated the Silver Jubilee of King George V. MacDonald retired from the prime ministership the following month, and Stanley Baldwin succeeded him. The new government was completely controlled by the Conservatives, although the term "National Government" continued to be used.

The 1935 Elections

The parliamentary election of November 1935 increased the Conservatives' domination of the National Government. Supporters of the National Government won 428 seats in the House of Commons, with 387 of them held by the Conservatives. The opposition included 157 Laborites, 17 Liberals, and a small group of independents.

The Crisis of the Throne

The death of King George V in January 1936 was followed by the accession of Edward VIII (r. 1936). The new king was unmarried, although he had established a relationship with Mrs. Wallis Warfield Simpson, a twice-married and once-divorced American woman, who soon secured a divorce from her second husband. For almost a year, a self-imposed press censorship left the British people largely unaware of the king's attachment.

When Edward VIII indicated his intention to marry Mrs. Simpson, Baldwin insisted that it was inappropriate for the monarch to marry a divorcée, a view that was supported by the cabinet, the three major political parties, most of the British public, the dominion prime ministers, and the Church of England.

In December 1936, Edward VIII abdicated and was succeeded by his younger brother, the duke of York, who became King George VI (r. 1936–1952). The former king, who became the duke of Windsor, went into exile, where he married Mrs. Simpson in 1937.

The Prime Ministership of Neville Chamberlain

Shortly after the formal coronation of King George VI in May 1937, Baldwin retired from the prime ministership. Neville Chamberlain, his successor, was well-equipped by temperament and experience to deal with domestic affairs, having served as minister of health in the 1920s and chancellor of the exchequer in the National Government of MacDonald and Baldwin. His misfortune was that he would be compelled to face difficult issues of foreign policy (see Chapter 21).

Imperial Affairs

The Dominions

Although the British dominions — Canada, Australia, New Zealand, and the Union of South Africa — were self-governing in their domestic affairs, Great Britain continued to control their foreign policy. The British government's decision to enter World War I in 1914 bound the dominions, and they had loyally supported the Allied war effort. However, the war also promoted a growing sentiment in the dominions in favor of autonomy in foreign affairs, and they entered the League of Nations as separate states.

The Imperial Conference of 1926

The Imperial Conference of 1926 defined formally the relationship between the dominions and Great Britain and, in particular, recognized the autonomy of the dominions in foreign policy. According to the definition of the Imperial Conference, the dominions were "autonomous communities within the British Empire, equal in status, in no way subordinate one to another in any aspect of their domestic or external affairs, though united by a common allegiance to the Crown, and freely associated as members of the British Commonwealth of Nations."

The Statute of Westminster of 1931

In 1931, Parliament endorsed this definition of dominion status in the Statute of Westminster, formally declaring that no act of the British Parliament would be binding on any dominion without its express consent.

Ireland

In the 1918 parliamentary election, Sinn Fein (see Chapter 19) won 73 of the 105 Irish seats in the House of Commons. Instead of going to London, the Sinn Feiners met in Dublin, where they formed their own parliament, the Dail Eireann, declared Irish independence, and proclaimed the establishment of an Irish republic.

Civil War

Ireland soon sank into civil war. The Irish Volunteers, now known as the Irish Republican Army, led by Michael Collins (1890–1922), fought the Royal Irish Constabulary, which was aided by a newly recruited force known as the Black and Tans. Other Irish leaders included Arthur Griffith (1872–1922), the founder of Sinn Fein, and Eamon de Valera (1882–1975).

ATLANTIC

OCEAN

North Channel

Londonderry

Foyle

Bann

NORTHERN

ULSTER

IRELAND

Belfast

Donegal Bay

Lough
Erne

STRANGFORD
L.

Sligo

Newry

Dundalk

CONNAUGHT

Drogheda

Bayne

Lough
Ree

IRISH

Dublin

IRISH SEA

Lough
Corrib

Galway

Athlone

Liffey

Kingstown

Galway Bay

FREE STATE

Aran Is.

LEINSTER

Wicklow

Lough
Derg

Nore

Barrow

Shannon

Slaney

Limerick

Kilkenny

Suir

Wexford

Tralee

MUNSTER

Waterford

St. Georges Channel

Dingle Bay

Blackwater

Cork

Lee

Queenstown

Bantry Bay

Cape Clear

ATLANTIC

OCEAN

Ireland, 1922

Partition

The Fourth Home Rule Bill, passed by Parliament in 1920, partitioned Ireland between the Catholic south and the six counties of predominantly Protestant Ulster. Each region would have its own single-chamber parliament to legislate in regard to internal affairs.

The Irish Free State and Ulster

While Ulster accepted the partition arrangement, the south rejected it, and the civil war continued. In an effort to end the conflict, Lloyd George offered dominion status to Ireland. Griffith and Collins accepted the offer, and a treaty signed in October 1921 established a virtually independent state, the Irish Free State. Ulster gained the right to withdraw, which it promptly did, remaining a part of what was now known as the United Kingdom of Great Britain and Northern Ireland.

Conflict between Moderates and Radicals

While the more moderate Sinn Feiners had accepted dominion status, de Valera continued to demand total independence and the establishment of an Irish republic. In 1922, open warfare broke out in the Irish Free State between the radicals and the moderates. The British left the Irish to fight it out among themselves. In December 1922, the Irish Free State was formally established, with William T. Cosgrave (1880–1965) as president of the executive council. While de Valera ended his resistance in 1923, he did not abandon his cause.

De Valera as Leader of Eire

In 1932, de Valera, the leader of the political party known as Fianna Fail, defeated Cosgrave's moderate Fine Gael Party and became head of the government of the Irish Free State. De Valera remained committed to securing full independence from Great Britain.

A new constitution, adopted in 1937, embodied de Valera's ideas. The country was declared to be an "independent and sovereign state" to be known as Eire. While de Valera's ultimate objective was an Irish republic embracing all of Ireland, Ulster remained a part of the United Kingdom.

India

World War I encouraged the further development of nationalism in India, and in 1917, the British agreed that India would eventually receive dominion status.

The Government of India Act of 1919

In 1918, Edwin S. Montagu (1879–1924), the secretary of state for India, and Lord Chelmsford (1868–1933), the viceroy, presented recommendations for constitutional reform. The Montagu-Chelmsford Report led to the passage of the Government of India Act of 1919, which introduced limited responsible government on the provincial level and also created a two-house legislature for India, most of whose members were elected. Nevertheless, real power remained in the hands of the British viceroy and his executive council.

The Indian National Congress and the Moslem League

Both the predominantly Hindu Indian National Congress, led by Mohandas K. Gandhi (1869–1948) and Jawaharlal Nehru (1889–1964), and the All-India Moslem League, led by Mohammed Ali Jinnah (1876–1948), found British concessions insufficient. During the 1920s, Gandhi, known as the Mahatma, began a campaign of nonviolent civil disobedience against British rule.

The Simon Report

In 1930, a commission headed by Sir John Simon (1873–1954) recommended the establishment of a federation of Indian provinces. Full responsible government would be granted on the provincial level only.

Two Round-Table Conferences, held in London in 1930 and 1931, sought to draft a constitution for India based on the Simon Report. Although agreement was reached on the establishment of an Indian federation, wide differences existed between the views of the Hindus, the Moslems, and the Indian princes. When Gandhi resumed his campaign of civil disobedience, he was imprisoned by the British.

The Government of India Act of 1935

The Government of India Act of 1935 created an Indian federation with limited representative government on both the provincial and federal levels. Great Britain retained control of financial, military, and foreign affairs. The act also separated Burma from India, and in 1937, Burma became a crown colony.

While many Conservatives believed the act went too far in the direction of autonomy for India, both the Labor Party and the Indian leaders criticized it for providing less than full dominion status. However, while the Indian National Congress wanted self-government for a united India, the Moslem League demanded the establishment of a separate Moslem state. The outbreak of World War II in 1939 interrupted the full implementation of the act.

Egypt

In 1922, the British agreed to end their protectorate over Egypt. While Egypt was now independent in principle, the British continued to exert a considerable degree of influence over Egyptian affairs. In particular, the British retained the authority to protect the Suez Canal and foreign interests in Egypt.

The Anglo-Egyptian Treaty of 1936 provided for the withdrawal of British troops from Egypt except for the area of the Suez Canal, and it established a twenty-year Anglo-Egyptian alliance.

Palestine

Following World War I, Palestine, which had been a part of the Ottoman Empire, became a British mandate (see Chapter 19). In the Balfour Declaration of 1917, the British government had endorsed the establishment in Palestine of "a national home for the Jewish People."

The Arabs strongly opposed an increase in the Jewish presence in Palestine, and, in an effort to placate the Arabs, the British imposed restrictions on Jewish immigration. The Nazi persecution of the Jews prior to and during World War II increased world pressure for the fulfillment of the pledge contained in the Balfour Declaration.

British Literature

Shaw, Wells, and Galsworthy

Three writers of the pre-World War I generation remained prominent in the postwar era: George Bernard Shaw (1856–1950), H. G. Wells (1866–1946), and John Galsworthy (1867–1933).

Saint Joan (1923) was among Shaw's successful plays produced during the 1920s. He won the Nobel Prize for literature in 1925.

In the postwar era, Wells's *Outline of History* (1920) won a wide readership, as did his futuristic novel *The Shape of Things to Come* (1933).

Galsworthy, who won the Nobel Prize for literature in 1933, is best known for his trilogy *The Forsyte Saga* (1922), which dealt with the decline of the English upper-middle class.

Virginia Woolf

Virginia Woolf (1882–1941) was a central figure in the circle of writers, critics, and artists known as the Bloomsbury Group. She used the stream-of-consciousness technique in such novels as *Jacob's Room* (1922) and *To the Lighthouse* (1927).

She was also an accomplished essayist. In *A Room of One's Own* (1929), her essays focus on a woman's need for independence and the opportunity for creative work.

D. H. Lawrence

D. H. Lawrence (1885–1930) shocked his contemporaries with his frankness about sexuality. His novel *Sons and Lovers* (1913) appeared on the eve of World War I. *Lady Chatterley's Lover* (1928), Lawrence's best-known novel, was widely condemned as pornographic and was banned in Great Britain and the United States for many years.

Aldous Huxley

Aldous Huxley (1894–1963) is best known for his novel *Brave New World* (1932), which presented a grim picture of a future "ideal" society. Among his other novels are *Crome Yellow* (1921), *Antic Hay* (1923), *Point Counter Point* (1928), and *Eyeless in Gaza* (1936).

Noel Coward

Noel Coward (1899–1973) was a witty and sophisticated playwright whose best-known works include *Private Lives* (1930) and *Blithe Spirit* (1941). He also wrote revues, songs, and several volumes of autobiography, and he was active in motion pictures as an actor, writer, director, and producer.

T. S. Eliot

The American-born T. S. Eliot (1888–1965) was among Britain's best-known poets, playwrights, and critics. In *The Waste Land* (1922), Eliot wrote of the barrenness of modern life. In his verse drama *Murder in the Cathedral* (1935), he told the story of the murder of Thomas à Becket, the twelfth-century archbishop of Canterbury (see Chapter 4).

James Joyce

The Irish writer James Joyce (1882–1941) first achieved recognition for *The Dubliners* (1914), a collection of short stories, and for *A Portrait of the Artist as a Young Man* (1916), an autobiographical novel. In *Ulysses* (1922), Joyce broke new ground, experimenting with the stream-of-consciousness technique and long interior monologues. Criticized for obscenity, *Ulysses* was banned in several countries. Joyce continued his literary experimentation in the complex novel *Finnegan's Wake* (1939).

In retrospect, British history during the interwar era can be seen as a portent of the future. Following World War I, serious problems plagued the British economy, once one of the world's strongest. Caused in large part by the dislocations resulting from the war, Great Britain's economic problems would be further exacerbated by World War II and would persist for decades after that war's end in 1945.

In politics, the Labor Party established its position as one of Britain's two major parties after World War I and controlled the government briefly in 1924 and again from 1929 to 1931. Following World War II, the first majority Labor government in British history came to power in 1945, and the post-World War II era produced three Labor prime ministers.

In imperial affairs, the growth of nationalism in the interwar years paved the way for the dissolution of the British Empire that took place after World War II.

Recommended Reading

Aldcroft, Derek Howard. *The Inter-War Economy: Britain, 1919–1939* (1970).

Bassett, R. *Nineteen Thirty-One: Political Crisis* (1958).

Blake, Robert. *The Unknown Prime Minister: The Life and Times of Andrew Bonar Law* (1954).

Boyce, D. G. *Englishmen and Irish Troubles: British Public Opinion and the Making of Irish Policy, 1918–22* (1972).

Branson, Noreen. *Britain in the Nineteen Twenties* (1975).

Branson, Noreen and Margot Heinemann. *Britain in the Nineteen Thirties* (1971).

Dockrill, Michael L. and J. Douglas Gould. *Peace Without Promise: Britain and the Peace Conferences, 1919–1923* (1981).

Donaldson, Frances. *Edward VIII* (1974).

Graves, Robert and Alan Hodges. *The Long Weekend: A Social History of Great Britain, 1918–1939* (1940).

Gray, Nigel. *The Worst of Times: An Oral History of the Great Depression in Britain* (1985).

Havighurst, Alfred F. *Britain in Transition: The Twentieth Century* (4th ed., 1985).

James, Robert Rhodes. *Churchill: A Study in Failure, 1900–1939* (1970).

Jones, Bill. *The Russia Complex: The British Labour Party and the Soviet Union* (1977).

Lloyd, T. O. *Empire to Welfare State: English History, 1906–1985* (3rd ed., 1986).

Marquand, David. *Ramsay MacDonald* (1977).

Marwick, Arthur. *Britain in the Century of Total War, 1900–1967* (1968).

Medlicott, W. N. *British Foreign Policy Since Versailles, 1919–1963* (2nd ed., 1968).

Middlemass, Keith and John Barnes. *Baldwin* (1969).

Morgan, Kenneth O. *Consensus and Disunity: The Lloyd George Coalition Government, 1918–1922* (1979).

Nicolson, Harold. *King George the Fifth, His Life and Reign* (1951).

Pugh, Martin. *The Making of Modern British Politics, 1867–1939* (1982).

Ramsden, John. *The Age of Balfour and Baldwin, 1902–1940* (1978).

Richardson, Harry W. *Economic Recovery in Britain, 1932–1939* (1967).

Robson, W. W. *Modern English Literature* (1970).

Skidelsky, Robert. *Politicians and the Slump: The Labour Government of 1929–1931* (1968).

Stevenson, John and Chris Cook. *The Slump: Society and Politics During the Depression* (1978).

Taylor, A. J. P. *English History, 1914–1945* (1965).

Thompson, J. A., ed. *The Collapse of the British Liberal Party: Fate or Self-Destruction?* (1969).

Wheeler-Bennett, J. W. *King George VI, His Life and Reign* (1958).

CHAPTER 21

Great Britain and the Second World War

Time Line

1931	Japan invades Manchuria
1933	Adolf Hitler comes to power in Germany
1935	Hitler denounces the disarmament clauses of the Treaty of Versailles
	Italy invades Ethiopia
1936	Germany remilitarizes the Rhineland
	The Spanish Civil War begins
1937	Japan attacks China
1938	Germany annexes Austria

	The Munich Conference awards the Sudetenland to Germany
1939	The Spanish Civil War ends
	Hitler destroys Czechoslovakia
	Great Britain and France pledge to aid Poland
	Germany and the Soviet Union sign a Nonaggression Pact
	Germany invades Poland
	Great Britain and France declare war on Germany
1940	The Germans conquer Denmark and Norway
	The Germans overrun the Netherlands, Belgium, and Luxembourg
	Winston Churchill becomes prime minister
	Italy enters the war as Germany's ally
	France signs an armistice with Germany
	The German *Luftwaffe* begins the Battle of Britain
	The Italians invade Egypt and Greece
1941	The Germans send Rommel's *Afrika Korps* to North Africa
	The Germans overrun Yugoslavia and Greece
	Germany invades the Soviet Union
	Churchill and Roosevelt issue the Atlantic Charter
	The Japanese attack Pearl Harbor
1942	The American navy halts the Japanese advance in the battles of the Coral Sea and Midway
	American and French forces land in French North Africa
1943	Churchill and Roosevelt meet at Casablanca

	The Battle of Stalingrad ends in a German defeat
	German and Italian forces in Tunisia surrender to the Allies
	American and British troops invade Sicily and Italy
	Churchill, Roosevelt, and Stalin meet at Teheran
1944	The Western Allies launch the invasion of Normandy
1945	Churchill, Roosevelt, and Stalin meet at Yalta
	Germany surrenders
	The last of the wartime Big Three Conferences meets in Potsdam
	Japan surrenders

In international relations, the 1930s proved to be a decade of intensifying crisis. Soon after taking power in 1933, Adolf Hitler seized the initiative in foreign affairs and met surprisingly little resistance from Great Britain and France. The French failure to resist Germany resulted in large part from their awareness of their own relative weakness. France believed it could act to contain Hitler only with the full support of the British. In Great Britain, however, there was a widespread belief that the Treaty of Versailles had been unduly harsh and that it should be revised in Germany's favor. In addition, both Great Britain and France were preoccupied with domestic economic problems resulting from the Great Depression, and in both of the Western democracies, intense memories of the carnage of World War I created a powerful desire to do everything possible to avoid another conflict.

It ultimately became clear, however, that Hitler's ambitions knew no limits, and Great Britain and France recognized they had no choice but to go to war.

The Second World War was truly a global conflict. During its first years, from 1939 to 1942, the Axis powers — Germany, Italy, and Japan — won a series of impressive victories in Europe, North Africa, Asia, and the Pacific. Then the tide began to turn as the Allies, led by the United States, Great Britain, and the Soviet Union, pushed forward to victory.

The Manchurian Crisis

The first international crisis of the 1930s resulted from events in Asia, rather than Europe. In September 1931, Japan invaded Manchuria, a region of northeastern China. Charging Japan with aggression, the Chinese appealed to the League of Nations.

Responding to the findings of a League investigating committee, headed by Britain's Lord Lytton (1871–1947), the League of Nations condemned the Japanese for the use of force but took no action to halt Japan's aggression. In protest, Japan withdrew from the League in 1933. Manchuria became the Japanese puppet state of Manchukuo.

Thus, in the Manchurian crisis, the League of Nations faced and failed the first major test of its ability to take action against aggression. This failure served to encourage aggression elsewhere.

In 1937, Japan attacked China proper, beginning a war that would continue until Japan's final defeat in 1945.

Hitler's Early Foreign Policy

The World Disarmament Conference

In February 1932, the World Disarmament Conference convened in Geneva, Switzerland. While the French demanded assurances of greater security before they would agree to disarmament, the Germans insisted that they should be allowed to rearm if others refused to disarm.

As the wrangling continued, Adolf Hitler (1889–1945) came to power in Germany in January 1933. At first, Hitler had to proceed with caution; Germany was not yet strong enough to risk provoking a strong response from Great Britain and France.

Charging that the World War I allies were not willing to treat Germany as an equal, Hitler withdrew Germany from both the League of Nations and the Disarmament Conference in October 1933. The conference soon collapsed.

German Rearmament

In March 1935, Hitler moved more boldly, flouting the disarmament clauses of the Treaty of Versailles by reintroducing military conscription and proclaiming the existence of a German air force, both of which were prohibited by the treaty. Great Britain and France protested the German action, and in April the League of Nations condemned it.

The Stresa Front and the Anglo-German Naval Treaty

Concerned about Germany's intentions, British, French, and Italian representatives met at Stresa, Italy, in April 1935 to discuss the possibility of joint action to contain Hitler. Nothing substantial came of this so-called Stresa Front, however. Instead, the British sought to win Hitler's agreement to a limitation of German naval expansion. The Anglo-German Naval Treaty of June 1935 provided that Germany would limit its navy to 35 percent of the British fleet. While this accord provided reassurances to the British, their acceptance of Germany's abrogation of the disarmament clauses of the Treaty of Versailles angered the French.

Italian Aggression in Ethiopia

In October 1935, Benito Mussolini (1883–1945), the Italian dictator, embarked on a war of aggression against Ethiopia.

League of Nations Action

In response to the Italian attack, Ethiopia's Emperor Haile Selassie (r. 1930–1974) appealed to the League of Nations, which branded Italy as an aggressor. The League also imposed limited economic sanctions on Italy, placing an embargo on the shipment of some goods to Italy. However, no embargo was placed on oil, which Italy desperately needed to continue its aggression. Having failed to take any effective action against Italy's aggression, the League of Nations, in effect, ceased to function. By May 1936, the Italians had completed their conquest of Ethiopia. Mussolini withdrew Italy from the League of Nations in 1937.

The Hoare-Laval Pact

In an effort to reach an accommodation with Mussolini, British Foreign Secretary Samuel Hoare (1880–1959) and French Premier

Pierre Laval (1883–1945) agreed in December 1935 to a treaty designed to appease the Italian dictator by allowing him to take about half of Ethiopia. When British public opinion reacted strongly against the Hoare-Laval Pact, Hoare resigned, and Anthony Eden (1897–1977) succeeded him.

Remilitarization of the Rhineland

In March 1936, Hitler remilitarized the Rhineland, thereby violating the terms of both the Treaty of Versailles and the Locarno Pact (see Chapter 20).

While the British were critical of the Nazi dictator's unilateral action, they also noted that the Germans had done nothing more than remilitarize their own territory. The British government thus refused to support either military or economic sanctions.

Although the French could have forced a German withdrawal at this stage, they would not act without British support. While the League of Nations Council condemned Germany's treaty violations, it took no further action. Hitler was thus proved correct in his belief that the British and French were unlikely to take any action other than to protest.

The Spanish Civil War

In July 1936, a civil war broke out in Spain, marking a culmination of several years of left–right conflict. General Francisco Franco (1892–1975) soon emerged as the leader of the rebels, who were known as the Nationalists.

Foreign Involvement

Great Britain and France joined in urging a policy of nonintervention in Spain. Italy and Germany provided aid to the Nationalists, while the Soviet Union assisted the Loyalists, the supporters of the Spanish republic.

The war became a divisive issue in British politics. Those who supported the Loyalists were often accused of being pro-Communist, while opponents of the nonintervention policy charged the government with helping the fascists win power in Spain.

Franco's Victory

The Nationalists gradually increased their control of Spain and captured Barcelona and Madrid, the last two Loyalist strongholds, in early 1939. The victory of Franco and the Nationalists was generally regarded as a victory for Hitler and Mussolini and a defeat for the cause of the democracies.

The Rome-Berlin-Tokyo Axis

The Rome-Berlin Axis

Anglo-French opposition to Italy's aggression in Ethiopia had enraged Mussolini and encouraged him to draw closer to Hitler, as did the fact that both Italy and Germany supported the Nationalist cause in Spain. In October 1936, Germany and Italy proclaimed the formation of the Rome-Berlin Axis. While this was not a formal alliance, it clearly indicated the shift in Italian foreign policy.

The Anti-Comintern Pact

In November 1936, Germany and Japan signed an agreement known as the Anti-Comintern Pact, in which they pledged to cooperate in opposition to Communism and the activities of the Communist International (Comintern). Italy joined the Anti-Comintern Pact in November 1937, thereby bringing into being the Rome-Berlin-Tokyo Axis. This represented the creation of a powerful bloc opposed to the maintenance of the international status quo.

German Annexation of Austria

In mid-March 1938, the Germans proclaimed the annexation (*Anschluss*) of Austria. Once again, the Western democracies took no action other than offering routine protests.

British Accord with Italy

Neville Chamberlain (1869–1940), who became prime minister in May 1937, hoped that he could strengthen Britain's position in dealing with Hitler by improving relations with Hitler's ally Mussolini.

In February 1938, Foreign Secretary Anthony Eden resigned in protest against Chamberlain's softness toward Mussolini. He was succeeded by Viscount Halifax (1881–1959).

In an accord signed in mid-April 1938, Great Britain and Italy agreed not to extend their bases in the eastern Mediterranean. In return for British support of recognition by the League of Nations of Italian control over Ethiopia, the Italians would withdraw their troops from Spain. The accord failed to foster Chamberlain's objective of weakening Mussolini's ties with Hitler.

The Czechoslovak Crisis

Sudeten German Demands

Soon after his absorption of Austria, Hitler turned his attention to Czechoslovakia, encouraging discontent among the German-speaking minority of the Sudetenland, located along the Czechoslovak border with Germany. The Sudeten Germans demanded autonomy for the Sudetenland.

During the summer of 1938, the Czech crisis intensified. On September 7, acting on orders from Hitler, the Sudeten Germans broke off negotiations with the Czech government. On September 12, Hitler demanded the right of self-determination for the Sudeten Germans and threatened intervention in Czechoslovakia.

Chamberlain's Meetings with Hitler

In an effort to resolve the crisis, Chamberlain proposed a meeting with Hitler. The British prime minister pursued a policy of appeasement, based on the mistaken belief that Hitler's demands were fundamentally just and that, if these demands were satisfied, Hitler would act as a responsible statesman and peace in Europe would be assured. Chamberlain's error was his failure to realize that Hitler's lust for conquest was incapable of being satisfied and that to give way in face of his demands would serve only to increase his appetite.

Berchtesgaden

On September 15, 1938, Chamberlain flew to Germany and conferred with Hitler at Berchtesgaden. Hitler demanded the German annexation of the Sudetenland and threatened to go to war against Czechoslovakia if this demand was not met.

Following this meeting, Chamberlain consulted with the French and then began efforts to persuade the Czech government to agree to the German annexation of the Sudetenland following a plebiscite in which the Sudeten Germans would presumably vote to unite with Germany.

Bad Godesberg

Chamberlain returned to Germany and met with Hitler on September 22 at Bad Godesberg. The prime minister was shocked to discover that Hitler now demanded the immediate annexation of the Sudetenland without a plebiscite. Hitler insisted that German forces enter the Sudetenland no later than October 1.

The Munich Conference

Great Britain, France, and Czechoslovakia refused to give way to Hitler's demands, and for a few days, war seemed inevitable. In a final, desperate attempt to preserve peace, Chamberlain asked Hitler for another meeting. At Mussolini's suggestion, Hitler invited Chamberlain, Premier Edouard Daladier (1884–1970) of France, and the Italian dictator to meet with him in Munich. The Soviet Union was not invited to participate.

The Munich Conference convened on September 29, 1938. Great Britain and France faced the choice of either sacrificing Czechoslovakia or risking war. They decided to sacrifice Czechoslovakia. The Munich agreement, signed in the early hours of September 30, granted Hitler's demand for the immediate annexation of the Sudetenland. The statesmen at Munich did not consult Czechoslovakia, which had no choice but to accept the decision.

British Reaction to the Munich Agreement

Most of the British public rejoiced in the belief that peace had been preserved, as did people in other countries. Chamberlain believed he had secured "peace in our time," but some in the House of Commons denounced the Munich agreement. Winston Churchill (1874–1965) described it as "a total and unmitigated defeat."

Hitler's Destruction of Czechoslovakia

In mid-March 1939, Hitler destroyed what was left of Czechoslovakia. Germany established its control over the western provinces of Bohemia and Moravia, while Slovakia became a separate puppet state.

The End of Appeasement

Hitler's action angered Chamberlain, who belatedly recognized that the German dictator's aggressive desires had no limits. Abandoning the policy of appeasement, Great Britain and France now pledged to come to the aid of Poland in the event of a German attack. The British and French offered similar guarantees to Romania, Greece, and Turkey.

Faced with the possibility of war, the British introduced conscription in order to expand their army, increased the production of military aircraft, and began a program of naval expansion. In addition, a civil defense program was initiated.

German-Italian Alliance

Jealous of Hitler's gains, Mussolini sought to achieve a success of his own. In early April 1939, the Italians conquered Albania. In May, Italy and Germany signed a full military alliance, which Mussolini dubbed the Pact of Steel.

The Polish Crisis
and the Outbreak of War

German Demands on Poland

In April 1939, soon after his destruction of Czechoslovakia, Hitler began to prepare an attack on Poland. He made demands that he believed Poland would not accept, including the return of the free city of Danzig to Germany and new access routes to East Prussia across the Polish Corridor.

Anglo-French Negotiations with the Soviet Union

As German pressure on Poland mounted during the spring and summer, Great Britain and France made a halfhearted attempt to form an alliance with the Soviet Union. On the one hand, the British and French wanted Soviet assistance in the event of war with Germany. On the other hand, the Western powers feared an expansion of Soviet power and the spread of Communism in Eastern Europe. Poland moreover was unwilling to allow Soviet troops into its territory. The Soviets, for their part, remained suspicious of the intentions of the Western powers.

German-Soviet Nonaggression Pact

As negotiations between the Soviets and the Western powers lagged, German-Soviet talks got under way. On August 23, 1939, Germany and the Soviet Union signed a Nonaggression Pact, which is often called the Hitler-Stalin Pact. A secret agreement accompanying the pact provided that, in the event of war between Germany and Poland, the Soviets would receive eastern Poland and a sphere of influence in Eastern Europe in return for their neutrality.

The Soviet commitment to remain neutral meant that Hitler did not face the danger of war on two fronts. With this threat removed, the German dictator could begin his war.

Declarations of War

On September 1, 1939, Germany invaded Poland. Two days later, on September 3, Great Britain and France fulfilled their guarantees to Poland and declared war on Germany. The Second World War had begun.

Hitler's March of Conquest
1939–1940

The Polish Campaign

In their onslaught against Poland, the Germans demonstrated the effectiveness of their *Blitzkrieg* (lightning war) technique, the use of tanks and airplanes to support the infantry. In less than a month, Poland was crushed. In accordance with their pact with Hitler, the Soviets invaded Poland from the east on September 17. At the end of the month, the Germans and Soviets partitioned Poland.

The Soviet Sphere of Influence

While the Soviets stood apart from the main conflict, they moved to establish a sphere of influence in Eastern Europe.

Finland

From November 1939 to March 1940, the Soviets fought the Winter War against Finland. The peace settlement forced the Finns to cede to the Soviet Union some 16,000 square miles of territory, primarily in Karelia near the Soviet city of Leningrad.

The Baltic Republics and Bessarabia

In the spring of 1940, the Soviets annexed the Baltic republics of Estonia, Latvia, and Lithuania. They also forced Romania to cede the province of Bessarabia.

The Phony War

The war in the West during the winter of 1939–1940 became known as the Phony War or the Twilight War. Hitler did not carry out his anticipated offensive against France. Although a British army went to France, the Anglo-French Allies did not move against Germany.

The Maginot Line

From their experience in World War I, the French had concluded that in a future war the advantage would lie with the defense. They had built the Maginot Line, a line of fortifications along their frontier with Germany, and expected to be able to repulse a German attack. The Maginot Line did not extend along the Franco-Belgian border, however.

Naval Action

Some action did occur at sea. While German submarines sank a number of British ships, the British scored several successes against Germany's surface fleet, effectively eliminating the threat of German raiders. In December 1939, British cruisers cornered the German pocket battleship the *Graf Spee* off Montevideo, Uruguay, and the ship was scuttled by her crew. The British also established a naval blockade of Germany, hoping to strangle their enemy's economy.

Hitler's Scandinavian Campaign

On April 9, 1940, the Germans overran Denmark and invaded Norway. In a vain effort to save Norway, the British landed troops at Trondheim and Narvik on the Norwegian coast, but they had to be withdrawn a few weeks later.

Replacement of Chamberlain by Churchill

The British failure in Norway led to an angry debate in the House of Commons on Prime Minister Chamberlain's conduct of the war. In the face of heavy criticism, Chamberlain stepped down. On May 10, 1940, Winston Churchill became prime minister, heading a coalition government.

The War in the West, 1940

On May 10, 1940, Hitler's long-awaited assault on Western Europe began, as the Germans overran Luxembourg and invaded the Netherlands and Belgium. The attack on the Low Countries outflanked the Maginot Line.

The Dunkirk Evacuation

Once again, the German *Blitzkrieg* proved irresistible. The Netherlands fell after five days. When Belgium surrendered at the end of May, a large Allied army was left stranded along the Belgian-French border near the English Channel. Between May 26 and June 4, the British succeeded in evacuating some 338,000 troops, two-thirds of them British, from the beaches of Dunkirk.

The Fall of France

On June 5, the Battle of France began. On June 10, Italy entered the war. When the war began, Italy, unprepared to fight a major war, had declared its nonbelligerency. Mussolini had grown jealous of Hitler's gains, however, and wanted to share in the spoils of victory.

On June 14, the Germans took Paris. The French government had fled south, and on June 16, the French cabinet decided to seek an armistice, which was signed on June 22.

The Vichy Government

Under the terms of the armistice, Germany occupied northern and western France. Unoccupied France was ruled by a collaborationist government, headed by Marshal Henri Philippe Pétain (1856–1951), with its capital at Vichy in central France.

The Free French

On the eve of the French surrender, General Charles de Gaulle (1890–1970) went to London, where he established the Free French movement, a government-in-exile committed to continuing the war.

The Battle of Britain

The defeat of France left Great Britain alone in the struggle against Hitler's Germany.

The RAF Against the *Luftwaffe*

Hitler began planning for Operation Sea Lion, his code name for an invasion of England. In order for the Germans to launch this invasion, it would be necessary for the *Luftwaffe,* the German air force, to win control of the airspace over the English Channel and southern England. During the first phase of the Battle of Britain, in August and September 1940, the *Luftwaffe* attempted to destroy Britain's Royal Air Force (RAF) and its bases. The RAF benefited both from the courage and determination of its pilots and the newly invented radar warning system. The Germans suffered heavy losses. Paying tribute to the RAF pilots, Churchill declared: "Never in the field of human conflict was so much owed by so many to so few."

Frustrated in their effort to win control of the air, in the early autumn of 1940, the Germans began bombing attacks on London and other British cities in an effort to destroy industry and to weaken civilian morale. The effort failed.

Hitler's Diversion to Russia

Hitler was not unduly troubled by his failure in the Battle of Britain. By the late summer of 1940, the Nazi leader was already deeply involved in his planning for Operation Barbarossa, the invasion of the Soviet Union scheduled for the spring of 1941. He believed that the British might soon be forced to make peace on his terms. If they did not, they would have no choice but to surrender once the Soviets had been defeated.

The Battle of the Atlantic

The German submarine fleet operating in the North Atlantic presented a serious threat to Great Britain. The ability of the British to remain in the war depended on imports of food and war materials, but German submarines were sinking British ships faster than they could be replaced.

American Aid to Great Britain

Revision of the Neutrality Act

When the war began in September 1939, the United States declared its neutrality. In November, Congress revised the Neutrality Act, making it possible for belligerents to purchase war materials in the United States on a cash-and-carry basis. Since the British had established a naval blockade of Germany, the revision of the Neutrality Act mainly benefited the Allies.

The Lend-Lease Act

Following the fall of France, the United States increased its aid to Great Britain. In September 1940, the United States sent fifty old American destroyers to the British in exchange for leases to British bases in the Western Hemisphere. The Lend-Lease Act of March 1941 authorized the President to provide aid to "any country whose defense the President deems vital to the defense of the United States."

Aid to British Shipping

After German submarine attacks on British convoys intensified in the spring of 1941, the United States began a naval patrol in the western North Atlantic to warn the British of the presence of German submarines. In September 1941, American ships in the North Atlantic began to convoy British ships carrying lend-lease goods.

Following the American entry into the war in December 1941, the United States stepped up its efforts in the Battle of the Atlantic.

Allied Victory in the Atlantic

The first turning point in the Battle of the Atlantic came in November 1942, the last month in which the Allied loss of ships exceeded new construction. The second turning point came in May 1943, the first time the Germans lost more submarines than they were able to put into service.

Victory in the Atlantic made possible the unimpeded shipment of manpower and supplies from the United States to the European and Mediterranean theaters of war.

The War in the Mediterranean

North African Campaigns

Italian Failures

Italy's entry into the war endangered British control of the eastern Mediterranean. In September 1940, the Italians invaded Egypt from their colony in Libya, hoping to advance to the Suez Canal. British forces, commanded by Field Marshal Sir Archibald Wavell (1883–1950), drove the invaders back.

Early in 1941, the British conquered Italy's East African Empire, occupying Italian Somaliland, Eritrea, and Ethiopia.

Rommel's Campaign

In order to stave off an Italian collapse in North Africa, the Germans, in early 1941, dispatched the *Afrika Korps,* commanded by Field Marshal Erwin Rommel (1891–1944), nicknamed the Desert Fox. In April 1941, Rommel's troops and their Italian allies renewed the attack, pushing the British back into Egypt. Wavell was replaced by General Sir Claude Auchinleck (1884–1981).

At this point, Hitler was committed in the Balkans (see p. 401) and was preparing his assault on the Soviet Union. Reinforcements were not sent to Rommel, who was unable to follow up on his successful advance.

During late 1941 and early 1942, the British once again moved into Libya. An Axis counterattack pushed Auchinleck's forces back, however, and by summer, Rommel had reached El Alamein, about 60 miles west of Alexandria, posing a serious threat to the Suez

Canal. By this time, Hitler was deeply involved in a new offensive in Russia, and once again reinforcements were not sent to Rommel.

Montgomery's Counterattack

General Sir Harold Alexander (1891–1969) replaced Auchinleck as head of the British Middle Eastern Command, while General Sir Bernard Montgomery (1887–1976) took direct command of the Eighth Army. In late October 1942, Montgomery counterattacked, forcing Rommel's forces to retreat.

Allied Victory in North Africa

On November 8, 1942, Anglo-American forces, commanded by General Dwight D. Eisenhower (1890–1969), carried out Operation Torch, the invasion of Morocco and Algeria in French North Africa. The German and Italian defenders were caught in a squeeze as Eisenhower's forces advanced from the west and the British pressed forward from the east. In May 1943, the remaining 250,000 Axis defenders surrendered in Tunisia.

Hitler's Balkan Campaign

Just as Mussolini's defeat in Egypt drew the Germans into North Africa, so, too, did Italian setbacks pull Hitler into the Balkans in early 1941.

In October 1940, Mussolini invaded Greece from Italian-occupied Albania. A Greek counterattack threatened to drive the Italians into the sea, while the Royal Navy defeated the Italian fleet at its base at Taranto in southern Italy and off Cape Matapan in Greece.

In order to save Mussolini from defeat, in April 1941 the Germans overran Yugoslavia and invaded Greece. The British rushed 58,000 troops to Greece from Egypt. In the face of an overwhelming German onslaught, however, the British evacuated these troops first to the island of Crete and then, after German airborne troops landed on Crete, back to Egypt.

Allied Invasion of Sicily and Italy

The Allied victory in North Africa in May 1943 led to the Anglo-American decision to invade Sicily and Italy. The invasion of Sicily in July was followed by the Italians' overthrow of Mussolini the same month. Conquering Sicily, the American and British armies invaded Italy at the beginning of September. The new Italian government surrendered on September 3. The Germans had anticipated the surrender, however, and quickly took control of about two-thirds of the country.

For the Allies, the Italian campaign proved long and frustrating as the German defenders took full advantage of the country's rugged terrain. The war in Italy lasted until the spring of 1945, ending only a few days before the final German surrender.

The Russo-German War

The Invasion of the Soviet Union

On June 22, 1941, Hitler's armies invaded the Soviet Union. By December, it appeared that Hitler might achieve his objective of a quick victory over the Soviets. However, on December 6, 1941, the Red Army launched a counterattack on the Moscow front and drove the Germans back from 50 to 100 miles before they were able to stabilize the front in early 1942.

Campaigns in 1942 and 1943

In the spring of 1942, the Germans launched a new offensive directed toward two objectives: the oil-rich Caucasus, lying between the Black and Caspian seas, and the city of Stalingrad on the Volga River. At Stalingrad, the German attackers and the Soviet defenders became engaged in one of the war's bloodiest battles. In February 1943, the remnants of the German Sixth Army surrendered.

In the early summer of 1943, the Germans launched their final offensive in the Soviet Union. A few days later, the Soviets counterattacked. By the end of the year, the Red Army had recaptured two-thirds of the Soviet territory the Germans had occupied.

The War in Europe
During 1944 and 1945

The Air War Against Germany

During 1944, American and British air raids on Germany intensified. The Americans specialized in daylight, high-altitude precision bombing, hitting at key targets, while the Royal Air Force concentrated on night area bombing.

Allied bombing did massive damage to Germany's cities and economy. However, the bombing was not decisive. Victory over the Germans was not won by air raids but rather on the fields of battle.

The Normandy Invasion

By 1944, an Allied victory was in sight. In Italy, American and British troops continued their slow advance, while the Red Army pushed into the Baltic States, Poland, and the Balkans.

On D-day, June 6, 1944, Operation Overlord, which was the invasion of Normandy, opened the long-awaited Second Front in France. In the largest amphibious operation in history, American troops landed on Omaha and Utah beaches, while British and Canadian troops assaulted Gold, Juno, and Sword beaches further to the east. General Eisenhower served as Supreme Allied Commander, with British Air Chief Marshal Sir Arthur Tedder (1890–1967) as his deputy.

Allied Advance in France

As Eisenhower's troops drove toward Paris, an American and French force landed in mid-August on the coast of southern France between Marseilles and Nice, and began to advance northward through the Rhone valley.

Following the liberation of Paris on August 25, Allied troops pushed into the Low Countries and toward the Rhine River frontier between Germany and France.

The Battle of the Bulge

The Allied victories in Western Europe, together with the Soviet push from the East, suggested that Germany might be defeated before the end of 1944. But this assessment proved overly optimistic.

In December, the Germans launched a powerful counterattack against the advancing Americans in the Ardennes Forest in Belgium. In the Battle of the Bulge, the Germans pushed the Americans back, but they were not able to achieve a breakthrough.

The V-Bombs

In his desperate effort to ward off defeat, Hitler launched his V-1 flying bombs against British cities during June 1944. Although they caused some loss of life and physical damage, neither the V-1s nor the more destructive V-2 rockets that began to hit Britain in September had any impact on the outcome of the war.

The End of the European War

In mid-January 1945, the Soviets took Warsaw, Poland's capital. The Red Army's advance continued, and on April 25, American and Soviet forces met on the Elbe River in central Germany. At the end of April, Germany's armies in Italy surrendered, while Italian partisans seized and murdered Mussolini.

The Red Army entered Berlin on April 19, and Hitler committed suicide in his bunker beneath the city on April 30. The Germans surrendered on May 7.

The War Against Japan

Early Japanese Aggression

The Invasion of China

Following their invasion of China in 1937, the Japanese succeeded in conquering most of the country's coastal areas, but their efforts to overrun the interior bogged down.

The Tripartite Pact

In early September 1940, the Japanese occupied the northern part of French Indochina. In the same month, Japan signed the Tripartite Pact, allying itself more closely with Germany and Italy.

American Economic Pressure on Japan

In an effort to contain the Japanese threat and to aid China, the United States began to apply economic pressure on Japan. In late September 1940, President Franklin D. Roosevelt (1882–1945) imposed an embargo on the shipment of scrap iron and steel to Japan. American sanctions also barred the sale of oil to the Japanese. In July 1941, the Japanese occupied the rest of French Indochina, and Roosevelt responded by freezing Japanese assets in the United States.

American economic and financial sanctions confronted the Japanese with a dilemma. In order to get what it needed from the

United States, Japan would have to cease its aggression. The alternative was for Japan to seize the oil resources of the Dutch East Indies, an action likely to evoke a strong American response.

Attack on Pearl Harbor

On December 7, 1941, Japanese aircraft attacked the American naval base at Pearl Harbor, Hawaii, inflicting heavy damage and casualties. The United States declared war on Japan the following day, and Great Britain and the dominions also entered the war against Japan. On December 11, Germany and Italy declared war on the United States.

Early Japanese Victories

Within a few days of the declarations of war, the Japanese sank two British warships, the *Repulse* and the *Prince of Wales*. The Japanese then moved quickly to conquer the British crown colony of Hong Kong, the American-ruled Philippines, British Malaya with its great port at Singapore, British Burma, and the Dutch East Indies. The conquest of Burma enabled the Japanese to seal off the Burma Road—which the Allies had used to send supplies to China—and to threaten India. Advancing into New Guinea, the Japanese threatened Australia.

The Battles of the Coral Sea and Midway

Two important naval battles took place in the Pacific in the spring of 1942. While the Battle of the Coral Sea, fought on May 7–8, ended in a draw, it removed the immediate Japanese threat to Australia.

The Battle of Midway, fought in the central Pacific from June 3–6, resulted in an American victory, which eliminated the threat to Hawaii.

Allied Victories

American Island-Hopping

The Allies pushed against Japan from several directions. In the Pacific, the American island-hopping campaign began with the invasion of Guadalcanal in August 1942. By early 1945, the Americans had seized Iwo Jima and Okinawa. The Americans also reconquered the Philippines.

The British in Southeast Asia

Lord Louis Mountbatten (1900–1979), the Supreme Allied Commander in Southeast Asia, launched an invasion of Burma in early 1945, first capturing Mandalay in Upper Burma and then seizing Rangoon, the capital.

The End of the War Against Japan

Despite the successful push against Japan, American military planners believed that Japan could be defeated only by an invasion, which they estimated would cost as many as 1 million casualties.

The Atomic Bombs

Concern about casualties was a major factor contributing to the American decision to use the atomic bomb against Japan. On August 6, 1945, the first atomic bomb was dropped on Hiroshima, causing massive destruction and heavy casualties. On August 9, a second atomic bomb hit Nagasaki. The following day, Emperor Hirohito (r. 1926–1989) decided that Japan had no choice other than to surrender. He set one condition: He must be permitted to keep his throne.

Japanese Surrender

The Allies agreed to accept Hirohito's condition, and the news of Japan's surrender became public on August 14. The formal surrender documents were signed on September 2 on board the American battleship *Missouri* anchored in Tokyo Bay. The Second World War had ended.

Allied Wartime Diplomacy

During the war, the Allies held a series of conferences in which they discussed military operations and their plans for the postwar world.

The Atlantic Charter

In August 1941, Prime Minister Churchill and President Roosevelt met aboard the British battleship *Prince of Wales* off the coast of Newfoundland. In the Atlantic Charter, the two leaders declared that neither Great Britain nor the United States sought any territorial gains from the war and endorsed the principle of national self-determination. They also called for freedom of the seas and greater freedom of trade, as well as for the reduction of arms and the establishment of a "permanent system of general security."

The Casablanca Conference

In January 1943, a few weeks following the Anglo-American invasion of French North Africa, Churchill and Roosevelt met at Casablanca in French Morocco. The two leaders agreed to demand the unconditional surrender of the Axis powers.

Churchill and Roosevelt disagreed about the future conduct of the war, however. While Roosevelt favored a cross-Channel assault on France at the earliest possible date, Churchill urged further operations in the Mediterranean, including an invasion of the Balkans, to hit at what he called "the soft underbelly" of Axis-dominated Europe. Churchill also hoped that a Balkan campaign by the Western Allies would restrict the expansion of Soviet power and influence in Eastern Europe.

The two leaders reached a compromise, agreeing to move forward with an invasion of Sicily and Italy once the Axis had been defeated in North Africa, but not to postpone plans for the launching of a Second Front in France.

The Cairo Conference

In November 1943, Churchill and Roosevelt met in Cairo, the capital of Egypt, with Chiang Kai-shek (1887–1975), the Chinese leader. In addition to discussing plans for the conduct of the war against Japan, the Allied leaders agreed that Japan would be required to return the territory it had taken from China and to surrender the North Pacific islands then under its control.

The Teheran Conference

In late November and early December 1943, Churchill and Roosevelt met with Joseph Stalin (1879–1953) in Teheran, Iran. This first meeting of the "Big Three" discussed plans for the Second Front in Western Europe, scheduled for the spring of 1944.

At Teheran, Stalin made clear his determination to extend Soviet power in Eastern Europe following the war, while Roosevelt sought to overcome the Soviet leader's suspicions of the West in an effort to win his cooperation in the postwar world.

The Yalta Conference

In February 1945, Churchill, Roosevelt, and Stalin met at Yalta in the Soviet Crimea in the most important of the wartime conferences.

The Big Three agreed on plans for the occupation of Germany and on voting procedures in the Security Council of the new United Nations, while the Soviets agreed to enter the war against Japan following Germany's defeat.

Disagreement on Poland

The question of Poland was the most difficult issue considered at Yalta. Great Britain and the United States had maintained relations with the Polish government-in-exile in London, while the Soviets had established a pro-Soviet, Communist-dominated government at Lublin in Poland.

At Yalta, Stalin agreed to permit a broadening of the Lublin government by adding to it representatives of the London Poles. The Polish government continued to be dominated by Communists, however, and although Stalin promised to permit free elections in Poland, they were never held.

Friendly Governments Versus Free Elections

The Big Three also agreed on the text of the Declaration on Liberated Europe, pledging that postwar governments in the liberated countries of Europe would be established on the basis of free elections.

There was a basic incompatibility between the Soviet demand for friendly governments in Poland and other Eastern European countries and the Anglo-American demand for free elections. In most of Eastern Europe, and certainly in Poland, free elections would almost inevitably have led to the establishment of governments hostile to the Soviet Union. Stalin therefore got the friendly governments he wanted by imposing Communist-dominated regimes on countries occupied by Red Army troops. The Western Allies protested Soviet actions, but Moscow ignored the protests.

The Potsdam Conference

New Participants: Truman and Attlee

On April 12, 1945, President Roosevelt died and was succeeded by his vice president, Harry S Truman (1884–1972). In mid-July 1945, Truman met with Churchill and Stalin in Potsdam, near Berlin, in the last of the wartime Big Three conferences. During the conference, Churchill was replaced by the newly elected Labor prime minister, Clement Attlee (1883–1967).

Decisions on German Occupation

By the time the Potsdam Conference met, the British, Americans, French, and Soviets had taken possession of their zones of occupation in Germany. The Big Three agreed to establish a four-power Allied Control Council to determine the policies to be executed in all of the four zones in Germany. In practice, however, the four powers failed to reach agreement on common policies, and thus each power proceeded to determine policy for its own zone.

The Cold War

The East-West disputes over Poland, free elections versus friendly governments in Eastern Europe, and the occupation of Germany marked the beginning of the breakdown of the wartime grand alliance that quickly led to the outbreak of a new international conflict — the Cold War.

The British Home Front

The Second World War brought an end to the depression that had afflicted the British economy. Instead of unemployment, there was a shortage of labor as growing numbers of men were inducted into the armed services, and wages increased.

Wartime Government

Soon after the outbreak of war in September 1939, the Chamberlain government assumed extensive powers. The Emergency Powers Acts of 1939 and 1940 gave the government extraordinary authority over British national life, while several new ministries were established, including the ministries of Economic Warfare, Shipping, Food, and Information.

When Churchill became prime minister, he created a five-member war cabinet, later increased to nine members, to direct the war effort.

Postwar Planning

While Churchill concentrated his attention on the war, others considered the issue of postwar reconstruction.

Employment Policy

Subsidies.   The government gave considerable attention to an effort to avoid the heavy unemployment that had plagued Great Britain during the interwar years. In a White Paper issued in 1942, the government committed itself to providing subsidies in an effort to create and maintain full employment.

Relocation.   In addition, a government committee made proposals regarding the relocation of industry and labor away from congested urban districts in an effort to distribute employment opportunities more equally across the country. The work of this committee resulted in the passage of the Location of Industries Act in 1945.

The Education Act of 1944.   The Education Act of 1944 also had implications for employment. By raising the minimum age for leaving school to fifteen, the act had the effect of reducing the number of relatively untrained young people entering the labor force.

The Town and Country Planning Act of 1944

Other committees studied agriculture, land utilization, and the redevelopment of depressed urban areas. Some of the proposals advanced by these committees were embodied in the Town and Country Planning Act of 1944.

The Beveridge Report

In 1942, a committee headed by Sir William Beveridge (1879–1963) recommended a substantial extension of social services and social insurance to provide the British people with "cradle-to-the-grave" protection. The Beveridge Report provided the foundation for the social reform program enacted by the postwar Labor government.

Great Britain and the Second World War   411

During the 1930s, Great Britain failed to act effectively to halt the spread of aggression. Then, following the declarations of war in September 1939, the British war effort appeared uncertain at best. However, under the leadership of Winston Churchill, one of the greatest war ministers in England's long history, the British people united with grim determination to win what quickly became a total war. Great Britain was one of the wartime Big Three and established a close "special relationship" with the United States. Nevertheless, the strain of a second world war within a generation ended Britain's position as a first-class power.

Recommended Reading

Adamthwaite, Anthony P. *The Making of the Second World War* (2nd ed., 1979).

Barker, A. J. *Dunkirk: The Great Escape* (1977).

Bryant, Arthur. *The Turn of the Tide, 1939–1943* (1957).

Bryant, Arthur. *Triumph in the West, 1943–1946* (1959).

Calder, Angus. *The People's War: Britain, 1939–1945* (1969).

Chalfont, Alun. *Montgomery of Alamein* (1977).

Churchill, Randolph and Martin Gilbert. *Life of Winston Churchill,* 7 vols. (1966–1986).

Churchill, Winston S. *The Second World War,* 6 vols. (1948–1954).

Cowling, Maurice. *The Impact of Hitler: British Politics and British Policy, 1933–1940* (1975).

Edwards, Jill. *The British Government and the Spanish Civil War, 1936–1939* (1979).

Feis, Herbert. *Roosevelt, Churchill, Stalin: The War They Waged and the Peace They Sought* (1957).

Fuller, J. F. C. *The Second World War, 1939–1945* (1959).

Gilbert, Martin. *Britain and Germany Between the Wars* (1964).

Gilbert, Martin. *The Roots of Appeasement* (1967).

Gilbert, Martin and Richard Gott. *The Appeasers* (2nd ed., 1967).

Lafore, Laurence. *The End of Glory: An Interpretation of the Origins of World War II* (1970).

Lee, J. M. *The Churchill Coalition, 1940–1945* (1980).

Lowenheim, Francis L., ed. *Peace or Appeasement? Hitler, Chamberlain and the Munich Crisis* (1965).

Macleod, Ian. *Neville Chamberlain* (1960).

Marwick, Arthur. *The Home Front: The British and the Second World War* (1977).

Mee, Charles L. *Meeting at Potsdam* (1975).

Pelling, Henry. *Britain and the Second World War* (1970).

Pelling, Henry. *Winston Churchill* (1974).

Rock, William R. *British Appeasement in the 1930s* (1977).

Shay, Robert Paul. *British Rearmament in the Thirties* (1979).

Snell, John L. *Illusion and Necessity: The Diplomacy of Global War, 1939–1945* (1963).

Taylor, Telford. *Munich: The Price of Peace* (1980).

Thorne, Christopher. *Allies of a Kind: The United States, Britain and the War Against Japan, 1941–1945* (1978).

Thorne, Christopher. *The Approach of War, 1938–1939* (1967).

Wilmot, Chester. *The Struggle for Europe* (1948).

Woodward, E. L. *British Foreign Policy in the Second World War* (1962).

CHAPTER 22

Socialist Britain

Time Line

1945–1951	Clement Attlee, a Laborite, serves as prime minister
1946–1948	The Labor government carries out a program of nationalization
1946	Parliament passes the National Insurance Act
	Parliament passes the National Health Service Act
1947	India and Pakistan become independent
1948	Great Britain withdraws from Palestine
	Burma and Ceylon become independent
1949	The Irish Free State becomes the Republic of Ireland

Great Britain becomes a member of the North Atlantic Treaty Organization (NATO)

1951–1955   Winston Churchill, a Conservative, heads his second ministry

1952   Elizabeth II becomes queen

1953   The Steel Act denationalizes the iron and steel industry

1954   Great Britain becomes a member of the Southeast Asia Treaty Organization (SEATO)

1955   Great Britain becomes a member of the Baghdad Pact

1955–1957   Anthony Eden, a Conservative, serves as prime minister

1956   Anglo-French intervention in the Suez Canal zone misfires

1957   The Gold Coast gains independence as Ghana

1957–1963   Harold Macmillan, a Conservative, serves as prime minister

1960   Nigeria becomes independent

1961   Tanganyika becomes independent

The Union of South Africa becomes the Republic of South Africa

1962   Kenya becomes independent

1963   French President Charles de Gaulle vetoes British entry into the Common Market

The Profumo Scandal undermines the Macmillan government

Sir Alec Douglas-Home, a Conservative, becomes prime minister

| 1964 | Nyasaland and Northern Rhodesia become independent as Malawi and Zambia, respectively |
| 1965 | Rhodesia issues its unilateral declaration of independence |

The Second World War completed the process begun by the First World War of reducing Great Britain to the status of a second-rate power. By war's end in 1945, two superpowers, the United States and the Soviet Union, had come to dominate international relations. In the Cold War, the great new international conflict that developed in the late 1940s, Great Britain firmly allied itself with the United States. Although the British participated in measures for collective security, they were reluctant to become involved in Western European economic integration.

In imperial affairs, the revolt against imperialism was in full swing in India and elsewhere in Asia, and by the late 1950s, it extended to Britain's African possessions as well.

The Labor Party won the 1945 elections for the House of Commons, and for the first time in British history, a majority Labor government took office. Labor promoted both extensive nationalization and a substantial expansion of the welfare state. In 1951, the Conservatives returned to power, inaugurating a period of thirteen years of Conservative domination of British politics.

The Attlee Government, 1945-1951

The 1945 Elections

In July 1945, for the first time since 1935, British voters elected a new House of Commons.

The Labor Party Program

In its program, *Let Us Face the Future,* the Labor Party called for the creation of "a new Socialist Commonwealth," including the establishment of a planned economy, assurances of full employment, an expanded system of social insurance, and the construction of more housing.

Labor benefited from its forthright endorsement of reform, as it did from the electorate's memory of the economic hard times of the prewar years when the Conservatives had dominated British politics.

Results

Labor won 393 seats in the new House of Commons to 189 for the Conservatives and 12 for the Liberals. Some 46 independents and members of splinter parties, including two Communists, also won seats, an unusually large number.

The Labor Government

Clement Attlee (1883–1967), the Labor Party's moderate leader, became prime minister. Ernest Bevin (1884–1951) served as foreign secretary. Hugh Dalton (1887–1962) became chancellor of the exchequer, and he was succeeded in that office in 1947 by Sir Stafford Cripps (1889–1952). While the members of the cabinet had served in the House of Commons for a number of years, most Labor members of the house were newly elected.

The Economy

The Cost of Victory

Though Great Britain was one of the victorious allies, the cost of victory was heavy. Some 357,000 Britons had lost their lives in the war, including some 30,000 merchant seamen and 60,000 civilians killed in air raids.

Although the loss of life was less than in the First World War (see Chapter 19), Great Britain suffered more physical damage than it had in the earlier conflict. German bombing had done heavy damage to the country's cities, railroads, and port facilities.

The cost of the war had led to a substantial increase in the national debt, which tripled to £23 billion.

Economic Problems

The British economic situation in 1945 was desperate. The war had resulted in the loss of Britain's export market, along with the loss of income from merchant shipping and overseas investments. The British were thereby deprived of the income necessary to pay for the imports of food and raw materials on which the country depended.

In an effort to overcome the crisis, Great Britain secured a $3.75 billion loan from the United States in June 1946 and a credit of some $1.25 billion from Canada.

The Austerity Program

Confronting the economic crisis, Attlee's government imposed an austerity program. Strict wartime economic controls remained in place in order to restrict imports, increase exports, and reduce the balance of payments deficit. The rationing of meat, sugar, clothing, gasoline, and tobacco continued.

Balance of Payments.   Since balance of payments problems would continue to plague Great Britain in the post-World War II era, it is useful to explain the term. The concept of balance of payments is derived from the older concept of balance of trade. While balance of trade involves the relationship between a country's imports and exports, balance of payments involves all payments between a country and its trading partners, including payments for goods and services, foreign loans and interest on those loans, and the transfer of gold. A deficit in the balance of payments can lead to an outflow of gold from the country and may threaten the stability of the country's currency.

Marshall Plan Aid.   In 1948, the United States initiated the Marshall Plan to assist in the economic recovery of Western Europe. Between 1948 and 1951, the British received some $2 billion in Marshall Plan aid, which helped stimulate a modest economic upswing.

Labor Legislation

The Labor government won repeal of the Trade Disputes Act of 1927 (see Chapter 20), which was strongly opposed by Britain's labor unions.

Nationalization

From 1946 to 1948, the Labor government nationalized the Bank of England, the coal industry, electric and gas production, civil aviation, telecommunications, and the railroads and other transport services.

Iron and Steel

In 1948, the government introduced a controversial bill to nationalize the iron and steel industry. While the Labor Party's large majority in the House of Commons ensured the bill's passage in the lower house, the House of Lords appeared ready to block the legislation. The government thus pushed through an amendment of the Parliament Act of 1911 (see Chapter 18), reducing the power of the House of Lords to block legislation from two years to one. The bill to nationalize iron and steel became law in 1949 to take effect in 1951.

Evaluation of Nationalization

While nationalization was a fundamental part of the Labor Party's program, it did not provide a solution to the country's economic problems. Nationalization was widely regarded as the only effective way to infuse necessary capital into the outmoded coal industry, but the industry nevertheless remained troubled. In other industries, nationalization was more a matter of political doctrine than economic necessity.

Nationalized industries were operated by public corporations rather than by government departments. In practice, they continued to operate much as they had under private ownership, and the workers gained little sense of control over or participation in decision-making in the industries where they labored.

Although most industries nationalized by Labor remained nationalized, there was little enthusiasm for further nationalization outside of the left wing of the Labor Party.

Social Insurance

The Labor government accepted a greatly expanded responsibility for the well-being of the British people.

The National Insurance Act of 1946

The National Insurance Act of 1946 carried out many of the recommendations of the wartime Beveridge Report (see Chapter 21). The act consolidated earlier social welfare legislation. It expanded coverage and increased benefits for a number of programs, including unemployment insurance, pensions for retirees, sickness insurance, maternity and widow's benefits, and death grants.

The Industrial Injuries Insurance Act of 1946

The Industrial Injuries Insurance Act of 1946 established a comprehensive and expanded program of workman's compensation for job-related injuries.

The National Assistance Act of 1948

The National Assistance Act of 1948 abolished the old poor laws and established in their place a government program of aid for the poor.

The National Health Service

The National Health Service Act of 1946 was the most famous of the social insurance measures of the Attlee government. The National Health Service, which went into effect in 1948, provided free medical care for the British people. It covered physicians' and dentists' services, prescription drugs, hospital care, eyeglasses, and dentures.

The National Health Service was directed by Aneurin Bevan (1897–1960), a radical Laborite, who served as minister of health.

The National Health Service provided the British people with better health care than most had been able to afford in the past, although the cost of the program was considerably greater than had originally been estimated.

Housing

More than 4 million housing units had either been destroyed or damaged by the wartime bombing, and the need for additional housing was considerable. The Housing Acts of 1946 and 1949 resulted in the construction of 806,000 new housing units by 1950, while the repair and conversion of older buildings provided another 333,000 units.

Imperial Affairs

Ireland

In 1949, the Irish Free State (Eire) withdrew completely from the Commonwealth of Nations, becoming the Republic of Ireland.

Palestine

In 1918, there had been about 50,000 Jews in Palestine. By 1946, close to 600,000 Jews lived alongside about 1 million Arabs. The

Balfour Declaration of 1917 had promised to establish in Palestine a national home for the Jewish people (see Chapter 20). In the wake of the Holocaust of World War II, in which the Nazis murdered some 6 million of Europe's Jews, the Zionists and their supporters demanded that the British fulfill this pledge.

The Arabs strongly opposed Jewish immigration, however, and increasingly violent clashes occurred among the Jews, Arabs, and British.

Establishment of Israel

In November 1947, the United Nations (UN) voted to partition Palestine into Arab and Jewish sections. But the conflict appeared to be beyond peaceful resolution, and the British withdrew from Palestine in May 1948.

The Jews now proclaimed the establishment of the State of Israel, accepting the frontiers proposed by the United Nations. The Arab League continued its refusal to accept partition, however, and went to war against Israel.

The Israeli war of independence ended in 1949 with an Israeli victory, and Israel extended its borders slightly beyond what the UN had originally proposed.

India

Conflict between Hindus and Moslems.   In 1942, a mission to India, led by Sir Stafford Cripps, promised dominion status for India after the war in return for Indian support of the British war effort. The Indian leaders, however, were divided on the question of the nature of the new India (see Chapter 20). While the predominantly Hindu Indian National Congress, led by Gandhi and Nehru, advocated a strong central government for all of India, the All-India Moslem League, led by Mohammed Ali Jinnah (1876–1948), called for the creation of a separate Moslem state.

Partition.   Following the war, Lord Louis Mountbatten (1900–1979) demonstrated his skill at diplomacy in achieving an agreement for the partition of India. In August 1947, two independent states came into being: India, with its capital at New Delhi, and Pakistan, with its capital at Karachi. The two states soon became involved in a protracted dispute over control of the province of Kashmir.

Assassination of Gandhi.   The achievement of independence was accompanied by violent communal conflict that took the lives of over 1 million people. Then, in January 1948, Gandhi was assassinated by a Hindu fanatic, and Nehru had to bear the primary responsibility for building the new state.

Transition to Republics.   The establishment of independence for India and Pakistan introduced a new era in the history of the Commonwealth of Nations. For the first time, countries whose populations were essentially non-European acquired independence within the Commonwealth. (The traditional term "dominion" began to fall into disuse.)

In addition, the desire of India to become a republic required a change in the formula set forth by the Imperial Conference of 1926, which declared that the dominions were united by a "common allegiance to the Crown." In 1949, a meeting of Commonwealth prime ministers eliminated this reference to the Crown and defined the monarch as "Head of the Commonwealth." India formally became a republic in 1950, while Pakistan did so in 1956.

Burma and Ceylon

In January 1948, Burma secured its independence outside the Commonwealth. The following month, Ceylon became independent as a member of the Commonwealth.

Foreign Affairs

The development of the Cold War frustrated Foreign Secretary Ernest Bevin's hopes of maintaining the wartime policy of cooperation with the Soviet Union. Soviet actions in Eastern Europe at the end of the war evoked protests from Great Britain and the United States (see Chapter 21), and during late 1945 and early 1946, East-West relations continued to deteriorate.

The Iron Curtain

In March 1946, in a speech at Westminster College in Fulton, Missouri, former Prime Minister Winston Churchill (1874–1965) introduced a new term to the political vocabulary when he declared: "From Stettin in the Baltic to Trieste in the Adriatic, an iron curtain has descended across the continent."

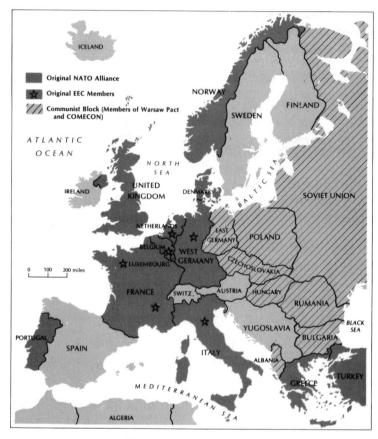

Europe During the Cold War

The Truman Doctrine

At the end of World War II, Great Britain had assumed a major responsibility in the eastern Mediterranean, providing assistance to the Greek government in its war against Communist rebels and to Turkey in its efforts to resist Soviet demands for a larger voice in the control of the Dardanelles. In February 1947, the British informed the United States that they no longer had the financial strength to continue this role. The United States would have to take over.

Appearing before a joint session of Congress on March 12, 1947, President Harry S Truman (1884–1972) called for the appropriation of $400 million for military and economic assistance to Greece and Turkey. The President also expressed what came to be known as the Truman Doctrine: "I believe that it must be the policy of the United States to support free peoples who are resisting attempted subjugation by armed minorities or by outside pressure." Congress quickly approved the President's appeal for aid to Greece and Turkey.

East-West Relations in Germany

Allied Occupation of Germany.   In the aftermath of Germany's defeat in May 1945, the British, Americans, French, and Soviets took control of their occupation zones. Berlin, the former capital lying within the Soviet zone, was divided into four occupation sectors. The western powers had access to their sectors by highway, railroad, and air routes through the Soviet zone.

Although the occupying powers had established the Allied Control Council to determine the policies to be executed in all four zones, in practice the four powers failed to reach agreement on common policies. Thus, each power proceeded to determine policy for its own zone.

Consolidation of Western Zones.   When the four-power Conference of Foreign Ministers failed to reach any agreement on a peace treaty with Germany, the Americans and British merged their zones for economic purposes in early 1947, creating a unit known as Bizonia. The French joined their zone several months later. In this way, the Western powers took the first steps toward the establishment of a separate West German state.

The Berlin Blockade.   The Soviets decided to apply pressure on the West where they could do so with the greatest ease, at Berlin. On June 20, 1948, the Soviets cut off the land routes between the Western zones and Berlin, thereby initiating the Berlin Blockade. The Western powers responded by establishing the Berlin Airlift, in order to provide the three Western sectors of the city with food, fuel, and other supplies.

Creation of Two German States.   The Berlin Airlift achieved a remarkable success in meeting the needs of the Western sectors, and the Soviets decided against escalating the crisis. In May 1949, the Soviets ended the blockade. The Western powers proceeded with their plans to establish the Federal Republic of Germany, which came into being in mid-1949. The Soviets responded by creating in their zone an East German state, the German Democratic Republic.

Western Defense

Mounting East-West tension gradually led the Western powers to join in a military alliance.

The Brussels Pact.   In March 1948, Great Britain signed the Brussels Pact, a treaty of alliance with France and the Benelux states (Belgium, the Netherlands, and Luxembourg).

The North Atlantic Pact.   In April 1949, representatives of twelve nations met in Washington to sign a defensive alliance, the North Atlantic Pact. The twelve signers included the five Brussels Pact states plus the United States, Canada, Iceland, Denmark, Norway, Italy, and Portugal. Greece and Turkey joined in 1952, and West Germany was added in 1955. The North Atlantic Pact established the North Atlantic Treaty Organization (NATO) to coordinate the activities of the alliance.

The Korean War

Background.   At the end of World War II, Japanese-ruled Korea was occupied by American and Soviet forces, with the line between the occupation zones established at the 38th parallel. In the south, the United States supported the creation of a government headed by Syngman Rhee (1875–1965), a conservative nationalist. In the north, the Soviets established a Communist government, led by Kim Il-Sung (b. 1912). Both occupying powers withdrew in 1949.

Course of the War.   On June 25, 1950, the army of Communist-ruled North Korea attacked South Korea. Acting promptly to support South Korea, the United States took advantage of a temporary Soviet absence from the UN Security Council to win that body's condemnation of North Korea as an aggressor and its endorsement of intervention. The Security Council's action made the Korean War officially a United Nations police action, although the bulk of the fighting was done by Americans and South Koreans.

Great Britain supported the intervention in Korea, sent a small force to South Korea, and increased its defense budget.

An armistice signed in 1953 left Korea divided at the 38th parallel.

The 1950 Elections

In the elections of February 1950, Labor won 315 seats in the House of Commons as compared to 298 for the Conservatives and 9 for the Liberals. Most of the independents and representatives of other parties who had been elected in 1945 lost their seats. The new House of Commons had only three independent members.

While the Attlee government remained in power, it held only a slender seven-seat majority over the combined opposition.

Problems of the Labor Government

The outbreak of the Korean War in 1950 led to increased expenditures for defense, which in turn resulted in tax increases. Since the government could not afford increased expenditures for both armaments and social services, the National Health Service established a charge of one shilling for each prescription and modest fees for eyeglasses and dentures.

In April 1951, the left-wing Laborites Aneurin Bevan and Harold Wilson (b. 1916) resigned from the government in protest against the National Health Service fees and increased defense spending.

Attlee's government was also weakened by the loss of other key members. Foreign Secretary Ernest Bevin died in 1951, while Sir Stafford Cripps, the chancellor of the exchequer, retired for reasons of health.

The 1951 Elections

In an effort to increase his majority in the House of Commons, Prime Minister Attlee called elections in October 1951. Although the Labor Party polled some 200,000 more votes than the Conservatives, Labor lost its majority in Parliament.

The Conservatives won 321 seats as compared to 295 for Labor and six for the Liberals. The new House of Commons also contained three independents.

The Second Churchill Government
1951-1955

Winston Churchill returned to the prime ministership. His leadership was largely titular, however, and power was in the hands of the key members of his cabinet. Anthony Eden (1897-1977), who had been Britain's wartime foreign secretary, returned to that office. R. A. "Rab" Butler (1902-1982) served as chancellor of the exchequer, while Harold Macmillan (1894-1986) was minister of housing and local government.

In February 1952, King George VI (r. 1936-1952) died and was succeeded by his daughter, Queen Elizabeth II.

Attitude toward Nationalization

The Conservative government did not attempt to undo Labor's nationalizations, with two exceptions. The Steel Act of 1953 denationalized the iron and steel industry, which had only recently been nationalized. There was also a partial denationalization of long-distance trucking, which allowed private firms to compete with the state-owned enterprise.

Social Welfare

Under the Conservatives, the social welfare program of Labor remained in place and was, in fact, expanded. The Churchill government increased family allowances and unemployment benefits, while Macmillan's ambitious housing program called for the construction of 300,000 units annually.

The Economy

Easing of Financial Problems

When the Conservatives took office in 1951, Great Britain faced a financial crisis resulting from increases in the balance of payments deficit and the depletion of gold and dollar reserves. Although the Conservatives advocated ending Labor's austerity program, in this situation it did not seem wise to remove economic controls. Over the course of the next year, the government succeeded in reducing imports and increasing exports, which eased the balance of payments problem.

Asia, 1989

Improvements in Economy

Controls were then relaxed, and the last of food rationing ended in 1953. The removal of controls, combined with lower interest rates, lower prices for raw materials, and the generally favorable international economic climate served to increase British production, employment, and standard of living. While business profits and wages increased, so, too, did inflation.

Foreign Affairs

During the 1950s, Great Britain supported American efforts to expand the Western alliance system that had begun with the creation of NATO in 1949.

SEATO

In September 1954, Great Britain joined with the United States, France, Australia, New Zealand, the Philippines, Thailand, and Pakistan in the Southeast Asia Treaty Organization. SEATO was intended to be the Asian equivalent of NATO.

The Baghdad Pact (CENTO)

The creation of the Baghdad Pact in 1955 marked the completion of the Western alliance system. Consisting of Great Britain, Turkey, Iraq, Iran, and Pakistan, the Baghdad Pact joined NATO and SEATO. Turkey, the easternmost member of NATO, was the westernmost member of the Baghdad Pact, while Pakistan, the westernmost member of SEATO, was the easternmost member of the Baghdad Pact.

In 1959, Iraq dropped out of the Baghdad Pact in the wake of an anti-Western coup. Since Baghdad was Iraq's capital, the alliance was renamed the Central Treaty Organization (CENTO).

The Eden Government, 1955-1957

In April 1955, Churchill retired from the prime ministership at the age of eighty and was succeeded by Anthony Eden.

The 1955 Elections

In May 1955, British voters elected a new House of Commons. The Labor Party was weakened by intraparty conflict between the moderates and the party's left wing, while Labor's program of economic controls and further nationalization won little popular support in a time of relative prosperity.

The Conservatives increased their majority in the House of Commons, winning 347 seats; Labor won 277, and the Liberals won six.

The Geneva Summit

Following the death of Soviet dictator Joseph Stalin (1879–1953) in March 1953, control of the Soviet government passed into the hands of a more moderate collective leadership. Communist party chief Nikita Khrushchev (1894–1971) and Premier Nikolai Bulganin (1895–1975) spoke of "peaceful coexistence" between the Soviet Union and the West.

In July 1955, Eden met with President Dwight D. Eisenhower (1890–1969) of the United States, Premier Edgar Faure (1908–1988) of France, and Khrushchev and Bulganin in Geneva, Switzerland. This was the first meeting in a decade of the heads of the major governments, who conducted their talks in a cordial atmosphere. Following this summit meeting, there was talk of a "Spirit of Geneva," although East and West had not reached any agreements on the major issues that divided them, notably German reunification and arms limitation.

The Suez Crisis

Although Eden had been Churchill's long-time heir apparent, he proved to be a disappointment as prime minister. Paradoxically, it was foreign affairs, his supposed area of expertise, that caused his downfall.

The Egyptian Revolution

In 1952, a revolution in Egypt overthrew King Farouk (r. 1936–1952). Gamel Abdul Nasser (1918–1970), an ardent nationalist and advocate of Arab unity, soon established his dictatorship. A new Anglo-Egyptian Treaty, signed in 1954, provided for the withdrawal of British troops from the Suez Canal area by June 1956.

Nationalization of the Suez Canal

Nasser developed an ambitious plan for Egypt's economic development, centered on the construction of a high dam at Aswan on the Nile River. Egypt received pledges of loans to help build the dam from the United States, Great Britain, and the World Bank.

When Nasser tried to play the two Cold War antagonists off against one another and secured arms and a loan from the Soviet Union, the United States responded in July 1956 by canceling American support for the Aswan high dam. Great Britain and the World Bank quickly followed suit.

At the end of July, Nasser retaliated by seizing the privately owned Suez Canal Company. Although Nasser agreed to compensate the company's owners, the British and French were troubled by Egyptian control of the strategically important canal.

Anglo-French Intervention

Great Britain and France entered into a scheme with Israel, which feared an Egyptian attack. Acting in accord with London and Paris, Israel launched a preemptive strike against Egypt on October 29, 1956. Britain and France moved into the canal zone on November 5, ostensibly to separate the antagonists but in reality to take control of the canal.

World opinion joined in condemnation of the British, French, and Israelis, and in Great Britain, the intervention was denounced by the Labor Party and most of the press. Isolated diplomatically, Great Britain, France, and Israel agreed to an armistice. Egypt paid the Suez Canal Company's stockholders $81 million for the canal, and the Soviets helped the Egyptians build the Aswan high dam.

Consequences of the Intervention

The British gained nothing from the intervention. The Egyptians blocked the Suez Canal, making it unusable. Britain's oil pipeline in Syria was cut, relations with the United States and the Arab countries were strained, and Britain's gold and dollar reserves dropped precipitously. In January 1957, Eden resigned.

The Macmillan Government 1957–1963

Harold Macmillan succeeded Eden in the prime ministership, quickly establishing his authority both in the Conservative Party and the country.

The Economy

Gains

Macmillan dealt effectively with the post-Suez balance of payments problems and lowered interest rates, which encouraged investment and economic expansion. Foreign trade increased, and the economy entered a period of expansion.

Problems

Despite the economic upturn, the British failed to modernize their industry as rapidly as did their competitors in the world market. Furthermore, British industry often lacked innovative management, and the economy continued to be hurt by labor-management conflict. As a consequence, the British experienced considerably less economic prosperity than did the United States and the highly industrialized countries of the European continent.

The Labor Party

The Conservatives benefited not only from Macmillan's leadership but also from the problems of the Labor Party. In 1955, Clement Attlee retired as the Labor Party's leader and was replaced by Hugh Gaitskell (1906–1963). The Labor Party remained divided between moderates and the left wing, which called for the disestablishment of the Church of England, unilateral disarmament, and further nationalization.

The 1959 Elections

The elections of October 1959 were the third in a row in which the Conservatives strengthened their hold on the House of Commons. The Conservatives won 365 seats, while Labor won 258 and the Liberals won six.

The Common Market

Although Great Britain was actively involved in Western defense, the British had been unwilling to participate in the economic integration of Western Europe, refusing to join either the European Coal and Steel Community (ECSC), formed in 1951, or the European Economic Community (EEC), popularly known as the Common Market, established in 1957. Many in Great Britain harbored a distrust of Europe and longed for the "splendid isolation" of the past. Instead of tying the British economy closer to that of the continent, there was a desire for stronger economic relations with the Commonwealth and the United States.

The European Free Trade Association

Fearing competition from the Common Market, in 1959 the British took the lead in organizing the European Free Trade Association (EFTA), a customs union with Sweden, Norway, Denmark, Switzerland, Austria, and Portugal. The EFTA quickly came to be called the "outer seven," contrasted with the "inner six" (France, Italy, West Germany, and the Benelux states) of the ECSC and EEC.

DeGaulle's Veto

In 1960, the British economy experienced a downturn and the balance of payments deficit increased. Recognizing the success of the Common Market, Macmillan believed that Great Britain stood to lose more by staying out than by joining and applied for British membership in the EEC. In January 1963, however, French President Charles de Gaulle (1890–1970) vetoed British entry. De Gaulle's reasons were political. He regarded Great Britain as not fully European, believed the British maintained too close a relationship with the United States, and feared that Great Britain would not be willing to play a subordinate role to France.

The Profumo Scandal

Macmillan's problems were compounded by the 1963 scandal involving John Profumo (b. 1915), his secretary of state for war. Profumo admitted that he had lied to the House of Commons when he denied having an affair with call girl Christine Keeler, who had also been involved with the Soviet naval attaché. Although fears of a possible breach of national security proved unfounded, the Profumo Scandal weakened both Macmillan and the Conservative Party.

Sir Alec Douglas-Home

In October 1963, Macmillan resigned and was succeeded by his foreign secretary, the earl of Home (pronounced Hume). Resigning his peerage, he became prime minister as Sir Alec Douglas-Home (b. 1903) and began an effort to rebuild support for the Conservative party.

The Commonwealth of Nations

During the late 1950s and 1960s, the breakup of the British Empire continued, and in 1966, the Colonial Office ceased being a separate ministry.

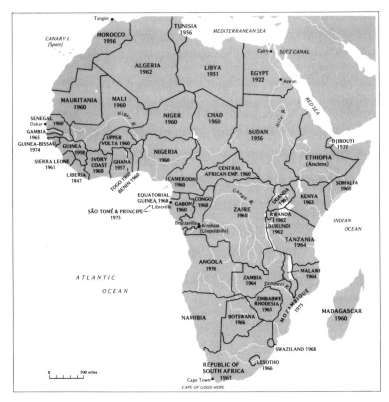

Africa, 1989

Cyprus

The island of Cyprus in the eastern Mediterranean contained a mixed Greek and Turkish population. Following World War II, conflict developed between the Greek majority, which favored union with Greece, and the Turks, who urged partition of the island.

Under the terms of a settlement reached in 1960, Cyprus became an independent republic and a member of the Commonwealth. Archbishop Makarios (1913–1977), a Greek Cypriot, became president, while a Turkish Cypriot served as vice president.

Violence continued on the island, however. In 1964, an international force organized by the United Nations succeeded in restoring order.

The Federation of Malaya

In 1948, a Communist insurgency broke out in Britain's Southeast Asian possession of Malaya. Although the insurgency was not suppressed until 1960, the Federation of Malaya became an independent state within the Commonwealth in 1957.

In 1963, Singapore, Sarawak, and Sabah were added to the federation, which was renamed the Federation of Malaysia. Singapore seceded peacefully from the federation in 1965, becoming an independent state.

Subsaharan Africa

By the late 1950s, nationalism had become a powerful force in Britain's African possessions south of the Sahara Desert.

The Sudan.   In 1956, the Sudan became an independent republic outside the Commonwealth.

The Gold Coast.   The British West African colony of the Gold Coast gained its independence within the Commonwealth in 1957 under the leadership of Kwame Nkrumah (1909–1972). It became the nation of Ghana.

Nigeria.   The British colony of Nigeria, also in West Africa, secured its independence within the Commonwealth in 1960.

Within a few years, Nigeria sank into a bitter civil war, the result of tribal conflict between the Moslem Hausas and the predominantly Christian Ibos. In 1967, the Ibos seceded and proclaimed the establishment of Biafra. The Ibos' bid for independence proved abortive, however, and the Nigerian government regained control of Biafra in 1970.

Sierra Leone and Gambia.   Elsewhere in West Africa, Sierra Leone became independent in 1961 and Gambia in 1965. Both remained members of the Commonwealth.

Tanzania.   British possessions in East Africa also chose membership in the Commonwealth when they acquired their independence.

Tanganyika became independent in 1961 under the leadership of Julius Nyerere (b. 1922). In 1964, the island colony of Zanzibar joined with Tanganyika to form the new country of Tanzania.

Uganda.   Uganda became independent in 1962 and gained worldwide notoriety during the 1970s, when the country was ruled by a former army sergeant, Idi Amin (b. 1925). During an eight-year reign of terror, Amin took thousands of lives and wrecked Uganda's economy. Tanzanian troops overthrew Amin in 1979, and Uganda regained constitutional government.

Kenya.   In Kenya, white settlers fought for several years against the terrorist Mau Mau organization. In 1962, however, Kenya gained its independence, and Jomo Kenyatta (1893–1978), a founder of the Mau Mau movement, became the country's first president.

Nyasaland and Northern Rhodesia.   In 1953, the British had joined Southern Rhodesia, Northern Rhodesia, and Nyasaland to form the Central African Federation.

This experiment collapsed in 1963, and Nyasaland and Northern Rhodesia became independent members of the Commonwealth in 1964, taking the names of Malawi and Zambia, respectively.

Rhodesia.   In Rhodesia (formerly Southern Rhodesia), the black population of some 6 million greatly outnumbered the white population of 250,000. The white minority, however, was determined to maintain its hold on power. When the British attempted to secure equal political rights for the black population, the Rhodesian Front government, headed by Ian Smith (b. 1919), issued a unilateral declaration of independence in 1965. Several years of controversy followed, and Rhodesia became a republic in 1970.

Finally, in 1980, a government controlled by the black majority took power, and Rhodesia became Zimbabwe.

The Union of South Africa.   In the Union of South Africa, the white minority, primarily of British and Dutch ancestry, numbered about 4 million. Those of Dutch ancestry, known as Afrikaners, became a majority of the white population in the post-World War II period and were determined to maintain white control, even though blacks and other nonwhites totaled some 18 million.

In 1948, the Afrikaner-dominated Nationalist Party, led by Dr. Daniel F. Malan (1874–1959), won control of the South African parliament. The Nationalists imposed and maintained a system of rigid racial segregation known as apartheid. Under apartheid, blacks were compelled to live in separate townships and had little opportunity for higher education or occupational advancement. Black activists were imprisoned, often without trial, and strict censorship laws were enforced.

In the face of mounting pressure from Great Britain and other members of the Commonwealth, the Union of South Africa pulled out of the Commonwealth in 1961, becoming the Republic of South Africa.

The Western Hemisphere

In the Western Hemisphere, several British possessions acquired independence within the Commonwealth. The island of Jamaica in the West Indies gained independence in 1962, as did Trinidad and Tobago. The island of Barbados acquired independence in 1966, while the Bahamas became independent several years later, in 1973.

On the mainland of South America, British Guiana became the independent country of Guyana in 1966.

From 1945 to 1951, the Labor government completed the process of building the welfare state, fulfilling the vision of the Beveridge Report of providing the British people with cradle-to-the-grave social insurance. Labor's program of nationalization brought a significant portion of the British economy under state control, but the country's serious economic problems persisted.

Apart from the denationalization of iron and steel and long-distance trucking, the Conservative governments from 1951 to 1964 left Labor's reforms largely intact. Like the Laborites before them, the Conservatives failed to achieve an enduring economic recovery.

In foreign affairs, the Suez Crisis of 1956 demonstrated the dramatic decline in Britain's power and position in world affairs, while the spread of nationalism in the post-World War II era resulted in the conversion of the British Empire into the loose association of independent states that constitute the Commonwealth of Nations.

Recommended Reading

Barker, Elizabeth. *The British Between the Superpowers, 1945–50* (1984).

Barnett, Corelli. *The Audit of War: The Illusion and Reality of Britain as a Great Power* (1986).

Bartlett, C. J. *A History of Post-War Britain, 1945–74* (1977).

Beer, Samuel H. *Modern British Politics: Parties and Pressure Groups in the Collectivist Age* (1982).

Brown, Judith M. *Modern India: The Origins of an Asian Democracy* (1985).

Bullock, Alan. *Ernest Bevin, Foreign Secretary, 1945–1951* (1983).

Burridge, T. D. *Clement Attlee: A Political Biography* (1985).

Cairncross, Alec. *Years of Recovery: British Economic Policy, 1945–51* (1985).

Charlton, David. *Anthony Eden: A Biography* (1982).

Chester, Norman. *The Nationalisation of British Industry, 1945–1951* (1975).

Eatwell, Roger. *The 1945–51 Labour Governments* (1980).

Fisher, Nigel. *Harold Macmillan: A Biography* (1982).

Foot, Michael. *Aneurin Bevin,* 2 vols. (1962–1973).

Frankel, Joseph. *British Foreign Policy, 1945–1973* (1975).

Fraser, Derek. *The Evolution of the British Welfare State* (1973).

Hopkins, Harry. *The New Look: A Social History of Britain in the 1940's and 1950's* (1964).

Kitzinger, U. W. *The Politics and Economics of European Integration: Britain, Europe, and the United States* (1964).

Lacey, Robert. *Majesty: Queen Elizabeth II and the House of Windsor* (1977).

Lindsey, Almont. *Socialized Medicine in England and Wales* (1962).

Louis, William Roger. *The British Empire in the Middle East, 1945–1951* (1985).

Milward, Alan S. *The Economic Effects of the Two World Wars on Britain* (1984).

Morgan, Kenneth O. *Labour in Power, 1945–1951* (1984).

Northedge, F. S. *Descent from Power: British Foreign Policy, 1945–1973* (1974).

Pandey, B. N. *The Break-Up of British India* (1969).

Sampson, Anthony. *Macmillan: A Study in Ambiguity* (1967).

Sked, Alan and Chris Cook. *Post-War Britain: A Political History* (2nd ed., 1984).

Thomas, Hugh. *Armed Truce: The Beginnings of the Cold War, 1945–1946* (1987).

Thomas, Hugh. *The Suez Affair* (1967).

Williams, Philip. *Hugh Gaitskell* (1979).

CHAPTER 23

Contemporary Britain

Time Line

1970–1974	Edward Heath, a Conservative, serves as prime minister
1972	The government of Northern Ireland is suspended
1973	Great Britain enters the Common Market
1974–1976	Wilson heads his second government
1975	The inflation rate reaches 25 percent
1976	The Employment Protection Act strengthens the position of Britain's labor unions
1976–1979	James Callaghan, a Laborite, serves as prime minister
1979–1990	Margaret Thatcher, a Conservative, serves as prime minister
1981	Racial rioting breaks out in several cities
	A split in the Labor Party leads to the creation of the Social Democratic Party
1982	Great Britain defeats Argentina in the Falkland Islands War
1984	A treaty with the People's Republic of China provides for the return of Hong Kong to China in 1997
	The coal miners' strike is broken
1987	Thatcher leads the Conservatives to their third consecutive election victory
1990	John Major, a Conservative, becomes prime minister
1991	Great Britain supports the United States-led coalition in the Persian Gulf War against Iraq

From 1964 to 1979, the Labor Party dominated the British government, with the exception of the years from 1970 to 1974, when the Conservatives held office. The welfare state remained intact during this period, and the Labor governments pressed forward with modest programs of further nationalization. Above all, however, chronic economic problems troubled both Labor and Conservative govern-ments during these years.

After 1979, the Conservative government headed by Margaret Thatcher charted a new course, seeking to trim the welfare state and denationalize a number of state-owned enterprises. While the vic-tory over Argentina in the Falkland Islands War of 1982 gave the British people a sense of renewed national power, economic prob-lems persisted, race relations were uneasy, and the conflict in North-ern Ireland remained unresolved.

The Wilson Government
1964–1970

The 1964 Elections

Sir Alec Douglas-Home (b. 1903), who became Great Britain's prime minister in late 1963 (see Chapter 22), demonstrated his political skill in rebuilding support for the Conservative Party and reducing Labor's commanding lead in the polls.

Nevertheless, in the October 1964 elections for the House of Commons, Labor eked out a narrow victory, winning 317 seats, while the Conservatives won 304 and the Liberals won nine.

Harold Wilson

Harold Wilson (b. 1916), who had become the leader of the Labor Party following the death of Hugh Gaitskell (1906–1963), took office as prime minister. Wilson had been active in the left wing of the Labor Party, but as prime minister he proved to be more a pragmatist than a doctrinaire left-winger.

Despite the slender Labor majority in the House of Commons, Wilson pressed for the enactment of some of the party's program. The government eliminated all charges imposed by the National Health Service and increased old age pensions.

The Economy

In its 1965 budget, the Wilson government attempted to deal with the serious balance of payments deficit it had inherited from the Conservatives. Efforts were made to encourage exports and reduce inflation. To cut consumer spending, restrictions were imposed on consumer credit. The budget also imposed the first tax in British history on long-term capital gains.

Despite government efforts to promote economic planning in order to encourage the modernization of industry and increase productivity, much of British industry remained technologically outmoded and productivity continued to lag.

The 1966 Elections

Hoping to increase the Labor majority in the House of Commons, Wilson called elections in March 1966. Labor won 363 seats to the 253 won by the Conservatives and the 12 won by the Liberals.

Renationalization of the Steel Industry

With Labor in firm control of the House of Commons, Wilson secured passage of a bill for the renationalization of the steel industry. British Steel, the new government-owned corporation, began operation in 1967.

Housing and Education

The Wilson government increased spending for housing and education. From 1964 to 1968, about 400,000 units of new housing were built annually. Wilson took pride in spending more for education than defense, and during his term of office, a number of new universities were established.

The Economy

Labor's enlarged majority made it no easier for the Wilson government to find solutions to the country's chronic economic problems. Inflation and inefficiency in industry persisted, and the balance of payments problem remained serious.

Economic Controls

In an effort to revive the economy, Wilson imposed strict economic controls. Interest rates were increased, consumer credit was tightened further, restrictions were placed on spending by British tourists abroad, and taxes were raised on gasoline and alcoholic beverages. An attempt was made to control inflation by imposing a temporary freeze on wages and prices in 1966.

The Common Market

In early 1967, as part of its effort to strengthen the economy, the Wilson government renewed British efforts to enter the Common Market. But once again, as in 1963, French President Charles de Gaulle (1890–1970) vetoed Britain's entry (see Chapter 22).

Consequences of the Six-Day War

The Six-Day War between Israel and its Arab neighbors in June 1967 compounded Britain's economic problems. The Suez Canal, which had been reopened following its closing at the time of the Suez Crisis of 1956 (see Chapter 22), was once again closed, and the Arab states imposed a three-month embargo on oil shipments.

As Britain's balance of payments deficit worsened, the government decided to reduce foreign spending by closing the last remaining British bases east of Suez by the mid-1970s. Great Britain remained committed to maintaining its position west of Suez, however. Above all, the British resisted Spanish demands for the return of Gibraltar at the western end of the Mediterranean Sea.

Devaluation of the Pound and Further Economic Controls

The economic controls imposed by the government proved unpopular, and the Labor Party suffered losses in municipal elections and parliamentary by-elections in 1967.

Despite the controls, the problems of inflation and the balance of payments deficit persisted and were made more serious by a strike of Liverpool and London dock workers in the fall of 1967.

These economic and financial problems forced the government in November 1967 to devalue the pound from $2.80 to $2.40. The weakness of the pound reflected the lack of foreign confidence in the British economy. Roy Jenkins (b. 1920), the chancellor of the exchequer, imposed further controls designed to cut the government's budget deficit, reduce consumer spending, and increase exports. Charges were reimposed on prescription drugs, interest rates were increased, and new restrictions were placed on consumer credit.

In addition, income and sales taxes were increased. By 1970, exports were increasing more rapidly than imports, and Great Britain enjoyed a modest balance of payments surplus.

Education

Acting to democratize education, the Wilson government won enactment of the Education Act of 1970, which resolved a long-standing controversy by creating a system of comprehensive secondary schools. This ended the practice of separating academically oriented students from those who were on a vocational track.

Immigration

During the early 1960s, the growing number of immigrants from the Commonwealth, especially India, Pakistan, and the West Indies, led to growing racial and social tensions in Great Britain.

The Commonwealth Immigration Act of 1962

In 1962, Macmillan's Conservative government won adoption of the first Commonwealth Immigration Act, which required prospective immigrants to obtain work permits before they would be admitted to the country.

Race Relations Acts

While the Wilson government imposed further restrictions on immigration, it also secured passage of the Race Relations Acts of 1965 and 1969, which banned racial discrimination in employment, housing, and public accommodations.

Enoch Powell

Despite the restrictions on immigration, the issue remained controversial, and Enoch Powell (b. 1912), a Conservative, became a leading figure in the anti-immigration movement. Breaking with his own party, Powell called not only for a ban on immigration but also urged the government to subsidize the repatriation of Asians and West Indians who had already settled in Great Britain.

Although Powell won only limited support, it was evident that racial issues were gaining a place in British politics.

British Society
During the 1960s

The 1960s were a time of considerable change in British society. In Great Britain, as in Western Europe and the United States, a more permissive society came into being. This was, first of all, the decade of the Beatles, the Rolling Stones, and other rock'n'rollers, as well as of miniskirts and the "mod" fashions of London's Carnaby Street. Church membership and attendance declined markedly, and the once-strict censorship of literature, the theater, and motion pictures was virtually eliminated. The decade also brought increases in the crime rate and the number of illegitimate births.

Legislation reflected the changes in social attitudes. In 1966, homosexual activities involving consenting adults were decriminalized, while in 1968, abortion became legal for women whose pregnancies endangered their physical and mental health. In 1969, capital punishment was abolished. In the same year, divorce was liberalized, and during the following decade, the number of divorces increased sharply. Also in 1969, the voting age and the age of legal majority were reduced from twenty-one to eighteen.

Also during the 1960s, the number of women working outside the home increased. In 1957, about one-fifth of married women were employed outside the home. By 1970, about one-third were. The Equal Pay Act, adopted in 1970, sought to establish equal pay and working conditions for men and women doing the same jobs.

The Heath Government
1970–1974

The 1970 Elections

In 1970, the balance of payments situation was favorable, the economy was stronger, and the polls indicated a Labor victory in the parliamentary elections scheduled for June. But the Conservatives won an upset victory, capturing 330 seats in the House of Commons to 287 seats for Labor and six seats for the Liberals. Seven seats were held by "others," including several Welsh and Scottish Nationalists. Their election reflected the growing strength of separatist movements in Wales and Scotland.

Edward Heath (b. 1916), who had succeeded Douglas-Home as the leader of the Conservative Party in 1965, became prime minister. During his term of office, he confronted both a crisis in Northern Ireland and the persistent problem of the economy.

Northern Ireland

Conflict between Catholics and Protestants

A new era in the history of Irish problems began in Northern Ireland (Ulster) in 1969. Terence O'Neill (b. 1914), Northern Ireland's prime minister since 1963 and a liberal Ulster Unionist, had sought to win enactment of reforms to end discrimination against Roman Catholics in Northern Ireland and to promote better relations with the Republic of Ireland. The reforms came too slowly to satisfy the increasingly more militant Catholic civil rights movement, led by Bernadette Devlin (b. 1947) and others, while the Protestant militants, led by the Rev. Ian Paisley (b. 1926), opposed all reforms.

British Intervention

As conflict mounted, O'Neill resigned the prime ministership in April 1969. James Chichester-Clark (b. 1923), his successor, attempted to continue the reform program with the support of the British government. In August 1969, violence broke out in Belfast and Londonderry, resulting in several deaths and the wounding of several hundred. Prime Minister Harold Wilson sent British troops to Northern Ireland to help the police quell the violence.

The Irish Republican Army

During the early 1970s, the conflict intensified as the "provisional wing" of the Irish Republican Army (IRA) increased its activities. While the civil rights movement had sought to eliminate discrimination against Roman Catholics in Northern Ireland, the goal of the IRA was to use violence, if necessary, to unite all of Ireland. Though the Republic of Ireland supported unity in principle, it opposed the use of force to attain that objective and had outlawed the IRA several years earlier.

IRA attacks on British troops in Northern Ireland resulted in the arrest and imprisonment without trial of IRA leaders. This, in turn, led to further IRA violence. In March 1972, the Heath government decided that the government of Northern Ireland was incapable of restoring and maintaining order and suspended it. Authority now passed into the hands of a British secretary of state for Northern Ireland who sought, without success, to find a compromise settlement. The unrest continued, with acts of violence committed both by the IRA and Protestant extremists.

The Economy

In an effort to stimulate the economy, the Heath government reduced income taxes and, in 1971, removed limits on bank interest rates and restrictions on consumer credit.

By 1972, the British economy was enjoying a considerable prosperity, which proved to be short-lived. An increase in world prices of raw materials, especially petroleum in the aftermath of the Arab-Israeli War of 1973, along with labor-management conflict and a shortage of skilled labor, led to an increase in the inflation rate and a slowdown of economic expansion. In an effort to restrain inflation, Heath imposed controls on wages and prices.

The Common Market

British Entry.   Although some Conservatives opposed any surrender of sovereignty to a supranational organization, Heath believed that British entry into the Common Market would provide a powerful impetus to the economy. In May 1971, he met in Paris with France's new president, Georges Pompidou (1911–1974), who agreed not to veto Britain's application, as de Gaulle had done on two occasions.

On January 1, 1973, Great Britain became a member of the Common Market, along with Ireland and Denmark.

Steps to Integrate Economy.   To facilitate the integration of Britain's economy with that of Western Europe, the government had introduced the metric system of weights and measures, while the Celsius temperature scale replaced Fahrenheit. The system of coinage was also reformed. In February 1971, the old system of twelve pence in a shilling and twenty shillings in a pound had been replaced by a decimal system of one hundred pence in a pound. In addition, the British followed the pattern of the other members of the Common Market by establishing a value-added tax (VAT) in place of the sales tax.

The Industrial Relations Act of 1971

The militancy of Britain's trade unions led to an increase in the number and frequency of strikes, which generally ended with inflationary wage increases. These, in turn, resulted in higher prices and demands from other workers for higher wages. In an effort to reduce the turmoil in labor-management relations, the government won passage of the Industrial Relations Act of 1971. The act established an Industrial Court empowered to impose a sixty-day cooling-off period to delay strikes that could result in a national emergency. The unions opposed this act, which had little practical effect, and antagonism mounted between organized labor and the Heath government.

Inflation

Inflation increased the cost of British exports, which resulted in a balance of payments deficit in 1972 after three years of surplus. The Heath government decided to let the British pound float on international money markets, and by 1974, the pound had fallen about 20 percent in relation to the major Western European currencies. While the decline in the pound's value encouraged exports, it also contributed to further inflation in Great Britain.

In late 1972, the government imposed restrictions on wages and prices and during 1973, the rate of inflation declined temporarily. Nevertheless, trade union militancy, especially a coal miners' strike in early 1974, undermined the government's efforts to control inflation.

The Second Wilson Government 1974-1976

The February 1974 Elections

The Campaign

While Heath's opposition to union militancy had gained him the enmity of the leaders of organized labor, it had won a favorable response from much of the British public. Hoping to benefit politically, the prime minister called elections for February 1974. During the campaign, Heath posed the question: "Who governs Britain?" Was it the government or the unions? Heath hoped the electorate would provide a resounding answer.

Results

The election proved indecisive, as no party won a clear majority in the House of Commons. The Labor Party took 301 seats and the Conservatives 296, although the Conservatives had won more popular votes than Labor. The Liberals polled close to twenty percent of the vote but won only 14 seats. The Northern Ireland Unionist parties captured 11 seats, demonstrating the political strength of the Protestant majority and its determination to maintain the union of Ulster with Great Britain. Seven Scottish Nationalists and two Welsh Nationalists also won seats. Harold Wilson once again became prime minister, heading a minority Labor government.

The Economy

Economic issues topped the agenda of the new government. The coal strike was ended on terms favorable to the miners. While Wilson maintained some controls on prices and rents, he did not attempt to control wages other than to encourage restraint. In practice, there was little wage restraint. The rate of inflation increased, and business profits and stock prices declined.

The October 1974 Elections

In an effort to strengthen his control of the House of Commons, Wilson called the second elections of the year for October. Polling barely three percent more of the popular vote than the Conservatives, Labor won 319 seats in the House of Commons to 277 for the Conservatives and 13 for the Liberals. Eleven Scottish Nationalists and two Welsh Nationalists gained seats, while the Northern Ireland Unionists captured ten seats.

The Economic Crisis

Although Wilson acknowledged the existence of an economic crisis, his government did little to resolve it. Above all, the Wilson government failed to take action to restrain the demands of the unions for inflationary wage increases.

The Employment Protection Act of 1976

The Employment Protection Act of 1976 strengthened the position of the unions, whose membership had been increasing. The act encouraged employers to negotiate closed shop agreements with the unions. Under these agreements, workers who refused to join the union would lose their jobs, and employers who fired an employee unfairly would be subject to a substantial fine. The act also required employers to give a ninety-day warning when they anticipated laying off 100 or more unionized workers and to provide women workers with six-month maternity leaves.

Nationalization

In accordance with the Labor Party's socialist doctrine, the government nationalized the shipbuilding and aircraft industries and carried out a partial nationalization of the oil industry. British Leyland, the auto manufacturer that had gone bankrupt, was also nationalized.

Taxes and Inflation

The Wilson government increased taxes on the wealthy. This "tax the rich" program served to undermine business confidence still further.

The economic crisis thus persisted. The inflation rate, which had been slightly under six percent in 1969, reached almost twenty-five percent in the summer of 1975, the highest in history. As the economy weakened, unemployment and the budget deficit increased. The intensity of the crisis forced the Trades Union Congress (TUC) to agree to limit wage increases during the next year, and the inflation rate declined slightly.

Nevertheless, the balance of payments deficit remained large, and the value of the pound continued to decline against major Western currencies, falling to about $1.70 in June 1976.

The Common Market

Although Great Britain had joined the Common Market in 1973, many left-wing Laborites continued to oppose British participation in what they viewed as a capitalist economic endeavor, while many unions feared that their traditional privileges would be undermined by Britain's association with countries that were less supportive of unions. In an effort to avoid open conflict within his own party over the issue, Wilson called for a national referendum, a unique occurrence in British history.

In the referendum held in June 1975, some sixty-seven percent of the British voters endorsed British membership in the EEC.

Wilson's Resignation

In March 1976, Wilson unexpectedly resigned the prime ministership. While he cited his age (he was sixty) and his long service in the House of Commons as reasons for retirement, he was also tired of harassment by his party's left wing.

The Callaghan Government
1976–1979

James Callaghan

The Labor M.P.'s (members of Parliament) chose James Callaghan (b. 1912), a moderate, as the new prime minister, rather than Michael Foot (b. 1913), the leader of the party's left wing. Callaghan had served as Wilson's foreign secretary.

Economic Problems

The new prime minister found it no easier than his predecessor had to come up with enduring solutions for the country's economic problems. The budget and balance of payments deficits remained high, and the value of the pound continued to fall.

The Callaghan government, like its predecessors, failed to find a means to promote the modernization of British industry and to take other measures needed to get the economy off its "stop-and-go" track, where a brief period of recovery was quickly followed by another downturn. Unemployment continued to grow, from slightly over 600,000 in 1974 to some 1.3 million by 1979.

Callaghan's Defeat

The persistence of economic problems undermined popular support for the Callaghan government. During 1976 and 1977, the Labor Party lost several by-elections, and its majority in the House of Commons was threatened. Callaghan became dependent on the support of the Liberals and Scottish Nationalists to retain his hold on power.

Then, during the 1978–1979 "winter of discontent," the government failed to contain the unions' demand for inflationary wage increases. The government's failure, the unions' attitude, and the wave of strikes angered the public.

In March 1979, the Conservatives proposed a "no confidence" motion in the House of Commons. With the support of the Liberals and Scottish Nationalists, the motion carried by a vote of 311 to 310. Callaghan's government resigned, and new elections were called.

The Thatcher Government 1979–1990

The 1979 Elections

The Labor Party

During the 1970s, the influence of the left wing had increased within the Labor Party. The left-wing Laborites, led by Michael Foot and Anthony Wedgwood Benn (b. 1925), argued that private industry had failed to make adequate capital investments to achieve a modernization of British industry. They urged a "Socialist transformation" of the economy, including the nationalization of the 200 largest industries. In addition, they advocated the abolition of private schools and the House of Lords, and they called for unilateral disarmament and a British withdrawal from NATO and the Common Market.

Results

The radical program of the left-wing Laborites held only a modest appeal for the electorate, and the 1979 elections returned the Conservatives to power with solid control of the House of Commons. The Conservatives won 339 seats to 268 for Labor and 11 for the Liberals. The Scottish and Welsh Nationalists won only two seats each, a sign that the separatist movements were losing some of their momentum. The Northern Ireland Unionists took ten seats.

Margaret Thatcher

Margaret Thatcher (b. 1925), who had succeeded Edward Heath as the Conservatives' leader in 1975, became prime minister. Not only was the "Iron Lady," as Thatcher soon came to be known, the first woman in British history to hold the prime ministership, but she also held that office longer than any person since Lord Liverpool in the early nineteenth century.

Policies of the Thatcher Government

While the Labor Party had moved to the left, the Conservatives under Thatcher's leadership had moved to the right, and Thatcher's policies marked a clear-cut departure from the policies of both the Labor and Conservative governments that preceded her. Emphasis was placed on bringing inflation under control, curbing the power of the unions, and reducing the role of the state in the economy.

Early Successes and Failures

During its first years, Thatcherism recorded both successes and failures. In its effort to control inflation, the government regulated the money supply and sought to contain increases in spending for social services, housing, and education.

Economic Stimulation

By 1982, the rate of inflation had declined to under eight percent, and there was a balance of payments surplus. This improvement resulted in large part from the increasing exploitation of North Sea oil, which made Great Britain both self-sufficient in energy and an exporter of petroleum.

In an effort to stimulate the economy by encouraging private initiative, income and inheritance taxes were substantially reduced. For the first time since World War II, restrictions on transferring money in and out of the country were removed.

People who rented public housing (council houses) were encouraged to buy their homes. Between 1979 and 1987, some 750,000 council houses were sold, and by 1988, two-thirds of the British people owned their own homes, up from about half in 1979.

Negative Effects

On the negative side of the ledger, Britain's achievement of self-sufficiency in energy resulted in an overvaluation of the pound in international exchange, which led in turn to a decline in exports. During the world recession of the early 1980s, the British were unable to find jobs for much of their work force, and unemployment increased from about four percent in 1979 to just over thirteen percent in 1983. While the government was able to control its spending for social services generally, expenditures for unemployment insurance increased considerably.

Race Riots

During the early 1980s, mounting unemployment fueled racial tensions, which had been growing for several years, and rioting broke out in the spring and summer of 1981 in London and several other cities. In these riots, unemployed black and Asian youths battled the police and unemployed white youths, although there were several instances in which blacks, Asians, and whites joined forces against the police. Similar outbreaks of racial violence swept a number of British cities in 1985.

Formation of the Social Democratic Party

In 1980, James Callaghan stepped down as the leader of the Labor Party and was succeeded by the left-winger Michael Foot. In response to the increasing radicalization of Labor, several former Labor cabinet members, including Roy Jenkins, David Owen (b. 1938), and Shirley Williams (b. 1930), broke with the party in 1981 and formed the Social Democratic Party (SDP). They intended the new party to be a center force in British politics between the Conservatives and the radicalized Labor Party.

The SDP won the support of several Labor M.P.'s, and SDP candidates won several by-elections. By 1982, the SDP had 28 members of the House of Commons who joined with the 12 Liberals, led by David Steel (b. 1938), in the SDP-Liberal Alliance.

The Falkland Islands War, 1982

Argentine Invasion

The Falkland Islands, located in the South Atlantic, were among Great Britain's few remaining crown colonies. Argentina claimed the Falklands, which the Argentines called the Malvinas, although the fewer than 2000 residents of the islands, many of them sheep farmers, were of British origin and desired to remain British.

After several years of fruitless negotiations, Argentine forces invaded the Falklands at the beginning of April 1982, forcing the surrender of a small contingent of British marines.

British Response

Thatcher responded strongly to the invasion with both diplomatic and military initiatives. The British appealed to the United Nations Security Council, which by a vote of ten to one called for an Argentine withdrawal.

The British dispatched a sizable fleet to the South Atlantic, while passenger ships, including the *Queen Elizabeth II,* were pressed into service as troop transports.

In late April, the British retook the island of South Georgia, a dependency of the Falklands, and then began to move against the Falkland Islands proper. In late May, British troops landed on East Falkland and captured Port Stanley, the capital of the Falklands, in mid-June.

British Victory

During the war, the British lost some 255 military dead and six ships. Apart from the left wing of the Labor Party, most Britons supported the government's vigorous action and rejoiced in the outcome. Not only did Great Britain defeat Argentine aggression and defend the Falkland islanders from Argentine rule, but the British also had asserted their power in a fashion reminiscent of the more glorious days of empire.

The Empire

While Thatcher maintained British rule over the Falkland Islands, the status of two other British possessions changed.

British Honduras

In Central America, British Honduras became an independent member of the Commonwealth, known as Belize, in 1981.

Hong Kong

A 1984 treaty with the People's Republic of China provided for the restoration of the thriving crown colony of Hong Kong to China in 1997. The Chinese promised that for at least fifty years after that date, Hong Kong would maintain its own economic and social systems.

The 1983 Elections

Victory in the Falklands War brought political dividends to Thatcher and the Conservative Party, but above all they profited from the unpopular left-wing program of the Labor Party and the defection from Labor of the Social Democrats.

In the elections of June 1983, the Conservatives won an overwhelming victory, capturing 397 seats in the House of Commons to 209 for Labor and 23 for the Social Democratic-Liberal Alliance. The Scottish and Welsh Nationalists won two seats each; the Northern Ireland Unionists captured 15 of the 17 Ulster seats.

While the Labor Party suffered an immense defeat, polling fewer than thirty percent of the popular votes, the election was also a disappointment for the SDP-Liberal Alliance. Although the Alliance polled just over twenty-five percent of the popular votes, it won relatively few seats.

The Economy

The productivity of the British economy increased during the 1980s, although unemployment remained high, especially in the English Midlands, once the center of Britain's industry, and in northern England, as well as in Scotland and Wales.

Financial Deregulation

In October 1986, the government deregulated the country's financial institutions, which enhanced London's already substantial position as an international financial center. Income from financial services and overseas investments provided Great Britain with its major source of income and promoted economic prosperity in the capital and the surrounding area in southeastern England.

Denationalization

Following the 1983 election, the Thatcher government pressed forward with its program of denationalization, or "privatization," of state-owned enterprises. The British Oil Corporation, British Gas, British Airways, British Telecom (the telephone services), Jaguar automobiles, the port facilities, and the cross-channel ferries were among the enterprises sold to private investors by 1987. The value of these enterprises totaled some $57 billion. Many of the shares of stock in these enterprises were sold to their employees. Between 1979 and 1987, the number of British stockholders grew from 3 million to about 9 million.

The 1984 Coal Strike

The Thatcher government acted to curb the power of the trade unions, outlawing political strikes and secondary boycotts, limiting the number of pickets at struck enterprises, and applying pressure on the unions to use the secret ballot in strike votes.

In 1984, the coal miners' union presented a powerful challenge to the Thatcher government. Nationalization had not brought solutions to the problems of Britain's troubled coal industry. Between 1947 and 1982, the number of coal miners declined from 700,000 to 200,000 as coal gave way to oil and gas. Over the years, the miners' union had succeeded in its efforts to win wage increases for the declining work force and had also fought off efforts to close some unnecessary coal mines.

Arthur Scargill (b. 1938), the radical president of the National Union of Mineworkers, called a strike that lasted from April 1984 to March 1985. While earlier strikes had forced concessions from the government, Thatcher stood firm, and the miners' strike was broken.

Following the strike, the Coal Board persuaded many older miners to accept generous terms for early retirement, and the work force was reduced further. By the late 1980s, a substantially smaller work force produced almost as much coal as had been mined a decade earlier.

The Trade Union Act of 1984

The Trade Union Act of 1984 further reduced the power of the union leaders by providing for their election by secret ballot at regular five-year intervals.

During the 1980s, union membership declined from more than one-half to a little over a third of the labor force. While the coal miners' strike attracted considerable attention, the number and frequency of strikes declined during the 1980s as militancy and confrontation were gradually replaced by consultation and negotiation.

The National Health Service

During the 1980s, the National Health Service remained intact, and, despite the government's efforts to effect savings, spending increased for health and for social services generally. The number of doctors and nurses employed by the National Health Service increased, as did the number of patients treated.

Northern Ireland

Assassination of Mountbatten

The problem of Northern Ireland persisted, and only a few months after Thatcher came into office, IRA terrorists assassinated Lord Mountbatten (1900–1979), the last British viceroy of India and uncle of Prince Philip (b. 1921), the husband of Queen Elizabeth II.

IRA Protests and Violence

From May to October 1981, Irish Republican Army members imprisoned in Belfast, the capital of Northern Ireland, staged a hunger strike. Ten died from starvation as Thatcher remained adamant in her refusal to treat imprisoned members of the IRA as political prisoners.

While the IRA abandoned hunger strikes, the violence continued. In October 1984, Thatcher herself became the target of IRA terrorism, escaping a bomb blast in a hotel in the seaside resort of Brighton where the Conservative Party was holding a conference.

Efforts at Peacemaking

In November 1985, Thatcher signed an agreement with the prime minister of Ireland. This agreement provided for meetings of British and Irish leaders to discuss the problems of Northern Ireland, especially the rights of the Roman Catholic minority in Ulster.

The Northern Ireland Protestants opposed this agreement, which had no practical effect in reducing the violence on both sides.

Foreign Affairs

During the early and mid-1980s, Thatcher remained a firm ally of President Ronald Reagan (b. 1911) in maintaining a hard-line stance in dealings with the Soviet Union. However, the prime minister was one of the first Western leaders to recognize Mikhail Gorbachev (b. 1931), who became the Soviet leader in 1985, as "a man we can do business with." Her visit to Moscow in April 1987 helped pave the way for East-West accords on arms reduction.

The 1987 Elections

As the 1987 elections approached, Thatcher and the Conservatives appeared to be in a relatively strong position, although for almost five years, the number of unemployed had remained at close to 3 million, about eleven percent of the work force. Nevertheless, most Britons had a sense of improved economic conditions, and the Conservatives also benefited from the divisions of the opposition.

The Labor Party

The radical program of the Labor Party continued to alienate a significant portion of the British electorate. Neil Kinnock (b. 1942), a left-wing Laborite known more for congeniality than militancy, had replaced Michael Foot as the party's leader. The Labor program, however, continued to urge unilateral nuclear disarmament, higher taxes on the wealthy, increased social spending, and the repeal of laws restricting the unions.

Results

Polling just over forty-two percent of the popular votes, the Conservatives won 375 seats to 229 seats for Labor (thirty-one percent) and 22 seats for the Social Democratic-Liberal Alliance (twenty-three percent). Scottish and Welsh Nationalists won three seats each, while the Northern Ireland Unionists gained 13.

Thatcher's Fall from Power

Although Prime Minister Thatcher's success in leading her Conservative Party to three election victories in a row represented a remarkable achievement, soon after the 1987 election, her power began to erode as a consequence of several developments, some of her own making.

Attitude Toward European Integration

Although Great Britain had entered the Common Market in 1973, many Britons, including Thatcher, resisted further European integration. In particular, the prime minister opposed both the European Community's plans to create a common European currency, which would deprive Great Britain of control of its own currency, and proposals for a future European political union. Her position weakened her support among members of her own party who believed that Britain's ties with the continent should be strengthened.

The Poll Tax

Local government in Great Britain was traditionally supported by taxes on property, known as the "rates." Town councils controlled by the Labor Party could increase these property taxes virtually at will in order to pay for expanded services.

In an effort to restrict these town councils, Thatcher won the passage of the "community charge." This flat, per-head tax, known as the poll tax, resulted in large tax reductions for wealthy property owners. However, for many lower-class and middle-class homeowners, the new poll tax was considerably higher than the old property tax. This disparity evoked strong popular opposition to the prime minister.

Economic Downturn

The inflation rate, which had been 4.2 percent at the time of the Conservatives' victory in the 1987 election, had increased to 10.9 percent by late 1990, and unemployment remained high. A further drop in the already slow rate of growth of the gross national product (GNP) was anticipated, and economists feared the onset of a recession.

Conservative Revolt

Despite her political success, Thatcher had never been truly popular. Even within her own party, there was considerable resentment at her arrogant and heavy-handed treatment of her associates.

Decline in Thatcher's Popularity.   A 1989 opinion poll showed that her approval rating had dropped to twenty-four percent, the lowest ever recorded for any prime minister. Polls also suggested that the Conservative Party under her leadership would lose the next election to Labor, while under any one of several other possible leaders, the Conservatives would win.

Contest for Succession.   Fearing the loss of the election that would come no later than July 1992, the prime minister's fellow Conservatives became restive. Michael Heseltine (b. 1933), who had earlier served as defense secretary in the Thatcher government, launched the challenge that led to the prime minister's downfall. In the race for the succession, Heseltine was soon joined by Douglas Hurd (b. 1930), a former foreign secretary, and John Major (b. 1943), the chancellor of the exchequer.

Thatcher's Resignation

Confronted with the challenge and fearing she would lose in a vote of the Conservative M.P.'s, Thatcher stepped down as leader of the Conservative Party and prime minister in late November 1990. She threw her support to Major.

John Major

Defeating Heseltine and Hurd, Major became party leader and prime minister. Although he was regarded as the most conservative of the contenders for the prime ministership, observers expected that he would be more sympathetic to social needs than Thatcher had been, would be more conciliatory regarding European economic and political union, and would actively seek a resolution of the poll tax problem.

During Major's first months in office, however, the crisis in the Middle East engaged most of his attention. On August 2, 1990, Iraq overran and annexed neighboring Kuwait. In response, the United Nations Security Council on August 6 condemned the Iraqi invasion, called for a complete and immediate Iraqi withdrawal, and imposed economic sanctions on Iraq. Then, on August 25, the Security Council authorized military action if necessary to compel an Iraqi withdrawal. The British government, still led by Thatcher, supported these decisions.

On January 16, 1991, a coalition led by the United States went to war against Iraq. Great Britain contributed units to the multinational force organized by the coalition.

When Margaret Thatcher left the prime ministership at the end of 1990, the record of her eleven-year tenure appeared mixed. Despite her efforts to trim government social spending, Great Britain remained very much a welfare state. Even many of Thatcher's supporters feared that any truly substantial reduction of welfare state benefits would come at the cost of increased social unrest.

Economic improvement during the Thatcher years proved to be modest, at best, and there seemed increasingly to be two Englands: a relatively prosperous southeast, centered on London, and the chronically depressed areas of the English Midlands and North, as well as Wales and Scotland, where unemployment had become an enduring way of life.

Recommended Reading

Cole, John. *The Thatcher Years* (1987).

Cosgrave, Patrick. *Thatcher: The First Term* (1985).

Daniel, W. W. *Racial Discrimination in England* (1968).

Davies, Christie. *Permissive Britain* (1975).

Harvie, Christopher. *No Gods and Precious Few Heroes: Scotland, 1918–1980* (1981).

Harvie, Christopher. *Scotland and Nationalism* (1977).

Hastings, Max and Simon Jenkins. *The Battle for the Falklands* (1983).

Hull, Rogert H. *The Irish Tangle: Conflict in Northern Ireland* (1975).

James, Robert Thodes. *Ambitions and Realities: British Politics, 1964–70* (1972).

Jones, Catherine. *Immigration and Social Policy in Britain* (1977).

Kavanagh, Dennis. *Thatcherism and British Politics* (1987).

Lewis, Russell. *Margaret Thatcher: A Personal and Political Biography* (rev. ed., 1984).

Lyons, F. S. L. *Ireland Since the Famine* (rev. ed., 1973).

McKie, David and Chris Cook, eds. *The Decade of Disillusionment: British Politics in the Sixties* (1972).

Morgan, Kenneth O. *Rebirth of a Nation: Wales, 1880–1980* (1981).

Norman, Philip. *Shout! The Beatles in Their Generation* (1981).

Riddell, Peter. *The Thatcher Decade: Britain in the 1980s* (1990).

Sampson, Anthony. *The New Anatomy of Britain* (1971).

APPENDIX 1

Monarchs since the Norman Conquest

Normans

1066–1087	William I
1087–1100	William II
1100–1135	Henry I
1135–1154	Stephen

Angevins (Plantagenets)

1154–1189	Henry II
1189–1199	Richard I
1199–1216	John
1216–1272	Henry III

1272–1307	Edward I
1307–1327	Edward II
1327–1377	Edward III
1377–1399	Richard II

Lancastrians

1399–1413	Henry IV
1413–1422	Henry V
1422–1461	Henry VI

Yorkists

1461–1483	Edward IV
1483	Edward V
1483–1485	Richard III

Tudors

1485–1509	Henry VII
1509–1547	Henry VIII
1547–1553	Edward VI
1553–1558	Mary I
1558–1603	Elizabeth I

Stuarts

1603–1625	James I
1625–1649	Charles I
1649–1660	Interregnum (Commonwealth and Protectorate)
1660–1685	Charles II

1685–1688	James II
1689–1702	William III
1689–1694	and Mary II
1702–1714	Anne

Hanoverians
(House of Windsor since World War I)

1714–1727	George I
1727–1760	George II
1760–1820	George III
1820–1830	George IV
1830–1837	William IV
1837–1901	Victoria
1901–1910	Edward VII
1910–1936	George V
1936	Edward VIII
1936–1952	George VI
1952–	Elizabeth II

APPENDIX 2

Prime Ministers
and Ministries

1721–1742	Sir Robert Walpole (Whig)
1742–1744	Earl of Wilmington and John Carteret (Whig)
1744–1754	Henry Pelham (Whig)
1754–1756	Duke of Newcastle (Whig)
1756–1757	Duke of Devonshire and William Pitt (Whig)
1757–1761	Duke of Newcastle and William Pitt (Whig)
1761–1762	Duke of Newcastle and the Earl of Bute (mainly Whig)
1762–1763	Earl of Bute (mainly Tory)
1763–1765	George Grenville (Coalition)

1765–1766	Marquess of Rockingham (Whig)
1766–1768	William Pitt, Earl of Chatham (Coalition)
1768–1770	Duke of Grafton (Whig)
1770–1782	Lord North (Tory)
1782	Marquess of Rockingham (Whig)
1782–1783	Earl of Shelburne (Whig)
1783	Duke of Portland, Lord North, Charles James Fox (Coalition)
1783–1801	William Pitt the Younger (Tory)
1801–1804	Henry Addington (Tory)
1804–1806	William Pitt the Younger (Tory)
1806–1807	Lord Grenville and Charles James Fox (Coalition)
1807–1809	Duke of Portland (Tory)
1809–1812	Spencer Perceval (Tory)
1812–1827	Lord Liverpool (Tory)
1827	George Canning (Tory)
1827	Viscount Goderich (Tory)
1828–1830	Duke of Wellington (Tory)
1830–1834	Earl Grey (Whig)
1834	Viscount Melbourne (Whig)
1834–1835	Sir Robert Peel (Tory)
1835–1841	Viscount Melbourne (Whig)
1841–1846	Sir Robert Peel (Tory)
1846–1852	Lord John Russell (Whig)
1852	Earl of Derby and Benjamin Disraeli (Tory)
1852–1855	Earl of Aberdeen (Whig-Peelite)
1855–1858	Viscount Palmerston (Whig)

1858–1859	Earl of Derby and Benjamin Disraeli (Tory-Conservative)
1859–1865	Viscount Palmerston (Whig-Liberal)
1865–1866	Earl Russell (Whig-Liberal)
1866–1868	Earl of Derby and Benjamin Disraeli (Tory-Conservative)
1868	Benjamin Disraeli (Tory-Conservative)
1868–1874	William E. Gladstone (Liberal)
1874–1880	Benjamin Disraeli (Conservative)
1880–1885	William E. Gladstone (Liberal)
1885–1886	Marquess of Salisbury (Conservative)
1886	William E. Gladstone (Liberal)
1886–1892	Marquess of Salisbury (Conservative)
1892–1894	William E. Gladstone (Liberal)
1894–1895	Earl of Rosebery (Liberal)
1895–1902	Marquess of Salisbury (Conservative-Unionist)
1902–1905	Arthur James Balfour (Conservative-Unionist)
1905–1908	Henry Campbell-Bannerman (Liberal)
1908–1916	Herbert Asquith (Liberal)
1916–1922	David Lloyd George (Coalition)
1922–1923	Andrew Bonar Law (Conservative)
1923–1924	Stanley Baldwin (Conservative)
1924	Ramsay MacDonald (Labor)
1924–1929	Stanley Baldwin (Conservative)
1929–1931	Ramsay MacDonald (Labor)
1931–1935	Ramsay MacDonald (National Government)
1935–1937	Stanley Baldwin (National Government)

1937–1940	Neville Chamberlain (Conservative)
1940–1945	Winston Churchill (Coalition)
1945–1951	Clement Attlee (Labor)
1951–1955	Winston Churchill (Conservative)
1955–1957	Anthony Eden (Conservative)
1957–1963	Harold Macmillan (Conservative)
1963–1964	Sir Alec Douglas-Home (Conservative)
1964–1970	Harold Wilson (Labor)
1970–1974	Edward Heath (Conservative)
1974–1976	Harold Wilson (Labor)
1976–1979	James Callaghan (Labor)
1979–1990	Margaret Thatcher (Conservative)
1990–	John Major (Conservative)

Index